THE SACRED BOOKS OF THE EAST

Translated by

VARIOUS ORIENTAL SCHOLARS

Edited by

F. MAX MÜLLER

VOLUME 12

SACRED BOOKS OF THE EAST

(50 VOLUMES)

Series Editor : *F. Max-Müller*

ISBN: 978-81-208-0101-1 (Set) Rs. 20000 (Each Vol. Rs. 400)

These volumes of the Sacred Books of the East series include translations of all the most important works of the seven non-Christian religions that have exercised a profound influence on the civilisations of the continent of Asia. The Vedic Brahmanic system claims 21 volumes, Buddhism 10, and Jainism 2; 8 volumes comprise Sacred Books of the Parsis; 2 volumes represent Islam; and 6 the two main indigenous systems of China. Translated by twenty leading authorities in their respective fields, the volumes have been edited by the late F. Max Müller. The inception, publication and the compilation of these books cover almost 34 years.

I. BUDDHISM

Vol. 49: Buddhist Mahayana Texts (2 Parts)
Vol. 11: Buddhist Suttas
Vol. 10: The Dhammapada and Sutta Nipata
Vols. 35 & 36: The Questions of King Milinda (2 Parts)
Vol. 21: The Saddharma Pundarika or the Lotus of the True Law
Vols. 13, 17 & 20: Vinaya Texts (3 Parts)

II. CHINESE

Vol. 19: The Fo-Sho-Hing-Tsan-King
Vols. 3, 16, 27, 28, 39 & 40: The Sacred Books of China (6 Parts)

III. A GENERAL INDEX

Vol. 50: A General Index to the Names and Subject-matter of the Sacred Books of the East

IV. ISLAM

Vols. 6 & 9: The Qur'an (2 Parts)

V. JAINISM

Vols. 22 & 45: The Jaina Sutras (2 Parts)

VI. PARSIS

Vols. 5, 18, 24, 37 & 47: Pahlavi Texts (5 Parts)
Vols. 4, 23 & 31: The Zend-Avesta (3 Parts)

VII. VEDIC-BRAHMANIC SYSTEM

Vol. 8: The Bhagavadgita with the Sanatsujatiya and the Anugita
Vols. 29 & 30: The Grihya-Sutras: Rules of Vedic Domestic Ceremonies (2 Parts)
Vol. 42: Hymns of the Atharva Veda together with Extracts from the Ritual Books and the Commentaries
Vol. 7: The Institutes of Vishnu
Vol. 25: The Laws of Manu
Vol. 33: The Minor Law Books
Vols. 2 & 14: The Sacred Laws of the Aryas as Taught in the Schools of Apastamba, Gautama, Vasishtha and Baudhayana (2 Parts)
Vols. 12, 26, 41, 43 & 44: The Satapatha Brahmana According to the Text of the Madhyandina School (5 Parts)
Vols. 1 & 15: The Upanishads (2 Parts)
Vols. 34 & 38: The Vedanta Sutras (2 Parts)
Vol. 48: The Vedanta-Sutras (with the commentary by Ramanuja)
Vols. 32 & 46: Vedic Hymns (2 Parts)

THE SATAPATHA—BRÂHMANA

ACCORDING TO THE TEXT OF THE MÂDHY ANDINA SCHOOL

Translated by

JULIUS EGGELING

PART I

BOOKS I AND II

MOTILAL BANARSIDASS PUBLISHERS
PRIVATE LIMITED • DELHI

9th Reprint : **Delhi, 2018**
First Published by the Clarendon Press: Delhi, 1982

ISBN: 978-81-208-0113-4

Also available at:
MOTILAL BANARSIDASS
41 U.A. Bungalow Road, Jawahar Nagar, Delhi 110 007
1 B, Jyoti Studio Compound, Kennedy Bridge, Nana Chowk, Mumbai 400 007
120 Royapettah High Road, Mylapore, Chennai 600 004
236, 9th Main III Block, Jayanagar, Bengaluru 560 011
8 Camac Street, Kolkata 700 017
Ashok Rajpath, Patna 800 004
Chowk, Varanasi 221 001

UNESCO COLLECTION OF REPRESENTATIVE WORKS—*Indian Series*
This book has been accepted in the Indian Translation Series of the UNESCO Collection of Representative Works, jointly sponsored by the United Nations Educational, Scientific and Cultural Organization (UNESCO) and the Government of India

Printed in India

by RP Jain at NAB Printing Unit,
A-44, Naraina Industrial Area, Phase I, New Delhi–110028
and published by JP Jain for Motilal Banarsidass Publishers (P) Ltd,
41 U.A. Bungalow Road, Jawahar Nagar, Delhi-110007

RASHTRAPATI BHAVAN,
NEW DELHI-4
June 10, 1962

I am very glad to know that the Sacred Books of the East, published years ago by the Clarendon Press, Oxford, which have been out-of-print for a number of years, will now be available to all students of religion and philosophy. The enterprise of the publishers is commendable and I hope the books will be widely read.

S. RADHAKRISHNAN

CONTENTS

INTRODUCTION.

THE translator of the *S*atapatha-brâhma*n*a can be under no illusion as to the reception his production is likely to meet with at the hand of the general reader. In the whole range of literature few works are probably less calculated to excite the interest of any outside the very limited number of specialists, than the ancient theological writings of the Hindus, known by the name of Brâhma*n*as. For wearisome prolixity of exposition, characterised by dogmatic assertion and a flimsy symbolism rather than by serious reasoning, these works are perhaps not equalled anywhere; unless, indeed, it be by the speculative vapourings of the Gnostics, than which, in the opinion of the learned translators of Irenæus, 'nothing more absurd has probably ever been imagined by rational beings[1].' If I have, nevertheless, undertaken, at the request of the Editor of the present Series, what would seem to be a rather thankless task, the reason will be readily understood by those who have taken even the most cursory view of the history of the Hindu mind and institutions.

The Brâhma*n*as, it is well known, form our chief, if not our only, source of information regarding one of the most important periods in the social and mental development of India. They represent the intellectual activity of a sacerdotal caste which, by turning to account the religious instincts of a gifted and naturally devout race, had succeeded in transforming a primitive worship of the powers of nature into a highly artificial system of sacrificial ceremonies, and was ever intent on deepening and extending its hold on the minds of the people, by surrounding its own vocation with the halo of sanctity and divine inspiration. A complicated ceremonial, requiring for its proper observance and

---

[1] A. Roberts and W. A. Rambaut, The Writings of Irenæus, vol. i. p. xv.

consequent efficacy the ministrations of a highly trained priestly class, has ever been one of the most effective means of promoting hierarchical aspirations. Even practical Rome did not entirely succeed in steering clear of the rock of priestly ascendancy attained by such-like means. There, as elsewhere, 'the neglect or faulty performance of the worship of each god revenged itself in the corresponding occurrence; and as it was a laborious and difficult task to gain even a knowledge of one's religious obligations, the priests who were skilled in the law of divine things and pointed out its requirements—the *pontifices*—could not fail to attain an extraordinary influence[1].' The catalogue of the duties and privileges of the priest of Jupiter might well find a place in the Talmud. 'The rule—that no religious service can be acceptable to the gods, unless it be performed without a flaw—was pushed to such an extent, that a single sacrifice had to be repeated thirty times in succession on account of mistakes again and again committed; and the games, which formed part of the divine service, were regarded as undone, if the presiding magistrate had committed any slip in word or deed, or if the music even had paused at a wrong time, and so had to be begun afresh, frequently for several, even as many as seven, times in succession[2].' Great, however, as was the influence acquired by the priestly colleges of Rome, 'it was never forgotten—least of all in the case of those who held the highest position—that their duty was not to command, but to tender skilled advice[3].' The Roman statesmen submitted to these transparent tricks rather from considerations of political expediency than from religious scruples; and the Greek Polybius might well say that 'the strange and ponderous ceremonial of Roman religion was invented solely on account of the multitude which, as reason had no power over it, required to be ruled by signs and wonders[4].'

The devout belief in the efficacy of invocation and sacri-

[1] Mommsen, History of Rome, translated by W. P. Dickson, vol. i. p. 181.
[2] Ibid. vol. ii. p. 400. [3] Ibid. vol. i. p. 179. [4] Ibid. vol. iii. p. 455.

ficial offering which pervades most of the hymns of the Rig-veda, and which may be assumed to reflect pretty faithfully the religious sentiments of those amongst whom they were composed, could not but ensure to the priest, endowed with the gift of sacred utterance, a considerable amount of respect and reverence on the part of the people. His superior culture and habitual communion with the divine rulers of the destinies of man would naturally entitle him to a place of honour by the side of the chiefs of clans, or the rulers of kingdoms, who would not fail to avail themselves of his spiritual services, in order to secure the favour of the gods for their warlike expeditions or political undertakings. Nor did the Vedic bard fail to urge his claims on the consideration and generosity of those in the enjoyment of power and wealth. He often dwells on the supernatural virtues of his compositions and their mysterious efficacy in drawing down divine blessings on the pious worshipper. In urging the necessity of frequent and liberal offerings to the gods, and invoking worldly blessings on the offerer, the priestly bard may often be detected pleading his own cause along with that of his employer, as Ka*n*va does when he sings (Rig-veda VIII, 2, 13), 'Let him be rich, let him be foremost, the bard of the rich, of so illustrious a Maghavan[1] as thou, O lord of the bay steeds!' Though the Dâna-stutis, or verses extolling, often in highly exaggerated terms, the munificence of princely patrons, and generally occurring at the end of hymns, are doubtless, as a rule, later additions, they at least show that the sacerdotal office must have been, or must gradually have become during this period, a very lucrative one.

Although there is no reason to suppose that the sacrificial ceremonial was in early times so fully developed as some scholars would have us believe, the religious service would seem to have been already of a sufficiently advanced nature to require some kind of training for the priestly office. In course of time, while the collection of hymns were faithfully

[1] Maghavan, the mighty or bountiful, is a designation both of Indra and the wealthy patron of priests. Here it is evidently intended to refer to both.

handed down as precious heirlooms in the several families, and were gradually enriched by the poetical genius of succeeding generations, the ceremonial became more and more complicated, so as at last to necessitate the distribution of the sacerdotal functions among several distinct classes of priests. Such a distribution of sacrificial duties must have taken place before the close of the period of the hymns, and there can be little doubt that at that time the position of the priesthood in the community was that of a regular profession, and even, to some extent, a hereditary one[1]. A post of peculiar importance, which seems to go back to a very early time, was that of the Purohita (literally 'praepositus'), or family priest to chiefs and kings. From the comparatively modest position of a private chaplain, who had to attend to the sacrificial obligations of his master, he appears to have gradually raised himself to the dignity of, so to say, a minister of public worship and confidential adviser of the king. It is obvious that such a post was singularly favourable to the designs of a crafty and ambitious priest, and must have offered him exceptional opportunities for promoting the hierarchical aspirations of the priesthood[2].

In the Rig-veda there is, with the single exception of the Purusha-sûkta, no clear indication of the existence of caste in the proper, Brâhmanical sense of the word. That institution, we may assume, was only introduced after the Brâhmans had finally established their claims to the highest

[1] See J. Muir, Original Texts, I, p. 239 seq.

[2] See Max Müller, History of Ancient Sanskrit Literature, p. 485 seq.; A. Weber, Indische Studien, X, 31 seq. In Rig-veda IV, 50, 8, Vâmadeva is made to say, 'That king alone, with whom the Brahman walks in front (pûrva eti), lives well-established in his house; for him there is ever abundance of food; before him the people bow of their own accord.' If Grassmann was right in excluding verses 7–11 as a later addition, as I have no doubt he was (at least with regard to verses 7–9), these verses would furnish a good illustration of the gradually increasing importance of the office of Purohita. Professor Ludwig seems to take the verses 7–11 as forming a separate hymn; but I doubt not that he, too, must consider them on linguistic grounds, if on no other, as considerably later than the first six verses. The fact that the last pâda of the sixth verse occurs again as the closing formula of the hymns V, 55; VIII, 40; and X, 121 (though also in VIII, 48, 13, where it is followed by two more verses) seems to favour this view.

rank in the body politic; when they sought to perpetuate their social ascendancy by strictly defining the privileges and duties of the several classes, and assigning to them their respective places in the gradated scale of the Brâhmanical community. The period during which the main body of the Vedic hymns was composed, in the land of the seven rivers, seems to have been followed by a time of wars and conquests. From the literary products of the succeeding period we can see that the centre of the Âryan civilisation had in the meantime shifted from the region of the Sindhu (Indus) to that of the Yamunâ (Jumna) and Gaṅgâ. As the conquered districts were no doubt mainly occupied by aboriginal tribes, which had either to retire before their Âryan conquerors, or else to submit to them as *S*ûdras, or serfs, it seems not unnatural to suppose that it was from a sense of the danger with which the purity of the Brâhmanical faith was threatened from the idolatrous practices of the aboriginal subjects, that the necessity of raising an insurmountable barrier between the Âryan freeman and the man of the servile class first suggested itself to the Brâhmans. As religious interests would be largely involved in this kind of class legislation, it would naturally call into play the ingenuity of the priestly order; and would create among them that tendency towards regulating the mutual relations of all classes of the community which ultimately found its legal expression, towards the close of this period, in the Dharma-sûtras, the prototypes of the Hindu codes of law.

The struggle for social ascendancy between the priesthood and the ruling military class must, in the nature of things, have been of long duration. In the chief literary documents of this period which have come down to us, *viz.* the Ya*g*ur-veda, the Brâhma*n*as, and the hymns of the Atharva-veda some of which perhaps go back to the time of the later hymns of the *Ri*k, we meet with numerous passages in which the ambitious claims of the Brâhmans are put forward with singular frankness. The powerful personal influence exercised by the Purohitas, as has already been indicated, seems to have largely contributed to the final success of the sacerdotal order. Thus we read in the Aitareya-brâhmana VIII, 24–25, 'Verily, the gods do not eat the food offered by the king who is without a Purohita: wherefore let the king, who wishes to sacrifice, place a Brâhman at the head (puro adhîta). . . .' 'Now Agni Vaisvânara, who is possessed of five destructive weapons, is the same as the Purohita. With them he constantly surrounds (protects) the king, even as the ocean surrounds the earth: the kingdom of such a ruler is undisturbed. His vital breath deserts him not before the (full term of) life, but he lives to old age, and attains to the full measure of life: he dies not (and is not born) again, whosoever possesses such a wise Brâhman for his Purohita, for the guardian of his realm.' And again, in the Atharva-veda III, 19, 'May this prayer of mine be accomplished; may perfect vigour and strength, may perfect, unceasing, and victorious power accrue to those whose Purohita I am. I perfect their kingdom, their might, their vigour, their strength. With this oblation I cut off the arms of their enemies . . . . Go forth, ye men, and conquer; may your arms be terrible! ye sharp-shafted, smite the weak-bowed; ye of terrible weapons and terrible arms, (smite) the feeble! when discharged, fly forth, O arrow, sped by prayer; vanquish the enemies; rush forward and slay all the best of them; let not one of them escape[1].'

The question as to how the Brâhmans ultimately succeeded in overcoming the resistance of the ruling class receives but little light from the contemporaneous records. Later legendary accounts of sanguinary struggles between the two classes, and the final overthrow, and even annihilation, of the Kshatriyas can hardly deserve much credence. At best they seem to contain some small kernel of historical fact. Perseverance and tenacity of purpose were probably the chief means by which the Brâhmans gained their ends. Not unfrequently, too, kings may have lent their countenance to the aspirations of the priesthood, as calculated to counteract the unruly spirit and ambitious designs of the military order. We certainly meet with not a few instances of kings

[1] Cf. J. Muir, Original Sanskrit Texts, I, p. 283.

figuring as the patrons of learned Brâhmans. As the old hymns were gradually assuming the character of divinely inspired utterances, additional matter might occasionally find its way into them, almost unconsciously, which more adequately expressed the actual scope of the aspirations of their priestly depositaries. That many such additions must have been made to the old hymns, prior to the age of diaskeuasts and exegetes, cannot be doubted.

Another, even more important, source of strength to the sacerdotal order was the sacrifice. The more complicated the ceremonial, the greater the dependence of the lay worshipper on the professional skill of the priests; and the greater the number of priests required for the proper performance of these ceremonies, the larger the gains derived by the priesthood generally from this kind of occupation. What more natural, therefore, than that the highest importance should have been ascribed to these performances, and an ever-increasing attention bestowed on the elaboration of the ceremonial. From clear indications in not a few hymns of the Rig-veda it appears, as has already been remarked, that a distribution of the sacrificial functions among different classes of priests had taken place before the final redaction of that collection. As to the time when such a step may have become necessary for the due performance of sacrifices, this is a question which will probably never be decided. The sacrifice is an old Indo-Iranian, if not Indo-Germanic, institution. Some of the chief Indian sacrifices undoubtedly go back, in some form or other, to the common Indo-Iranian period, notably the Soma-sacrifice, and, if we may judge from the coincidence of name between the âprî-hymns[1] and the âfrî-gân of the Pârsî ritual, the animal sacrifice.

As regards the third great division of Indian sacrifices, the haviryag*ñ*as (or offerings of milk, butter, grain-food, and similar materials), of which the present volume treats, we have hardly any evidence to fall back upon. It is,

[1] See Haug's Essays, p. 241; Max Müller, History of Ancient Sanskrit Literature, p. 463 seq.

however, highly probable that these sacrifices also reach at all events far back into the Vedic antiquity. Perhaps the careful preservation of the pravara-lists[1], or lists of ancestors required at the ishti, the normal form of offering which underlies the haviryagñas, might be adduced in favour of the antiquity of the latter. This, however, is a point which requires further investigation. Neither has the last word been spoken regarding the traditional arrangements of the hymns. It is well known that the majority of the single collections of which the first seven Mandalas (and to some extent those of the tenth) are made up, begin with hymns addressed to Agni, which, as a rule, are followed by hymns addressed to Indra. These, again, are in many cases followed by hymns to the Visve Devâh (and Maruts)[2]. Now, in the later dogmatic literature we find the three Âryan castes, the Brahman, the Kshatra, and the Vis, identified with Agni, Indra, and the Visve Devâh (all the gods, or, as a special class, the All-Gods)[3] respectively. This identification is a very natural one. Agni, the sacrificial fire, the bearer of oblations and caller of the gods, is, like the priest, the legitimate mediator between God and man. Penetrating brilliance (tegas) and holy lustre (varkas) are the common attributes of the Brahman. Again, Indra, the valiant hero, for ever battling with the dark powers of the sky, is a not less appropriate representative of the knightly order. According to Professor Roth, this truly national deity of the Vedic Âryans would seem to have superseded

[1] See the present volume, p. 115 note.

[2] See Max Müller, History of Ancient Sanskrit Literature, p. 461 seq.

[3] See especially Taitt. S. VII, 1, 1, 4. 5; Weber, Ind. Stud. X, pp. 8, 26. In Sat. Br. II, 4, 3, 6. 7, Indra and Agni are identified with the Kshatra (? power in general) and the Visve Devâh with the Vis. Sometimes Brihaspati or Brahmanaspati, the lord of prayer or worship, takes the place of Agni, as the representative of the priestly dignity (especially Taitt. S. IV, 3, 10, 1–3; Vâg. S. 14, 28–30); and in several passages of the Rik this god appears to be identical with, or at least kindred to, Agni, the purohita and priest (see Max Müller, Translation of Rig-veda, I, 77; J. Muir, Original Sanskrit Texts, V, p. 272 seq.) In Rig-veda X, 68, 9, where Brihaspati is said to have found (avindat) the dawn, the sky, and the fire (agni), and to have chased away darkness with his light (arka, sun), he seems rather to represent the element of light and fire generally (das Ur-licht, cf. Vâg. S. IX, 10–12). In the second

the older Indo-Iranian god Trita[1], and to have gradually encroached on the province of Varu*n*a, who perhaps was originally one of the highest deities of the Âryan (Indo-Germanic) pantheon. The warlike chiefs and clansmen evidently saw in Indra a more congenial object of their adoration. It can scarcely be without significance that of all the Vedic *Ri*shis, Vasish*th*a, the priest *par excellence*, has ascribed to him by far the greatest number of hymns addressed to Varu*n*a (and Mitra-Varu*n*a), while there is not a single hymn to Varu*n*a in the family collection of the royal *Ri*shi Vi*s*vâmitra, whose religious enthusiasm is divided almost exclusively between Agni, Indra, and the Vi*s*ve Devâ*h*. Lastly, the identification of the common people with a whole class of comparatively inferior deities would naturally suggest itself. Hence we also find the Maruts[2], the constant companions and helpmates of Indra, the divine ruler, employed in a similar

Ma*nd*ala the hymns to B*ri*haspati are placed immediately after those to Agni and Indra. Though the abstract conception represented by this deity may seem a comparatively modern one, it will by no means be easy to prove from the text of the hymns addressed to him, that these are modern. It would almost seem as if two different tendencies of adoration had existed side by side from olden times; the one, a more popular and sensuous one, which, in Vedic times, found its chief expression in Indra and his circle of deities; and the other, a more spiritual one, represented originally by Varu*n*a (Mitra, &c.; cf., however, *S*at. Br. IV, 1, 4, 1–4), and in Vedic times, when the sacerdotal element more and more asserted itself, by B*ri*haspati, and especially by Agni. The identification of this god with the priestly office was as happy as it was natural; for Agni, the genial inmate of every household, is indeed vai*s*vânara, the friend of all men. Shadowy conceptions, such as B*ri*haspati and Brahman, on the other hand, could evoke no feelings of sympathy in the hearts of the people generally. Of peculiar interest, in this respect, are the hymns in which Agni is associated with Indra (see Max Müller's Science of Language, Second Series, p. 495; J. Muir, Original Sanskrit Texts, V, pp. 219, 220), and the passages in which Agni has ascribed to him functions which legitimately belong to Indra; viz. the slaying of V*ri*tra and destruction of the enemies' cities. The mutual relation of Indra and Varu*n*a has been well discussed in Dr. Hillebrandt's treatise 'Varu*n*a and Mitra,' p. 97 seq. It is most concisely expressed by Vasish*th*a, Rig-veda VII, 83, 9, 'The one (Indra) slays the enemies in battles; the other (Varu*n*a) ever defends the ordinances.'

[1] See the present volume, p. 48 note; R. Roth. Zeitsch. der D. M. G., VI, p. 73 seq.

[2] The Maruts are identified with the vi*s*a*h*, or clans, in *S*at. Br. II, 5, 1, 12; 2, 24; 27; 35, etc. In *S*âṅkh. 16, 17, 2–4 the heaven of the Maruts is assigned to the Vai*s*ya (Ind. Stud. X, p. 26).

sense. The identification of the Vis with the Visve Devâh, which ultimately obtained, was probably determined chiefly by etymological considerations.

The same triad of divinities, as representative of the mutual relations of the social grades of the Âryan community, is repeatedly met with in the sacrificial ritual, and especially in its dogmatic exposition. This identification finds its most complete expression in the well-known passages of the Taittirîya-samhitâ (VII, 1, 1, 4–5) and the Tândya-brâhmana (VI, 1, 6–11)[1]. According to these authorities, Pragâpati, the lord of creatures, created from his mouth the Brâhmana, together with Agni, the trivrit stoma, the gâyatrî metre (and the rathantara sâman and he-goat, according to the first source; or the spring, according to the other). From his breast and arms he created the Râganya, together with Indra, the pañkadasa stoma, the trishtubh metre (and the brihat sâman, and the ram; or the summer respectively). From the middle part of his body he created the Vaisya, together with the Visve Devâh, the saptadasa stoma, the gagatî metre (and the vairûpa sâman, and the kine; or the rainy season respectively). Finally, from his feet he created the Sûdra, together with the ekavimsa stoma and the anushtubh metre (and the vairâga sâman and the horse, according to the Taitt. S.), but no deity, and no season. In accordance with these speculations, single objects of those here enumerated are frequently found elsewhere identified with their respective deities and castes. On the same principle, the three savanas, or morning, mid-day, and evening libations[2] at the Soma-sacrifice, as well as the first three days of the

[1] See Weber, Ind. Stud. X, p. 8.

[2] In Ath.-veda IX, 1, 11, the three savanas are assigned to the Asvins, Indra-Agni, and the Ribhus (cf. Ait. Br. VI, 12) respectively; and in another passage of the same collection, VI, 47, 1, to a. Agni; b. the Visve Devâh, Maruts and Indra; and c. the Bards (kavi). In Vâg. S. XIX, 26, also, the morning libation is assigned to the Asvins (? as the two Adhvaryus of the gods, cf. Sat. Br. I, 1, 2, 17; IV, 1, 5, 15; Ait. Br. I, 18); but in Taitt. S. II, 2, 3, 1; Ait. Br. III, 13; Sat. Br. II. 4, 4, 12; IV, 2, 4, 4–5 they are referred to Agni, Indra, and the Visve Devâh respectively. See, also, Sat. Br. IV, 3, 5, 1, where the Vasus (related to Agni III, 4, 2, 1; VI, 1, 2, 10), Rudras, and Âdityas (cf. VI, 1, 2, 10, and Ait. Br. III, 13) are connected with the three libations.

Dvâdasâha[1], are generally assigned to Agni, Indra, and the Visve Devâh respectively. If in the ekâdasinî, or traditional order of eleven victims that have to be immolated at the Soma-sacrifice, the victim sacred to Agni is placed first, while those to the Visve Devâh and to Indra only come sixth and seventh respectively, we have probably to assume that this order was too firmly established (just as the so-called âprî-hymns are) by long usage to have been easily altered; the more so as the privileged position of the sacerdotal class was not thereby affected.

At the haviryagñas not less prominent a place is assigned to the divine representatives of the two leading classes. The first oblation at every ishti belongs to Agni. The second oblation at the new-moon sacrifice is offered either to Indra, or to Indra[2] and Agni; at the full-moon sacrifice, to Agni and Soma, the latter of whom constitutes Indra's chief source of strength. Indra also plays an important part at the Seasonal offerings which indeed, according to the dogmatic, and by no means improbable, explanation of the Brâhmanas, are performed with special reference to Indra's struggle with Vritra, the demon of drought. At the Agny-upasthâna, or worship of the fires, which succeeds the Agnihotra, the first prayer is addressed to Agni, the second to Indra and Agni[3]. Indeed, while Agni appears everywhere as the Purohita, the 'yagñasya deva ritvik,' or divine priest of the sacrifice, Indra is the god of sacrifice[4], the Maghavan, or munificent patron of the priest.

From these indications it would appear far from improbable that the arrangement of the hymns in which the collections of the Rig-veda were finally handed down, was intended, as far as the leading deities are concerned, to

[1] See, for instance, Ait. Br. IV, 29; 31; V, 1.

[2] The special oblations of the offering of first-fruits consist of a rice-cake to Indra and Agni, and a pap of rice-grains to the Visve Devâh.

[3] See Vâg. S. III, 12-13; Sat. Br. II, 3, 4, 11-12. 'Indra-Agni are everything,—Brahman, Kshatra, and Vis,' Sat. Br. IV, 2, 2, 14.

[4] See, for instance, Sat. Br. I, 4, 5, 4; II, 3, 1, 38; 3, 4, 38; and especially IV, 1, 2, 15, 'for Indra, indeed, is the Maghavan the ruler (netri) of the sacrifice.' He is, as it were, the divine representative of the human sacrificer or patron, who is the yagñapati or lord of sacrifice.

exhibit a social gradation of the Hindu community which was either already firmly established or was steadily kept in view by the sacerdotal class as 'a consummation devoutly to be wished.' In either case the claims of the priests could not fail to be materially strengthened by the pre-eminent position assigned to their divine prototype in the inspired utterances of the *Ri*shis. The question, whether the present arrangement is entirely the result of the final redaction, or whether it was already a feature of the earlier redactions, will perhaps never receive a quite satisfactory answer. It cannot, however, be denied that there is some force in Professor Ludwig's[1] argument,—that, if the arrangement of the several collections had lain with the authors of the final redaction, the result would probably have been a far greater uniformity than they now present.

The idea of bringing together the different family collections would seem first to have suggested itself to the priests at a time when the hitherto divided Âryan tribes had moved from the Panjab to the eastern plains and became consolidated into larger communities, and the want of a more uniform system of worship would naturally make itself felt. To the same period, then, we may refer the first attempts at a systematic arrangement of the entire ceremonial of worship, and the definite distribution of the sacrificial duties among four classes of priests,—viz. the Adhvaryu, or performer of the material part of the sacrifice; the Udgât*ri*, or chanter of hymns; the Hot*ri*, or reciter of solemn sacrificial prayers; and the Brahman, or superintendent of the entire performance. Though some of these offices had no doubt existed for a long time, we possess no definite information as to the exact extent of the duties entrusted to them[2]. The institution of the office

[1] Der Rig-veda, vol. iii. p. 45.

[2] Compare the following remarks of M. Haug, who believed in the identity of the Vedic Adhvaryu and the Zota and Rathwi of the Zend-Avesta:—'At the most ancient times it appears that all the sacrificial formulas were spoken by the Hotar alone; the Adhvaryu was only his assistant, who arranged the sacrificial compound, provided the implements, and performed all manual labour. It was only at the time when regular metrical verses and hymns were introduced into the ritual, that a part of the duties of the Hotar devolved on the Adhvaryu.

of Brahman, doubtless the latest of all, marks a new era in the development of the sacrificial system. While the other priests were only required to possess an accurate knowledge of their own special departments, the Brahman was to be the very embodiment of the sacrificial art and Vedic lore in general, so as to be able to advise the other priests on doubtful points and to rectify any mistakes that might be committed during the performance of sacrifices. Neither had the Hot*ri* priest any special manual of his formulas assigned to him. He was rather expected to have acquired a thorough knowledge of the whole of the *Ri*k-sa*m*hitâ, from which the sacrificial prayers recited by him were exclusively selected. It was probably out of this class—or the Bahv*rik*as, as the followers of the Rig-veda came to be called—more than from any other, that individual priests would fit themselves for the office of Brahman.

As regards the two remaining classes of priests—the Udgât*ri*s and Adhvaryus—we have no means of determining in what form and to what extent the stock of chants and sacrificial formulas used by them may have existed from the time of the institution of their offices down to the formation of the collections that have been handed down, viz. the Sâma-veda-sa*m*hitâ and the Ya*g*ur-veda. From the close connection that exists between the Sâman and the eighth and ninth ma*nd*alas of the *Ri*k, as well as from the fact that most of the hymns of these two ma*nd*alas are ascribed to authors whose family collections (including, in several instances, hymns of their own) are contained in earlier ma*nd*alas,—we may perhaps assume that already at the time when the first nine ma*nd*alas were collected the then existing hymns of the eighth and ninth ma*nd*alas were set apart for the purpose of being chanted at the Soma-sacrifice. In course of time—hand in hand with the fuller development of the Soma ritual and the gradual influx of new hymn material which was either incorporated with the old collections or formed into a new ma*nd*ala—additional chants (or more suitable ones in the place of those hitherto

There are in the present ritual traces to be found, that the Hotar actually must have performed part of the duties of the Adhvaryu.' Ait. Br. I, p. 31.

used) might be required and selected from the hymns of other mandalas. In its original connected form, the material of these chants would naturally remain all along an essential part of the *Ri*k-sa*m*hitâ, for the use of the Hot*ri* and Brahman priests; and thus each of these two collections would henceforth have a history of its own, and discrepancies in the texts common to both would gradually become more and more numerous.

The sacrificial texts used by the Adhvaryu priest are contained in the Ya*g*ur-veda, of which several recensions have come down to us. These texts consist, in about equal parts, of verses (*rik*) and prose formulas (ya*g*us). The majority of the former are likewise found in the *Ri*k-sa*m*hitâ, though not unfrequently with considerable variations, which may be explained partly from a difference of recension, and partly as the result of the adaptation of these verses to their special sacrificial purpose[1]. With the prose formulas, on the other hand, save a few isolated sacrificial calls alluded to in the *Ri*k[2], we meet for the first time in this collection. In the older recensions of the Ya*g*ur-veda the texts are, as a rule, followed immediately by their dogmatic explanation. Now, these theological treatises, composed chiefly with the view of elucidating the sacrificial texts and explaining the origin and hidden meaning of the various rites, form one of the most important departments of the literature of the period which succeeded the systematic arrangement of the sacrificial ceremonial, and in which we must place the gradual consolidation of the Brâhmanical hierarchy. Such as they lie before us, they contain the accumulated wisdom and speculations of generations of Indian divines. They are essentially digests of a floating mass of single discourses or *dicta* on various points of the ceremonial of worship, ascribed to individual teachers, and handed down orally in the theological schools. Single discourses of this kind were called brâhma*n*a,—probably either because they were intended for the instruction and guidance of priests

[1] See A. Weber, History of Indian Literature, pp. 9, 115.
[2] See M. Haug, Ait. Br. I, p. 34.

(brahman) generally; or because they were, for the most part, the authoritative utterances of such as were thoroughly versed in Vedic and sacrificial lore and competent to act as Brahmans or superintending priests[1]. In later times a collection or digest of such detached pieces came to be likewise called a Brâhma*n*a. Works of this kind have come down to us in connection with all the Vedic Sa*m*hitâs, generally in more than one version which, though on the whole betraying a common stock of material, often vary considerably, both in their arrangement and their treatment of these materials. Nay, owing as they do their origin to different schools of the same Veda, these recensions not unfrequently take the very opposite view of single points of ceremonial. Originally the number of such recensions, more or less differing from each other, must have been much larger; but the practical tendencies of a later age, which led to the production of concise manuals of ceremonial rules—the Kalpa-sûtras—adapted to the sacrificial practices of more than one school, were not favourable to the perpetuation of these bulky cyclopædias of theological school-wisdom: thus only the Brâhma*n*as of the schools which had the greatest number of followers survived; while others were probably never committed to writing, or at best had a precarious existence down to more recent times.

While the Brâhma*n*as are thus our oldest sources from which a comprehensive view of the sacrificial ceremonial can be obtained, they also throw a great deal of light on the earliest metaphysical and linguistic speculations of the Hindus. Another, even more interesting feature of these works, consists in the numerous legends scattered through them. From the archaic style in which these mythological tales are generally composed, as well as from the fact that not a few of them are found in Brâhma*n*as of different schools and Vedas, though often with considerable varia-

[1] See Max Müller, History of Ancient Sanskrit Literature, p. 172; Rig-veda-sa*m*hitâ IV, p. vi. Professors Weber (History of Sanskrit Literature, p. 11), Whitney, Westergaard, and other scholars derive brâhma*n*a from bráhman, 'prayer, worship.'

tions, it is pretty evident that the ground-work of many of them goes back to times preceding the composition of the Brâhmanas. From a mythological, and to some extent from a linguistic, point of view these legends thus form a connecting link between the latter and the Vedic hymns. In the case of some of these legends—as those of Sunahsepha [1] and the fetching of the Soma from heaven [2]—we can even see how they have grown out of germs contained in the Vedic hymns; their relation to the latter being thus not unlike that of the Sagas of the younger Edda to the songs of the older Edda. The Kaushîtaki Brâhmana [3], at the end of a story of this kind about Soma, remarks that it is thus told by those versed in legend (âkhyânavidah). We may perhaps infer from this passage that there was a class of people who took a special interest in such legends, and made it their business to collect and repeat them. Indeed, many of the elaborate mythical stories with which we meet in the later epical and Purânic literature doubtless owe their origin to simple popular legends of this kind [4].

Besides the genuine myths which we find in the Brâhmanas, there is also a large number of stories which were evidently invented by the authors of these treatises for the purpose of supplying some kind of traditional support for particular points of ceremonial [5]. However small the intrinsic merit of such passages, they, too, are not entirely devoid of interest, especially from a linguistic point of view, since the style of narrative and the archaic mode of diction which they affect, readily lend themselves to syntactic turns of expression rarely indulged in by the authors in the purely explanatory and exegetic parts of their works. And, indeed, whatever opinion the general reader may form of the Brâhmanas, as purely literary com-

[1] See R. Roth in Weber's Ind. Stud. I, 475 seq.; II, 111 seq.; Max Müller, History of Ancient Sanskrit Literature, p. 408 seq.

[2] See the present volume, p. 183. Compare also Professor Aufrecht's remarks on the myth of Apâlâ, Ind. Stud. IV, p. 8.

[3] K. B. III, 25; cf. Weber, Ind. Stud. II, 313.

[4] Cf. Max Müller, Upanishads, I, p. 39 note.

[5] See, for instance, Sat. Br. II, 4, 3, 1, where a legend of this kind seems to be directly ascribed to Yâgñavalkya.

positions—and, assuredly, it cannot be a very high one—to the Sanskrit student these works (together with their supplements, the Âra*n*yakas; and their metaphysical appendages, the Upanishads) are of the highest importance as the only genuine prose works which the Sanskrit, as a popular language, has produced. For the comparative study of syntax, which has been taken up with such signal success by Professor Delbrück and other scholars, the Brâhma*n*as offer a rich field of enquiry. Nor is the style of these compositions—with its compact grammatical forms and expressive particles, and its habitual employment of the *oratio directa* instead of dependent clauses—without a certain rough beauty of its own, which, however, almost entirely evaporates in a rendering into modern analytical speech. And notwithstanding the general emptiness of the speculations of the Indian theologians, 'there are,' as Professor Max Müller observes [1], 'passages in the Brâhma*n*as full of genuine thought and feeling, and most valuable as pictures of life, and as records of early struggles, which have left no trace in the literature of other nations.'

Although the Adhvaryus, who had to perform all the manual work connected with the sacrifice, were originally looked upon as a subordinate class of priests, their office seems to have risen in the general estimation with the increasing importance that was attributed to the endless details of the ceremonial. In a passage of the Taittirîya Upanishad (2, 3), the Ya*g*us is said to be the head, the *Ri*k the right side, the Sâman the left side, the Âde*s*a [2] the soul, and the Atharvâṅgiras (Atharva-veda) the tail. With better reason the Ya*g*ur-veda might be called the body of the sacrifice, since it contains almost the entire apparatus of sacrificial formulas, while the other ritualistic works are concerned, either chiefly or entirely, with the Soma-sacrifice. As a matter of fact, no other Veda has given rise to so large a number of schools as the Ya*g*ur-

[1] History of Ancient Sanskrit Literature, p. 408.

[2] That is, the Brâhma*n*a, according to *S*aṅkara. In *S*at. Br. IV, 6, 7, 6, the *Rik* and Sâman are identified with Speech, and the Ya*g*us with the Mind.

veda[1]. The numerous subdivisions of the Adhvaryus trace their origin to either of two principal schools, an older and a younger one, the latter of which is itself an offshoot of the former. The oral transmission of the large body of exegetic and legendary matter attached to the sacrificial formulas could hardly fail, in course of time, to produce considerable variations, in different localities, both as regards the wording and the arrangement of these works. Different schools would naturally arise,—each with its own approved recension of the traditional texts,—which in their turn would sooner or later become liable to the same process of disintegration. Such, indeed, has been the case, more or less, with all the Vedic texts, until mechanical means were devised to arrest this process of change. The names of many such subdivisions of the older Yagur-veda are recorded; but hitherto the recensions of only three of them have come to light,—viz. the Kâthaka, the Maitrâyanî-samhitâ, and the Taittirîya-samhitâ. The two former texts belong to subdivisions of the Kathas and Maitrâyanîyas, two branches of the old school of the Karâkas or Karakâdhvaryus. The Taittirîyas, on the other hand, seem to have been an independent branch of the old Yagus[2], the origin of which is ascribed to a teacher named Tittiri. Their text has come down to us in the recension of one of its subdivisions[3], the Âpastambins.

The chief characteristic of the old Yagus texts consists, as has already been indicated, in the constant inter-

[1] Except, perhaps, the Sâma-veda, which, in the Karanavyûha, is said to have counted a thousand schools; though that work itself enumerates only seven schools, one of them with five subdivisions. The number of teachers mentioned in connection with this Veda is, however, very considerable.

[2] As such, at least, the Taittirîyas are mentioned in the Karanavyûha. The term Karaka, however, is also (e.g. in the Pratigñâ-sûtra) applied to the schools of the Black Yagus generally. If the Berlin MS. of the Kâthaka professes, in the colophon, to contain the Karaka text of the work (which Professor Weber takes to refer to the Kârâyanîyâh), the Karaka-sâkhâ of the Kâthaka has perhaps to be understood in contradistinction to those portions of the Kâthaka which have been adopted by the Taittirîyas and incorporated into their Brâhmana.

[3] The Taittirîyas divide themselves into two schools, the Aukhîyas and the Khândikîyas; the Âpastambins are a subdivision of the latter branch. We have also the list of the contents (anakramanî) of the Âtreyas, a subdivision of the Aukhîyas.

mingling of the sacrificial formulas and the explanatory or Brâhma*n*a portions. It was with the view of remedying this want of arrangement, by entirely separating the exegetic matter from the formulas, that the new school of Adhvaryus was founded. The name given to this school is Vâ*g*asaneyins, its origin being ascribed to Yâ*gñ*avalkya Vâ*g*asaneya. The result of this new redaction of the Ya*g*us texts was the formation of a Sa*m*hitâ, or collection of mantras, and a Brâhma*n*a. This re-arrangement was doubtless undertaken in imitation of the texts of the Hot*ri* priests, who had a Brâhma*n*a[1] of their own, while their sacrificial prayers formed part of the *Ri*k-sa*m*hitâ. Indeed, the Taittirîyas themselves became impressed with the desirability of having a Brâhma*n*a of their own,—and attained their object by the simple, if rather awkward, expedient of applying that designation to an appendage to their Sa*m*hitâ, which exhibits the same mixture of mantra and brâhma*n*a as the older work. They also incorporated a portion of the Kâ*th*aka text into their Brâhma*n*a and its supplement, the Taittirîyâra*n*yaka. Of all the schools of the old Ya*g*us those of the Taittirîyas seem to have attracted by far the greatest number of adherents; and in southern India their texts have continued pre-eminently the subject of study till the present day. In northern India, on the other hand, they have been largely superseded by their later rivals. On account of the lucid arrangement of their sacred texts, the Vâ*g*asaneyins called them the White (*s*ukla) Ya*g*ur-veda; the term of Black or Dark (k*ri*sh*n*a) Ya*g*ur-veda being, for the opposite reason, applied to the texts of the older schools. In later times, an absurd story was invented (doubtless by followers of the White Ya*g*us), in which the origin of the name Taittirîya is connected with the word tittiri[2], in the sense of 'partridge.'

[1] It has come down to us in two different recensions, the Aitareya and the Kaushîtaki (or *S*âṅkhâyana) Brâhma*n*a.

[2] Professor Weber, however, thinks there may be some reason for this derivation; the name of Taittirîya having perhaps been applied to this school on account of the motley (partridge-like) character of its texts. According to the story alluded to, Yâ*gñ*avalkya, having been taught the old Ya*g*us texts by Vai*s*ampâyana, incurred the displeasure of his teacher, and was forced by him to disgorge the sacred science which, on falling to the ground, became soiled

The Brâhma*n*a of the Vâ*g*asaneyins bears the name of *S*atapatha, that is, the Brâhma*n*a 'of a hundred paths,' because it consists of a hundred lectures (adhyâyas). Both the Vâ*g*asaneyi-sa*m*hitâ and the *S*atapatha-brâhma*n*a have come down to us in two different recensions, those of the Mâdhyandina and the Kâ*n*va schools. Of the latter recension of the Brâhma*n*a, however, three books out of seventeen are wanting in the European libraries and have, as far as I know, not yet been discovered in India. The Mâdhyandina text both of the Sa*m*hitâ and the Brâhma*n*a has been edited by Professor Weber; the former with the various readings of the Kâ*n*va recension. To the same scholar we owe a German translation of the first adhyâya of the first kâ*nd*a[1]; and he has, moreover, subjected the entire accessible literature of the White Ya*g*ur-veda—with the exception of the Kâ*n*va text of the Brâhma*n*a—to a careful examination, and has extracted from it all that seems calculated to throw light on its history, so that in this respect little remains to those who come after him but to state the results of his enquiries. Professor Max Müller, in his History of Ancient Sanskrit Literature, has also fully discussed the questions regarding the date and authorship of these texts, and has done much to clear up what was obscure in their relations to the older Ya*g*us texts and to Vedic literature generally. Many points, however, still remain doubtful; and, above all, opinions are as divided as ever regarding the approximate date of the teacher with whose name tradition connects the origin of the modern school of the Adhvaryus.

The schools of the Vâ*g*asaneyins are stated to have been either fifteen or seventeen; and their names are given, though with considerable variations, in different works. No distinct traces, however, have as yet been discovered of any recensions besides the two already referred to. As regards the names of these two,—the Mâdhyandina and Kâ*n*va,—the latter is the name of one of the chief families of *Ri*shis

(hence Black Ya*g*us), and was picked up by Yâ*gñ*avalkya's condisciples, who had assumed the form of partridges. This story seems first to occur in the Purâ*n*as; see Wilson's translation of the Vish*n*u Purâ*n*a (ed. Hall), III, p. 54. Pâ*n*ini (IV, 3, 102) and Pata*ñg*ali only know of the Taittirîya texts as 'promulgated by Tittiri.'

[1] Zeitsch. der D. M. G., IV, p. 289 seq.; reprinted in Indische Streifen I, p. 31 seq.

of the *Ri*k-sa*m*hitâ; and certain orthoepic peculiarities of the Ya*g*us texts of the Kâ*n*vas would seem to favour the assumption of a connection of this school with the redaction of the *Ri*k. The name of the Mâdhyandinas, literally 'meridional,' on the other hand, does not occur in the older literature. Nor can we draw any definite conclusions, as to the probable date of their recension, from Lassen's identification of this name with the Μανδιαδινοί, mentioned by Megasthenes (as quoted by Arrian) as a people on the banks of a tributary of the Ganges; or from Professor Weber's conjecture that the Mâdhyandina school may have taken its origin among that people.

The Mâdhyandina text of the *S*atapatha is divided into fourteen books (kâ*nd*a). For several reasons, however, some of these books have to be assigned to a later period than the others. In the first place, the twelfth kâ*nd*a is called madhyama, 'the middle one;' a fact which in itself would suggest the idea that, at the time when this nomenclature was adopted, the last five books (or perhaps books 11–13) were regarded as a separate portion of the work [1]. Besides, Pata*ñg*ali, in a kârikâ or memorial couplet to Pâ*n*. IV, 2, 60, mentions the words shash*t*ipatha ('consisting of sixty paths') and *s*atapatha, with the view of forming derivative nouns from them, in the sense of one who studies such works. Now, as the first nine books of the *S*atapatha, in the Mâdhyandina text, consist of sixty adhyâyas, it was suggested by Professor Weber that it was probably this very portion of the work to which Pata*ñg*ali applied the term 'shash*t*ipatha,' and that consequently the first nine books were at that time considered as, in some sense, a distinct work and were studied as such. This conjecture has been generally accepted. There is indeed a possibility that Pata*ñg*ali may have been acquainted with some other

[1] The Kâ*n*va text is divided into seventeen books. Kâ*n*das 12–15 correspond to Mâdhyandina 10–13; and kâ*nd*a 16, which treats o the Pravargya ceremony, corresponds to the first three adhyâyas of the last kâ*nd*a of the Mâdhyandinas. Thus, in the Kâ*n*va recension the fourteenth kâ*nd*a, called 'madhyama,' is the middle one of kâ*nd*as 12–16; the seventeenth kâ*nd*a, or B*ri*hadâra*n*yaka, being apparently considered as a supplement. Perhaps this division is more original than that of the Mâdhyandinas.

recension of the Brâhma*n*a of the Vâ*g*asaneyins which consisted of only forty adhyâyas; but even in that case the latter would in all probability correspond to the first nine books of the Mâdhyandina text. As regards the Kâ*n*va recension, we are unfortunately not yet able, owing to the want of some of its kâ*nd*as, to determine its exact extent; and have to rely on a list added by a scribe on the front page of one of the kâ*nd*as in the Oxford MS.[1], according to which that text consists of 104 adhyâyas. Still further evidence regarding the mutual relations of the several portions of our Brâhma*n*a is contained in a passage of the Mahâbhârata (XII, 11739), where Yâ*g*ñavalkya relates that, at the inspiration of the Sun, he composed (*k*akre) the *S*atapatha, including[2] the Rahasya (mystery), the Sa*m*graha (epitome), and the Pari*s*ish*t*a (supplement). Now the tenth book is really called Agni-rahasya; while the eleventh contains a kind of summary of the preceding ritual; and kâ*nd*as 12–14 treat of various other subjects. This relation between the first nine and the remaining five books is also fully borne out by internal evidence, as well as by a comparison with the Vâ*g*asaneyi-sa*m*hitâ. The latter consists of forty adhyâyas, the first eighteen of which contain the formulas of the ordinary sacrifices—the Haviryа*g*ñas and Soma-sacrifice—and correspond to the first nine books of the *S*atapatha-brâhma*n*a. The succeeding adhyâyas have been clearly shown by Professor Weber[3] to be later additions. As a rule only those formulas which are contained in the first eighteen adhyâyas are found in the Taittirîya-sa*m*hitâ; while those of the later adhyâyas are given in the Taittirîya-brâhma*n*a.

At the end of the *S*atapatha the White Ya*g*us is said to have been promulgated (â-khyâ) by Yâ*g*ñavalkya Vâ*g*asaneya. Now the name of this teacher is indeed more frequently met with in the Brâhma*n*a than that of any other;

[1] The accuracy of this list cannot be relied upon, as several mistakes occur in the number of ka*nd*ikâs there given. It is, however, unlikely that the scribe should have committed any mistake regarding the number of adhyâyas.

[2] Literally 'together with the rahasya (sarahasyam),' &c.

[3] History of Indian Literature, p. 107 seq.

especially in some of the later books where his professional connection with *G*anaka, king of Videha, and his skill in theological disputations are favourite topics. As regards the earlier portion of the work, however, it is a remarkable fact that, while in the first five books Yâ*gñ*avalkya's opinion is frequently recorded as authoritative [1], he is not once mentioned in the four succeeding kâ*nd*as (6–9). The teacher whose opinion is most frequently referred to in these books, is *S*â*nd*ilya. This disagreement in respect of doctrinal authorities, coupled with unmistakable differences [2], stylistic as well as geographical and mythological, can scarcely be accounted for otherwise than by the assumption of a difference of authorship or original redaction. Now the subject with which these four kâ*nd*as are chiefly concerned, is the agni*k*ayana, or construction of the sacred fire-altar. For reasons urged by Professor Weber, it would appear not improbable that this part of the ceremonial was specially cultivated in the north-western districts; and since the geographical allusions in these four kâ*nd*as chiefly point to that part of India, while those of the other books refer almost exclusively to the regions along the Ganges and Jumna, we may infer from this that the fire-ritual, adopted by the Vâ*g*asaneyins at the time of the first redaction of their texts—that is, of the first nine kâ*nd*as, as far as the Brâhma*n*a is concerned—had been settled in the north-west of India.

Here, however, we meet with another difficulty. The tenth book, or Agnirahasya, deals with the same subject as the preceding four kâ*nd*as; and here also Sâ*nd*ilya figures as the chief authority, while no mention is made of Yâ*gñ*avalkya. Moreover, at the end of that kâ*nd*a, a list of teachers is given in which the transmission of the sacrificial science (either in its entirety, or only as regards the fire-ritual) is traced from a teacher Tura Kâvasheya —who is said to have received it from the god Pra*g*âpati—downwards, through two intermediate teachers, to Sâ*nd*i-

[1] See, however, *S*at. Br. II, 5, 1, 2–3, where Yâ*gñ*avalkya's opinion is referred to as being contrary to the Rig-veda.

[2] See Weber, Ind. Stud. XIII, p. 266 seq.

lya; and from thence, through six intermediate teachers, to *S*â*m*g*î*vî-putra. Tura Kâvasheya is referred to in another passage of the tenth kâ*nd*a (X, 6, 5, 9) as having built a fire-altar[1] to the gods at Kârotî; and in the Aitareya-brâhma*n*a he is mentioned as the high-priest who officiated at the inauguration-ceremony of king *G*aname*g*aya Pârikshita, renowned in epic legend. From these indications we may, it seems to me, take it for certain that Tura Kâvasheya and *S*â*nd*ilya (the latter of whom is also held in high repute by the *Kh*andogas or Sâman-priests) were regarded by the Vâ*g*asaneyins as the chief arrangers, if not the originators, of the fire-ritual such as it was finally adopted by that school. On the other hand, we saw that the first nine books of the *S*atapatha, if their identification with Pata*ñg*ali's 'shash*t*ipatha' be correct, must have been regarded as, in some particular sense, a complete work. Now this combination of the fire-ritual in kâ*nd*as 6–9 with the complete exposition of the Haviryag*ñ*a and Soma-sacrifice, contained in the first five books, would seem to presuppose some kind of compromise between the two schools recognising Yâ*g*ñavalkya and Sâ*n*-*d*ilya respectively as their chief authority. What, then, are we to understand to be the exact relations between the later kâ*nd*as, especially the tenth, and the earlier portion of the work? We do not, and could not, meet with such a term as '*k*atvâri*ms*at-patha,' or work of forty paths, as applying to the last five kâ*nd*as of the *S*atapatha; their nature was too well understood for that, as we see from the passage of the Mahâbhârata, above referred to. The list of teachers at the end of the tenth kâ*nd*a shows no sign of any amalgamation of the two schools up to the time of Sâ*mg*îvî-putra, the last teacher mentioned in it: with one exception, it belongs exclusively to the *S*â*nd*ilya school. It contains, however, an additional remark to the effect that from Sâ*mg*îvî-putra downward the list is 'identical,'—viz. with some other list. Now this remark can only refer to the va*m*sa given at the end of the last kâ*nd*a. In this list the

[1] The author of this passage would seem to imply, though he does not exactly express it, that this was the first fire-altar built in the proper way.

transmission of the science of the Adhvaryus is traced—as far as human agency is concerned—from Ka*s*yapa Naidhruvi, through nine teachers, to Yâ*g*ñavalkya, and thence, through four other teachers, to Sâ*mg*îvî-putra[1]. The only name which this list has in common with the former one, previous to Sâ*mg*îvî-putra, is that of Ku*s*ri. According to the former list, he was the teacher of *S*â*nd*ilya, who, in his turn, taught Vâtsya[2]. But since in the same book (X, 5, 5, 1) he is referred to as Vâ*g*a*s*ravasa, and in the list at the end of the *S*atapatha he is set down as the pupil of Vâ*g*a*s*ravas, the same teacher is evidently referred to in both lists; and if we can at all rely on the authenticity of these va*ms*as, we should have to infer from this coincidence, that there was already some connection between the two schools prior to both Yâ*g*ñavalkya and *S*â*nd*ilya.

The two lines of teachers meet once more in the name of Sâ*mg*îvî-putra. In the later list the succession of teachers

---

[1] I here give, side by side, the lists, in inverted order, from Sâ*mg*îvî-putra upwards. For the complete lists, see Max Müller, History of Ancient Sanskrit Literature, p. 438 seq.

End of Book XIV.	End of Book X.
58. Âditya.	(52) Brahman Svayambhu.
57. Ambi*n*î.	
56. Vâ*k*.	(51) Pra*g*âpati.
55. Ka*s*yapa Naidhruvi.	
54. *S*ilpa Ka*s*yapa.	(50) Tura Kâvasheya.
53. Harita Ka*s*yapa.	
52. Asita Vârshaga*n*a.	
51. *G*ihvâvat Bâdhyoga.	(49) Ya*g*ñava*k*as Râ*g*astambâyana.
50. Vâ*g*a*s*ravas.	
49. Ku*s*ri.	(48) Ku*s*ri.
48. Upave*s*i.	(47) *S*â*nd*ilya.
47. Aru*n*a.	(46) Vâtsya.
46. Uddâlaka (Âru*n*eya).	(45) Vâmakakshâya*n*a.
45. Yâ*g*ñavalkya (Vâ*g*asaneya).	
44. Âsuri.	(44) Mâhitthi.
43. Âsurâya*n*a.	(43) Kautsa.
42. Prâ*s*nî-putra (Âsurivâsin).	(42) Mâ*nd*avya.
41. Kâr*s*akeyî-putra.	(41) Mâ*nd*ûkâyani.
40. Sâ*mg*îvî-putra.	(40) Sâ*mg*îvî-putra.
Follow 39 names formed by the addition of 'putra' to the mother's name.	(Same as elsewhere.)

[2] In the B*ri*had-âra*n*yaka (Kâ*n*va) VI, 5, 4 the order is Ku*s*ri, Vâtsya, *S*â*n*(*d*)ilya.

is then continued by forty-nine more names—all of them formed by the addition of 'putra' (son) to the mother's name—which, it appears, we are to supply in the former list. According to Professor Max Müller[1], 'Sâmgîvî-putra seems to have united two lines of teachers.' That this must have been the case, cannot be doubted, provided, of course, that the vamsas are trustworthy[2]. Nay, I should even be inclined to assign to the time of Sâmgîvî-putra the final adjustment of the ritual and its dogmatic exposition such as we find them in the Shashtipatha (and the first eighteen adhyâyas of the Vâgasaneyi-samhitâ), and consequently the first redaction of that part of the Satapatha. Not that all the matter contained in the latter part of the work must necessarily be more modern. There can, on the contrary, be little doubt that much of it is quite as old as anything in the earlier books; and of the Madhukânda, which forms part of the Brihad-âranyaka in the last book, we know at any rate, from a reference to the Madhu-brâhmana in the fourth kânda, that some such tract existed at that time. But such matter as, for some reason or other, was not included in the systematic exposition of the ceremonial, would naturally be in a less settled condition and more liable to modifications and additions.

According to the two lists, Sâmgîvî-putra is removed from Sândilya by six intermediate teachers, the three older[3] of whom are referred to in kândas 6–9; and from Yâgña-

[1] History of Ancient Sanskrit Literature, p. 437.

[2] Professor Weber, Ind. Stud. II, 201 note, expresses his conviction that 'the vamsas are, on the whole, quite authentic; though they do not of course belong to the text, but are later additions; judging from the great number of names, some vamsas must have been added at a very late time.' It seems to me, however, that if the vamsas are at all authentic—and I see no reason for doubt as far as the two lists above referred to are concerned—we have rather to assume that the lists were kept from early times and gradually added to. On the other hand, little can be made of the two vamsas at the end of the Madhu and Yâgñavalkîya kândas. They look rather like attempts—and very unsuccessful ones—at throwing several independent lists into one.

[3] Viz., Vâtsya IX, 5, 1, 62; Vâmakakshâyana VII, 1, 2, 11; Mâhitthi VI, 2, 2, 10; VIII, 6, 1, 16 seq.; IX, 5, 1, 57. Not mentioned are Kautsa, Mândavya, and Mândûkâyani. A Mândavya occurs in the twelfth book of the Mahâbhârata, as a contemporary of Ganaka and Yâgñavalkya.

valkya by four intermediate teachers, the first of whom (Âsuri)[1] is repeatedly quoted in the second (and once each in the first, fourth, and fourteenth) kâ*nd*as. Although these indications do not, of course, supply more than a *terminus a quo* for the final settlement of this part of the work, they would nevertheless seem to favour the supposition that the combination of the fire-ritual with the sacrificial system cannot have taken place at a time far removed from that of Sâ*mg*îvî-putra. The custom of forming metronymics by means of 'putra' is of some interest. It first shows itself in the predecessor of Sâ*mg*îvî-putra's teacher in the Yâ*gñ*a-valkya line, and continues from thence down to the very end of the va*ms*a. Unfortunately, however, we have no means of ascertaining whether this custom had already been commonly practised, in certain localities, before that time, or whether, as seems to me more probable, it was a fashion of recent date. If the latter alternative could be proved, it might help to settle the chronological relations between Yâ*gñ*avalkya and Pâ*n*ini, since it would appear from Pâ*n*. IV, 1, 159[2] (and VI, 1, 13), that the great grammarian was well acquainted, not only with the practice of forming metronymics of this kind, but also with that of forming patronymics from such metronymics.

The relative date of Pâ*n*ini and Yâ*gñ*avalkya has been discussed more than once by Sanskrit scholars[3]; but no agreement has as yet been come to on what Goldstücker justly called 'one of the most important problems of Sanskrit literature.' The chief difficulty of this problem lies in the ambiguity of Kâtyâyana's well-known vârttika to Pâ*n*. IV, 3, 105. According to Pâ*n*ini's rule the names

[1] He is also the *Ri*shi of Vâ*g*. S. III, 37.

[2] This rule, which applies to the people of the north, is not explained in the Mahâbhâshya. The Kâ*s*ikâ V*ri*tti gives the patronymics of Gârgîputra and Vâtsîputra, both of whom occur in our va*ms*a. It is worthy of remark that Kavasha Ailûsha, who is mentioned in Ait. Br. II, 19, and to whom the hymns Rig-veda X, 30-34 are ascribed, is called Kavasha Ailûshîputra in the Kâ*th*aka 25, 7. Cf. Weber, Ind. Stud. III, pp. 459, 157, 485.

[3] See especially Max Müller, History of Ancient Sanskrit Literature, p. 360 seq.; Goldstücker, Pâ*n*ini, p. 132 seq.; Weber, Ind. Stud. V, 65 seq.; XIII, 443; Bühler, Sacred Laws of the Âryas, I, p. xxxix note.

of Brâhmanas and Kalpas proclaimed by old (sages) are formed by the addition of the affix in (to the sages' names). As instances of Brâhmanas, the names of which are formed in this way, the Kâsikâ Vritti gives Bhâllavinah (proclaimed by Bhallu), Sâtyayaninah, Aitareyinah. In accordance with this rule the texts of the White Yagus are called Vâgasaneyinah. This name does not, however, occur in any of Pânini's rules, but follows only from the word 'vâgasaneya' being included in the gana 'saunakâdi' to Pân. IV, 3, 106; and since we have no evidence as to whether any of the words in a gana except the first really belong to Pânini, it must remain doubtful whether or not he knew of the existence of the school known by that name. Kâtyâyana's vârttika runs thus: 'Among the Brâhmanas and Kalpas proclaimed by the old, there is an exception in regard to Yâgñavalkya and others, on account of contemporaneousness: hence (Yâgñavalkya's Brâhmanas are called, not Yâgñavalkinah, but) Yâgñavalkâni Brâhmanâni; Saulabhâni B.' The question, then, is, Does Kâtyâyana mean to say that the Brâhmanas proclaimed by Yâgñavalkya do not fall under this rule, because he was contemporary with Pânini,—and therefore not an old sage in the sense of the rule,—or, that those works should have been excepted by Pânini from his rule, because they are of the same age as those (old) Brâhmanas to which the rule applies? The former alternative was the one generally accepted, until the late Professor Goldstücker made known the text of Patañgali's and Kaiyata's comments[1] on this vârttika. He showed that Kaiyata, at least, clearly interprets it in the sense that Pânini should have excepted works like the Yâgñavalkâni Brâhmanâni, since they, too (api), are of the same age as the Sâtyâyaninah and others. The Mahâbhâshya, on the other hand, is not quite so explicit. It merely says that the Yâgñavalkâni Brâhmanâni &c. ought to have been excepted, because they, too (api), are of the same age. Goldstücker naturally took this explanation to convey the same meaning as that of Kaiyata. This view was, however, controverted by

[1] Pânini, p. 138.

Professor Weber in his review of Goldstücker's 'Pâ*n*ini.' The interpretation of the vârttika adopted in the Kâ*s*ikâ V*ri*tti—according to which Pâ*n*ini's rule does not apply to those works, because Yâ*gñ*avalkya and others are not old authorities in the sense of Pâ*n*ini's rule—is likewise rejected by him, since in that case Kâtyâyana's exception would be no exception at all. On the other hand, Professor Weber thinks that, if we accept Kaiya*t*a's interpretation, Kâtyâyana's additional remark 'on account of contemporaneousness' would be entirely superfluous. He, therefore, proposes, in the passage of the Mahâbhâshya, to take 'api' in the sense of 'even,' and to interpret the passage thus[1]: 'Among the Brâhma*n*as and Kalpas proclaimed by the ancients, Pâ*n*ini ought to have made an exception in regard to Yâ*gñ*avalkya &c., because the Brâhma*n*as and Kalpas proclaimed by them, though indeed going back to ancient (sages), are nevertheless contemporaneous (with Pâ*n*ini himself).' This rather paradoxical argumentation, on the part of Patañ*g*ali, would have to be understood to mean, that the Yâ*gñ*avalkâni Brâhma*n*âni and similar works, though ascribed to old authorities, are in reality modern productions; or—if we may venture to express it in somewhat different words—Pâ*n*ini ought to have made an exception in regard to works which, in point of fact, are no exception at all. Now, if this be the correct interpretation, I can only say this—that, had Patañ*g*ali been anxious to conceal his real meaning, he could scarcely have done so more effectually than by choosing words which, at first sight, look as clear as day.

Professor Bühler[2], who has recently touched upon this controversy, sides with Kaiya*t*a and Goldstücker; and I, too, can take no other view. But, like him, I see no necessity for accepting the inferences which Goldstücker has drawn from this vârttika, viz. that we have to assume so long an interval between Pâ*n*ini and Kâtyâyana, that authors, whom Kâtyâyana considered as far older than Pâ*n*ini, were in reality his contemporaries. This assumption, surely, would involve a degree of ignorance, on the part of

[1] Ind. Stud. V, 68 seq.; XIII, 443.
[2] Sacred Laws of the Âryas, I, p. xxxix note.

Kâtyâyana, regarding the age of Pâ*n*ini, such as would seem altogether unaccountable. The weakness of Goldstücker's argument lies in his identification of the Yâ*g*ñavalkâni Brâhma*n*âni with the Brâhma*n*a of the Vâ*g*asaneyins. With Professor Weber I believe that Pâ*n*ini was perfectly well acquainted with the term 'Vâ*g*asaneyina*h*,' but saw no occasion for specially mentioning it in his rules. Surely, if his silence could possibly have been construed into an act of negligence, Kâtyâyana, who was so intimately connected with the White Ya*g*us that, on Goldstücker's own showing, he composed the Vâ*g*asaneyi-prâti*s*âkhya before he wrote his vârttikas, would have been the first to notice it. The Yâ*g*ñavalkâni Brâhma*n*âni, in their relation to the sacred canon of the school, seem to me to stand somewhat on a par with the 'Tittiri*n*â proktâ*h* *s*lokâ*h*[1],' which, in Patañ*g*ali's time, were excluded from the term 'Taittirîyâ*h*' as uncanonical, and which Professor Weber would identify, perhaps rightly, with some portions of the Taittirîyâra*n*yaka. Both kinds of tracts probably belong to the last floating materials of Adhvaryu tradition, which had not yet been incorporated with the canon. Whether or not the Yâ*g*ñavalkâni Brâhma*n*âni form part of the text of the *S*atapatha which has come down to us, and what exact portions of that text we have to understand by this designation, must remain uncertain for the present. Most probably, however, we have to look for them to certain portions of the last book (or books) in which Yâ*g*ñavalkya figures so prominently. If we had a complete copy of the Kâ*n*va recension, we might perhaps be in a better position for forming an opinion on this subject; for if that version should really turn out to consist of 104 adhyâyas, four of these adhyâyas may have to be considered as a later interpolation; and the fact might have become obscured in the Mâdhyandina recension by a different division of the text[2]. But, however this may

[1] Mahâbhâshya on Pâ*n*. IV, 2, 66; 3, 104.

[2] Possibly, however, this redundancy may have been caused by the insertion of the third or uddhârî-kâ*nd*a, consisting of 124 ka*nd*ikâs, to which there seems to be nothing corresponding in the Mâdhyandina text. We have no MS. of this particular kâ*nd*a. I may also mention that, while in the first kâ*nd*a (or second Kâ*n*va), the Mâdhyandinas count 9, and the Kâ*n*vas 8 adhyâyas,—in the fourth kâ*nd*a (or

be, it appears to me quite intelligible why such portions should have been considered as of equal age to the body of the work; in fact they would probably go back to about the same time as some of the earlier portions; only that, owing to a longer state of uncertain transmission, they may have been more liable to changes and additions. If these tracts are not mentioned by Pâ*n*ini, it may be an accidental omission on his part, or he may not have been aware of their existence, for geographical or other reasons: we can hardly expect Pâ*n*ini to have been so intimately acquainted with the Ya*g*us texts as Kâtyâyana. As regards the dates of Kâtyâyana and Pata*ñg*ali, I accept with Professor Bühler and others, as by far the most probable, the fourth and the middle of the second century B.C. respectively.

Under the title of Vâ*g*asaneyaka, the *S*atapatha-brâhma*n*a is quoted once in Lâ*t*yâyana's *S*rauta-sûtra IV, 12, 12; but I have not been able to find the passage either in the Mâdhyandina text or in that part of the Kâ*n*va text which I have hitherto had at my disposal, viz. kâ*nd*as I, II, IV–VII (Kâ*n*va). Far more frequently the work is quoted, either as Vâ*g*asaneyaka or as Vâ*g*asaneyi-brâhma*n*a, by Âpastamba, both in his *S*rauta and his Dharma-sûtras. On comparing one of these quotations in the Dharma-sûtras (I, 4, 12, 3) with the corresponding passage in the Mâdhyandina recension, Professor Bühler found that 'its wording possessed just sufficient resemblance to allow us to identify the passage which Âpastamba meant, but differed from the *S*atapatha-brâhma*n*a in many details[1].' From this he naturally inferred that Âpastamba probably took his quotations from the Kâ*n*va recension. Now, although I have not been able to compare this particular passage with the Kâ*n*va text[2], I have done so regarding a number of other passages quoted from Âpastamba in Karka's commentary on the Kâtîya-*S*rauta-sûtra. The result was that in no single case did Âpastamba's quotations agree with the corresponding passages in the Kâ*n*va,

fifth Kâ*n*va), on the other hand, the Kâ*n*vas have 8, instead of 6 adhyâyas; and in the fifth kâ*nd*a (or sixth and seventh Kâ*n*vas) they have together 7, instead of 5 adhyâyas.

[1] Bühler, loc. cit. p. xxv. [2] The passage occurs in Mâdhyandina XI, 5, 6, 3.

any more than they did with those of the Mâdhyandina text[1]. In some cases they came nearer to the one text, in others to the other. To several quotations, again, I could find nothing corresponding in either text. Now, supposing the quotations, as given by Karka, to be on the whole correct, there seem to be only two ways of accounting for these discrepancies, viz. either Âpastamba did not mean to quote the passages literally, but only to give the substance of them; or he had a third recension of the Satapatha before him. While some passages would seem to be in favour of the former alternative, others would scarcely admit of this explanation. This question, however, requires further investigation, before it can be definitely settled. In connection with this question the fact will also have to be taken into account, that Kâtyâyana, in composing his Vâgasaneyi-prâtisâkhya, seems to have had before him a different recension of the Samhitâ, from those of the Kânva and Mâdhyandina schools[2].

Professor Bühler appears to be inclined to place Âpastamba somewhere about the fifth century B.C.; and though probably he himself does not consider the reasons he adduces as conclusive, they seem at any rate to show that that writer cannot have lived later than the third century B.C. From

---

[1] I select a few passages:—

1. Âp. (Kâty. VII, 1, 36). prâgvamsasya madhyamam sthûnârâgam âlabhya gapatîti vâgasaneyakam.
   Mâdhy. III, 1, 1, 11. sa pûrvârdhyam sthûnârâgam abhipadyaitad yagur âha.
   Kânva IV, 1, 1, 7. sâ yâsau varshishthâ pûrvârdhe sâlâsthûnâ bhavati tâm abhipadya gapati.
2. Âp. (Kâty. V, 3, 6). atrâpi mesham ka meshîm ka karotîti vâgasaneyakam.
   Mâdhy. II, 5, 2, 15. tatrâpi mesham ka meshîm ka kurvanti.
   Kânva I, 5, 1, 13. mesham ka vâ api meshîm ka kurvanti.
3. Âp. (Kâty. VII, 2, 34). (vritrasya kanînikâsîti traikakudenâñganenâṅkte) yadi traikadukam nâdhigakkhed yenaiva kenâñganenâñgîti vâgasaneyakam.
   Mâdhy. III, 1, 3, 12. (traikadukam bhavati; yatra vâ indro vritram ahams tasya yad akshy âsît tam girim trikakudam akarot....) yadi traikakudam na vinded apy atraikakudam eva syât samânî hy evâñganasya bandhutâ.
   Kânva IV, 1, 3, 10. (tat traikakudam syât; yatra vâ indro vritram ahams tasya ha yâ kanînakâsa yak kakshus tam etam girim kakâra trikakudam; sa yat traikakudam bhavati kakshushy evaitak kakshur dadhâti); yadi traikakudam na vinded api yad eva kiñka syât.
4. Âp. (Kâty. VII, 3, 28). ûshnîshena pradakshinam siro veshtayata iti vâgasaneyakam.
   Mâdhy. III, 2, 1, 16-17. sa prornute.
   Kânva IV, 2, 1, 11-12. athainam prornoti,—sa prornoti.

[2] See Weber, Ind. Stud. IV, p. 69.

the fact that *S*vetaketu, the son of Uddâlaka Âru*n*i, the reputed teacher (and rival[1]) of Yâ*gñ*avalkya, is counted by Âpastamba among the Avaras or moderns, Dr. Bühler infers that the promulgator of the White Ya*g*us cannot have preceded Âpastamba 'by a longer interval than, at the utmost, two or three hundred years.' That the two authors may not have been separated from each other by a longer interval seems likely enough; but, on the other hand, Âpastamba, by his remark, pays no very great compliment to the inspired texts of his own school, since Aru*n*a Aupave*s*i, the grandfather of *S*vetaketu Âru*n*eya, is twice referred to in the Taittirîya-sa*m*hitâ[2].

The geographical and ethnical allusions contained in the *S*atapatha-brâhma*n*a have been carefully collected by Professor Weber[3]. With the exception of those in kâ*nd*as 6–10, as I have already remarked, they point almost exclusively to the regions along the Ganges and Jumna. In the legend about Videgha Mâthava[4], and his Purohita Gotama Râhûga*n*a, tradition seems to have preserved a reminiscence of the eastward spread of Brâhmanical civilisation. Among the peoples that occupied those regions, a prominent position is assigned in the *S*atapatha to the closely-allied Kuru-Pa*ñk*âlas. The Kurus occupied the districts between the Jumna and Ganges—the so-called Madhyade*s*a or middle country—and the Pa*ñk*âlas bordered on them towards the south-east. According to *S*at. Br. XIII, 5, 4, 7, the Pa*ñk*âlas were in olden times called Krivi; and a tribe of this name is evidently referred to in Rig-veda VIII, 20, 24; (22, 12)[5], in connection with the rivers Sindhu and Asiknî. The Kurus, on the other hand, are not directly referred to in the *Ri*k; but a king Kuru*s*rava*n*a, 'glory of the Kurus,' and a patron with the epithet Kaurayâ*n*a are mentioned in the hymns. In Aitar. Br. VIII, 14, the Uttara (northern) Kurus, together with the Uttara-Madras, are said to dwell beyond the Himâlaya.

[1] See B*ri*h. Âr. 3, 5, where he is defeated by Yâ*gñ*avalkya in disputation.

[2] Taitt. S. VI, 1, 9, 2; 4, 5, 1.

[3] Ind. Stud. I, 187 seq.

[4] See the present volume, p. 104, with note. It would have been safer to give the name as Videgha Mâthava, instead of Mâthava the Videgha.

[5] See Ludwig, Rig-veda III, p. 205; Zimmer, Altindisches Leben, p. 103.

From these indications Professor Zimmer infers that, in the times of the hymns, the Kurus and Krivis—whose names evidently are merely variations of the same word—may have lived together in the valleys of Kâ*s*mîr, on the upper Indus; and he also offers the ingenious conjecture, that we may have to look for the Kuru-Krivis in the twin-people of the Vaikar*n*au, mentioned in Rig-veda VII, 18, 11. The names of the principal teachers of the *S*atapatha mark them as belonging to the land of the Kuru-Pa*ñk*âlas; and as in I, 7, 2, 8, preference is given to a certain sacrificial practice on the ground that it is the one obtaining among these peoples, it seems highly probable that the redaction of the work, or at least of the older portion of it, took place among the Kuru-Pa*ñk*âlas[1]. A prince[2] of Pa*ñk*âla, Pravâha*n*a *G*aivali, is mentioned XIV, 9, 1, 1, in connection with Yâ*gñ*avalkya's teacher, Uddâlaka Âru*n*i.

East of the Madhyade*s*a, we meet with another confederacy of kindred peoples, of hardly less importance than the Kuru-Pa*ñk*âlas, at the time of the redaction of the Brâhma*n*a, viz. the Kosala-Videhas. In the legend above referred to they are said to be the descendants of Videgha Mât[illegible]va, and to be separated from each other by the river Sadânîrâ (either the modern Ga*nd*akî or Karatoyâ). The country of the Videhas, the eastern branch of this allied people, corresponding to the modern Tirhut or Puraniya, formed in those days the extreme east of the land of the Âryas. In the later books of the *S*atapatha, king *G*anaka of Videha appears as one of the principal promoters of the Brâhmanical religion, and especially as the patron of Yâ*gñ*avalkya. In XI, 6, 2, 1, *G*anaka is repre-

[1] The passage III, 2, 3, 15, where the Kuru-Pa*ñk*âlas are apparently placed in the north—in direct contradiction to XI, 4, 1, 1, where they are placed in opposition to the Northerners (udî*k*ya*h*)—seems to go against this supposition. Professor Weber, Ind. Stud. I, 191, tries to get over this difficulty by translating Kurupa*ñk*âlatrâ by 'as among the Kuru-Pa*ñk*âlas,' instead of 'among the Kuru-Pa*ñk*âlas;' so that the meaning of the passage would be that 'the same language is spoken in the northern region, as among the Kuru-Pa*ñk*âlas.' Unfortunately, however, the Kâ*n*va text of the passage is not favourable to this interpretation. It runs as follows (K. IV. 2, 3, 10):—udî*k*îm pathyayâ svastyâ vâg vai pathyâ svastis tasmâd atrottarâhai vâg vadatîtyâhu*h* kurupa*ñk*âleshu kurumahâvisheshv ity etâ*m* hi tayâ di*s*a*m* prâgânann eshâ hi tasyâ dik pra*gñ*âtâ.

[2] He is styled râganyabandhu in *Kh*ândogyop. V, 3, 5.

sented as meeting, apparently for the first time, with *S*vetaketu Âru*n*eya, Soma*s*ushma Sâtyaya*gñ*i, and Yâ*gñ*avalkya, while they were travelling (dhâvayadbhi*h*). Probably we are to understand by this that these divines had then come from the west to visit the Videha country. A considerable portion of the B*ri*hadâra*n*yaka deals with learned disputations which Yâ*gñ*avalkya was supposed to have held at *G*anaka's court with divers sages and with the king himself. In B*ri*h. Âr. II, 1, 1 (and Kaush. Up. IV, 1) *G*anaka's fame as the patron of Brâhmanical sages is said to have aroused the jealousy of his contemporary, A*g*âta*s*atru, king of the Kâ*s*is[1]. The name *G*anaka is also interesting on account of its being borne likewise by the father of Sîtâ, the wife of Râma. Unfortunately, however, there is not sufficient evidence to show that the two kings are identical. With the legend of the other great epic, the *S*atapatha offers more points of contact; but on this subject also no definite results have as yet been obtained, it being still doubtful whether the internecine strife between the royal houses of the Kurus and Pa*ñk*âlas which, according to the late Professor Lassen, forms the central fact of the legend of the Mahâbhârata, had not yet taken place at the time of the *S*atapatha-brâhma*n*a, or whether it was already a thing of the past[2]. In the Mahâbhârata, I, 4723, Pâ*nd*u, in speaking to his wife Kuntî, mentions *S*vetaketu, the son of the Maharshi Uddâlaka, as having lived 'not long ago[3].'

As regards the two recensions of the *S*atapatha-brâhma*n*a, this is hardly the place to enter into any detailed discussion of their mutual relations. Nor is my acquaintance with the Kâ*n*va text as yet sufficiently extensive to do justice to this important question. I intend, however, to publish before long a number of extracts from several kâ*nd*as of this recension,—including the text of all the

[1] They occupied the country about the modern Benares (Kâ*s*î).

[2] Dh*ri*tarâsh*t*ra Vai*k*itravîrya, whose sons and nephews form the chief parties of this great feud, is mentioned in the Kâ*th*aka 10, 6. From this passage—which, unfortunately, is not in a very good condition in the Berlin MS.—it would appear that animosities had then existed between the Kurus and Pa*ñk*âlas. It is doubtful, however, whether this part of the Kâ*th*aka is older than the bulk of the *S*atapatha. See Weber, Ind. Stud. III, 469 seq.

[3] See Weber, Ind. Stud. I, 176.

legends as well as other portions which seemed to me of special interest,—from which Sanskrit scholars will be able to form an opinion regarding the exact nature of the variations between the two versions. In my notes to the present translation of the first two kândas, I have considered it desirable occasionally to notice some of the variae lectiones of the Kânva school; it should, however, be understood that these readings have been given solely on the authority of the Oxford MS., for the loan of which I am deeply indebted to the liberality of the Curators of the Bodleian Library. With the aid of the Paris MS., the use of which has also just been kindly granted to me, I hope soon to be able to verify these extracts. For most of the kândas, from the fourth[1] onwards, our materials have been lately enriched by a copy which Mr. Whitley Stokes has had made for Professor Weber from a Benares MS.

The various readings of the Kânva recension of the Vâgasaneyi-samhitâ have been given in Professor Weber's edition, at the end of each kânda. They may be said to consist either of mere verbal variations or of additional mantras. In regard to these readings the Brâhmana of the same school exhibits a feature which may have an important bearing on the textual criticism of the Samhitâ. While the Brâhmana generally shows the same verbal variations in the sacrificial texts as the Samhitâ, it, as a rule, takes no notice whatever of the additional mantras, but agrees in this respect pretty closely with the Mâdhyandina text. Indeed, so far as I am able to judge, the two relations seem to coincide almost entirely, as far as the subject-matter is concerned; the differences, considerable as they sometimes are, being rather of a grammatical and stylistic nature. Occasional omissions, which I have hitherto noticed[2], may perhaps turn out to be due to the carelessness of scribes. As regards the additional mantras referred to, they may have found their way into the Samhitâ at the time when the Sûtras

[1] Viz. kândas 4–7, 9, 10, 12, 14–17.

[2] For instance, the brâhmanas Mâdhy. I, 4, 3; II, 3, 2 and 3; IV, 5, 10; 6, 8 are wanting in the Oxford MS.; see p. 338, note 3.—In the fourth (fifth Kânva) kânda, the Kânvas, on the other hand, have two brâhmanas (V, 7, 5; 8, 2, the latter of which treats of the adâbhya graha, Vâg. S. VIII, 47–50) which are not found in the Mâdhyandina text.

were composed; though, it is true, they do not as a rule appear in the Kâtîya-sûtra, and no other sûtra of the White Yagus, as far as I know, has hitherto come to light[1]. On the other hand, as there are also not a few mantras in the Mâdhyandina Sa*m*hitâ[2], which are not noticed in the Brâhma*n*a of that school, this question must be left for future investigation.

I have already referred to the connection which seems to have existed between the Kâ*n*va school of the White Yagus and the redactors of the *Ri*k-sa*m*hitâ. One of the chief points of contact between our existing recension of the *Ri*k and the Kâ*n*va text of the Yagur-veda is the use of the letters *l* and *lh* instead of *d* and *dh* used by the Mâdhyandinas. Besides, the *rik*s of the Kâ*n*va text generally approach more nearly to the readings of the Rig-veda than those of the other school. Another, even more interesting, feature which the Kâ*n*va recension has in common with the *Ri*k, is the constant[3] employment of the ordinary genitive and ablative of feminine bases, where the other Sa*m*hitâs and Brâhma*n*as generally use the dative; thus the Kâ*n*vas read 'tasyâ*h*' instead of 'tasyai' (M. I, 1, 4, 16); 'gâyatryâ*h*' instead of 'gâyatryai' (I, 7, 1, 1); 'p*ri*thivyâ*h*' instead of 'p*ri*thivyai' (I, 2, 5, 18); 'kumbhyâ bhastrâyâ*h*' instead of 'kumbhyai bhastrâyai' (I, 1, 2, 7); 'stîr*n*âyâ vede*h*' instead of 'stîr*n*âyai vede*h*' (IV, 2, 5, 3); 'dheno*h*' instead of 'dhenvai' (III, 1, 2, 21), &c. Thus the Kâ*n*va text is in this respect more in accordance with the *Ri*k-sa*m*hitâ than even the Aitareya-brâhma*n*a[4]. Again, the Kâ*n*vas seem to form the dative of feminine i-bases in accordance with the usual and older practice of the *Ri*k; at least I find everywhere 'âhutaye' and 'guptaye' (as also in the Atharvan) instead of 'âhutyai' and 'guptyai' as the Mâdhyandinas (and Taittirîyas) read[5]. Of minor points of grammatical

[1] Professor Weber thinks that the sûtra of Vaigavâpa, of which mention is occasionally made in the commentaries on the Kâtîya-sûtra, may belong to the White Yagus. See History of Indian Literature, p. 142. Professor Bühler, Sacred Laws, I, p. xxvi, remarks that 'Kâ*n*va is considered the author of the still existing Kalpa-sûtras of the Kâ*n*va school;' but I have found no notice of these sûtras anywhere.

[2] That is, in those adhyâyas to which the Brâhma*n*a forms a running commentary.

[3] I have not met with any exception in the kâ*nd*as hitherto examined.

[4] See Aufrecht, Ait. Br. p. 428. [5] See also the form 'dheno*h*' mentioned above.

differences may be mentioned the form 'nililye,' which occurs once in the Mâdhyandina text (I, 2, 3, 1), and is otherwise only found in the Mahâbhârata; while the Kâṇva recension has the periphrastic form (nilayâm *k*akre), which the Mâdhyandina text also offers in the other two cases (I, 6, 4, 1; IV, 1, 3, 1) in which the word occurs. On the other hand, the Kâṇvas seem to read invariably 'âtmani (dhâ or kri),' where the Mâdhyandinas have 'âtman,' which is also (doubtless on metrical grounds) the more usual formation in the Rig-veda[1]. Of cases of material differences I can only at present adduce the passage I, 1, 4, 12 (M.), where the Mâdhyandina text is guilty of a transposition of the second and third castes, while that of the Kâṇvas gives them in the proper order. Though most of these points of difference between the two schools would seem to tell in favour of the higher antiquity of the Kâṇva text, there will always be great difficulty in deciding this question, as it is by no means impossible that these variations are entirely due to different local or family traditions. In favour of the latter alternative one or two other points may be mentioned. The Mâdhyandina text, as has already been remarked, offers not a few grammatical and other differences between the first five and the succeeding four kâṇḍas, or, as we may say, between the Yâgñavalkya and the Sâṇḍilya books of the Shashṭipatha. Though I cannot speak with confidence on this point, as I have not yet examined the Kâṇva text of the Sâṇḍilya kâṇḍas, I may refer here to at least two points in which the Kâṇvas, in the Yâgñavalkya portion, agree with the Sâṇḍilya portion of the Mâdhyandina text, viz. the use of the imperfect (aspardhanta) instead of the perfect (paspridhire) in the opening clause of legends; and the frequent employment of the particle 'vâva' in the place of 'vai.'

As regards the present translation of the first two kâṇḍas,

[1] Another curious feature of the Kâṇva text is the frequent insertion of an 'ity uvâ*k*a' in the middle of speeches, much like the colloquial 'says he.' As an instance I may adduce K. IV, 2, 3, 3 (M. III, 2, 3, 5):—Sâ hovâ*k*â 'ham eva vo yagñam amûmuham iti hovâ*k*a yad eva mayi tanvânâ iti mâm yagñâd antaragâta tenaiva vo yagñam amûmuham iti te mahyam nu bhâgam kalpayatety atha vo yagñah praro*k*ishyata iti tatheti ho*k*us, &c. The Kâṇvas also insert much more frequently an 'iti' in the middle of speeches.

I need hardly say that I am fully aware of its shortcomings. My chief endeavour has been to translate as literally as seemed at all compatible with the English idiom. If, in consequence of this, many passages should be found to read somewhat awkwardly, I hope at least that the wish to follow the original as closely as possible, has not rendered them unintelligible. Those who have given any attention to the Brâhma*n*as and the sacrificial system of the Hindus, know how difficult the task is, and how easy it is to commit mistakes regarding the intricate minutiae of the ceremonial. The Brâhma*n*as presuppose a full knowledge of the course of sacrificial performance, and notice only such points as afford an opportunity for dogmatic and symbolic explanations, or seem to call for some authoritative decision to guard them against what were considered as heretical practices. In order to enable the reader to follow the course of the performance with something like completeness, I have supplied in my notes the chief details from Kâtyâyana's Kalpa-sûtras. That not a few of these details did not belong to the sacrificial ceremonial of the *S*atapatha, but were the result of later development, or of an adaptation of sacrificial practices of other schools, can scarcely be doubted. Dr. Hillebrandt[1] is of opinion that sacrificial manuals, somewhat similar to the later Prayogas, must have existed as early as the time of the composition of the Brâhma*n*as. In the absence of any direct evidence, speculation on this point can scarcely lead to any definite results. I may say, however, that it seems to me quite sufficient to assume that the performance of sacrifices was taught as a practical art, and that the theoretic instruction, supplied by the Brâhma*n*as, was conveyed orally in connection with such practical performances. That the latter was the case, is sufficiently evident from the constant occurrence in the Brâhma*n*as of demonstrative pronouns and particles of a 'deictic' force[2].

I have occasionally referred to corresponding passages of the Taittirîyas: an exhaustive comparison of the two branches of the Ya*g*ur-veda, however interesting this might be, lay outside the scope of my notes. A general view of

[1] Das Altindische Neu- und Vollmondsopfer, p. xv.

[2] See, for instance, *S*at. Br. I, 3, 1, 7; 8, 1, 14.

the sacrificial system might be considered desirable in this place; but I have found it necessary to defer this part of my duty as translator to some future opportunity. Those who desire further information on this point, I may refer to Professor Weber's general survey of Hindu sacrifices, in vols. x and xiii of his Indische Studien. No other scholar has contributed so much to our knowledge of the sacrificial ceremonial of the Hindus. I need hardly say that I have also obtained much useful information from the late Professor Haug's notes to his translation of the Aitareya-brâhma*n*a, although on many points the practices of modern *S*rotriyas, on which he chiefly relied, are manifestly at variance with those enjoined by the old ritualistic authorities. For the first kâ*nd*a, I have also been able to avail myself of Dr. Hillebrandt's careful exposition of the new and full-moon sacrifice; and though I had already worked myself through that part of the ritual before the appearance of his treatise, his constant references to the Sûtras of the Black Ya*g*ur-veda have been of great assistance to me.

The Brâhma*n*as and Kalpa-sûtras treat of the so-called *S*rauta or Vaidik sacrifices, requiring for their performance three sacrificial fires; while the Pâka-ya*gñ*as, or simple oblations of cooked food prepared on the domestic fire, are dealt with in the G*ri*hya-sûtras. The present volume contains that portion of the Brâhma*n*a which deals with the Haviryа*gñ*as—or offerings of milk, butter, rice, barley, and similar materials—as distinguished from the animal and Soma sacrifices. The new and full-moon offering being considered as the normal type of an ish*t*i, or simplest form of a complete sacrificial performance, the place of honour is assigned to it in most texts of the Ya*g*us; only points of difference being generally noted regarding the performance of ish*t*is, as parts of subsequent sacrifices. In point of time, the Dar*s*a-pûr*n*amâsau ought to be preceded—as indeed they are in the Kâ*n*va text of the Brâhma*n*a—by the Agnyâdhâna, or establishment of a sacred fire on the part of a young householder; and by the Agnihotra, or morning and evening libations.

*S*ATAPATHA-BRÂHMA*N*A.

FIRST KÂ*ND*A.

THE DAR*S*APÛR*N*AMÂSA-ISH*T*Î OR NEW AND FULL-MOON SACRIFICES.

FIRST ADHYÂYA. FIRST BRÂHMA*N*A.

A. THE VOW OF ABSTINENCE.

EACH of the two half-monthly sacrifices, the regular performance of which is enjoined on the Brâhma*n*ical householder for a period of thirty years from the time of his performance of the ceremony of agny-âdhâna, or setting up of a fire of his own,—according to some authorities even for the rest of his life—usually occupies the greater part of two consecutive days. Whilst the first day—the upavasatha or fast-day—is chiefly taken up with preparatory rites, such as the sweeping and trimming of the fire-places and lighting of the fires; and the formal taking of the vow of abstinence (vrata) by the sacrificer and his wife; the second day is reserved for the main performance of the sacrifice. As to the exact days of the month appointed for these ceremonies, there is some difference of opinion among native authorities, some of them deciding in favour of the last two days of each half of the lunar month, whilst the generality of ritualistic writers consider the first day of the half-month—or the first and sixteenth day of the month respectively—to be the proper time for the main performance. The personal restrictions involved in the householder's entering on the vrata include chiefly the abstention from certain kinds of food, especially meat, and from other carnal pleasures; the cutting (optional, according to some) of the beard and hair, except the crest-lock; the sleeping on the ground in one of the chief fire-houses; and the observance of silence during the ceremonies. It was, however, permitted to compress the two-days' rites of the Full-moon sacrifice into one single day, in which case some of these restrictions would of course not be applicable.

The ceremonies begin with the preparation of the sacrificial fires. [First, the fivefold lustration successively of the Âhavanîya and Dakshinâgni fire-places, to render them fit for receiving the fire from the Gârhapatya or householder's fire, viz. by thrice sweeping the hearths; thrice besmearing them with gomaya; drawing three lines across them from west to east, or south to north, with the wooden sword (sphya); removing the dust from the lines with the thumb and ring-finger; and thrice sprinkling the lines with water[1].] Then the Adhvaryu performs the agny-uddharana, or twice taking out of the fire from the Gârhapatya, and putting it successively on the forepart of the Âhavanîya and Dakshinâgni hearths. After this takes place the agny-anvâdhâna, or putting (fuel) on the fires, by either the householder or the Adhvaryu; two logs being put on each of the three fires. This may be done in three different ways, viz. first on the Âhavanîya, then on the Gârhapatya, and last on the Dakshinâgni, in which case the first log is put on by him whilst muttering the verse Rig-veda X, 128, 1 (Taitt. S. IV, 7, 14, 1), 'Let there be lustre, O Agni, at my invocations!' &c., the second log silently. Or the first logs are put on with one of the three mystical words 'bhûr, bhuvah, svar' on the Gârhapatya, Dakshinâgni, and Âhavanîya successively, and the second logs again silently. Or both logs may be put on silently, the order of fires being in that case the one in which they originate, viz. Gârhapatya, Âhavanîya, and Dakshinâgni.

In the afternoon the householder and his wife partake of the vratopanîya or fast-day food (prepared chiefly of rice, barley, or mudga beans) with clarified butter; whereupon they take the vow in the manner prescribed in the Brâhmana. In the evening, immediately after sunset, and on the following morning just before sunrise, the householder has, as usual, to perform the Agnihotra, a burnt-offering of fresh milk, which has to be made by him twice daily, with certain exceptions, from the Agnyâdhâna to the end of his life.

1. He who is about to enter on the vow, touches water[2], whilst standing between the Âhavanîya

[1] The statements enclosed in brackets [ ] are drawn from the comments and Paddhati on Kâtyâyana's Srauta-sûtra.

[2] I.e. 'he dips his hand into water contained in a vessel,' Schol. Kâty. Sr. S. I, 10, 14. According to the general rule there given,

and Gârhapatya fires, with his face turned towards east. The reason why he touches water is, that man is (sacrificially) impure on account of his speaking untruth; and because by that act an internal purification (is effected),—for water is indeed (sacrificially) pure. 'After becoming sacrificially pure, I will enter on the vow,' thus (he thinks); for water is indeed purifying. 'Having become purified through the purifying one, I will enter on the vow,' thus (he thinks, and) this is the reason why he touches water.

2. Looking towards the (Âhavanîya) fire[1], he enters on the vow, with the text (Vâ*g*. S. I, 5 a): 'O Agni, Lord of Vows! I will keep the vow! may I be equal to it, may I succeed in it!' For Agni is Lord of Vows to the gods, and it is to him therefore that he addresses these words. In the words, 'I will observe the vow; may I be equal to it; may I succeed in it,' there is nothing that requires explanation.

3. After the completion (of the sacrifice) he divests himself (of the vow), with the text (Vâ*g*. S. II, 28 a), 'O Agni, Lord of Vows! I have kept the vow; I have been equal to it; I have succeeded in

the same purificatory act has to be repeated whenever, in the course of ceremonial performances, a sacrificial formula or prayer has been used, which is addressed to, or directed against, Rudra, the Rakshas and Asuras, and the Manes; or one directed against some specified enemy of the sacrificer with the view of exorcising or averting the evil influences with which the latter is supposed to be threatened from that quarter; or lastly, when a touching of one's self has taken place, either accidentally or as part of the ceremonial.

[1] 'Stepping between the Gârhapatya and Dakshi*n*a fires (aparâgnî), and standing west of the Âhavanîya, with his face turned eastward and looking at the fire.' Kâty. *S*r. S. II, 1, 11.

it;' for he who has attained the completion of the sacrifice, has indeed been equal to it; and he who has attained the completion of the sacrifice, has succeeded in it. It is in this way that most (sacrificers) will probably enter on the vow; but one may also enter on it in the following way.

4. Twofold, verily, is this, there is no third, viz. truth and untruth. And verily the gods are the truth, and man is the untruth. Therefore in saying (Vâ*g*. S. I, 5 b), 'I now enter from untruth into truth,' he passes from the men to the gods[1].

5. Let him then only speak what is true; for this vow indeed the gods do keep, that they speak the truth; and for this reason they are glorious: glorious therefore is he who, knowing this, speaks the truth.

6. After the completion (of the sacrifice) he divests himself (of the vow), with the text (Vâ*g*. S. II, 28 b): 'Now I am he who I really am.' For, in entering upon the vow, he becomes, as it were, non-human; and as it would not be becoming for him to say, 'I enter from truth into untruth;' and as, in fact, he now again becomes man, let him therefore divest himself (of the vow), with the text: 'Now I am he who I really am.'

7. Now then of the eating (or) fasting[2]. And on this point Âshâ*dh*a Sâvayasa, on the one hand, was of opinion that the vow consisted in fasting. For assuredly, (he argued,) the gods see through the mind of man; they know that, when he enters on this

[1] I.e. 'he obtains a divine body (devatâ*s*arîram),' Mahîdh.; 'man's existence is untruth on account of its perishableness,' id.

[2] The discussion which here follows refers to the evening meal which the sacrificer is allowed to take after he has performed the Agnihotra. Cf. Kâty. *S*r. S. II, 1, 13.

vow, he means to sacrifice to them the next morning. Therefore all the gods betake themselves to his house, and abide by (him or the fires, upa-vas) in his house; whence this (day) is called upa-vasatha[1].

8. Now, as it would even be unbecoming for him to take food, before men (who are staying with him as his guests) have eaten; how much more would it be so, if he were to take food before the gods (who are staying with him) have eaten: let him therefore take no food at all.

9. Yâ*gñ*avalkya, on the other hand, said: 'If he does not eat, he thereby becomes a sacrificer to the Manes; and if he does eat, he eats before the gods have eaten: let him therefore eat what, when eaten, counts as not eaten.' For that of which no offering is made, even though it is eaten, is considered as not eaten. When he therefore eats, he does not become a sacrificer to the Manes; and by eating of that of which no offering is made, he does not eat before the gods have eaten.

10. Let him therefore eat only what grows in the forest, be it forest plants or the fruit of trees. And in regard to this point Barku Vârsh*n*a said: 'Cook ye beans for me, for no offering is made of them!' This, however, he should not do; for pulse

---

[1] The primary meaning of upa-vas probably is 'to dwell or abide near (? the gods or fires);' its secondary and technical meaning being 'to fast,' whence upavasatha, 'a fasting or fast-day,' literally 'the abiding near (? or honouring, the gods or fires).' Cf. III, 9, 2, 7. The term is more usually applied to the preliminary fast-day of the Soma-sacrifice; but the latter being considered the most solemn and efficacious of sacrificial rites, a strong tendency prevails to establish some kind of connection between it and the other ceremonies. Cf. Kâty. *S*r. S. IV, 15, 36.

serves as an addition to rice and barley; and hence he increases the rice and barley by means of it: let him therefore eat only what grows in the forest.

11. Let him sleep that night in the house of the Âhavanîya fire or in the house of the Gârhapatya fire. For he who enters on the vow approaches the gods; and he sleeps in the midst of those very gods whom he approaches. Let him sleep on the ground[1]; for from below, as it were, one serves one's superior.

B. The Preparation of the Offerings.

After the morning's performance of the Agnihotra and the subsequent rising of the sun, the sacrificer chooses his Brahman, or superintending priest. [In the first place he gets six seats ready, covered with sacrificial grass: two of these, to be used by the Brahman and sacrificer during the ceremony of election, are placed somewhere on the north side of the sacrificial ground; another south of the Âhavanîya fire, to serve for the Brahman's permanent seat (brahmasâdanam), and west of the latter (placed so as to be quite close to the altar to be constructed hereafter, cf. Kâty. Sr. I, 8, 28), the sacrificer's permanent seat; finally a seat north of each of the two fires, the Gârhapatya and the Âhavanîya, to be used by the Adhvaryu on certain occasions. The sacrificer and future Brahman then having seated themselves on the two first-mentioned seats on the north side, the former with his face turned northward, and the latter looking toward east; the sacrificer, holding the wooden sword (sphya) in his left hand, touches the right knee of the Brahman with his right hand, in which he holds barley-corns and] chooses him for his Brahman with the formula: ['Thou, of such and such a family, N. N. Sarman! we are about to perform the Full-moon sacrifice,'] 'O Lord of the earth! Lord of the world! Lord of the great universe! we choose thee for our Brahman!' The chosen one then mutters (cf. Vâg. S. p. 57): 'I am the lord of the earth, I lord of the world, I lord of the great universe (mahâbhûta)! earth! ether! heaven! O God Savitri, thee they choose for their Brahman, their lord of prayer (Brihaspati)!' &c., 'Brihaspati is Brahman to the gods, I to the men!' He (or, according

[1] A shake-down of grass (âstaranam, ? a blanket) is not forbidden. Paddh. on Kâty. Sr. II, 1.

to some, the sacrificer) further says, 'O Lord of speech, protect the sacrifice!' after which he betakes himself to the Brahman's seat (south of the Âhavanîya), and whilst [standing north of it, with his face turned eastward and] looking on it, he mutters: 'Avaunt! unholy one (daidhishavya, lit. son of a re-married woman)! take thee away from here and seat thee on another's seat who is less exalted (pâkatara) than we!' He takes one blade of grass from the seat and flings it towards south-west (the region of the Rakshas or evil spirits) with the formula: 'Expelled is sin with him whom we detest!' and then sits down with the formula: 'Here I sit on the seat of Brihaspati, at the command of the divine Savitri! This I proclaim to the fire, this to the wind, this to the earth!' Here he remains seated, with his face towards the Âhavanîya fire, to watch the progress of the ceremony and give directions, whenever he is appealed to. When the full or new-moon sacrifice is performed for the first time, it should be preceded by the Anvârambhanîyâ offering, performed in much the same way as the Paurnamâsî, except that the oblations themselves consist of a rice cake on eleven potsherds for Agni and Vishnu, a potful of boiled (rice) grains (karu) for Sarasvatî; and a rice cake on twelve potsherds for Sarasvat; the priest's fee on this occasion consisting of a cow four years old, or a pair of cattle, instead of the Anvâhârya mess. Kâty. Sr. IV, 5, 22–23.

12. By way of his first act on the following morning he (the Adhvaryu priest) betakes himself to the water, and brings water forward[1]: for

[1] He, in the first place, pours water into a jug [usually made of varana wood (Cratæva Roxburghii), four-cornered, about a span or twelve fingers' breadths deep and four fingers' breadths square, and furnished with a handle], puts it down north of the Gârhapatya fire, and touches it with the formula: 'I, the existent, will operate with thee (?tvâ karishyâmi), O existent one!' He then addresses himself to the Brahman: 'O Brahman! shall I bring the water forward?' and to the patron or sacrificer: 'Sacrificer, restrain thy speech!' The Brahman,—after muttering the mantra (as he does, with certain modifications, on similar occasions when his permission is asked in the course of the performance): 'Lead on the sacrifice! gladden the deities! May the sacrificer be on the vault of heaven! Where the world of the seven pious Rishis is, thither do thou lead this sacrifice and sacrificer!'—replies aloud: 'Hail (õm)! bring forward!'

water is (one of the means of) sacrifice. Hence by this his first act he approaches (engages in) the sacrifice; and by bringing (water) forward, he spreads out (prepares) the sacrifice.

13. He brings it forward with those mysterious words (Vâg. S. I, 6): 'Who (or Pragâpati) joins (or yokes) thee (to this fire)[1]? He joins thee. For what (or, for Pragâpati) does he join thee? For that (or him) he joins thee!' For Pragâpati is undefined[2] (mysterious); Pragâpati is the sacrifice: hence he thereby yokes (gets ready for the performance) Pragâpati, this sacrifice.

14. The reason why he brings forward water is, that all this (universe) is pervaded by water[3]; hence by this his first act he pervades (or gains) all this (universe).

15. And whatever here in this (sacrifice) the Hotri, or the Adhvaryu, or the Brahman, or the Âgnîdhra, or the sacrificer himself, does not succeed in accomplishing, all that is thereby obtained (or made good).

16. Another reason why he brings forward water is this: whilst the gods were engaged in performing sacrifice, the Asuras and Rakshas forbade (raksh)

---

[1] 'Ka (i. e. who? or Pragâpati) joins thee (i. e. places thee, O water, by the side of the Âhavanîya fire)? (!) . . . Kasmai (i. e. for what purpose? or, for whom? or, for Pragâpati) does he join thee? (!)' Mahîdh. Dark is the meaning of these words because of the ambiguity of ka, the interrogative pronoun, which speculative theology also takes for a mystic name of Pragâpati. Cf. XI, 5, 4, 1 seq.; Max Müller, History of Ancient Sanskrit Literature, p. 433.

[2] Cf. also I, 6, 1, 20, where Sâyana says that Pragâpati is anirukta, because he represents all deities.

[3] A play on the word âpah (ap), 'water,' and the root âp, 'to obtain, to pervade.'

them, saying, 'Ye shall not sacrifice!' and because they forbade (raksh), they are called Rakshas.

17. The gods then perceived this thunderbolt, to wit, the water: the water is a thunderbolt, for the water is indeed a thunderbolt; hence wherever it goes, it produces a hollow (or depression of ground); and whatever it comes near, it destroys (lit. it burns up). Thereupon they took up that thunderbolt, and in its safe and foeless shelter they spread (performed) the sacrifice. And thus he (the Adhvaryu priest) likewise takes up this thunderbolt, and in its safe and foeless shelter spreads the sacrifice. This is the reason why he brings forward water.

18. After pouring out some of it (into the jug) he puts it down north of the Gârhapatya fire. For water (ap) is female and fire (agni) is male; and the Gârhapatya is a house: hence a copulation productive of offspring is thereby effected in this house. Now he who brings forward the water, takes up a thunderbolt; but when he takes up the thunderbolt, he cannot do so unless he is firmly placed; for otherwise it destroys him.

19. The reason then why he places it near the Gârhapatya fire is, that the Gârhapatya is a house, and a house is a safe resting-place; so that he thereby stands firmly in a house, and therefore in a safe resting-place: in this way that thunderbolt does not destroy him,—for this reason he places it near the Gârhapatya fire.

20. He then carries it north of the Âhavanîya fire[1]. For water is female and fire is male: hence

[1] After the water has been brought forward by the Adhvaryu from the house of the Gârhapatya fire, its technical name is Pra*n*îtâ*h*,

a copulation productive of offspring is thereby effected. And in this way alone a regular copulation can take place, since the woman lies on the left (or north) side of the man.

21. Let nobody pass between the water (and the fire), lest by passing between them he should disturb the copulation which is taking place. Let him set the water down without carrying it beyond (the north side of the fire, i.e. not on the eastern side); nor should he put it down before reaching (the north side, i.e. not on the western side). For, if he were to put the water down after carrying it beyond,—there being, as it were, a great rivalry between fire and water,—he would cause this rivalry to break forth on the part of the fire; and when they (the priests and the sacrificer) touch the water of this (vessel), he would, by carrying it and setting it down beyond (the northern side), cause the enemy to rise (spirt) in the fire. If, on the other hand, he were to put it down before gaining (the northern side), he would not gain by it the fulfilment of the wish for which it has been brought forward. Let him therefore put it down exactly north of the Âhavanîya fire.

22. He now strews sacrificial grass all round (the fires)[1], and fetches the utensils, taking two at a

---

'brought forward.' On putting it down north of the Âhavanîya, he covers the jug over with sacrificial grass.

[1] Kâty. Sr. II, 3, 6: 'Having strewn sacrificial grass around the fires, beginning on the east side,' which the Comm. interprets: 'He strews eastward and northward-pointed grass around first the Âhavanîya, then the Gârhapatya, and last the Dakshiṇâgni, beginning each time on the eastern side, and then moving around from left to right, and turning his right side towards the fire, so as to end on the north side' (cf. Kâty. IV, 13, 15). The Paddhati, on

time, viz. the winnowing basket and the Agnihotra ladle, the wooden sword and the potsherds, the wedge and the black antelope skin, the mortar and the pestle, the large and the small mill-stones. These are ten in number; for of ten syllables consists the Virâ*g* (metre), and radiant (virâ*g*)[1] also is the sacrifice: so that he thereby makes the sacrifice resemble the Virâ*g*. The reason why he takes two at a time is, because a pair means strength; for when two undertake anything, there is strength in it. Moreover, a pair represents a productive copulation, so that a productive copulation (of those respective objects) is thereby effected.

SECOND BRÂHMA*N*A.

1. Thereupon he takes the winnowing basket and the Agnihotra ladle[2], with the text (Vâ*g*. S. I, 6 b): 'For the work (I take) you, for pervasion (or accomplishment) you two!' For the sacrifice is a work: hence, in saying 'for the work you two,' he says, 'for the sacrifice.' And 'for pervasion you two,' he says,

---

the other hand, following Âpastamba, interprets it to the effect that on the eastern and western sides he strews the grass with its tops turned northward, and on the southern and northern sides with the tops turned eastward.

[1] Or, 'and the sacrifice also is Virâ*g*,' as the scholiast interprets the passage on the ground that at the performance of the *G*yotish*t*oma 190 stotriyâ verses are used, and that this number is dividable by ten, the number of syllables in the Virâ*g* metre; cf. Weber, Ind. Streifen I, 36, note 4. See also X, 4, 3, 21, where the fire is identified with the virâ*g* on the ground that there are ten fires, viz. eight dhish*n*ya fires and the Âhavanîya and Gârhapatya. In VIII, 4, 5, 5 virâ*g* is explained as 'that which rules.'

[2] For the Agnihotra-hava*n*î or ladle used for making the morning and evening milk-oblations, see note on I, 3, 1, 1. For the winnowing basket (*s*ûrpa), see I, 1, 4, 19 seq.

because he, as it were, pervades (goes through, accomplishes) the sacrifice.

2. He then restrains his speech; for (restrained) speech means undisturbed sacrifice; so that (in so doing) he thinks: 'May I accomplish the sacrifice!' He now heats (the two objects on the Gârhapatya), with the formula (Vâg. S. I, 7 a): 'Scorched is the Rakshas, scorched are the enemies!' or (Vâg. S. I, 7 b): 'Burnt out is the Rakshas, burnt out are the enemies!'

3. For the gods, when they were performing the sacrifice, were afraid of a disturbance on the part of the Asuras and Rakshas: hence by this means he expels from here, at the very opening[1] of the sacrifice, the evil spirits, the Rakshas.

4. He now steps forward (to the cart[2]), with the text (Vâg. S. I, 7 c): 'I move along the wide aërial realm.' For the Rakshas roams about in the air, rootless and unfettered in both directions (below and above); and in order that this man (the Adhvaryu) may move about the air, rootless and unfettered in both directions, he by this very prayer renders the atmosphere free from danger and evil spirits.

5. It is from the cart that he should take (the rice required for the sacrifice). For at first the cart (is the receptacle of the rice) and afterwards this hall;

[1] Literally, 'from the very mouth,' which refers both to the mouth or hollow part of the two vessels (from which the enemies are, as it were, burnt out), and to the opening of the sacrifice. The same symbolical explanation is met with on the occasion of the heating of the sacrificial spoon, I, 3, 1, 5.

[2] The cart containing the rice or barley, or whatever material may be used instead, stands behind (i. e. west of) the Gârhapatya, fitted with all its appliances (except the oxen). Kâty. Sr. II, 3, 12. Rice-grains, as the most common material, will be assumed to constitute the chief havis (sacrificial food) at the present sacrifice.

and because he thinks 'what was at first (in the cart, and hence still unimpaired by entering the householder's abode), that I will operate upon;' for that reason let him take (rice) from the cart.

6. Moreover, the cart represents an abundance; for the cart does indeed represent an abundance: hence, when there is much of anything, people say that there are 'cart-loads' of it. Thus he thereby approaches an abundance, and for this reason he should take from the cart.

7. The cart further is (one of the means of) the sacrifice; for the cart is indeed (one of the means of) sacrifice. To the cart, therefore, refer the (following) Yagus-texts, and not to a store-room, nor to a jar. The *Ri*shis, it is true, once took (the rice) from a leathern bag, and hence, in the case of the *Ri*shis, the Yagus-texts applied to a leathern bag. Here, however, they are taken in their natural application. Because he thinks 'from (or, by means of) the sacrifice I will perform the sacrifice,' let him, therefore, take (rice) from the cart.

8. Some do indeed take it from a (wooden) jar. In that case also he should mutter the Yagus-texts without omitting any; and let him in that case take (the rice) after inserting the wooden sword[1] under

[1] The sphya is a straight sword (kha*d*ga) or knife, a cubit long, carved out of khadira wood (Mimosa Catechu). Kâty. *S*r. I, 3, 33; 39. It is used for various purposes calculated to symbolically insure the safe and undisturbed performance of the sacrifice. On the present occasion it represents the yoke, by touching which (par. 10) the cart is connected with the sacrifice. At the close of the sacrifice also the offering spoons are, as it were, unyoked (or relieved of their duties), by being placed on the yoke, if the rice was taken from the cart; or on the wooden sword lying on the jar, if it was taken from the latter. See I, 8, 3, 26.

(the jar). He does so, thinking 'where we want to yoke, there we unyoke;' for from the same place where they yoke, they also unyoke.

9. (Like) fire, verily, is the yoke of that very cart; for the yoke is indeed (like) fire: hence the shoulder of those (oxen) that draw this (cart) becomes as if burnt by fire. The middle part of the pole behind the prop represents, as it were, its (the cart's) altar[1]; and the enclosed space of the cart (which contains the rice) constitutes its havirdhânam (receptacle of the sacrificial food)[2].

10. He now touches the yoke, with the text (Vâg. S. I, 8 a): 'Thou art the yoke (dhur); injure (dhûrv) thou the injurer! injure him that injures us! injure him whom we injure!' For there being a fire in the yoke by which he will have to pass when he fetches the material for the oblation, he thereby propitiates it, and thus that fire in the yoke does not injure him when he passes by.

11. Here now Âruni said: 'Every half-moon[3] I destroy the enemies.' This he said with reference to this point.

---

[1] The pole of an Indian cart consists of two pieces of wood, joined together in its forepart and diverging towards the axle. Hence, as Sâyana remarks, it resembles the altar in shape, being narrower in front and broader at the back, the altar measuring twenty-four cubits in front and thirty cubits at the back. At the extreme end of the pole a piece of wood is fastened on, or the pole itself is turned downwards, so as to serve as a prop or rest (popularly called 'sipoy' in Western India, and 'horse' in English).

[2] The havirdhâna (-mandapa) is a temporary shed or tent erected on the sacrificial ground for the performance of the Soma-sacrifice, in which the two carts containing the Soma-plants are placed. These carts themselves, however, are also called havirdhâna. Cf. IV, 6, 9, 10 seq.; III, 5, 3, 7.

[3] I. e. at the time of the new and the full moon. Schol.

12. Thereupon, whilst touching the pole behind the prop, he mutters (Vâg. S. I, 8 b–9 a): 'To the gods thou belongest, thou the best carrying one, the most firmly joined[1], the most richly filled[2], the most agreeable (to the gods), the best caller of the gods!' 'Thou art unbent, the receptacle of oblations; be thou firm, waver not!' Thus he eulogises the cart, hoping that he may obtain the oblation from the one thus eulogised and pleased. He adds (Vâg. S. I, 9 b), 'May thy Lord of Sacrifice not waver!' for Lord of Sacrifice is the sacrificer, and it is for the sacrificer, therefore, that he thus prays for firmness.

13. He now ascends (the cart by the southern wheel), with the text (Vâg. S. I, 9 c): 'May Vishnu ascend thee!' For Vishnu is the sacrifice; by striding (vi-kram) he obtained for the gods this all-pervading power (vikrânti) which now belongs to them. By his first step he gained this very (earth), by the second the aërial expanse, and by the last step the sky. And this very same pervading power Vishnu, as sacrifice, by his strides obtains for him (the sacrificer).

14. He then looks (at the rice) and (addressing the cart) mutters (Vâg. S. I, 9 d): 'Wide open (be

---

[1] Sasni-tama (?'the most bountiful'); sasni is explained by Mahîdhara (in accordance with Yâska, Nir. V, 1) by samsnâta, from snâ, 'to purify, cleanse,' or from snâ (snai), 'to envelop, wrap round;' hence 'cleanest or purest,' or 'most firmly secured by being tied (with thongs, &c.)' The latter was probably the meaning connected with the word in this sacrificial formula; though the correct derivation is no doubt from san, 'to acquire, gain,' and 'to bestow' (Roth, Nirukta notes, p. 52). In modern Indian carts the yoke is fastened on to the pole by a string.

[2] Papritama, 'most filled with rice,' &c. Schol.

thou) to the wind!' For wind means breath; so that by this prayer he effects free scope for the air of the (sacrificer's) breath.

15. With the text (Vâg. S. I, 9 e), 'Repelled is the Rakshas!' he then throws away whatever (grass, &c.) may have fallen on it. But if nothing (have fallen on it), let him merely touch it. He thereby drives away from it the evil spirits, the Rakshas.

16. He touches (the rice), with the text (Vâg. S. I, 9 f), 'Let the five take!' for five are these fingers, and fivefold also is the sacrifice[1]; so that he thereby puts the sacrifice on it (the cart).

17. He then takes (the rice), with the text (Vâg. S. I, 10 a, b): 'At the impulse (prasavana) of the divine Savitri, I take thee with the arms of the Asvins, with the hands of Pûshan, thee, agreeable to Agni!' For Savitri is the impeller (prasavitri) of the gods: therefore he takes this as one impelled by Savitri. 'With the arms of the Asvins,' he says, because the two Asvins are the Adhvaryu priests (of the gods). 'With the hands of Pûshan,' he says, because Pûshan is distributer of portions (to the gods), who with his own hands places the food before them. The gods are the truth, and men are the untruth: thus he thereby takes (the rice) by means of the truth.

[1] According to Sâyana, because there are five kinds of oblations (havish-paṅkti) at the Soma-sacrifice. Cf. Ait. Br. II, 24, with Haug's translation. Compare also the distinction of five different parts in the victim at animal sacrifices: Sat. Br. I, 5, 2, 16; Ait. Br. II, 14; III, 23; and the five kinds of victims, viz. man, horse, bullock, ram, and he-goat: Ath. V. XI, 2, 9; Sat. Br. I, 2, 3, 6. 7; VI, 2, 1, 6. 18; VII, 5, 2, 10; Taitt. S. IV, 2, 10; Khând. Up. II, 6, 1.

18. He now announces (the oblation) to the deity (for whom it is intended). For when the Adhvaryu is about to take the oblation, all the gods draw near to him, thinking, 'My name he will choose! my name he will choose!' and among them who are thus gathered together, he thereby[1] establishes concord.

19. Another reason for which he announces (the oblation) to the deity, is this: whichever deities are chosen, they consider it as an obligation that they are bound to fulfil whatever wish he entertains whilst taking (the oblation); and for that reason also he announces it to the deity. After taking the oblations (to the other deities) in the same way as before[2],—

20. He touches (the rice that is left), with the text (Vâg. S. I, 11 a): 'For existence (or, abundance,—I leave) thee, not for non-offering[3]!' He thereby causes it to increase again.

[1] Viz. by calling out the names, since, without this being done, quarrels would arise among the deities as to whom the offering might be intended for. Mahîdh.

[2] Viz. as in the case of the oblation to Agni, and substituting the name of the respective deity in the formula used above (par. 17), 'Thee, agreeable to (Agni)!' The oblations prescribed for the full-moon sacrifice are a cake on eight potsherds for Agni, and one on eleven potsherds for Agni and Soma: for each of these cakes he takes four handfuls from the cart [and throws them into the Agnihotra ladle lying on the winnowing basket which he holds with his left hand. With each of the first three handfuls of each of the two oblations he repeats the above text, whilst the fourth handful is thrown in silently. After the oblation for Agni is taken, he pours it from the ladle into the winnowing basket so as to lie on the southern side; and then takes out the oblation for Agni-Soma, which is afterwards poured into the basket so as to lie north of the first heap]. Kâty. Sr. II, 3, 20–21 and Scholl.

[3] Thus Mahîdhara (i.e. 'to serve for future oblations, or as food for the priests'). Perhaps the meaning is, 'For a (divine or human) being thee, not for the evil spirit!' Cf. St. Petersburg Dict. s. v. bhûta.

21. He now (whilst seated on the cart) looks towards east, with the text (Vâg. S. I, 11 b): 'May I perceive the light!' For that cart being covered up, its eye is thereby, as it were, affected with evil. Light, moreover, represents the sacrifice, the day, the gods, and the sun; so that he thereby perceives this same (fourfold) light.

22. He then descends (from the cart), with the text (Vâg. S. I, 11 c): 'May those provided with doors stand firm on the earth!' Those provided with doors are the houses: for the houses of the sacrificer might indeed be capable of breaking down behind the back of his Adhvaryu, when he walks forward (from the cart) with the sacrifice, and might crush his (the sacrificer's) family. By this (text), however, he causes them to stand firmly on this earth, so that they do not break down and crush (his family); for this reason he says: 'May those provided with doors stand firm on the earth!' He then walks forward (north of the Gârhapatya fire), with the text (Vâg. S. I, 11 d), 'I move along the wide aërial realm;' the application of which is the same (as before; see par. 4).

23. In the case of one (viz. householder) whose Gârhapatya fire they (the priests) use for cooking oblations, they place the utensils in the Gârhapatya (house); and let him (the Adhvaryu) in that case put (the winnowing basket with the rice) down at the back (or west) side of the Gârhapatya. But in the case of one whose Âhavanîya they use for cooking oblations, they place the utensils together in the Âhavanîya; and let him in that case put it (the rice) down at the back of the Âhavanîya. He should (in either case) do so, with the text (Vâg. S. I, 11 e), 'On the navel of the earth I place thee!' for

the navel means the centre, and the centre is safe from danger: for this reason he says, 'On the navel of the earth I place thee!' And further, 'In the lap of Aditi (the boundless or inviolable earth)!' for when people guard anything very carefully, they commonly say that 'they, as it were, carried it in their lap;' and this is the reason why he says, 'In the lap of Aditi!' And further, 'O Agni, do thou protect this offering!' whereby he makes this oblation over for protection both to Agni and to this earth: for this reason he says, 'O Agni, do thou protect this offering!'

Third Brâhma*n*a.

1. He now prepares two strainers (pavitra)[1], with the text (Vâ*g*. S. I, 12 a): 'Purifiers (or strainers, pavitra) are ye, and belonging to Vish*n*u!' For Vish*n*u is the sacrifice; so that he thereby says, 'You belong to the sacrifice.'

2. Two there are of them: for means of cleansing (pavitra) is this (wind) which here ventilates (pavate); and this, it is true, ventilates as one only; but on entering into man, it becomes a forward and a backward one, and they are these two, to wit, the prâ*n*a (breathing out) and the udâna (breathing up or in)[2]. And as this (clarifying process) takes place

[1] These strainers (or clarifiers) are to consist of two blades of Ku*s*a grass, with unbroken or undecayed tops, and without buds on them; and they must be severed from their roots by means of other Ku*s*a blades, so as to be of equal length (viz. one prâde*s*a, or span of thumb and fore-finger, long). Kâty. *S*r. II, 3, 31.

[2] Thus Sâya*n*a here takes the terms prâ*n*a (i*d*âpiṅgalâdinâ*d*î-dvârâ bahir nirga*kkh*an prâ*n*a*h* prâṅ) and udâna (tathaiva dvârâ punar anta*h* pravi*s*an pratyaṅ). In Ait. Br. II, 29, and *Kh*ând. Up. I, 3, 3, prâ*n*a, apâna, and vyâna are mentioned as the

in accordance with the measure of that (process of breathing), therefore there are two (strainers).

3. There may also be three: for the vyâna (or pervading vital air)[1] is a third (kind of breathing); but in reality there are only two. Having then strained the sprinkling water[2] with these two (strainers), he sprinkles with it. The reason why he strains it with the two (strainers) is this:

4. Vritra in truth lay covering all this (space) which here extends between heaven and earth. And because he lay covering (vri) all this, therefore his name is Vritra.

5. Him Indra slew. He being slain flowed forth stinking in all directions towards the water; for in every direction lies the ocean. And in consequence of this, some of the waters became disgusted, and, rising higher and higher, flowed over: whence (sprung) these grasses (of which the strainers are made; for they represent the water which was not putrified. With the other (water), however, some

three vital airs; where prâna is taken by Professors Haug and Müller as 'in-breathing' ('respiration' or 'expiration,' Röer), and apâna as 'out-breathing' ('inspiration,' Röer). Five vital airs are generally enumerated (Sat. Br. IX, 2, 2, 5); but theological speculation evidently considered these bodily processes a very convenient source of symbolism, as we find mention made in the Sat. Br. of six (XIV, 1, 3, 32); seven (III, 1, 3, 21; XIII, 1, 7, 2); nine (I, 5, 2, 5); and ten (XI, 6, 3, 7) breaths or vital airs.

[1] 'A combination of the out-breathing and in-breathing;' but as there is no distinction between this kind of breath and the others (combined), two must be considered as the normal number of strainers. Schol.

[2] He pours water into the Agnihotra ladle (in which some of the awn of the rice remains), and after cleaning it with the two strainers, he sprinkles with it. Kâty. II, 3, 33 seq. The details of this process are given in par. 6 seq.

matter has become mixed up, inasmuch as the putrid Vritra flowed into it. This he now removes from it by means of these two strainers; whereupon he sprinkles with the (sacrificially) pure water. This is the reason why he strains it through them.

6. He strains it, with the text (Vâg. S. I, 12 b): 'By the impulse of Savitri I purify thee with this flawless purifier (or ventilator, pavitra), with the rays of the sun!' For Savitri is the impeller (prasavitri) of the gods, so that he strains this (water) as one impelled by Savitri. 'With this flawless purifier (ventilator, pavitra),' he says, because this (wind) which here ventilates (or purifies, pavate) is a flawless purifier. 'With the rays of the sun,' he says, because they, the rays of the sun, are certainly purifying; and for this reason he says, 'With the rays of the sun.'

7. Having taken it (the water with the ladle) in his left hand, he makes it spirt upwards with his right hand, and eulogises and glorifies it, with the text (Vâg. S. I, 12 c): 'Shining (or divine) waters! ye the first-going, the first-drinking[1] ones!' For the waters are shining; and for this reason he says, 'Shining waters!' 'First-going,' he calls them, because they flow towards the sea and are therefore going in front (or forwards). 'First-drinking,' he calls them, because they are the first that drink of king Soma[2] and are therefore 'drinking first.' And further: 'Forward now lead this sacrifice[3],

---

[1] Agrepuvah; Mahîdhara allows to it the alternative meaning 'first-purifying.'

[2] 'Because, for the sake of extracting the juice from the Soma-plants, water is poured on them, so that the water drinks of the juice before the gods do.' Sây.

[3] I. e. 'carry the sacrifice through without hindrance.' Mahîdh.

forward the Lord of Sacrifice, the liberal, god-loving Lord of Sacrifice!' whereby he says, 'Well (lead) the sacrifice, well the sacrificer!'

8. And further (Vâg. S. I, 13 a): 'You Indra chose (for his companions) in the battle against Vritra!' For Indra, when he was battling with Vritra, did choose them (the waters) and with their help he killed him; and for this reason he says, 'You Indra chose in the battle against Vritra!'

9. 'You chose Indra in the battle against Vritra!' for they, too, chose Indra when he was battling with Vritra, and with them he killed him: therefore he says, 'You chose Indra in the battle against Vritra!'

10. And further (Vâg. S. I, 13 d): 'Consecrated by sprinkling are ye!' With these words he makes amends to them [1]. He then sprinkles the (first) oblation [2]. One and the same meaning applies to the (whole process of) sprinkling, viz. he thereby makes sacrificially pure that (which he sprinkles).

11. He sprinkles, with the text (Vâg. S. I, 13 e): 'Thee, agreeable to Agni, I sprinkle!' Thus for whichever deity the oblation is intended, for that one he thereby renders it sacrificially pure. When he has in the same way as before sprinkled (all) the oblations,—

12. He then sprinkles the sacrificial vessels [3],

[1] He, in the first place, sprinkles the sprinkling water in the ladle with itself; and the guilt incurred in the act of consecrating it with itself, that is, with something unconsecrated, is made amends for by the accompanying formula, Sây. Similarly Mahîdhara: 'The unconsecrated (water) cannot consecrate other (water).'

[2] Before doing so he asks the Brahman's permission (cf. p. 7, note 1), 'O Brahman! shall I sprinkle the oblation?' when the latter, after muttering the mantra, 'Sprinkle the sacrifice! gladden the deities,' &c., gives the permission by 'Ôm! sprinkle!' Paddh. on Kâty. II, 3, 36.

[3] According to some authorities the vessels are placed together

with the text (Vâg. S. I, 13 g), 'Be ye pure for the divine work, for the sacrifice to the gods!' for it is for the divine work, the sacrifice to the gods, that he consecrates them. 'Whatever, that belongs to you, the impure have defiled by touching, that I hereby purify for you!' For whatever belonging to them some impure one—either a carpenter or some other impure person—has on this occasion desecrated by touching, that he thereby renders sacrificially pure for them by means of the water; and therefore he says, 'Whatever, that belongs to you, the impure have defiled by touching, that I hereby purify for you[1]!'

FOURTH BRÂHMANA.

1. He now takes the black antelope skin[2], for completeness of the sacrifice. For once upon a time the sacrifice escaped the gods, and having become a black antelope roamed about. The gods having thereupon found it and stripped it of its skin, they brought it (the skin) away with them.

---

on one heap, and are then consecrated together by one sprinkling. According to others, each vessel must be consecrated separately. Kâty. Sr. II, 3, 39.

[1] After he has done the sprinkling, he puts the remaining water away in some place where nobody is allowed to walk [as between the pranîtâs and the Âhavanîya; or (according to Âpastamba) before, or east of, the Gârhapatya, since nobody is allowed to pass between the Gârhapatya and Âhavanîya. The two strainers also remain in the sprinkling water]. Kâty. Sr. II, 3, 40.

[2] The skin of the black antelope may be regarded as one of the symbols of Brâhmanical worship and civilisation. Thus it is said in Manu II, 22–23: 'That which lies between these two mountain ranges (the Himâlaya and the Vindhya), from the eastern to the western ocean, the wise know as Âryâvarta (the land of the Âryas). Where the black antelope naturally roams about, that should be known as the land suitable for sacrifice; what lies beyond that is the country of the Mlekkhas (barbarians).'

2. Its white and black hairs represent the *Rik*-verses and the Sâman-verses; to wit, the white the Sâman and the black the *Rik*; or conversely, the black the Sâman and the white the *Rik*. The brown and the yellow ones, on the other hand, represent the Yagus-texts.

3. Now this same threefold science is the sacrifice; that manifold form, that (varying) colour of this (science) is what is (represented by) this black antelope skin. For the completeness of the sacrifice (he takes the skin): hence the rite of initiation (for the Soma-sacrifice) is likewise performed on the black antelope skin;—for the completion of the sacrifice: hence it is also used for husking and bruising (the rice) on, in order that nothing of the oblation may get spilt; and that, if any grain or flour should now be spilt on it, the sacrifice would still remain securely established in the sacrifice. For this reason it is used for husking and bruising upon.

4. He thus takes the black antelope skin, with the text (Vâg. S. I, 14 a): 'Bliss-bestowing (sarman) art thou!' For karman ('hide') is the name of that (skin of the) black deer used among men, but sarman (bliss) is (that used) among the gods; and for this reason he says, 'Bliss-bestowing art thou!' He shakes it, with the text (Vâg. S. I, 14 b), 'Shaken off is the Rakshas, shaken off are the enemies!' whereby he repels from it the evil spirits, the Rakshas. He shakes it whilst holding it apart from the vessels[1]; whereby he shakes off whatever impure matter there may have been on it.

[1] According to some exegetes the Adhvaryu himself must step beyond (i. e. aside from) the vessels when he shakes the skin; according to others, he should not move, but only hold the skin

5. He spreads it (on the ground with the hairy side upwards, and) with its neck-part turned to the west[1], with the text (Vâg. S. I, 14 c): 'The skin of Aditi art thou! May Aditi acknowledge thee!' For Aditi is this earth, and whatever is on her, that serves as a skin to her: for this reason he says, 'The skin of Aditi art thou!' And 'may Aditi acknowledge thee!' he says, because one who is related (to another) acknowledges (him). Thereby he establishes a mutual understanding between her and the black antelope skin, (thinking) 'they will not hurt each other.' While it is still being held down with his left hand,—

6. He at once takes the mortar with his right hand, fearing lest the evil spirits, the Rakshas, might rush in here in the meantime. For the priest (brâhmana)[2] is the repeller of the Rakshas: therefore, whilst it is still being held down with his left hand,—

7. He puts the mortar (on it), with the text (Vâg. S. I, 14 d, e): 'A wooden stone (adri) art thou!'

---

apart from the vessels, so that no impure matter should fall on them. Some also maintain that the skin should only be shaken once, whilst others think it should be done three times. Cf. Kâty. Sr. II, 4, 2. Schol.

[1] Special mention is here made of this feature, since as a rule (Kâty. I, 10, 4) the skin is spread with its neck-part turned eastwards. He lays it down on the north side of the sacrificial ground, either west of the utkara (the mound formed by the earth dug out in constructing the altar, and by other rubbish) or exactly north of the Gârhapatya. Schol. on Kâty. II, 4, 3.

[2] Only a Brâhman can perform sacrifice. If, as is permitted in certain ceremonies, a Kshatriya or Vaisya officiates, he, as it were, becomes a Brâhman (and is addressed as such) for the occasion, by means of the dîkshâ, or rite of initiation. Cf. Sat. Br. III, 2, 1, 39; XIII, 4, 1, 3.

or 'A broad-bottomed stone (grâvan) art thou!' For, just as there (in the Soma-sacrifice) they press king Soma out with stones (grâvan), thus here also he prepares the oblation (haviryagña) by means of the mortar and pestle, and the large and small mill-stones[1]. Now 'stones (adrayah)' is the common name of these, and therefore he says, 'a stone art thou.' And 'wooden,' he calls it, because this one (the mortar) really is made of wood[2]. Or, he says, 'a broad-bottomed stone (grâvan) art thou,' because it is both a stone and broad-bottomed. He adds: 'May Aditi's skin acknowledge (receive) thee!' whereby he establishes a mutual understanding between it (the mortar) and the black antelope skin, thinking: 'they will not injure each other.'

8. He then pours the (two portions of) rice (from the winnowing basket into the mortar), with the text (Vâg. S. I, 15 a): 'Thou art the body of Agni, thou the releaser of speech!' For it is (material for) sacrifice, and hence (by being offered in the fire) it becomes Agni's body. 'The releaser of speech,' he adds, because he now releases that speech which he restrained when he was about to take the rice (from the cart). The reason why he now releases his speech, is that the sacrifice has now obtained a firm footing in the mortar, that it has become diffused; and for this reason he says, 'the releaser of speech!'

[1] Here, as in I, 5, 2, 11 (haviryagñe 'tha saumye 'dhvare), we have the simple division of the Srauta-sacrifices into oblations (of ghee, milk, rice, barley, &c.) and libations (of Soma). More usually the pasubandhu, or animal-sacrifice, is added as a third division. See also I, 7, 2, 10.

[2] The mortar (ulûkhala) and pestle (musala) are to be made of very hard wood, viz. both of varana wood (Cratæga Roxburghii), or the mortar of palâsa wood (Butea Frondosa), and the pestle of

9. Should he, however (by some accident), utter any human sound before this time, let him in that case mutter some *Rik* or Ya*g*us-text addressed to Vish*n*u[1]; for Vish*n*u is the sacrifice, so that he thereby again obtains a hold on the sacrifice, and penance is thereby done by him (for not keeping silent). He adds: 'For the pleasure of the gods I seize thee!' for the oblation is taken with the intention 'that it shall gladden the gods.'

10. He now takes the pestle, with the text (Vâ*g*. S. I, 14 b), 'A large, wooden stone art thou!' for it is a large stone, and made of wood, too. He thrusts it down, with the text (Vâ*g*. S. I, 14 c), 'Do thou prepare this oblation for the gods[2]! do thou prepare it thoroughly!' thereby saying, 'Get this oblation ready for the gods! get it quite ready!'

11. He then calls the Havishk*ri*t[3] (preparer of the sacrificial food), 'Havishk*ri*t, come hither! Havishk*ri*t, come hither!' The Havishk*ri*t[4] no doubt is speech, so that he thereby frees speech from

---

khadira wood (Acacia Catechu). The former is to be of the height of the knee, and the latter three aratnis (cubits) long. Schol. on Kâty. I, 3, 36; M. Müller, Die Todtenbestattung bei den Brahmanen, Zeitsch. der D. Morg. Ges. IX, p. xl.

[1] Kâty. *S*r. II, 2, 6–7 lays down the general rule, that if the Brahman or Adhvaryu (and according to some, the sacrificer also) by some slip were to utter any sound during the time for which restraint of speech (vâg-yama) is enjoined, they must atone for the transgression by muttering some mantra addressed to Vish*n*u, such as the couplet (Vâ*g*. S. V, 38, 41), 'Widely, O Vish*n*u, stride!' &c., or the formula (ib. I, 4), 'O Vish*n*u, preserve the sacrifice!'

[2] Or 'for the god,' 'for the goddess,' as the case may be.

[3] Or, he pronounces the havishk*ri*t formula, see next note. According to Kâty. *S*r. II, 4, 13 he calls out three separate times.

[4] Havishk*ri*t denotes not only the person that prepares the oblation, but also this formula by which that person is called.

restraint. And speech, moreover, represents sacrifice[1], so that he thereby again calls the sacrifice to him.

12. Now there are four different forms of this call, viz. 'come hither (ehi)!' in the case of a Brâhman; 'approach (âgahi)!' and 'hasten hither (âdrava)!' in the case of a Vaisya and a member of the military caste (râganyabandhu[2]); and 'run hither (âdhâva)!' in that of a Sûdra. On this occasion he uses the call that belongs to a Brâhman, because that one is best adapted for a sacrifice, and is besides the most gentle: let him therefore say, 'come hither (ehi)!'

13. Now in former times it was no other than the wife (of the sacrificer) who rose at this (call, to act) as Havishkrit; therefore now also (she or) some one (priest)[3] rises in answer to this call. And at the time when he (the Adhvaryu) calls the Havishkrit, one of the priests[4] beats the two mill-stones.

---

[1] Viz. in the shape of the sacrificial formulas.

[2] This inversion of the order of the second (or Kshatriya) and third (or Vaisya) castes is rather strange. The Sûtras of Bhâradv., Âpast., and Hirany. assign the same formulas to the several castes as here. Cf. Hillebrandt, Neu- und Vollmondsopfer, p. 29.

[3] According to the Schol. on Kâty. Sr. II, 4, 13, either the wife of the patron or the Âgnîdhra (the priest who kindles the fire) acts as Havishkrit. Mahîdh. on Vâg. S. I, 15 includes the patron (sacrificer) himself, unless yagamânah patnî is a misprint for yagamânapatnî. According to Âpastamba, 'either a maid-servant or the wife grinds; or the wife threshes and the Sûdra woman grinds' (cf. Schol. on Kâty. Sr. II, 5, 7). Similarly Bhâradv. and Hirany.; cf. Hillebrandt, p. 38, n. 2. Similar cases of differences between the ritualistic practices of the present time and those of former times are very frequently alluded to in the ritualistic books; and are of especial interest, as they afford some insight into the gradual development of the sacrificial ceremonial. Cf. Weber, Ind. Stud. X, 156 seq.

[4] Viz. the Âgnîdhra, whilst seated north of the expansion

The reason why they produce this discordant noise, is this:

14. Manu was in possession of a bull[1]. Into him had entered an Asura-killing, foe-killing voice; and by his snorting and roaring the Asuras and Rakshas were continually being crushed. Thereupon the Asuras said to one another: 'Evil, alas! this bull inflicts upon us! how can we possibly destroy him?' Now Kilâta and Âkuli were the two priests (brahman) of the Asuras.

15. These two said, 'God-fearing, they say, is Manu: let us two then ascertain!' They then went to him and said: 'Manu! we will sacrifice for thee!' He said: 'Wherewith?' They said: 'With this bull!' He said: 'So be it!' On his (the bull's) being killed the voice went from him.

16. It entered into Manâvî, the wife of Manu; and when they heard her speak, the Asuras and Rakshas were continually being crushed. Thereupon the Asuras said to one another: 'Hereby even greater evil is inflicted on us, for the human voice speaks more!' Kilâta and Âkuli then said: 'God-fearing, they say, is Manu: let us then ascertain!' They went to him and said: 'Manu! we will sacrifice for thee!' He said: 'Wherewith?'

(vihâra) of the fires; he strikes with the wedge (samyâ, a stick of khadira wood, usually some six or eight inches long, used for placing under the lower grindstone on the north side, so as to make it incline towards east) twice the lower and once the upper grindstone. Schol. on Kâty. Sr. II, 4, 15.

[1] This bull of Manu has been compared by Dr. Kuhn (Zeitschrift für Vergl. Sprachf. IV, 91 seq.) with the Minotaur of the Greeks. Cf. also J. Muir, Original Sanskrit Texts, vol. i. p. 188 seq.; and Professor Weber's Translation of the first Adhyâya, Ind. Streifen, I, p. 50.

They said: 'With this thy wife!' He said: 'So be it!' And on her being killed that voice went from her.

17. It entered into the sacrifice itself, into the sacrificial vessels; and thence those two (Asura priests) were unable to expel it. This same Asura-killing, foe-killing voice sounds forth (from the mill-stones when they are beaten with the wedge). And for whomsoever that knows this, they produce this discordant noise on the present occasion, his enemies are rendered very miserable.

18. He beats the mill-stones with the wedge, with the text (Vâg. S. I, 16 a): 'A honey-tongued cock (kukkuta[1]) art thou (O wedge)!' For honey-tongued indeed was he (the bull) for the gods, and poison-tongued for the Asuras: hence he thereby says: 'What thou wert for the gods, that be thou for us!' He adds: 'Sap and strength do thou call hither! with thy help may we conquer in every battle!' In these words there is nothing that is obscure.

19. Thereupon[2] he (the Adhvaryu) takes the winnowing basket, with the text (Vâg. S. I, 14 b): 'Rain-grown art thou!' For rain-grown it is indeed, whether it be made of reeds or of cane or of rushes, since it is the rain that makes these grow.

---

[1] Mahîdhara offers the following etymological derivation of this word: 1. from kva kva, 'where? where?' ['He who, wishing to kill the Asuras, roams about everywhere, crying "where, where are the Asuras?"']; 2. from kuk, 'a hideous noise,' and kut, 'to spread;' or 3. one who, in order to frighten the Asuras, utters a sound resembling that of the bird called kukkuta (cock). Professor Weber translates it by 'Brüller' (roarer, crier).

[2] Viz. when the rice has been husked (by the Havishkrit in the mortar). Schol. on Kâty. Sr. II, 4, 16.

20. He then pours out the (threshed) rice (from the mortar into the winnowing basket), with the text (Vâg. S. I, 16 c): 'May the rain-grown acknowledge (receive) thee!' For rain-grown also are these (grains), whether they be rice or barley, since it is the rain that makes them grow. By these words he establishes an understanding between them and the winnowing basket, in the hope 'that they will not injure each other.'

21. He now winnows (the rice), with the text (Vâg. S. I, 16 d): 'Cleared off is the Rakshas! cleared off are the evil-doers!' The husks (which have fallen on the ground) he throws away[1], with the text (Vâg. S. I, 16 e), 'Expelled is the Rakshas!' for those evil spirits, the Rakshas, he thereby expels.

22. He then separates (the husked grains from the unhusked), with the text (Vâg. S. I, 16 f): 'May the wind separate you!' For it is that wind (which is produced by the winnowing) which here purifies (or blows, pavate); and it is the wind that separates everything here (on earth) that undergoes separation: therefore it also separates here those (two kinds of grain) from each other. Now when they are undergoing this process, and whilst he is separating[2] (the husked, so as to drop them into a pot),—

[1] He puts them into the central one of the potsherds for the Agni cake, and throws them on the utkara, or heap of rubbish (cf. p. 25, note 1). Schol. on Kâty. Sr. II, 4, 19. Before he proceeds with his work, he has to touch water; cf. p. 2, note 2.

[2] He separates them whilst holding the mouth of the winnowing basket sideways or horizontally, and makes the husked ones fall into the pot. Schol. on Kâty. Sr. II, 4, 20. According to the Paddhati, he now puts the unhusked once more into the mortar and threshes them again, and then pouring them back into the basket repeats the same process.

23. He addresses (those in the pot) thus (Vâg. S. I, 16 g): 'May the divine Savitri, the golden-handed, receive you with a flawless[1] hand!' By this he says: 'May they be well received!' He then cleans them thrice[2]; for threefold is the sacrifice.

24. Here now some clean them with the formula: 'For the gods get clean! for the gods get clean!' But let him not do so: for this oblation is intended for some particular deity; and if he were to say, 'For the gods get clean!' he would make it one intended for all the deities, and would thereby raise a quarrel among the deities. Let him therefore do the cleaning silently!

SECOND ADHYÂYA. FIRST BRÂHMANA.

1. Now the one (viz. the Âgnîdhra) puts the potsherds on (the Gârhapatya fire); the other (viz. the Adhvaryu) the two mill-stones (on the black antelope skin): these two acts are done simultaneously. The reason why they are done simultaneously (is this):

2. The head of this sacrifice is (represented by) the rice-cake[3]: for those potsherds (kapâla), no doubt, are to this (rice-cake) what the skull bones (kapâla) are to the head, and the ground rice is

[1] Viz. with the fingers joined together so as not to allow any grains to fall to the ground. Mahîdh.

[2] By removing the minute husks and grains (kana) he makes the husked grains (tandula) free from dust and shiny (this is apparently done by repeated winnowings). Schol. on Kâty. Sr. II, 4, 22.

[3] This idea was no doubt suggested by the derivation of the word purodâs (rice-cake), from puras, 'before, in front, at the head,' and dâs, 'to offer' (see I, 6, 2, 5); the double meaning of kapâla (shell or cup and skull) being made use of to complete the simile.

nothing else than the brain. Now this (combination of skull and brain) certainly forms one limb: 'Let us put that (which is) one together! Let us make it one!' thus they think; and therefore the two acts are done simultaneously.

3. He who puts the potsherds on (the fire), takes the shovelling-stick (upavesha), with the text (Vâg. S. I, 17 a): 'Bold (dhrishti) art thou!' For since with it he, as it were, attacks the fire boldly, therefore it is called dhrishti[1]. And since with it he touches (the coals) at the sacrifice, since with it he attends to (upa-vish) this (Gârhapatya fire), therefore it is called upavesha.

4. With it he shifts the coals to the fore-part[2] (of the khara or hearth-mound), with the text (Vâg. S. I, 17 b): 'O fire! cast off the fire that eateth raw flesh! drive away the corpse-eating one!' For the raw flesh-eating (fire) is the one with which men cook what they eat; and the corpse-eating one is that on which they burn (the dead) man: these two he thereby expels from it (the Gârhapatya).

5. He now pulls toward himself[3] one coal, with the text (Vâg. S. I, 17 c): 'Bring hither that (fire) which maketh offerings to the gods!' He thinks: 'On that (fire), which makes offerings to the gods, we

[1] The upavesha, or dhrishti, is made of fresh varana or palâsa wood, a cubit (aratni) or span (vitasti) long; one of its ends having the shape of a hand (hastâkriti), to serve as a coal shovel; cf. Mahîdh. and Schol. on Kâty. I, 3, 36; II, 4, 26. Dhrishti is apparently derived from the root dhrish, 'to be bold.'

[2] The burning coals have been hitherto lying on the western side of the Gârhapatya hearth, and as this side, which has been well heated by this time, will be used for the potsherds to be put on, he shifts the coals to the eastern or fore-part of the hearth.

[3] Viz. to the centre of the cooking-place.

will cook the oblations! on that one we will perform the sacrifice!' and for this reason he pulls (one of the coals) toward himself.

6. On it he places the central potsherd[1]. For

[1] In Yâgñika Deva's commentary on Kâty. II, 4, 37, full explanations are given regarding the manner of arranging the potsherds (kapâlas) on which the sacrificial cakes are spread, and which vary in number and shape. The Adhvaryu is first to describe a circle, the diameter of which is six aṅgulas (an aṅgula or thumb's breadth = about $\frac{3}{4}$ inch). This circle he then divides into three parts by drawing across, from west to east, two parallel lines at a distance of two aṅgulas from one another, so as to make the two outer (or southern and northern) segments of equal size. The middle division he then covers with three equal square potsherds (measuring two aṅgulas on each side), by laying down first the central one, then the one behind or west of it, and lastly the front or eastern one. He then lays down another (the fourth) south of the first or central one; after which he divides the still remaining potsherds equally between the southern and the northern segments, or, in case of that number being uneven, assigns the odd potsherd to the southern division. Thus, in the present case, where in the first place a cake on eight potsherds is to be offered to Agni; after laying down the three intermediate ones and the fourth, or central one of the southern division, he divides the remaining four equally between the southern and northern segments, beginning, in laying them down, in the south-east corner, and moving around from right to left, so as to end in the north-east. Similarly in the case of the cake on eleven potsherds for Agnîshomau, after laying down the first four potsherds, he assigns four of the remaining seven to the southern, and three to the northern division. Thus with cakes requiring an uneven number of potsherds, the number of those of the southern division exceeds that of the northern one by two; and in the case of an even number, by one only. This is the rule applying to cakes requiring at least six potsherds. When one potsherd only is required, it is to be of the size of a hand; when two, they are to form a circle divided into two equal parts by a line drawn from south to north; when three, the circle is divided into three sections from south to north; when four or five, it is divided into two halves from west to east; and in the one case three potsherds are placed in the southern and one (of half-moon shape) in the northern half; in the other case three in the northern and two in the southern division. The potsherds,

the gods, when they were performing sacrifice, were in fear of a disturbance from the Asuras and Rakshas. They were afraid lest those evil spirits, the Rakshas, might rise from below them. Now Agni (fire) is the repeller of the Rakshas, and for this reason he thus places (the potsherd) on it. The reason why it is just this (coal) and no other (on which the potsherd is put) is, that this one, having been consecrated by the (above) sacrificial formula, is sacrificially pure: that is why he places the central potsherd on it.

7. He puts it on, with the text (Vâ*g*. S. I, 17 d): 'Thou art firm; make thou the earth firm!' For under the form of the earth he renders this same (sacrifice) firm; by it he chases away the spiteful enemy. He adds: 'Thee, devoted to the brahman, devoted to the kshatra, devoted to the (sacrificer's) kinsmen, I put on for the destruction of the enemy!' Manifold, indeed, are the prayers for blessing in the sacrificial texts (ya*g*us): by this one he prays for the priestly and military orders, those two towers of strength (vîrye, energies)[1]. 'Thee, devoted to the (sacrificer's) kinsmen,' he says, because kinsmen mean wealth, and wealth he thereby prays for. When he says, 'I put thee on for the destruction of the enemy,' whether or not he wishes to exorcise, let him say, 'for the destruction of so

though mostly irregular in shape, must always exactly fit one another, so as not to leave any space between. This is effected by rubbing the edges. The cake itself is to be of the shape of a tortoise; the convex shield, or carapace, of the latter consisting of plates arranged in a somewhat similar way as the potsherds of most cakes, viz. in a central (dorsal) and two lateral sets.

[1] For special prayers for the two highest castes, in the Vâ*g*as. Sa*m*h., cf. Weber, Ind. Stud. X, 27.

and so!' The moment it (the potsherd) has been put down (and while it is still being touched) with the (fore-)finger of his left hand,—

8. He seizes a (second) coal, lest the evil spirits, the Rakshas, should in the meantime rush in here. For the Brâhman is the repeller of the Rakshas[1]: hence, the moment it (the potsherd) has been put down (and while it is still being touched) with the finger of his left hand,—

9. He pushes the coal on it, with the text (Vâg. S. I, 18 a): 'Accept, O Agni, this holy work (brahman)[2]!' He says this, lest the evil spirits, the Rakshas, should rush in here before; for Agni is the repeller of the Rakshas: this is the reason why he pushes it on (the potsherd).

10. He then puts on that (potsherd) which is (to stand) behind (or west of the first or central one), with the text (Vâg. S. I, 18 b): 'A support art thou! make firm the aërial region!' Under the form of the atmosphere he makes this (sacrifice) firm; by this he chases away the spiteful enemy. He adds: 'Thee, devoted to the brahman, devoted to the kshatra, devoted to the (sacrificer's) kinsmen, I put on for the destruction of the enemy!'

11. He then puts on that one which is (to stand) before (i. e. east of the first potsherd), with the text (Vâg. S. I, 18 c): 'A stay art thou! do thou make firm the sky!' Under the form of the sky he makes this same (sacrifice) firm; by it he chases away the spiteful enemy. He adds: 'Thee, devoted to the brahman, devoted to the kshatra, devoted to the kinsmen, I put on for the destruction of the enemy!'

[1] Cf. I, 1, 4, 6.

[2] Mahîdhara admits the alternative interpretation, 'Receive (me) the priest!'

12. He now puts on the one that is (to stand) on the right (i.e. south of the first), with the text (Vâg. S. I, 18 d): 'For all the regions I put thee on!' What fourth (world) there is or is not beyond these (three) worlds, by that indeed he thereby chases away the spiteful enemy. Uncertain, no doubt, is what fourth (world) there is or is not beyond these (three) worlds, and uncertain also are all those regions; for this reason he says, 'For all the regions I put thee on!' The remaining potsherds he puts on[1] either silently, or with the text (Vâg. S. I, 18 e): 'Layer-forming are ye! heap-forming are ye!'

13. He then covers them over with (hot) coals, whilst muttering the text (Vâg. S. I, 18 f): 'May ye be heated with the heat of the Bhrigus and

[1] Viz. dividing them in the manner explained at p. 34, note 1, and beginning (south)-east, and moving around from left to right (i.e. following the course of the sun). Mr. Ralph Griffith (Translation of the Rámáyan, I, p. 90) has compared this Hindu rite of pradakshina or dakshinîkarana with the Gaelic deasil, as described in the following passage of Sir W. Scott's The Two Drovers: '"But it is little I would care for the food that nourishes me, or the fire that warms me, or for God's blessed sun itself, if aught but weel should happen to the grandson of my father. So let me walk the deasil round you, that you may go safe out into the far foreign land, and come safe home." Robin Oig stopped, half embarrassed, half laughing, and signing to those near that he only complied with the old woman to soothe her humour. In the meantime she traced around him, with wavering steps, the propitiation, which some have thought has been derived from the Druidical mythology. It consists, as is well known, in the person, who makes the deasil, walking three times round the person who is the object of the ceremony, taking care to move according to the course of the sun.' Cf. note at p. 45. Note also the etymological connection between dakshina and deiseil (Old Ir. dessel, from dess, Gael. deas, south or right side). For the corresponding rite (dextratio) at the Roman marriage ceremonies see Rossbach, Römische Ehe, pp. 315, 316; Weber, Ind. Stud. V, p. 221.

Aṅgiras[1]!' for it is indeed the brightest light, that of the Bhrigus and Aṅgiras. He covers them with the view that 'they shall be well heated.'

14. Now he[2] who puts the two mill-stones on (the black antelope skin), (in the first place) takes up the black antelope skin, with the text (Vâg. S. I, 19): 'Bliss-bestowing art thou!' He shakes it, with the text (ib.): 'Shaken off is the Rakshas, shaken off are the enemies!' the import and application of which is the same (as above, I, 1, 4, 4). He spreads it (on the ground) with the neck-part turned towards west, whilst muttering the text (ib.): 'The skin of Aditi (the inviolate or boundless earth) art thou! May Aditi acknowledge (receive) thee!' the import (of this formula) being the same (as before, I, 1, 4, 5).

15. He then puts the lower mill-stone on it, with the text (Vâg. S. I, 19): 'A rock-bowl art thou! May the skin of Aditi acknowledge thee!' for it is a bowl (dhishanâ) and a rock too; and by saying, 'May the skin of Aditi acknowledge thee,' he establishes an understanding between it and the black antelope skin, so that 'they will not hurt each other.' This one (the lower mill-stone) represents the earth.

16. He now puts upon (the west side of) it the wedge[3] with its point turned towards north, whilst

[1] The old families of the Bhrigus and Aṅgiras are frequently mentioned together, and often also in conjunction with the Atharvans: it is indeed to these three families that the native authorities attribute the texts and ritual of the Atharva-veda, or fourth Veda, which is generally referred to in the later Vedic writings under the designation Atharvâṅgirasas. It is probable that the Bhrigu-Aṅgiras in the above formula of the Vâgas. Samhitâ are intended as equivalent to the latter term. Cf. Weber, Omina et Portenta, p. 346.

[2] Viz. the Adhvaryu; cf. I, 2, 1, 1.

[3] According to the corresponding rule of Kâtyâyana (II, 5, 4)

muttering the text (Vâ*g*. S. I, 19): 'The stay of the sky art thou!' that is to say, it represents the atmosphere; for by means of the atmospheric region those two, the sky and the earth, are firmly kept asunder; and for this reason he says, 'The stay of the sky art thou!'

17. He then puts the upper mill-stone on (the lower one), with the text (Vâ*g*. S. I, 19): 'A rock-born bowl art thou! May the rock acknowledge thee!' For this one being smaller is, as it were, the daughter (of the lower mill-stone)[1]; for this reason he calls it 'rock-born.' 'May the rock acknowledge thee!' he says, because one of the same kin acknowledges (receives the other): thereby he establishes an understanding between those two mill-stones, thinking 'they will not hurt one another!' This one, as it were, represents the sky; (or) the two mill-stones are, as it were, the two jaws, and the wedge is the tongue: that is why he beats (the mill-stones) with the wedge[2], for it is with the tongue that one speaks.

18. He now pours the rice on (the lower stone), with the text (Vâ*g*. S. I, 20): 'Grain (dhânyam) art thou! do thou gratify (dhi)[3] the gods!' for it is

and to his commentators (and Mahîdhara on Vâ*g*. S. I, 19) and the Black Yagur-veda, he does not lay the wedge on the lower mill-stone, but inserts it under the west or back-part of the stone, so as to make the latter incline towards east and to steady it.

[1] In the Gobhilîya G*ri*hya-sûtra II, 1, 16 the upper stone is similarly called 'the son or child' of the lower one [d*ri*shatputra], which the editor, *K*andrakânta, interprets as 'd*ri*shad and its son;' or optionally, 'the son of the d*ri*shad.' Cf. Weber, Ind. Stud. V, p. 305 note.

[2] See I, 1, 4, 13.

[3] Mahîdhara derives dhânya from the root dhi; and apparently allows to it here the double meaning 'corn or grain,' and 'that which satisfies or pleases.'

grain; and it is with the intention 'that it may gratify the gods' that the rice-oblation is taken.

19. He then grinds it, with the text (Vâg. S. I, 20): 'For out-breathing (I grind) thee! for in-breathing thee! for through-breathing (pervading vital air)[1] thee! May I impart a long duration to the life (of the sacrificer)[2]!' He pours it (the ground rice on the skin), with the text (ib.): 'May the divine Savitri, the golden-handed, receive thee with a flawless hand[3]!' 'For his (the sacrificer's) eye (I look at) thee[4]!'

20. The reason why he thus grinds it, is that the sacrificial food of the gods is living, is amrita (ambrosia, or not dead) for the immortals. Now with the mortar and pestle, and with the two mill-stones they kill this rice-offering (haviryagña).

21. When he now says: 'For out-breathing thee! for in-breathing thee!' he thereby again imparts out-breathing and in-breathing (to it), and by saying 'for through-breathing thee!' he imparts through-breathing (to it). By 'may I impart a long duration to the life!' he bestows life on it. By 'may the divine Savitri, the golden-handed, receive thee with a flaw-

---

[1] On the three kinds of breathing, see I, 1, 3, 2–3.

[2] According to Kâtyâyana (II, 5, 7) and Mahîdhara, this last formula ('May I,' &c.) should be joined to the one that follows, and pronounced by the Adhvaryu whilst he pours the ground rice on the skin. Mahîdhara interprets it thus: 'I put thee, (O rice! on the black antelope skin) for (increasing) the life (of the sacrificer) with a view to a long continuance (of the sacrificial work);' or 'I place thee along the long expanse (i.e the skin) for thy (the rice's) long life!'

[3] See I, 1, 4, 23.

[4] Thus, according to Kâty. or Mahîdh., whilst he looks at the ground rice on the skin.

less hand!' he says: 'May they be well received!' By 'for the eye thee!' he bestows eye-sight on it. Now these (attributes) are those of a living being; and thus that sacrificial food for the gods is indeed living, is amrita (ambrosia, or not dead) for the immortals. This is the reason why he thus grinds (the rice). (Whilst) they are grinding the (ground) grains[1], (and whilst) they are heating the potsherds,—

22. Some one[2] pours clarified butter (into the âgyasthâlî, or butter-pot). Now whatever oblation, in being taken, is announced to a (particular) deity, that belongs to the respective deity, that he takes with a special prayer; but in taking this oblation, to wit, the butter, he does not announce it to any particular deity, and therefore takes it with an undefined formula, viz. with (Vâg. S. I, 20): 'Juice of the great ones art thou!' For 'the great ones' some (take to be) a name for the cows; and their juice indeed it is: for this reason he says, 'The juice of the great ones art thou!' And thus, moreover, is some of that (butter) taken with a sacrificial formula: and for this reason also he says, 'The juice of the great ones art thou!'

---

[1] Pimshanti pishtâni; the grinding of the ground or grinding of flour (pishta-peshana) is a common expression in later Sanskrit for doing a useless work ('carrying owls to Athens,' or 'coals to Newcastle'). In the present passage, however, the phrase has to be understood, according to Sâyana, as meaning 'whilst they (the sacrificer's people) carry on the work of grinding begun by the Adhvaryu.'

[2] The Âgnîdhra or somebody else, according to Sâyana; but according to the Schol. on Kâty. II, 5, 9, it is done by the sacrificer himself, who thereupon prepares the veda or bunch of sacrificial grass, tied in the middle, and cut straight at each end, and used for sweeping, &c. Cf. Kâty. I, 3, 21-22; II, 5, 9.

SECOND BRÂHMA*N*A.

1. He pours (the ground rice) into that which contains the strainers—viz. into a dish (pâtrî) on which he has laid the two strainers—with the text (Vâ*g*. S. I, 21): 'At the impulse of the divine Savi*tri* I pour thee out, with the arms of the A*s*vins, with the hands of Pûshan!' The import of this formula is the same (as before, I, 1, 2, 17).

2. He now sits down somewhere inside the altar (vedi)[1]. Then some one (viz. the Âgnîdhra) comes with the kneading-water[2] and brings it to him. He (the Adhvaryu) receives it through the strainers, with the text (Vâ*g*. S. I, 21): 'Let the waters mingle with the plants!' for thereby the water unites with the plants, viz. with the ground rice,—'The plants with the sap!' for the plants thereby unite with the sap; viz. that ground rice with the water, for water is their sap,—'The shining (or wealthy ones) with the moving!' for the shining ones are the waters, and the moving ones are the plants, and these two are thereby mixed together,—'Let the sweet mingle with the sweet!' whereby he says, 'let the savoury be mixed with the savoury!'

3. He then mixes (the two) together, with the text (Vâ*g*. S. I, 22): 'For generation I unite thee!' for, in order that it (the dough or the sacrificial cake prepared from it) may bring offspring to the sacri-

---

[1] 'He sits down (with the dish) either behind the cooking fire, or inside the altar,' Kâty. II, 5, 11. According to Mahâdeva, the former alternative is the one favoured by the Kâ*n*vas.

[2] According to Kâty. II, 5, 1, the kneading-water (or mixing-water, upasar*g*anî) has been put on the (Gârhapatya) fire (by the Agnîdh) at the time of, or previously to, the spreading of the black antelope skin.

ficer, for his prosperity, for food, and so on,—for these reasons he mixes them together. And he also mixes them together with the intention of placing it (the dough) on (the fire): hence, in order that it (the sacrificial cake) may be produced over the fire, for that purpose also he mixes them together.

4. He now divides it into two halves, if there be two oblations: at the full-moon sacrifice there really are two oblations. He then touches them,—where (by so doing) he would not again mix (the two) together,—with the (respective) formulas (Vâg. S. I, 22): 'This to Agni!' 'This to Agni-Soma!' Separately indeed they take that sacrificial food (from the cart) in the first place[1]; then they thresh it together, then they grind it together, then he again divides it: for this reason he thus touches (them separately). The one (the Adhvaryu) now places the cake over (the fire), the other (the Âgnîdhra) puts the clarified butter on:

5. These two acts are done simultaneously. The reason why these two acts are done simultaneously is that one half of the body of the sacrifice no doubt is that butter, and the other half is this rice-offering. 'That half and this half, these two let us now take to the fire!' thus (they think): for this reason those two acts are done simultaneously, and thus this body of the sacrifice is joined together.

6. That one (the Âgnîdhra) puts the butter on, with the text (Vâg. S. I, 22): 'For sap—thee!' When he says 'for sap thee!' he says it for the sake of rain; therefore he takes it off again, with the text (Vâg. S. I, 30): 'For juice—thee!' What juice is

[1] See I, 1, 2, 17 seq., especially p. 17, note 2.

derived (by the plants) from the rain, for that he says this.

7. Now he (the Adhvaryu) puts on (adhi-vrig) the cake, with the text (Vâg. S. I, 22): 'Heat (or a hot vessel, gharma) art thou!' whereby he makes it (a means of) sacrifice, and puts it on in the same way as if he were putting the (pravargya) cauldron (gharma)[1] on,—'Life-sustaining (visvâyus)!' he adds, whereby he obtains life (for the sacrificer).

8. He spreads it (over the respective potsherds), with the text (Vâg. S. I, 22): 'Spread widely, thou wide-spreading one!' whereby he causes it to spread. He adds: 'May thy Lord of Sacrifice spread widely (prosper)!' Lord of Sacrifice, namely, is the sacrificer: hence it is for the sacrificer that he thereby prays for blessing.

9. Let him not make it too broad; for he would make it a human (profane, common cake), if he were to make it (too) broad. Unlucky for (or, excluded from) the sacrifice indeed is that one, to wit, the common (cake). 'That I may not do anything that

[1] Gharma, literally 'heat,' is also the technical term for a kind of cauldron (also called mahâvîra) used at the Pravargya ceremony, a preparatory rite of the Soma-sacrifice: the empty cauldron is there put on the fire, and when thoroughly heated (whence its name), fresh milk is poured into it. The technical phrase for putting on the cauldron is pra-vrig, from which pravargya is derived; and the same verb, though with a different preposition (viz. adhi-vrig), being technically used for the putting on of the sacrificial cake, this verbal coincidence has probably suggested this connection of the two ceremonies, there being a constant tendency to establish some kind of relation between ordinary offerings and the Soma-sacrifice, as the most solemn one; cf. III, 4, 4, 1; X, 2, 5, 3 seq.; Ait. Br. I, 18 seq. Previously to the spreading of the cake, the cinders are swept off from the potsherds with the grass-brush (veda), Hilleb. p. 41, note 7.

is unlucky at the sacrifice,' thus (he thinks, and) for that reason he should not make it too broad.

10. And some now say: 'He should make it of the size of a horse's hoof!' But who knows how large is a horse's hoof? Let him make it of such a size as in his own mind he does not think would be too broad.

11. He then touches it over with water, either once or three times: for whatever in this (rice-offering) they either injure or tear asunder in the threshing or grinding of it, that—water being (a means of) expiation (or purification)—he thereby expiates with water, that is, with (the means of) expiation; that he thereby makes good: for this reason he touches it over with water.

12. He touches it over, with the text (Vâ*g*. S. I, 22): 'May the fire not injure thy skin!' for on the fire he is now going to heat it: 'May that (fire) not injure thy skin!' this is what he thereby says.

13. He now carries fire round it[1]. By this he encloses it with an unbroken fence, lest the evil

[1] The paryagnikara*n*am consists in performing pradakshi*n*â (see p. 37, note 1) on an object whilst holding a fire-brand or burning coal; or (according to the Paddhati) in moving one's hand, which holds the burning coal, round the oblation, from left to right. According to Kâty. II, 5, 22, the Adhvaryu does so on the present occasion, whilst muttering the formula, 'Removed is the Rakshas! removed are the enemies!' (Taitt. S. I, 1, 8, 1.) This practice of paryagnikara*n*am may be compared with the carrying of fire round houses, fields, boats, &c., on the last night of the year, a custom which, according to Mr. A. Mitchell (The Past in the Present, p. 145), still prevails in some parts of Scotland, and which he thinks is probably a survival of some form of fire-worship, and intended to secure fertility and general prosperity. The obvious meaning of the ceremony would seem to be the warding off of the dark and mischievous powers of nature.

spirits, the Rakshas, should seize upon it; for Agni (fire) is the repeller of the Rakshas: this is the reason why he carries fire round it.

14. He bakes[1] it, with the text (Vâ*g*. S. I, 22): 'Let the divine (or God) Savit*ri* bake thee!' for it is not a man that bakes it, but a god it is: therefore it is the God Savit*ri* that bakes it[2]. He adds: 'In the highest heaven!' He means to say 'among the gods,' when he says 'in the highest heaven.' He touches it: 'I will ascertain whether it is done!' thus (he thinks, and) for that reason he touches it.

15. He touches it, with the text (Vâ*g*. S. I, 23): 'Be not afraid! shrink not!' He thereby says: 'Do not thou be afraid, do not thou shrink, because I, a man, touch thee that art not human!'

16. When it is done, he covers it over (with hot ashes): 'Lest the evil spirits, the Rakshas, should espy it,' thus (he thinks); and 'Lest it should lie, as it were, naked and despoiled!' thus also (he thinks):—that is the reason why he covers it over.

17. He covers it over, with the text (Vâ*g*. S. I, 23): 'May the sacrifice not be liable to languish, nor the sacrificer's race liable to languish!' 'That the sacrifice or the sacrificer may not languish after this, when I cover this over,' thus (he thinks, and) for this reason he covers it over in this manner (i. e. with the above text).

---

[1] On the upper side it is baked by burning straw put on or held over it, whereby it takes a crust (tva*k*, 'skin'). Schol. on Kâty. II, 5, 23.

[2] With the name of no other God the epithet deva ('shining,' 'God') is so frequently used as with that of Savit*ri*: hence, according to the author's reasoning, it is he that must be intended, whenever a god not otherwise specified is alluded to.

18. He then pours out for the Âptya deities the water with which the dish has been rinsed and that in which he has washed his fingers[1]. The reason why he pours it out for the Âptyas (is this):

Third Brâhmana.

The Preparation of the Altar.

1. Fourfold, namely, was Agni (fire) at first. Now that Agni whom they at first chose for the office of Hotri priest passed away. He also whom they chose the second time passed away. He also whom they chose the third time passed away[2]. Thereupon the one who still constitutes the fire in our own time, concealed himself from fear. He entered into the waters. Him the gods discovered and brought forcibly away from the waters. He spat upon the waters, saying, 'Bespitten are ye who are an unsafe place of refuge, from whom they take me away against my will!' Thence sprung the Âptya deities, Trita, Dvita, and Ekata.

2. They roamed about with Indra, even as nowadays a Brâhman follows in the train of a king. When he slew Visvarûpa, the three-headed son of Tvashtri, they also knew of his going to be killed; and straightway Trita slew him. Indra, assuredly, was free from that (sin), for he is a god[3].

---

[1] The washing of the fingers and the dish, and has taken place after the putting on and touching over of the cake, and before the paryagnikaranam is performed.

[2] In I, 3, 3, 13–16, the three former Agnis (or the three brothers of Agni, acc. to Mahîdh., Vâg. S. II, 2) are said to have fled from fear of the thunderbolt, in the shape of the vashat formula.

[3] Cf. I, 6, 3, 1 seq. In the Taitt. Samh. II, 5, 1, 1, Visvarûpa, the Tvâshtra, is said to have been a sister's son of the Asuras, and

3. And the people thereupon said: 'Let those be guilty of the sin who knew about his going to be killed! 'How?' they asked. 'The sacrifice shall wipe it off upon (shall transfer it to) them!' they said. Hence the sacrifice thereby wipes off upon them (the guilt or impurity incurred in the preparation of the offering), when they pour out for them the water with which the dish has been rinsed, and that in which he (the Adhvaryu) has washed his fingers.

4. And the Âptyas then said: 'Let us make this pass on beyond us!' 'On whom?' they asked. 'On him who shall make an offering without a dakshinâ (gift to the officiating priests)!' they said. Hence one must not make an offering without a dakshinâ; for the sacrifice wipes (the guilt) off upon the Âptyas, and the Âptyas wipe it off upon him who makes an offering without a dakshinâ.

5. Thereupon the gods ordained this to be the

house-priest (purohita) to the gods, and to have been killed by Indra, because he had secretly contrived to let the oblations go to the Asuras, instead of to the gods. Thus by killing him, Indra (or Trita, according to our version of the legend) became guilty of that most hideous crime, the brahmahatyâ, or killing of a Brâhmana. Trita, the Âptya (i.e. probably 'sprung from, or belonging to the ap, or waters of the atmosphere'), seems to have been a prominent figure of the early Indo-Iranian mythology, the prototype, in many respects, of Indra, the favourite god of the Vedic hymns. The notion of wishing evil and misfortune away to Trita, or far, far away, is a familiar one to the Vedic bards. The name Traitana also occurs once in Rig-veda (I, 158, 5), though in a rather dark passage. On the connection between Trita (? Traitana) and the Iranian Thraetona (Ferîdûn), son of Athvya, see E. Burnouf, Journ. Asiat. V, 120; R. Roth, Zeitschr. d. Deutsch. Morg. Ges. II, p. 216 seq. Dvita (the second) and Ekata are no doubt later abstractions suggested by the etymology of the name Trita (the third), although the former, Dvita, occurs already in the Vedic hymns.

dakshinâ at the new- and full-moon sacrifices, to wit, the Anvâhârya mess of rice[1], 'lest the oblation should be without a dakshinâ.' That (rinsing water) he pours out (for each Âptya) separately: thus he avoids a quarrel among them. He makes it hot (previously)[2]: thus it becomes boiled (drinkable) for them. He pours it out with the formulas, 'For Trita thee!' 'For Dvita thee!' 'For Ekata thee!' —Now it is as an animal sacrifice that this sacrificial cake is offered[3].

[1] The Anvâhârya consists of boiled rice prepared from the rice-grains that remain after the sacrificial cakes have been prepared. It is put on the Dakshina fire by the Adhvaryu for cooking after covering over the cakes and pouring out the water. Kâty. II, 5, 27. Sâyana explains the term as 'that which takes away (anvâ-hri) from the sacrificer the guilt incurred by mistakes during the sacrifice;' but the St. Petersburg Dictionary offers the more probable explanation of it as 'that which serves to supplement (anvâ-hri) the sacrifice.'

[2] According to Sâyana 'he makes the poured-out water hot with a coal.' Kâtyâyana (II, 5, 26) and his commentators, on the other hand, supply the following particulars: 'Having heated (with straw lighted in the Gârhapatya) the water which has been used for washing the dish and hands, he pours it out for the Âptyas (from east to west into three lines drawn with the wooden sword from west to east, north of the sacrificial ground) in such a manner that it does not flow together, with the formulas, "For Trita thee!" &c., respectively.'

[3] That is to say, the sacrificial cake is a substitute or symbol (pratimâ) for the animal sacrifice (as this it would seem was originally a substitute for the human sacrifice) by which the sacrificer redeems himself from the gods. Cf. Sat. Br. XI, 1, 8, 3; Taitt. Br. III, 2, 8, 8. The initiation (dîkshâ) of the sacrificer constitutes his consecration as the victim at the animal sacrifice (Sat. Br. XI, 7, 1, 3; Ait. Br. II, 3; 9; 11; Taitt. Br. II, 2, 82; T. S. VI, 1, 11, 6; Kaush. Br. X, 3; XI, 8), or as the sacrificial food at the haviryagña (Sat. Br. III, 3, 4, 21; Taitt. Br. III, 2, 8, 9), or as the horse at the horse-sacrifice (Taitt. Br. III, 9, 17, 4–5), &c. See, also, Taitt. S. VII, 2, 10, 4; Kâth. 34, 11, where it is said that one must

6. At first, namely, the gods offered up a man as the victim[1]. When he was offered up, the sacrificial essence went out of him. It entered into the horse. They offered up the horse. When it was offered up, the sacrificial essence went out of it. It entered into the ox. They offered up the ox. When it was offered up, the sacrificial essence went out of it. It entered into the sheep. They offered up the sheep. When it was offered up, the sacrificial essence went out of it. It entered into the goat. They offered up the goat. When it was offered up, the sacrificial essence went out of it.

7. It entered into this earth. They searched for it, by digging. They found it (in the shape of) those two (substances), the rice and barley: therefore even now they obtain those two by digging; and as much

not perform the dvâdasâha for any one, since in having to eat of the victim, the cake, &c., one would eat the sacrificer's own flesh, &c. Cf. Weber, Ind. Streifen, I, p. 73. In accordance with these notions it would seem that man originally sacrificed his equal, as the best substitute for his own self; and that, as advancing civilisation rendered human sacrifices distasteful, the human victim was supplied by domestic animals, ennobled by constant contact with man; and finally by various materials of human diet.

[1] On this legend and the one in the Ait. Br. II, 8, but slightly differing from ours, see Max Müller's History of Ancient Sanskrit Literature, p. 420; A. Weber's Ind. Streifen, I, p. 55; Haug's Transl. of the Ait. Br. p. 90; J. Muir's Original Sanskrit Texts, IV, p. 289 note. Professor Max Müller remarks: 'The drift of this story is most likely that in former times all these victims had been offered. We know it for certain in the case of horses and oxen, though afterwards these sacrifices were discontinued. As to sheep and goats, they were considered proper victims to a still later time. When vegetable offerings took the place of bloody victims, it was clearly the wish of the author of our passage to show that, for certain sacrifices, these rice-cakes were as efficient as the flesh of animals.' Cf. also II, 1, 4, 3.

efficacy as all those sacrificed animal victims would have for him, so much efficacy has this oblation (of rice &c.) for him who knows this. And thus there is in this oblation also that completeness which they call 'the fivefold animal sacrifice.'

8. When it (the rice-cake) still consists of rice-meal, it is the hair [1]. When he pours water on it, it becomes skin [2]. When he mixes it, it becomes flesh: for then it becomes consistent; and consistent also is the flesh. When it is baked, it becomes bone: for then it becomes somewhat hard; and hard is the bone. And when he is about to take it off (the fire) and sprinkles it with butter, he changes it into marrow. This is the completeness which they call 'the fivefold animal sacrifice.'

9. The man (purusha) whom they had offered up became a mock-man (kim-purusha [3]). Those two, the horse and the ox, which they had sacrificed,

[1] According to Sâyana, because, like the hair of the victim, the particles of the ground rice are minute and numerous. According to Ait. Br. II, 9, on the other hand, the awn or beard of the rice represents the hair; the husks the skin; the minute particles of chaff removed by the final winnowings, the blood; the ground rice the flesh; and 'whatever other substantial part is in the rice' are the bones of the victim.

[2] 'Because it becomes as flexible as skin,' Sâyana.

[3] It is doubtful what particular kind of being the term kimpurusha (depraved man) is here intended to denote. The authors of the St. Petersburg Dictionary, whom Professor Weber follows (Ind. Stud. IX, 246), take it (probably correctly) to denote 'a monkey.' Professor Haug, on the other hand, in his translation of the corresponding passage in the Ait. Br. II, 8, thinks 'the author very likely meant a dwarf,' whilst Professor Max Müller (History of Ancient Sanskrit Literature, p. 420) translates it by 'a savage.' Perhaps one of the species of apes which particularly resemble man, is intended by it. Cf. Weber, Omina et Portenta, p. 356.

became a bos gaurus and a gayal (bos gavaeus) respectively. The sheep which they had sacrificed, became a camel. The goat which they had sacrificed, became a *s*arabha [1]. For this reason one should not eat (the flesh) of these animals, for these animals are deprived of the sacrificial essence (are impure).

Fourth Brâhmana.

1. When Indra hurled the thunderbolt at V*ri*tra, that hurled one became fourfold. Of (three parts of) it the wooden sword (sphya) represents one-third or thereabouts, the sacrificial post one-third or thereabouts, and the chariot one-third or thereabouts. That piece, moreover, with which he struck him, was broken off (*sri*); and on falling down it became an arrow (*s*ara): hence the designation arrow, because it was broken off. And in this way the thunderbolt became fourfold.

2. In consequence of this, the priests make use of two (of these pieces) at the sacrifice, and men of the military caste (râ*g*anyabandhu) also make use of two of them in battle: viz. the priests make use of the sacrificial post and the wooden sword, and the men of the military caste of the chariot and the arrow.

3. Now when he takes up the wooden sword [2], he raises that thunderbolt against the wicked, spiteful enemy, even as Indra at that time raised the thunderbolt against V*ri*tra: that is the reason why he takes the wooden sword.

4. He takes it, with the text (Vâ*g*. S. I, 24): 'At the impulse of the divine Savit*ri*, I take thee with

[1] A fabulous kind of deer with eight legs, which was supposed to kill elephants and lions.

[2] See note on I, 1, 2, 8.

the arms of the Asvins, with the hands of Pûshan; thee that performs sacred rites to the gods!' Savitri, namely, is the impeller of the gods: thus he thereby takes that (wooden sword) as one impelled by Savitri. 'With the arms of the Asvins,' he says, because the Asvins are the two Adhvaryu priests (of the gods): with their arms he therefore takes it, not with his own. Pûshan is distributer of portions (to the gods): with his hands he therefore takes it, not with his own; for it is the thunderbolt, and no man can hold that: he thus takes it with (the assistance of) the gods.

5. 'I take (thee) that performs sacred rites to the gods,' he says, because a sacred rite means a sacrifice: 'that performs sacrifices to the gods,' he thereby says. After taking it in his left hand and touching it with his right, he murmurs—by what he murmurs he makes it sharp,—

6. He murmurs (Vâg. S. I, 24): 'Thou art Indra's right arm!' for Indra's right arm no doubt is the most powerful one, and for that reason he says: 'Thou art Indra's right arm!' 'The thousand-spiked, hundred-edged!' he adds, for a thousand spikes and a hundred edges had that thunderbolt which he hurled at Vritra: he thereby makes it to be that (thunderbolt).

7. 'The sharp-edged Vâyu (wind) art thou!' he adds; for that indeed is the sharpest edge, to wit, that (wind) which here blows: for that one sweeps right across these worlds. He thereby makes it sharp. When he (further) says: 'The killer of the enemy!' let him, whether he wishes to exorcise or not, say: 'The killer of so and so!' When it has been sharpened, he must not touch either himself or the earth with it: 'Lest I should hurt either myself or the earth with that sharp thunderbolt,' thus he thinks, and for

that reason he does not touch either himself or the earth with it.

8. The gods and the Asuras, both of them sprung from Pra*g*âpati[1], were contending for superiority. The gods vanquished the Asuras; and yet these afterwards harassed them again.

9. The gods then said: 'We do, no doubt, vanquish the Asuras, but nevertheless they afterwards again harass us. How then can we vanquish them so that we need not fight them again?'

10. Agni then said: 'By fleeing northwards they escape from us.' By fleeing northwards they had indeed escaped from them.

11. Agni said: 'I will go round to the northern side, and you will then shut them in from here[2]; and whilst shutting them in, we will put them down by these (three) worlds; and from what fourth world there is beyond these (three) they will not be able to rise again.'

12. Agni thereupon went round to the northern side; and they (the other gods) shut them in from here; and whilst shutting them in, they put them down with these (three) worlds; and from what fourth world

---

[1] Pra*g*âpati is called the father of the gods and Asuras, I, 5, 3, 2; and they are represented as entering on his inheritance, I, 7, 2, 22; IX, 5, 1, 12. Not only the gods and Asuras, but also the men derive their origin from Pra*g*âpati, XIV, 8, 2, 1. He has created all beings, I, 6, 3, 35; Ait. Br. III, 36.

[2] I. e. 'from the sacrificial ground,' Sâya*n*a. It seems doubtful to me whether it does not rather mean 'you will then shut them in, or block them up, within that place,' that is to say, north of the altar, where the utkara, or heap of rubbish, lies. The four worlds by which he puts down the enemies are represented by the loose soil which is dug up by the sphya being flung four separate times at the grass-bush lying on the altar (vedi), and which is then thrown on the utkara.

there is beyond these (three) they did not rise again. Now this same (expulsion of the Asuras) is virtually the same act as the flinging away of the grass-bush [1].

13. The Âgnîdhra goes round to the north, for he is virtually the same person as Agni himself. The Adhvaryu then shuts them in from here; and whilst shutting them in, he puts them down by means of these (three) worlds; and from what fourth world there is beyond these (three) they do not rise again. Thus now also they do not rise again, for by the same means by which the gods kept them off, the priests now also keep them off during the sacrifice.

14. And whoever has evil designs upon the sacrificer and hates him, him he thereby puts down by means of these (three) worlds, and what fourth world there is beyond these. And in putting him down with these (three) worlds, and what fourth world there is beyond these, he flings everything away from this (earth), for on it all these worlds rest: for what would he fling away, if he were to fling (the grass-bush) away with the words, 'The air I throw away, the heaven I throw away!' therefore he flings everything away from this (earth) [2].

15. Thereupon, after putting the grass-bush between [3], he flings (the wooden sword at it). 'Lest I

---

[1] The ceremony called stambayagus (-haranam) consists in 'the throwing away of the grass-bush after cutting it by the (flinging of the) wooden sword, with the simultaneous reciting of Yagus-texts' [yagurmantrako darbhah stambayaguh, takka stambarûpam sphyena bhittvotkaradese haret, Sây., Taitt. S. I, 1, 9].

[2] This passage, in which the author seems to argue against some other ritualistic authority, is not quite clear to me. The Taitt. Br. has, 'from the atmosphere he drives him away (by the second throw), from the sky he drives him away (by the third throw).'

[3] That is, between himself, or the wooden sword, and the altar. According to Kâty. II, 6, 15, he lays the grass-bush down on the

should injure the earth with this sharp thunderbolt!' thus (he thinks, and) for that reason he flings after putting the grass-bush between.

16. He flings it, with the text (Vâ*g*. S. I, 25): 'O earth, that affordest the place for making offerings to the gods! may I not injure the root of thy plant!' He thereby makes her, as it were, with roots remaining in her[1]. Whilst he takes up (the earth dug up by the sword), he thus addresses her: 'May I not injure the roots of thy plants!'—And in further saying, 'Go to the fold, the abode of the cows!' when he is about to throw it away (on the heap of rubbish), he causes it not to forsake him; for that which is within the fold[2] does not forsake him: for that reason he says, 'Go to the fold, the abode of the cows!'—He further says (whilst looking at the hole in the ground): 'May the sky rain on thee!' Wherever, in digging into her, they wound and injure her—water being (a means of) expiation—that he thereby expiates by the water which is (a means of) expiation; that he thereby makes good by means of the water: that is the reason why he says: 'May the sky rain on thee!'—'Tie him down, O divine Savit*ri*, to the furthest end of the earth!' he says (whilst throwing on the heap of rubbish the soil dug up); he thus

altar with its top pointing northwards, with the text: 'The armour of the earth art thou!'

[1] Sâya*n*a explains it by uttaramûlâm iva karoti; 'p*ri*thivîm uparibhâgâvasthitamûlayuktâm ivâ' (? 'with the roots remaining in its (the earth's) upper part, or surface'). Cf. also Sây. on Taitt. S. I, 1, 9 (p. 155).

[2] The Taitt. Br. (III, 2, 9, 3) identifies the fold (pen, stable) with the metres (? which enclose the altar in the shape of the first set of lines), cf. *S*at. Br. I, 2, 5, 6 seq. This identification rests on the double meaning of go (in gosthânam) as 'cow' and 'metre.'

says to the divine Savitri: 'Tie him down to blind darkness!' when he says 'to the furthest end of the earth,'—'With a hundred fetters!' by this he means to say, 'so that he cannot free himself.'—'Him who hates us and whom we hate, do not release from there!' Whether or not he wishes to exorcise, let him say: 'So and so . . . do not release from there!'

17. He then throws (the wooden sword) a second time, with the text (Vâg. S. I, 26): 'May I drive Araru away from the earth, the place of offerings!' Araru[1], namely, was an Asura and Rakshas. Him the gods drove away from this (earth), and in the same way he (the Adhvaryu) thereby drives him away from this (earth). He adds (whilst repeating the several corresponding acts): 'Go to the fold, the abode of the cows! May the sky rain on thee! Tie him down, O divine Savitri, to the furthest end of the earth, with a hundred fetters, him who hates us and whom we hate, do not release him from there!'

18. The Âgnîdhra presses it down (on the heap of rubbish), with the text (Vâg. S. I, 26): 'O Araru! thou shalt not fly up to heaven!' For when the gods drove away Araru, the Asura-Rakshas, he wished to fly up to heaven. Agni pressed him down, saying, 'O Araru, thou shalt not fly up to heaven!' and he did not fly up to heaven. In the same way the

[1] Of this demon we have no further particulars except that in Rig-veda X, 99, 10, he is said to have four feet; see also Taitt. Br. III, 2, 9, 4 seq. Perhaps there is some connection between Araru and the Arurmaghas in Ait. Br. VII, 28, and the Arunmukhas in Kaushît. Up. 3, 1; both of them enemies of Indra. Cf. M. Haug's and Max Müller's translations of these works; and Weber, Ind. Stud. I, 411.

Adhvaryu thereby cuts him off from this world, and the Âgnîdhra from the side of heaven. That is the reason why he does this.

19. He then throws (the wooden sword) a third time, with the text (Vâg. S. I, 26): 'Let thy drop not spring up to the sky!' Her (the earth's) drop no doubt is that moisture of hers upon which the creatures subsist. 'Let this thine (moisture) not fly away to the sky!' he thereby says.—He adds (whilst again repeating the several acts): 'Go to the fold, the abode of the cows! May the sky rain on thee! Tie him down, O divine Savitri, to the furthest end of the earth, with a hundred fetters, him who hates us and whom we hate, do not release him from there!'

20. Three times he throws it, with the sacrificial formula (Yagus); for three are these worlds, and with these worlds he thereby puts him (the evil spirit) down [1]. And what these worlds are, that in truth is the Yagus: for that reason he throws it thrice with the sacrificial formula.

21. Silently (he throws) a fourth time [2]. What fourth world there may or may not be beyond these (three), by that one he thereby drives away the spiteful enemy. For uncertain indeed is what fourth world there may or may not be beyond these (three); and uncertain also is what (is done) silently: for that reason (he throws) silently a fourth time.

---

[1] In the corresponding passage of the Black Yagus (Taitt. Br. III, 2, 9, 5 seq.) the Adhvaryu is represented as driving the enemy away from the four worlds by throwing the sword four times.

[2] When, together with the dug-out soil, he throws the grass-bush on the heap of rubbish. Kâty. II, 6, 24.

FIFTH BRÂHMANA.

1. The gods and the Asuras, both of them sprung from Pragâpati, were contending for superiority. Then the gods were worsted, and the Asuras thought: 'To us alone assuredly belongs this world!'

2. They thereupon said: 'Well then, let us divide this world between us; and having divided it, let us subsist thereon!' They accordingly set about dividing it with ox-hides from west to east.

3. The gods then heard of this, and said: 'The Asuras are actually dividing this earth: come, let us go to where the Asuras are dividing it. For what would become of us, if we were to get no share in it?' Placing Vishnu, (in the shape of) this very sacrifice, at their head, they went (to the Asuras).

4. They then said: 'Let us share in this earth along with yourselves! Let a part of it be ours!' The Asuras replied rather grudgingly: 'As much as this Vishnu lies upon, and no more, we give you!'

5. Now Vishnu was a dwarf[1]. The gods, however,

[1] This legend is given in Muir's Original Sanskrit Texts, IV, p. 122, where it is pointed out that we have here the germ of the Dwarf Incarnation of Vishnu; and in A. Kuhn's treatise, 'Ueber Entwickelungsstufen der Mythenbildung,' p. 128, where the following remarks are made on the story: 'Here also we meet with the same struggle between light and darkness: the gods of light are vanquished and obtain from the Asuras, who divide the earth between themselves, only as much room as is covered by Vishnu, who measures the atmosphere with his three steps. He represents (though I cannot prove it in this place) the sun-light, which, on shrinking into dwarf's size in the evening, is the only means of preservation that is left to the gods, who cover him with metres, i. e. with sacred hymns (probably in order to defend him from the powers of darkness), and in the end kindle Agni in the east—the dawn—and thereby once more obtain possession of the earth.' Compare also the corresponding legend in Taitt. Br. III, 2, 9, 7,

were not offended at this, but said: 'Much indeed they gave us, who gave us what is equal in size to the sacrifice.'

6. Having then laid him down eastwards, they enclosed him on all (three) sides with the metres, saying (Vâ*g*. S. I, 27), on the south side, 'With the Gâyatrî metre I enclose thee!' on the west side: 'With the Trish*t*ubh metre I enclose thee!' on the north side: 'With the *G*agatî metre I enclose thee[1]!'

7. Having thus enclosed him on all (three) sides, and having placed Agni (the fire) on the east side, they went on worshipping and toiling with it (or him, i.e. Vish*n*u, the sacrifice). By it they obtained (sam-vid) this entire earth; and because they obtained by it this entire (earth), therefore it (the sacrificial ground) is called vedi (the altar). For this reason they say, 'As great as the altar is, so great is the earth;' for by it (the altar) they obtained this entire (earth). And, verily, he who so understands this, wrests likewise this entire (earth) from his rivals, excludes his rivals from sharing in it.

8. Thereupon this Vish*n*u became tired; but being enclosed on all (three) sides by the metres, with the

where the gods are granted by the Asuras as much as they can enclose; and by the Vasus being placed in the south, the Rudras in the west, the Âdityas in the north, and Agni in the east, they obtain the whole of the earth.

[1] In the actual performance of the sacrifice this represents the pûrva-parigraha, or first enclosing of the altar by a single line being drawn with the wooden sword on each of the three sides (viz. S.W. to S.E.; S.W. to N.W.; N.W. to N.E.) whilst muttering the respective texts. Before doing so he has, however, to ask and receive the permission of the Brahman, mutatis mutandis, in the usual way (cf. p. 7 note): the same forms have to be gone through at the marking of the second and third enclosures. Kâty. II, 6, 25 seq. On the ritualistic application of the metres, see note on I, 3, 2, 9.

fire on the east, there was no (means of) escaping: he then hid himself among the roots of plants.

9. The gods said: 'What has become of Vish*n*u? What has become of the sacrifice?' They said: 'On all (three) sides he is enclosed by the metres, with Agni to the east, there is no (way of) escaping: search for him in this very place!' By slightly digging they accordingly searched for him. They discovered him at a depth of three inches (or thumb's breadths): therefore the altar should be three inches deep; and therefore also Pâ*ñk*i[1] made the altar for the Soma-sacrifice three inches deep.

10. This, however, one must not do. Among the roots of the plants he (Vish*n*u) hid himself: therefore let him (the Adhvaryu) bid (the Âgnîdhra) to cut out the roots of the plants. And since they found (anu-vid) Vish*n*u in that place, therefore it is called vedi (altar).

11. When they had found him, they enclosed him with a second enclosure, saying (Vâ*g*. S. I, 27), 'Of good soil art thou, and auspicious art thou!' on the south side; for when they had thus obtained this earth they made it of good soil and auspicious;—'Pleasant art thou, and soft to sit upon!' they said on the west side, for when they had thus obtained this earth, they made it pleasant and soft to sit upon;—'Abounding in food and drink art thou!' they said on the north side, for when they had thus obtained this earth, they made it abounding in food and drink.

[1] This teacher is mentioned again, *S*at. Br. II, 1, 4, 27, along with two others, viz. Âsuri and Mâdhuki, but nothing further is known of him. According to the Black Ya*g*us the altar is made four (not three) aṅgulas deep.

12. Threefold[1] he draws round the first line of enclosure, threefold the second: hence sixfold (the two); for six seasons there are in the year, and the year, as Pragâpati (Lord of Creation), is the sacrifice[2]. As large as the sacrifice, as wide as its extent is, so wide does he thereby enclose it.

13. With six sacred words[3] he draws around the first line of enclosure, with six the second: thus (together) twelvefold, for twelve no doubt are the months of the year; and the year, as Pragâpati, is the sacrifice. As large as the sacrifice, as wide as its extent is, so wide does he thereby enclose it.

14. 'Let it (the altar) measure a fathom[4] across on the west side,' they say: that, namely, is the size of a man, and it (the altar) should be of (the) man's size. 'Three cubits long (should be) the

[1] Viz. each enclosing line consists of three divisions corresponding to the three sides (S., W., N.) of the altar.

[2] Pragâpati (Lord of Creation) is here, as elsewhere, identified with the year (probably as the representative of the eternal process of regeneration) and consequently with the annual cycle of sacrificial performance, or the sacrifice itself. Cf. Sat. Br. I, 5, 2, 16; X, 4, 3, 1.

[3] According to Sâyaṇa, because each of the three mantras, 'gâyatreṇa (traishṭubhena, gâgatena resp.) tvâ khandasâ pari gṛihṇâmi,' consists of two parts, the first ending with tvâ, the second with gṛihṇâmi, which makes together six. Similarly with the second triad of mantras. In the former case the Taittirîya text (Taitt. S. I, 1, 9, 3), 'The Vasus may enclose thee with the Gâyatrî metre, the Rudras with the Trishṭubh metre, the Âdityas with the Gagatî metre!' would furnish a more natural explanation of the six sacred words.

[4] Vyâma, the space between the extreme ends of the outstretched arms. It is doubtful whether it is here intended for a fixed measure, or whether it is a relative one, depending on the size of the respective sacrificer. The size of a man was supposed to be equal to the extent of his outstretched arms.

"easterly line[1]," for threefold is the sacrifice,' (so they say, but) in this there is no (fixed) measure: let him make it as long as he thinks fit in his own mind!

15. The two shoulders (of the altar) he carries along both sides of the (Âhavanîya) fire. For the altar (vedi, fem.) is female and the fire (agni, masc.) is male; and the woman lies embracing the man: thereby a copulation productive of offspring is obtained. For this reason he carries the two shoulders (of the altar) along both sides of the fire.

16. It (the altar) should be broader on the west side, contracted in the middle, and broad again on the east side; for thus shaped they praise a woman: 'broad about the hips, somewhat narrower between the shoulders, and contracted in the middle (or, about the waist).' Thereby he makes it (the altar) pleasing to the gods.

17. It should be sloping towards east, for the east is the quarter of the gods; and also sloping towards north, for the north is the quarter of men. To the south side he sweeps the rubbish (loose soil), for that is the quarter of the deceased ancestors. If it (the altar) were sloping towards south, the sacrificer would speedily go to yonder world; and thus (by making the altar in the prescribed way) the sacrificer lives for a long time: for this reason he sweeps the loose soil to the south side. Let

[1] I.e. a line drawn from the middle of the western side through the centre of the altar to the Âhavanîya fire. The same line prolongated from the western side of the altar westwards to the Gârhapatya would measure eight (eleven or twelve) steps (prakrama or vikrama, of two feet or pada each) from fire to fire. See I, 7, 3, 23–25.

him then cover it (the altar) over with (fresh) rubbish: for rubbish means cattle, and well-stocked with cattle he thereby makes it[1].

18. He (the Âgnîdhra) smooths it down (from east to west). The gods, namely, when they were preparing for the contest, said to one another: 'Come, let us remove to the moon for safety what imperishable place of worship there is on this earth; so that if the Asuras, on vanquishing us, should drive us away from here, we may afterwards, by praising and mortifying, prevail again!' They accordingly removed to the moon what imperishable place of worship there was on this earth. That now is the black (spots) in the moon: hence they say, 'In the moon is the place of worship for this earth.' It is in this place of worship also that his sacrifice is performed: for that reason he smooths (the altar) down[2].

19. He smooths it down, with the text (Vâg. S. I, 28): 'Before the bloody (battle) with its rushings hither and thither[3], O mighty one!' the bloody one no doubt is the battle, for in battle

---

[1] Purîsha, rubbish; 'sandy or gravel-like soil,' Sây. on Taitt. Br. III, 2, 9, 12; purîsha also means 'fæces, manure,' in which sense it is probably taken symbolically for 'cattle.' The Taitt. Br. better: 'well supplied with cattle he thereby makes him (the sacrificer).'

[2] ? By stroking along the altar he shifts it to the moon.

[3] The interpretation of purâ krûrasya visripah here given by the author, and also by Mahîdhara on Vâg. S. I, 28, is more than doubtful. Sâyana on Taitt. S. I, 1, 9 is probably more correct in taking purâ visripah (abl. or gerund) krûrasya to mean 'before the sneaking away of the cruel enemy (Araru, lying fettered on the heap of rubbish)'—he supplies: 'thou, O altar, containest merely the divine oblations, but since his removal thou containest everything.' Cf. also Weber, Ind. Streifen, II, p. 463.

bloody deeds are done, and slain lie man and horse; and before that battle they removed it (the altar to the moon); therefore he says, 'Before the bloody (battle) with its rushings hither and thither, O mighty one!'—'lifting up the life-bestowing earth,' for after lifting up what was living on this earth, they removed it to the moon; therefore he says, 'lifting up the life-bestowing earth;'—'which they raised to the moon by prayers,' 'which they placed in the moon by worship,' he thereby says,—'that (earth) the wise still point out and worship,' to that they accordingly address their worship; and the offering of him also who so understands this, is performed in that place of worship.

20. He now says (to the Âgnîdhra; Vâg. S. I, 28), 'Put the sprinkling-water down (on the altar)!' That thunderbolt, the wooden sword, and the priest (brâhmana) have hitherto defended that sacrifice. Now the water also is a thunderbolt: that thunderbolt he thereby lays down for its defence. While the sprinkling-water is being held close above the wooden sword, he takes up the latter. If he were to set the sprinkling-water down, while the wooden sword is still lying, the two thunderbolts would come into collision with each other; but in this way the two thunderbolts do not come into collision with each other: for that reason he takes up the wooden sword, while the sprinkling-water is being held close above it.

21. He pronounces this (entire) speech:—'Put the sprinkling-water down (on the altar)! put fuel and barhis (sacrificial grass) beside it! wipe the ladles! gird the (sacrificer's) wife! come hither with the clarified butter!' This is a direction (given to

the Âgnîdhra); he (the Adhvaryu) may pronounce it, if he choose; or, if he so choose, he may omit it: for he (the Âgnîdhra) himself knows that this work has now to be done.

22. He then flings the wooden sword northwards (on the heap of rubbish). If he wishes to exorcise[1], (he does so), with the text, 'I fling thee as a thunderbolt for so and so!' and as a thunderbolt the wooden sword accordingly strikes down (the enemy).

23. He then washes his hands[2]; for what there was bloody (or injured) on it (the altar) that he thereby removes from it: that is why he washes his hands.

24. Now those who made offerings in former times, touched (the altar and oblations) at this particular time, while they were sacrificing. They became more sinful. Those who washed (their hands) became righteous. Then unbelief took hold of men: 'Those who sacrifice become more sinful, and those who sacrifice not become righteous,' they said. No sacrificial food then came to the gods from this world: for the gods subsist on what is offered up from this world[3].

25. The gods thereupon said to Brihaspati Âṅgirasa, 'Verily, unbelief has come upon men; ordain thou the sacrifice to them!' Brihaspati Âṅgirasa then went and said, 'How comes it that you do not sacrifice?' They replied, 'From a desire for what

[1] Otherwise he uses the text (Vâg. S. I, 28): 'A killer of the enemy art thou!' Kâty. II, 6, 42.

[2] He does so (on the utkara) and then lays down the wooden sword west of the pranîtâ water. Kâty. II, 6, 43.

[3] Men, on the other hand, subsist on what is bestowed on them from yonder world. Taitt. S. III, 2, 9, 7; Taitt. Br. II, 2, 7, 3.

should we sacrifice, since those who sacrifice become more sinful, and those who sacrifice not become righteous?'

26. Brihaspati Âṅgirasa then said, 'What we have heard of as produced[1] for the gods that is this sacrifice, that is to say, the cooked oblations and the prepared altar; therewith you have performed while touching: that is why you have become more sinful. Sacrifice therefore without touching, for thus you will become righteous!' 'How long?' they asked. 'Till the spreading of the sacrificial grass (on the altar),' he said. By the sacrificial grass, namely, it (the altar) becomes appeased. If, therefore, before the spreading of the sacrificial grass anything were to fall on it, let him only remove it at the time when he spreads the sacrificial grass; for when they spread the sacrificial grass, then they also step on it with the foot. He who knowing this sacrifices without touching, becomes indeed righteous: let him therefore sacrifice, without touching (the altar and oblations).

THIRD ADHYÂYA. FIRST BRÂHMANA.

1. He (the Âgnîdhra) now brushes the spoons[2] (with the grass-ends). The reason why he brushes

[1] Parishûtam, which Sâyana interprets by parigrihîtam, 'hedged round' [? 'set apart']. The Kânva MS. reads parishutam.

[2] Besides the Agnihotra-havanî, or milk ladle used at the morning and evening oblations (see p. 11, note 2; and II, 3, 1, 17), three different sruk or offering-spoons are used, viz. the guhû, upabhrit, and dhruvâ. They are made each of a different kind of wood, of an arm's length (or, according to others, a cubit long), with a bowl of the shape and size of the hand, and a hole cut through the bark and front side of the bowl and fitted with a spout some eight or nine inches long, and shaped like a goose's bill. The sruva or dipping-spoon, on the other hand, chiefly used for ladling the clarified

the spoons is that the course[1] pursued among the gods is in accordance with that pursued among men. Now, when the serving up of food is at hand among men,—

2. They rinse the vessels, and having rinsed them, they serve up the food with them: in the same way is treated the sacrifice to the gods, that is to say, the cooked oblations and the prepared altar; and those vessels of theirs, the sacrificial spoons.

3. Now, when he brushes (the spoons), he in reality rinses them, thinking, 'with these rinsed ones I will proceed.' He thereby rinses them with two substances for the gods, and with one for men; viz. with water and the brahman (spirit of worship) for the gods,—for the water is (represented by) the sacrificial grass[2], and the brahman (by) the sacrificial formula;—and with one for men, that is with water alone: and thus this takes place separately[3].

4. He, in the first place, takes the dipping-spoon

butter (or milk) from the butter vessel into the offering-spoons, is of khadira wood (Acacia Catechu), a cubit long, with a round bowl measuring a thumb's joint across, and without a spout. In our text the term sruk is used both in the general sense of 'spoon' and in the narrower one of 'offering-spoon,' as distinguished from the sruva or 'dipping-spoon.'

[1] The brushing of the spoons is here compared with the rinsing of vessels preparatory to their being used for serving up the food. At the same time, we shall see further on (I, 8, 3, 26–27) that the two principal offering-spoons, the guhû and upabhrit, are looked upon as yoke-fellows, they being the two horses that are supposed to convey the sacrifice (and consequently the sacrificer himself) to the world of the gods; hence this process of cleaning also corresponds to the rubbing down of the horses preparatory to the setting out of the sacrificer on his progress to the world of the gods.

[2] See I, 1, 3, 5.

[3] It is doubtful to me whether this last passage merely refers to the several spoons, or whether it refers to the symbolical meaning

(sruva, masc.) and makes it hot (on the Gârhapatya fire), with either of the texts (Vâg. S. I, 29), 'Scorched is the Rakshas, scorched are the enemies!' or, 'Burnt out is the Rakshas, burnt out are the enemies!'

5. For when the gods were performing sacrifice they were afraid of a disturbance on the part of the Asuras and Rakshas. Hence by this means he, from the very opening of the sacrifice, expels from here the evil spirits, the Rakshas[1].

6. He brushes it thus inside with the (grass-)tops (cut off from the grass in tying the veda), with the text (Vâg. S. I, 29), 'Not sharp[2] art thou, (but yet) a destroyer of the enemies!' he says this in order that it may unceasingly destroy the enemies of the sacrificer. Further, 'Thee, the food-abounding (masc.), I cleanse for the kindling of food[3]!'—'thee that art suitable for the sacrifice, I cleanse for the sacrifice,' he thereby says. In the same way he brushes all the spoons, saying, 'Thee, the food-abounding (fem.) ...,' in the case of the offering-spoon (sruk, fem.). The prâsitraharana[4] (he brushes) silently.

of the wiping with sacrificial grass and the accompanying formula. In the latter case it might mean: 'and thus that (act) becomes different (i.e. has a different significance).'

[1] Cf. I, 1, 2, 3, and note.

[2] A-nisita, 'not sharpened,' from sâ (so), 'to sharpen' (thus also Mahîdh.). If, however, anuparata, 'unceasing,' in the text is intended by the author to explain anisita, he would seem to identify the root sâ with sâ (so), 'to bring to an end, to finish.' The spoon is sharpened by the wiping, cf. Taitt. Br. III, 3, 1, 1.

[3] Vâgedhyâyai, 'for the lighting (brightening) of the sacrifice (by means of the butter which is poured into the fire), the sacrifice being the food of the gods,' Mahîdh. The St. Petersburg Dictionary suggests vâgetyâyai, 'thee, the courser, I wipe for the race!' Cf. p. 68, note 1.

[4] The prâsitraharana is a pan of khadira wood, either

7. Inside he brushes with the (grass-)tops thus (viz. from the handle to the top, or in a forward, eastward direction from himself); outside with the lower (grass-)ends thus (viz. in the opposite or backward direction, towards himself)[1]: for thus (viz. in the former way) goes the out-breathing, and thus (in the opposite way) the in-breathing. Thereby he obtains out-breathing and in-breathing (for the sacrificer): hence these hairs (on the upper side of the elbow) point that way, and these (on the lower side) point that way[2].

8. Each time he has brushed and heated (a spoon), he hands it (to the Adhvaryu). Just as, after having rinsed (the eating vessels) while touching them, one would finally rinse them without touching them, so here: for this reason he hands over each (spoon) after heating it[3].

---

square or round (? oval, of the shape of a cow's ear, Sây.; of the shape of a mirror, Kâty.), used for holding the Brahman's portion (prâ*s*itra) of the sacrificial cake. According to Kâty. II, 6, 49, the *sri*tâvadânam (cake-cutter) and (purodâ*s*a-)pâtrî (cake-dish) also have to be cleaned on this occasion.

[1] While brushing the spoons he stands east of the Âhavanîya fire-house, looking toward east. The way of brushing, prescribed by the Black Yagus (Taitt. Br. III, 3, 1, 3–4; comm. on Taitt. S. I, 1, 10), seems to be more complicated.

[2] Viz. the former ('aratner uparibhâgasya lomâni'), according to Sâya*n*a, point in a forward direction (away from the body), and the latter ('p*ri*sh*th*abhâgasya lomâni') in a backward direction. The Taitt. Br. III, 3, 1, 4 has 'on the elbow (aratnau) the hairs above (point) forward, those below backward,' which Sâya*n*a (Taitt. S. I, 1, 1, 10) explains by 'the short hairs above the wrist (? ma*n*i-bandhâd ûrdhvam) are forward-pointed (prâṅmukha), but those below are backward-pointed (pratya*ñk*).'

[3] That is to say, the heating of the spoons corresponds to the usual final rinsing of household vessels with water without touching them. Sâya*n*a.

9. The dipping-spoon (sruva, masc.) he brushes first, and then the other spoons (sruk, fem.). The offering-spoon (sruk), namely, is female, and the dipping-spoon is male, so that, although in this way several women meet together, the one that is, as it were, the only male youth among them, goes there first, and the others after him. This is the reason why he brushes the dipping-spoon first, and afterwards the other (offering-)spoons.

10. Let him brush them so as not to spatter anything towards the fire, as he would thereby bespatter him, to whom he will be bringing food, with the slops of the vessels: therefore let him brush them so as not to spatter anything towards the fire, that is to say, after stepping outside (the Âhavanîya fire-house) towards the east.

11. Here now some throw the grass-ends used for cleaning the spoons into the (Âhavanîya) fire. 'To the veda (grass-bunch) they assuredly belonged, and the spoons have been cleaned with them: hence it is something that belongs to the sacrifice, and (we throw it into the fire) in order that it should not become excluded from the sacrifice,' thus (they argue). Let him, however, not do so, since he would thereby make him to whom he will offer food, drink the slops of the vessels[1]. Let him therefore throw them away (on the heap of rubbish).

12. He (the Âgnîdhra) then girds the wife (of the

[1] The Black Yagus (Taitt. Br. III, 3, 2, 1) prescribes that the grass-ends, after the brushing, should be thrown into the fire, and not on the heap of rubbish, as some do; or at all events they should not be thrown on the utkara, without their having been previously washed with water, as they would otherwise bring ill-luck to the cattle.

sacrificer)[1]. She, the wife, truly is the hinder part of the sacrifice. 'May the sacrifice go on increasing before me!' thus (she thinks while) he girds her, thinking, 'may she sit thus girt by my sacrifice!'

13. He girds her with a cord (yoktra): for with a cord (yoktra) they yoke the draught-animal (yogya). Impure indeed is that part of woman which is below the navel; and therewith she will be facing the sacrificial butter: that part of her he thereby conceals with the cord, and only with the pure upper part of her body she then faces the sacrificial butter. This is the reason why he girds the wife[2].

14. He girds her over the garment. Now the garment represents the plants, and (the cord represents) Varuna's noose[3] (raggu): hence he thereby places the plants between (her and the noose), and

[1] The mistress of the house is seated south-west of the Gârhapatya fire [with bent (or raised) knees and her face turned towards north-east]. The Âgnîdhra then girds her round the waist, outside the garment, with a triple cord of reed-grass (muñga). Kâty. II, 7, 1; and Sâyana on our passage.

[2] According to Taitt. Br. III, 3, 3, 2–3 the symbolical meaning of this act is, that it represents the vratopanayana, or initiation of the wife into the sacred rite. The girding of the wife would thus possess a significance similar to that of the ordinary upanayana, or investiture of the youth with the sacred cord.

[3] The noose (pâsa) is one of the chief attributes of God Varuna, the symbol of his supreme power and his abhorrence of sin. Thus we read in Atharva-veda IV, 16, 4 seq.: 'And if one were to flee far beyond the sky, one would not escape from king Varuna. From heaven his spies issue forth to this (world), and with their thousand eyes survey the earth. King Varuna sees all that happens between heaven and earth and beyond them: the very twinklings of the eyes of men are numbered by him. . . . May all those baleful nooses of thine, O Varuna, that are thrown sevenfold and three-

thus that noose of Varuna does not injure her. This is the reason why he girds her over the garment.

15. He girds her, with the text (Vâg. S. I, 30), 'A zone art thou for Aditi!' Aditi, indeed, is this earth. She is the wife of the gods, and that one is his (the sacrificer's) wife. It is for the latter, accordingly, that he makes it a zone instead of a noose (or string). A zone means a girdle, and he thereby makes it this for her.

16. Let him not make a knot[1], for the knot is Varuna's (attribute); and Varuna would lay hold on the (sacrificer's) wife, if he were to make a knot. For this reason he does not make a knot.

17. He twists it through upwards[2], with the text (Vâg. S. I, 30), 'The pervader[3] of Vishnu art thou!' Let her not sit to the west of the sacrifice, with her face towards the east. For Aditi is this earth[4], she is the wife of the gods, and she indeed sits on the west of the sacrifice of the gods, with her face turned

---

fold, ensnare him who speaks untruth, and pass by him who speaks the truth!'

[1] Taitt. Br. III, 3, 3, 4, on the contrary, prescribes a knot (granthim grathnâti), as the symbol which is to secure all blessings for her.

[2] He winds the cord round her waist from left to right (pradakshinam), and having fixed the southern end by twice twisting round the northern one, he draws the southern end through the encircling cord upwards (so as to hang down, uparishtâl lambayet, Sâyana. Kâty. II, 7, 1, &c., Scholl.).

[3] Veshya=vyâpaka, Mahîdh.; 'perhaps a headband,' St. Petersb. Dict. It is apparently an etymological play on the name of Vishnu (? the all-pervading sun). The formula, according to Mahîdhara, is addressed to the southern end of the cord which is drawn through the girdle (? the pervading ray of Vishnu).

[4] Aditi is the earth and therefore the altar, which represents the earth: hence Aditi, in the shape of the altar, looks towards the east.

towards the east: and this lady would, therefore, raise herself to her (Aditi), and would speedily go to yonder world. And thus (viz. by sitting in the prescribed way) she lives for a long time, thus she propitiates her (Aditi), and thus the latter harms her not. For this reason let her sit somewhat to the south.

18. She looks down upon the sacrificial butter[1]; for assuredly that wife is a woman, and the butter (represents) seed: hence a productive union is thereby brought about. For this reason she looks towards the butter.

19. She looks, with the text (Vâg. S. I, 30), 'With an unimpaired eye I look on thee;' whereby she says, 'with an uninjured eye I look on thee.'—'Agni's tongue art thou!' for when they offer up that (butter) in the fire, then Agni's tongues, as it were, issue forth: therefore she says, 'Agni's tongue art thou!'—'A good caller[2] of the gods,' whereby she says, 'well for the gods;'—'be thou for every dainty (or, sacrificial site, dhâman), for every prayer of mine!' whereby she says, 'for every sacrifice of mine be thou (a good caller)!'

20. Having then taken up the butter (from the

[1] He takes the pot containing the clarified butter from the fire, with the text (Vâg. S. I, 30): 'For juice thee!' [see I, 2, 2, 6,] puts it down on the ground before the sacrificer's wife and bids her look down on it. Kâty. II, 7, 4.

[2] Suhûh. The Kânva recension and Taitt. S. I, 1, 10, 3 have subhûh, 'well-being, good,' which reading seems also to be presupposed by our author's explanation 'well (or good) for the gods.' The Black Yagus assigns this entire mantra to the Adhvaryu, when he has taken the butter from the Âhavanîya, and puts it down north of the altar. In other respects also it differs considerably from the order followed by our author.

ground), he (the Âgnîdhra) carries it eastwards. In the case of one whose Âhavanîya fire is used for the cooking, he (now in the first place) puts it on the Âhavanîya, thinking, 'My oblation shall be entirely cooked on the Âhavanîya[1]!' The reason why he first puts it thereon (viz. on the Gârhapatya) is, because he will have to make the wife look at it: for it would not be proper, if he were to take it (from the Âhavanîya) to the west in the midst of the performance, for the purpose of making the wife look at it; and if he were not to let the wife look at it at all, he would thereby exclude her from the sacrifice. And in this way, then, he does not exclude the (sacrificer's) wife from the sacrifice: therefore he does not take it eastwards till after melting it close by the wife (on the Gârhapatya), and making her look at it. In the case of one who (through death or from other causes) has not his wife with him, he puts it from the very beginning on the Âhavanîya. He then takes it again from thence and puts it down within the altar.

21. Here now they say,—'He must not place it within the altar; for from that (butter) they make the oblation to the wives of the gods[2]: he therefore excludes the wives of the gods from the company (of

[1] According to the ritual of the Black Yagus, the butter, after the sacrificer's wife has looked at it, is again heated on the Gârhapatya fire, in order to remove the impurity which has thereby been imparted to it.

[2] The patnîsamyâgas are four oblations of butter to Soma, Tvashtri, the wives of the gods, and Agni Grihapati respectively, made at the end of these sacrifices. See I, 9, 2, 1. It would seem that, according to the ritual of the Black Yagus, the butter is not put on the altar, but on a line drawn with the wooden sword north of the altar. See p. 74, note 2.

their husbands)[1], and thereby his (the sacrificer's) wife becomes dissatisfied with her own husband.' Yâgñavalkya, however, said in reference to this point, 'Let it be so as it has been prescribed for the wife! who would care whether his wife may consort with other men[2]?' 'As the altar is (part of the) sacrifice, and the butter is (part of the) sacrifice, I will build up the sacrifice from out of the sacrifice!' thus thinking, let him place it within the altar.

22. The two strainers are lying in the sprinkling water. He takes them from thence and purifies (ut-pû) the butter with them. Now one of them is related to the wind (that blows) upwards (utpavana)[3], so that he thereby makes it (the butter) sacrificially pure.

23. He clarifies it, with the text (Vâg. S. I, 31), 'By the impulse of Savitri I purify thee with a flawless purifier (strainer), with the rays of the sun!' The meaning (of this formula) is the same (as before).

24. He then purifies the sprinkling water with the strainers covered with butter, with the text (Vâg. S.

[1] Avasabhâh karoti=avagatagaanasamûhâh karoti, Sây.; the gods are supposed to be assembled around the altar (cf. I, 3, 3, 8): hence by placing the butter, from which the oblations to the wives of the gods are to be made, within the altar, the Adhvaryu would separate the wives from their husbands.

[2] I am not quite certain as to whether this last scornful remark is really to be assigned to Yâgñavalkya. The Kânva text has,—Yâgñavalkya, however, said, 'Let him place it within the altar!' thus he said. 'Let it be so as it has been prescribed for the wife,' thus (thinking) let him place it, whether or not she consort with other men.

[3] Probably the same as ud-âna (breathing upwards or inspiration), which one of the strainers is said to represent in I, 1, 3, 2. See also I, 1, 3, 6; Taitt. Br. III, 3, 4, 4. The St. Petersburg Dictionary proposes the meaning 'an implement for cleaning' for utpavana in this passage.

I, 31), 'By the impulse of Savitri I purify you (O waters) with a flawless purifier, with the rays of the sun!' The meaning is the same (as before).

25. The reason why he purifies the sprinkling water with the strainers covered with butter is, that he thereby puts milk into the water, and that the milk thereby (becomes) beneficial [1] in the water, for, when it rains, plants are thereby produced; and on eating the plants and drinking the water, vital fluid (serum) results therefrom: and thus (he does this) in order to supply the vital fluid (of the sacrificer).

26. He then looks down on the butter. Here now some make the sacrificer look down. Yâgñavalkya, however, said in reference to this point,—'Why do not (the sacrificers) themselves become (act as) Adhvaryu priests? and why do not they (the sacrificers) themselves recite when far higher blessings are prayed for [2]? How can these (people) possibly have faith in this [3]? Whatever blessing the officiating priests invoke during the sacrifice that is for the benefit of the sacrificer alone.' The Adhvaryu should accordingly look down on it.

[1] A play on the word hitam, which means both 'put, placed,' and 'beneficial, salutary.'

[2] The Kânva text has as follows,—Here now some make the sacrificer eye it, arguing, 'whatever blessing (resides therein) that he should himself pray for.' Yâgñavalkya, however, said in reference to this point, 'Why then does not he himself become Adhvaryu? and why does he not recite (the solemn prayers of the Hotri priest), and that when they pray for higher blessing? Whatever blessing the priests invoke at the sacrifice, that they invoke for the sacrificer alone;' thus he said. The Adhvaryu, therefore, should look down on it.

[3] Teshâm sâkhinâm atraivâvekshanam yagamânenaiva kartavyam iti kasmât kâranât sraddhâ gâtâ, evam tâm sraddhâm prahasya, Sây. The Kânva text omits this derisive remark.

27. He looks down on it. The eye assuredly is the truth, for the eye is indeed the truth. If, therefore, two persons were to come disputing with each other and saying, 'I have seen it!' 'I have heard it!' we should believe him who said, 'I have seen it!' and not the other: hence he thereby causes it (the butter) to increase by means of the truth.

28. He looks down on it, with the text (Vâ*g*. S. I, 31), 'Lustrous art thou! resplendent art thou! immortal (or, ambrosia) art thou!' That prayer is indeed true, for that (butter) is lustrous, it is resplendent, it is immortal: hence he thereby causes it to increase by that (prayer) which is true.

SECOND BRÂHMA*N*A.

1. Now the sacrifice is the man. The sacrifice is the man for the reason that the man spreads (performs) it; and that in being spread it is made of exactly the same extent as the man[1]: this is the reason why the sacrifice is the man.

2. The *g*uhû (spoon) further belongs to that (man-shaped sacrifice), and so does the upabh*ri*t; and the dhruvâ[2] represents its trunk. Now it is from the

[1] The sacrifice is the representation of the sacrificer himself; and hence its dimensions are to be those of a man, viz. the altar (vedi) on its western side is to measure a fathom, or space between the extreme ends of the outstretched arms (? of the sacrificer), which is supposed to be equal to the size of a man; see I, 2, 5, 14. Originally these measurements were no doubt relative to the size of the sacrificer; but it is doubtful whether this was still the case at the time of our author.

[2] For a description of these spoons, see p. 67, note 2. The *g*uhû is supposed to represent the right, and the upabh*ri*t the left arm, and the dhruvâ the trunk.

trunk that all these limbs proceed, and for this reason the entire sacrifice proceeds from the dhruvâ.

3. The dipping-spoon (sruva, masc.) is no other than the breath. This breath passes through (or, goes to) all the limbs, and for that reason the dipping-spoon goes to all the offering-spoons (sru*k*, fem.).

4. That *g*uhû further is to him no other than yonder sky, and the upabh*ri*t this atmosphere, and the dhruvâ this same (earth). Now it is from this (earth) that all the worlds originate: and from the dhruvâ, therefore, the whole sacrifice proceeds.

5. The dipping-spoon then is no other than that blowing one (the wind); it is this that sweeps across all these worlds: and for that reason the sruva goes to all the offering-spoons.

6. Now when this sacrifice is being performed, it is performed for the gods, the seasons, and the metres (or sacred texts). To the gods belongs what sacrificial food there is, to wit, king Soma and the sacrificial cake: all this he takes, while announcing it with the formula, 'I take thee, agreeable to so and so!' for thus it becomes theirs.

7. And whatever oblations of butter are taken, they are taken for the seasons and the metres. Every one of them he takes in the form of butter without announcing it (to any particular deity). In the *g*uhû he takes of it four times (with the sruva from the pot), in the upabh*ri*t eight times[1].

8. Now when he takes of it four times (with the sruva) in the *g*uhû, he takes it for the seasons, since

[1] He takes butter in the *g*uhû and upabh*ri*t by four or eight ladlings with the dipping-spoon. As we learn further on, the quantity taken in the *g*uhû, by ladling four times, should exceed that in the upabh*ri*t, although the latter requires eight ladlings. Cf. Kâty. II, 7, 13.

he takes it for the fore-offerings[1], and the fore-offerings are the seasons: all this he takes in the form of butter without making any announcement, in order to avoid sameness; for if he were to take it with the formulas 'For Spring (I take) thee!' 'For Summer—thee!' he would commit (the fault of) a repetition[2]: he therefore takes it in the form of butter without making any announcement.

9. When, on the other hand, he takes eight times (with the sruva) in the upabhrit, he takes it for the metres[3], since it is for the after-offerings[1] that he takes it; and the after-offerings are the metres: all this he takes in the form of butter without making any announcement, in order to avoid sameness; for were he to take it with the formulas 'For the Gâyatrî—thee!' 'For the Trishtubh—thee!' he would commit a repetition: he therefore takes it in the form of butter without making any announcement.

10. Again, when he takes four times (with the sruva)

[1] On the prayâgas, or oblations of clarified butter introductory to, and the anuyâgas, oblations of the same material made subsequently to, the chief sacrifice, see I, 5, 3, 1 seq., and I, 8, 2, 1 seq.

[2] Repetition of one and the same sacrificial act on the same day is to be avoided, as far as possible. The repetition in the present case would consist in his announcing the butter-oblations to the several deities in the same way as he has done in regard to the rice-portions. See I, 1, 2, 17–18.

[3] On the frequent symbolical employment of the metres in the ritual, as the embodiment of supreme harmony and the efficacy of prayer, see Weber, Ind. Stud. VIII, 8 seq. The three principal Vedic metres are the gâyatrî (three times eight syllables), the trishtubh (four times eleven syllables), and the gagatî (four times twelve syllables); and three anuyâgas there are at these sacrifices, viz. to the barhis or sacrificial grass, to Narâsamsa and Agni Svishtakrit respectively. In the present instance (see par. 16) the trishtubh and gagatî metres are taken together as one, and as a fourth is added the anushtubh (four times eight syllables).

in the dhruvâ, he takes it for the whole sacrifice, and all this he takes in the form of butter without making any announcement. To whom indeed should he announce it, since he cuts it off for all the deities? He therefore takes it in the form of butter without making any announcement.

11. Now the sacrificer stands behind the *g*uhû, and he who means evil to him stands behind the upabh*ri*t. The eater stands behind the *g*uhû, and what (or, he who) is to be eaten stands behind the upabh*ri*t. And the *g*uhû, indeed, is the eater, and the upabh*ri*t is that which is to be eaten. In the *g*uhû he takes four times (with the sruva), and in the upabh*ri*t eight times.

12. Now when he takes four times (butter) in the *g*uhû, he thereby makes the eater more limited, smaller; and when he takes eight times in the upabh*ri*t, he makes that which is to be eaten more unlimited, more abundant: for a flourishing condition indeed exists where the eater is smaller and that which is to be eaten more abundant.

13. In taking four times in the *g*uhû, he takes (altogether) more butter, and in taking eight times in the upabh*ri*t he takes less butter.

14. For when, in taking four times (butter with the sruva) in the *g*uhû, he takes more butter, he thereby, in making the eater more limited, smaller, imparts vigour and strength to him. And when, in taking eight times in the upabh*ri*t, he takes less butter, he thereby, in making that which (or, him who) is to be eaten more unlimited, more abundant, makes it (or, him) vigourless and weaker. And thus a king who has established himself among a numberless people, subdues them even from a single dwelling,

and takes possession of whatever he likes[1]: with that very same energy (the Adhvaryu acts) when he takes a greater quantity of butter in the guhû. Now what he takes in the guhû, that he offers with the guhû; and what he takes in the upabhrit, that also he offers with the guhû.

15. And in reference to this point they say: 'Wherefore then is he to take it in the upabhrit, if he does not offer it with the upabhrit?' Now, if he were to offer it with the upabhrit, those subjects (of the king) would assuredly become separated from him, nor would there be either an eater or what is to be eaten. When, on the other hand, he pours (the butter) together and thus offers it with the guhû, thereby the people pay tribute to the Kshatriya. Hence by what he takes in the upabhrit, the Vaisya (man of the people), under the rule of the Kshatriya, becomes possessed of cattle; and when he pours (the butter) together and offers it with the guhû, thereby the Kshatriya, whenever he likes, says, 'Hallo Vaisya, just bring to me what thou hast stored away!' Thus he both subdues him and obtains possession of anything he wishes by dint of this very energy.

16. These butter-portions, then, are taken for the metres. Now what he takes in the guhû (by ladling) four times (with the sruva), that he takes for the gâyatrî; and what he takes in the upabhrit (by ladling) eight times, that he takes for the trishtubh and gagatî; and what he takes in the dhruvâ (by

[1] Tasmâd uta râgâpârâm visam prâvasâyâpy ekavesmanaiva ('by one who has a single dwelling, i.e. by himself,' Sâyana) ginâti tvad yathâ tvat kâmayate tathâ sakate. The MS. of the Kânva text has: 'Tasmât kshatriyo râgotâpârâd visam prâvasâya ginâti tvad yathâ tva(t) kâmayate tat karoti.'

ladling) four times, that he takes for the anush*t*ubh. For the anush*t*ubh is speech, and from speech all this (universe) springs: hence it is from the dhruvâ that the whole sacrifice originates. The anush*t*ubh also is this (earth), and from it all this (universe) originates: hence it is from the dhruvâ that the whole sacrifice originates.

17. He takes (butter with the sruva), with the text (Vâ*g*. S. I, 31), 'Verily, thou art the favourite resort (or, dainty) of the gods!' He thereby makes that butter the most favourite resort of the gods: for this reason he says, 'verily, thou art the favourite resort of the gods!'—'An unassailable means of worship!' the butter is indeed a thunderbolt: therefore he says, 'an unassailable means of worship!'

18. Once he puts (butter with the sruva) into the *g*uhû with this formula, three times silently. With the same formula he puts (butter) once into the upabh*ri*t, seven times silently. With the same formula he puts once (butter) into the dhruvâ, three times silently. Now, as to this, they say, 'Thrice he should take with the formula in each case, for threefold is the sacrifice.' Nevertheless (it is done) only once with each (spoon), for it is just in this way that the taking thrice (with a formula) is accomplished.

THIRD BRÂHMA*N*A.

1. The Adhvaryu takes the sprinkling-water, and sprinkles in the first place the fire-wood[1], with the

[1] The fire-wood had been brought by the Âgnîdhra and laid down on the altar. The Adhvaryu now unties and sprinkles it. [Before doing so he has, as usual, to ask and obtain the permission of the Brahman. The same is the case in regard to the barhis, but not in regard to the altar.] Kâty. II, 7, 19.

text (Vâg. S. II, 1), 'A black deer, living in the den, art thou[1]; I sprinkle thee, agreeable to Agni!' He thereby makes it sacrificially pure for Agni.

2. He then sprinkles he altar, with the text (Vâg. S. II, 1), 'Thou art the altar; I sprinkle thee, agreeable to the barhis (sacrificial-grass covering)!' He thereby makes it sacrificially pure for the grass covering.

3. He (the Âgnîdhra) then hands the sacrificial grass[2] to him (the Adhvaryu). The latter puts it down (on the altar) with the knot turned to the east, and sprinkles it, with the text (Vâg. S. II, 1), 'Barhis art thou! I sprinkle thee, agreeable to the spoons!' He thereby makes it sacrificially pure for the spoons.

4. Thereupon he pours the sprinkling-water

---

[1] ? Âkhare-shtha; it probably has a double meaning in this place, viz. 'that which dwells in a den (âkhara)' and 'that which has its place on the hearth (khara).'

[2] 'At the beginning of the sacrifice the Adhvaryu makes of the load of Darbha or sacred grass, which has been brought to the sacrificial compound, seven mushtis or bunches, each of which is tied together with a stalk of grass, just as the Baresma (Barsom) of the Parsis. The several names of these seven bunches are, 1. Yagamânamushti, the bunch kept by the sacrificer himself in his hand as long as the sacrifice lasts. 2. Three bunches from the Barhis, or the covering of the Vedi on which the sacrificial vessels are put. These are unloosened and spread all over the Vedi. 3. Prastara. This bunch, which must remain tied, is put over the Darbha of the Vedi. 4. Paribhoganî. From this bunch the Adhvaryu takes a handful out for each priest, and the sacrificer and his wife, which they then use for their seat. 5. The Veda. This bunch is made double in its first part; the latter part is cut off and has to remain on the Vedi; it is called parivâsana. The Veda itself is always wandering from one priest to the other, and is given to the sacrificer and his wife. It is handed over to the latter only when one of the priests makes her recite a mantra.' Haug's translation of the Ait. Br. p. 79.

which is left on the roots of the (grass) plants, with the text (Vâg. S. II, 2), 'A moistening art thou for Aditi!' Aditi, indeed, is this earth; hence it is for the latter that he thus moistens the roots of the plants: thereby these plants become root-moistened; and even if their tops are dry, their roots at least remain moist.

5. Having thereupon untied the knot, he takes the prastara bunch from the front (of the barhis), with the text (Vâg. S. II, 2), 'Vishnu's crest art thou!' Vishnu, namely, is the sacrifice, and this (the prastara) is his top-knot or crest: this he thereby makes it at this sacrifice[1]. From the front he takes it, because this top-knot also is (worn) on the front (of the head): for this reason he takes it from the front.

6. He then undoes the band (of the barhis). 'His (the sacrificer's) wife is sure to bring forth without difficulty[2],' thinking thus he undoes the band. He puts it down on the right hip (of the altar); for this represents his (the sacrificer's) waist-band, and it is on the right side that the waist-band is (tied): this is the reason why he puts it down on the right hip. He again covers it over (with sacrificial grass); for the waist-band also is covered (by the upper garment): for this reason he again covers it.

7. He now spreads the barhis (on the altar). For the prastara is the top-knot; and this other

---

[1] Because, according to Sâyana, it lies on the front, or eastern side of the altar, near the Âhavanîya fire, and men also wear their top-knot (in the form of a ball or lump) on the fore-part of their head. The prastara he hands to the Brahman-priest. Kâty. II, 7, 22.

[2] Prakliptam; Sâyana takes it in the sense of 'a completely formed (child).'

sacrificial grass is for this (sacrifice) what other hair there is below that (top-knot, viz. the beard, &c.) :—that (hair) he thereby puts on it, and for this reason he spreads the barhis.

8. Now the altar (vedi, fem.) is a woman, and around her sit the gods and those priests who have studied and teach revealed lore[1]; and as they thus sit around her, he makes her not naked: hence it is in order to avoid nudity (on her or the altar's part) that he spreads the barhis.

9. As large as the altar is, so large is the earth; and the plants (are represented by) the barhis; so that he thereby furnishes the earth with plants; and those plants are firmly established in this earth: for this reason he spreads the barhis.

10. Here now they say, 'Let him strew abundantly; for where the plants are most abundant on her, there the means of subsistence are most amply afforded by her: let him therefore strew abundantly!' It is in favour of him (the sacrificer) who procures (the sacrificial grass), then, (that this is done.) He strews it threefold[2], for threefold is the sacrifice. Or he may also spread it whilst lifting up (the tops)[3]; for

[1] 'Around her on the south sit the gods and those man-gods (manushyadevâh), the priests who have studied and teach revealed lore.' Kânva recension.

[2] Viz. in three layers, one beside the other, each consisting of one handful of grass. He first spreads a layer on the east side from the southern to the northern shoulder of the altar, with the tops of the blades turned towards the east; then a second one west of it, so as to cover the roots of the first with the tops of the second layer; and in the same way a third one on the west side of the altar. If he thinks fit, he may make more than three layers, but their number should be uneven. Kâty. II, 7, 22-26 (schol.).

[3] That is to say, he is to begin on the west side, and in laying down the successive layers, he is to lift up (with a stick or some

it has been said by the seer (Vâg. S. VII, 32), 'They spread the barhis continuously.' He spreads it with the roots below (the tops); for it is with their roots below that those plants are firmly established in this earth: for this reason he spreads it with the roots below.

11. He spreads it, with the text (Vâg. S. II, 2), 'I spread thee, soft as wool, pleasant to sit upon for the gods!'—when he says 'thee, soft as wool,' he thereby means to say 'agreeable to the gods;' and by 'pleasant to sit upon for the gods,' he means to say 'forming a good seat for the gods.'

12. He now trims the fire[1]. The Âhavanîya, doubtless, is the head of the sacrifice, for the head is the fore-part[2]: that fore-part of the sacrifice he thereby trims. He trims it while holding the prastara (which he has received back from the Brahman) close over it; for the prastara is the top-knot, and it is this which he thereby puts on it: for this reason he trims (the fire) while holding the prastara close over it.

13. He then lays the (three) enclosing-sticks (paridhi) around (the fire). The reason why he lays the enclosing-sticks around (is this). When at first the gods chose Agni for the office of Hotri, he said: 'Verily, I am not equal to this, that I should be your Hotri, and that I should carry your oblation. Already you have chosen three before,

other object) the heads of the preceding layer and push the roots of the succeeding one under them. Ib. 27 (schol.).

[1] He takes one stick from the fuel and gets the fire ready (for the oblations, either by throwing the stick into it, or by stirring it with the stick). Ib. 29.

[2] The Âhavanîya is at the foremost or eastern end of the sacrificial ground.

and they have passed away[1]. Restore them to me: then I shall be equal to this, that I should be your Hotri and that I should carry your oblation!' They said, 'So be it!' and they restored to him those (three former Agnis): they are these enclosing-sticks.

14. He then said, 'The thunderbolt, (in the shape of) the vashat-call[2], has struck these down: I am afraid of that thunderbolt, the vashat-call. Lest that thunderbolt, the vashat-call, should strike me down, enclose me by those (three Agnis, or paridhis); and thus that thunderbolt, the vashat-call, will not strike me down.' They said, 'So be it!' and they enclosed him with those (three sticks), and that thunderbolt, the vashat-call, did not strike him down. When he encloses Agni with those (sticks) he buckles armour on him.

15. They (the other three Agnis) then said, 'If you join us with the sacrifice in this wise, then let us also have a share in the sacrifice!'

16. The gods said: 'So be it! What shall fall outside the enclosure, that is offered unto you; and what they shall offer just upon you, that will sate

---

[1] See I, 2, 3, 1.

[2] The call 'vashat' (or vaushat), apparently signifying 'may he (Agni) carry it (the oblation) up!' (from vah, to bear, carry), is pronounced by the Hotri at the end of the yâgyâs or offering prayers (see note on I, 5, 1, 16). Professor Weber has somewhere proposed to derive it from vaksh, to grow, increase, hence 'may it prosper, or agree, with you!' Different, but quite fanciful, interpretations of vashat are given Sat. Br. I, 5, 2, 18; Ait. Br. 3, 6. As to the awful solemnity of this formula, and the danger arising from a careless use of it, see Ait. Br. 3, 8, on which Haug remarks, 'Up to the present day the Shrotriyas or sacrificial priests never dare to pronounce this formula save at the time of sacrificing. They say that if they would do so at any other time, they would be cursed by the gods.'

you; and what they shall offer up in the fire that will sate you!' Thus what they offer up in the fire, that satisfies them (the Agnis); and what they offer up just upon them (the enclosing-sticks, or Agnis), that satisfies them; and what is spilled outside the enclosure, that is offered to them[1]: hence no sin attaches to what (butter) is spilt; for into this earth they entered (when they, the Agnis, passed away), and whatever is spilt here,—all that remains indeed in her.

17. That which is spilt he touches, with the formulas (Vâg. S. II, 2), 'To the Lord of the Earth—svâhâ!' 'To the Lord of the World—svâhâ!' 'To the Lord of Beings—svâhâ!' These, indeed, are the names of those Agnis,—to wit, Lord of the Earth, Lord of the World, and Lord of Beings. Thus in like manner as that (oblation) which is accompanied by 'Vashat' is offered up (to the particular deity to which it is announced), so is this (offered up) on his (the sacrificer's) part to those Agnis.

18. Here now some people take the sticks they lay around from the fire-wood; but let him not do so, for unsuitable for laying around are those which they take from the fire-wood, since the fire-wood is prepared for the purpose of being put upon (the fire); but what other (kind of sticks) they bring to him, called 'enclosing-sticks (paridhis),' they are indeed suitable for his purpose: let them therefore bring others.

19. Indeed, they should be of Palâsa wood

[1] The Kânva text has as follows:—They said, 'So be it! what shall fall outside the enclosure that shall be yours! and what they shall offer just upon you that shall sate you!' for what they offer just upon them that does indeed sate them (enân); and what they offer up in the fire that is theirs (eshâm, ? the gods'); and what falls outside the enclosure by that he shall incur no guilt, &c.

(Butea Frondosa); for the Palâsa tree, doubtless, is the Brahman[1], and Agni also is the Brahman: for this reason the Agnis should be of Palâsa wood.

20. Should he be unable to procure them of Palâsa wood, they may be of Vikankata wood (Flacourtia Sapida); and if he be unable to procure any of Vikankata, they may be of Kârshmarya wood (Gmelina Arborea); and if he be unable to procure any of Kârshmarya wood, they may be of Vilva (Aegle Marmelos), or of Khadira (Acacia Catechu), or of Udumbara wood (Ficus Glomerata). These, doubtless, are the trees that are suitable for sacrificial purposes, and from these trees they (the enclosing-sticks) are therefore (taken).

FOURTH BRÂHMANA.

1. They should be green (fresh); for that is (what constitutes) their living element, by that they are vigorous, by that possessed of strength: for this reason they should be green.

2. The middle stick he lays down first (on the west side of the fire), with the text (Vâg. S. II, 3), 'May the Gandharva Visvâvasu[2] lay thee around

[1] The Brahman, or supreme spirit (? or, sacred writ), is more than once identified with the Palâsa tree in the Satapatha Br., as in V, 2, 4, 18; VI, 6, 3, 7; XII, 7, 2, 15; and with the leaf of that tree (palâsasya palâsam) in II, 6, 2, 8. [? Cf. Rig-veda X, 31, 7, 'Which was the wood, which was the tree, out of which they fashioned heaven and earth?' and Taitt. Br. II, 8, 9, 6, 'Brahma was the wood, Brahma was that tree out of which they fashioned heaven and earth;' also Ath.-veda X, 7, 38, 'The gods form part of the divine essence (Skambha-Brahma) as branches of a tree.']

[2] The genius Visvâvasu is already mentioned in Rig-veda X, 85, 21 seq., and X, 139, 4, where Grassmann identifies him with the rainbow (cf. Roth, Nirukta notes, p. 145). See also Sat. Br. III, 2, 4, 2; XIV, 9, 4, 18.

for the security of the All! Thou art a fence to the sacrificer, thou (art) Agni, invoked and worthy of invocation!'

3. He then lays down the southern one, with the text (ib.), 'Thou art Indra's arm for the security of the All! Thou art a fence to the sacrificer; thou Agni, invoked and worthy of invocation!'

4. He then lays down the northern one, with the text (ib.), 'May Mitra-Varuna lay thee around in the north with firm law for the security of the All! Thou art a fence to the sacrificer, thou Agni, invoked and worthy of invocation!' They are indeed Agnis, and for that reason he says, 'Agni, invoked and worthy of invocation!'

5. Thereupon he puts on (the fire) a samidh (kindling-stick). He first touches with it the middle enclosing-stick: thereby he first kindles those (three Agnis). After that he puts it on the fire: thereby he kindles the visible fire.

6. He puts it on[1], with the gâyatrî stanza (Vâg. S. II, 4), 'Thee, O Sage, who callest (the gods) to the feast, we will kindle so as to shine brilliantly; thee, O Agni, mighty at the sacrifice!' He thereby kindles the gâyatrî[2]; the gâyatrî, when kindled, kindles the other metres; and the metres, when kindled, carry the sacrifice to the gods.

---

[1] According to Sâyana, the two sticks or pieces of wood are put on the fire in a manner similar to that in which the two âghâras or sprinklings of clarified butter are made (see I, 4, 4–5); viz. the first in the direction north-west to south-east, and the second from south-west to north-east.

[2] The gâyatrî is the first of the three principal metres, cf. p. 80, note 3. It consists of three octo-syllabic pâdas, of which Rig-veda I, 164, 25 says,—'The gâyatra, they say, has three flames (or firebrands, samidh): therefore it excelled in grandeur and power.'

7. By the second kindling-stick (samidh), which he now puts on, he kindles the spring; the spring, when kindled, kindles the other seasons; and the seasons, when kindled, cause living beings to be produced and the plants to ripen. He puts it on, with the formula (Vâg. S. II, 5), 'A kindler (samidh) art thou!' for the spring is indeed a kindler.

8. When he has put it on, he murmurs (ib.), 'May the sun guard thee from the east against any imprecation!' for the enclosing-sticks serve for protection on all (the other three) sides; and thereby he makes the sun the protector on the east side, fearing 'lest the evil spirits, the Rakshas, should rush in from the east:' for the sun is the repeller of the evil spirits, the Rakshas.

9. By that third kindling-stick, then, which he puts on at the after-offerings[1], he kindles the officiating priest (brâhmana); and he, the priest, when kindled, carries the sacrifice to the gods.

10. He now returns to the altar covered (with sacrificial grass). Having taken two stalks of grass, he lays them down across (the barhis or grass covering, with the tops to the north), with the formula (Vâg. S. II, 5), 'Savitri's arms[2] are ye!' The prastara bunch is indeed the top-knot (of the sacrifice); and he now lays down these two crosswise as its eye-brows: thereby these two (represent) the transverse eye-brows. The prastara, further,

---

[1] See I, 8, 2, 3.

[2] Bâhû, 'the two arms,' is apparently taken here by our author both in its natural sense and as the arms of the bow or arch, formed by the eye-brows. The barhis, or grass covering of the altar, was, as we saw (I, 3, 3, 7), identified with the beard and other hair of the body.

(represents) the kshatra (or military class); and the other barhis the vi*s* (or, the common Âryan people);—(and the two stalks he puts down between them) for the sake of separating (vidh*ri*ti) the kshatra and the vi*s*: for this reason he lays them down crosswise; and for this reason these two (stalks) are called vidh*ri*ti.

11. On them he spreads the prastara, with the formula (Vâ*g*. S. II, 5), 'I spread thee, soft as wool, pleasant to sit upon for the gods!' When he says 'thee, soft as wool,' he means to say 'agreeable to the gods;' and by 'pleasant to sit upon for the gods' he means to say 'forming a good seat for the gods.'

12. He presses it down (with his left hand), with the text (ib.), 'May the Vasus, the Rudras, the Âdityas sit on thee!' These three, that is, the Vasus, the Rudras, and the Âdityas, namely, are (classes of) gods; and these, he means to say, are to sit down on it. While it is still being held down with his left hand,—

13. He seizes the *g*uhû with his right, fearing 'lest the evil spirits, the Rakshas, should enter there in the meantime;' for the officiating priest (brâhma*n*a) is the repeller of the Rakshas: therefore, while it (the prastara) is still being held down with his left hand,—

14. He seizes the *g*uhû, with the text (Vâ*g*. S. II, 6), 'Fond of butter art thou, *G*uhû by name!' for fond of butter indeed it is, and *G*uhû by name;—'Sit down here with the favourite resort[1] (or dainty) on the favourite seat!' The upabh*ri*t (he takes), with the formula (ib.), 'Fond of butter art thou, Upabh*ri*t

[1] Viz. the butter, which is the dear resort, or home, of the gods; see I, 3, 2, 17. Possibly, however, dhâman may here mean 'dainty.'

by name!' for fond of butter indeed it is, and Upabhrit by name;—'Sit down here with the favourite resort on the favourite seat!' The dhruvâ (he takes) with 'Fond of butter art thou, Dhruvâ by name!' for fond of butter indeed it is, and Dhruvâ by name;—'Sit down here with the favourite resort on the favourite seat!' What other sacrificial food there is, (he puts down on the prastara), with the formula, 'With the favourite resort sit down on the favourite seat!'

15. He lays the guhû down on (the prastara), and the other spoons down below, (viz. on the barhis, north of the guhû, and so as not to touch it or one another); for the guhû assuredly is the kshatra, and the other spoons (sruk) are the vis: he thereby makes the kshatra superior to the vis. Hence the people here serve, from a lower position, the Kshatriya seated above them: for this reason he places the guhû upon (the prastara) and the other spoons down below it.

16. He touches the offerings, with the text (Vâg. S. II, 6), 'Safely they have sat down,' for safely indeed they sat down;—'in the lap (yoni) of divine truth!' for the sacrifice is indeed the lap of divine truth, and in the sacrifice they sat down;—'Protect these, O Vishnu! protect the sacrifice! protect the lord of sacrifice!' thereby he refers to the sacrificer;—'Protect me, the leader of the sacrifice!' thereby he does not exclude himself either from the sacrifice. Vishnu, assuredly, is the sacrifice: hence it is to the sacrifice that he makes all that over for protection. This is the reason why he says, 'Protect these, O Vishnu!'

FIFTH BRÂHMANA.

THE KINDLING OF THE FIRE, THE PRAVARA, AND THE TWO LIBATIONS (ÂGHÂRA) OF BUTTER.

1. With the fire-wood (idhma, lighting material) the Adhvaryu lights (indh) the fire: hence it is called fire-wood. And with the kindling verses (sâmidhenî) the Hotri kindles (sam-indh, to make blaze): hence they are called kindling verses.

2. He (the Adhvaryu[1]) says (to the Hotri): 'Recite to the fire as it is being kindled!' for it is to the fire, when it is being kindled, that he recites.

3. Here now some people say, 'O Hotar, recite to the fire as it is being kindled!' But let him not say so; for that (priest) is not a Hotri as yet; only when he (the sacrificer) elects him[2], does he

---

[1] The Adhvaryu, in the first place, prepares a seat for the Hotri, either west of the altar or north of its left hip; and covers it with dry Kusa grass. [He then calls, 'O Hotri, come!'] The Hotri, having rinsed his mouth north-east of the Âhavanîya, with his face to the east, turns round from left to right and betakes himself to the sacrificial ground, always keeping his right foot before the left. He finally takes up his position so as to have the heel of the right foot in a line with the north hip of the altar, and the toes on the barhis; whilst he keeps the hands on a level with the heart, spread open and joined together, and looks towards the junction of the earth and sky. The Adhvaryu then takes a samidh (kindling-stick) and calls on him as above. The Hotri now mutters the formulas 'Adoration to the teacher! Adoration to the observer! Adoration to the promulgator!' &c. (Âsv. Srautas I, 2, 1). The sacrificer then takes the wooden sword and says, 'Recite for me, as it were, stretching along (i. e. continuously)!' whereupon the Hotri, having asked and received the permission of the Brahman, proceeds to recite the kindling verses. Kâty. III, 1, 1 seq.; Âsv. I, 1, 4 seq.

[2] This does not take place until the pravara or invitation addressed to Agni, the Hotri of the gods, to assist in calling the

become a Hotri. Let him therefore say, 'Recite to the fire as it is being kindled!'

4. He recites (verses) addressed to Agni: he accordingly kindles it (the fire) with the aid of its own deity. In the gâyatrî metre (are the verses which) he recites; for the gâyatrî is Agni's metre: by means of its own metre he thereby kindles it. The gâyatrî is vigour, the gâyatrî is the brahman[1] (the priestly order): with vigour he thereby kindles it.

5. Eleven (verses) he recites; for of eleven syllables consists the trishtubh metre. The gâyatrî is the brahman and the trishtubh is the kshatra (or military order)[2]. With the aid of these two energies he thus kindles it: for this reason he recites eleven (verses).

5. Thrice he recites the first verse, and thrice the last one; for of threefold beginning are sacrifices, and of threefold termination: therefore he recites thrice the first and the last (verses).

7. Fifteen sâmidhenî verses result (from this repetition of the first and last of the eleven verses). The fifteen-versed chant[3], doubtless, is the thunderbolt,

---

gods to the sacrifice, cf. Sâyana and Sat. Br. I, 5, 1, 1 seq. According to some authorities, however, the choosing of the Hotri seems to take place at this particular time, or even before, at the time of the agnyanvâdhâna; cf. Hillebrandt, p. 73.

[1] The gâyatrî (though it is not the most frequent metre) is considered as the first, as it is the shortest, of Vedic metres. The hymns addressed to Agni are mostly in the gâyatrî metre.

[2] The hymns celebrating the heroic deeds of Indra and his associates, the wind-gods, are almost entirely composed in the trishtubh, the most frequent of Vedic metres.

[3] The pañkadasa-stoma, or form of recitation in fifteen verses at the Soma-sacrifice, is sacred to Indra (Nirukta 7, 10), the wielder of the thunderbolt.

and the thunderbolt means strength; so that he thereby converts the sâmidhenîs into strength: hence, if he should hate any one, he may crush him with his great toes[1] at the time when those (verses) are recited. By saying, 'I here crush so and so!' he crushes him with that thunderbolt.

8. Fifteen nights indeed there are in a half-moon; and growing by half-moons the year passes: hence he thereby obtains the nights.

9. Now in the fifteen gâyatrî verses there are indeed three hundred and sixty syllables[2]; and three hundred and sixty days there are in a year: hence he thereby obtains the days, he thereby obtains the year.

10. For an ishti (which is performed in order to obtain the fulfilment of a special wish)[3] let him recite seventeen sâmidhenî verses; for in a low voice he sacrifices to the deity to which he offers an ishti.

---

[1] Or, with his thumbs (aṅgushthâbhyâm). The Kânva text has 'pâdyâbhyâm aṅgushthâbhyâm;' but Kâty. III, 1, 7 has 'aṅgushthâbhyâm pâdyâbhyâm vâ,' which would seem to leave a choice between the thumbs and the great toes; the commentator, however, takes vâ in a restrictive sense. The sacrificer is to press down the earth with his great toes (or thumbs) each time when a kindling verse is recited.

[2] The gâyatrî verse consists of three times eight syllables, and $24 \times 15 = 360$. In the place of the last sâmidhenî (called paridhânîyâ), however, the Vâsishthas have a trishtubh stanza (4×11 syllables), so that the above computation of syllables does not hold good in their case. One might be inclined to infer from this that the trishtubh was the more original, a gâyatrî being substituted later to yield the above symbolical number of syllables. Cf. Taitt. S. II, 5, 7 seq.; Taitt. Br. III, 5, 3.

[3] The kâmyeshtis, and ishtis generally, are performed with certain modifications, on the model of the new- and full-moon sacrifice, of which they are therefore said to be vikritis or modifications.

Twelve months, namely, there are in a year, and five seasons[1]: this (makes) the seventeenfold Pragâpati. For verily Pragâpati is all: hence for what wish he performs the ishti, that wish he thus accomplishes by means of the All. In a low voice he sacrifices to the deity; for what is spoken in a low voice is undefined (indistinct), and undefined is the 'All:' hence for whatever wish he performs the ishti, that wish he thus accomplishes by means of the All. This is the practice in regard to an ishti.

11. Some people say: 'Let him recite twenty-one sâmidhenî verses also at the full- and new-moon sacrifice.' Twelve, doubtless, are the months of the year, five the seasons, and three these worlds: this (makes) twenty; and the twenty-first is this very (sun) that here shines: he is the resort, he the stay; thereby he (the sacrificer) obtains this resort, this stay. He may therefore recite twenty-one.

12. Let him recite them only for one of established prosperity (gatasrî), who would not wish to become either better or worse. For, what he for whom they recite is like, like that he will either be or worse[2], for whom, that knows this, they recite

[1] In other passages, and in later times generally, six seasons, comprising two months each, are counted, but the transitional season between winter and spring, sisira, is not unfrequently, as in our passage, combined with the winter season (hemanta), or partially with that and the spring (vasanta). On the identification of Pragâpati with the year, cf. note on I, 2, 5, 12.

[2] The condition of one who is gatasrî cannot be improved, but only impaired. The construction of this paragraph is somewhat doubtful to me. It runs thus: Tâ haitâ gatasrer evânubrûyâd ya ikkhen na sreyânt syâm na pâpîyân iti yâdrisâya haiva sate 'nvâhus tâdrin vâ haiva bhavati pâpîyân vâ yasyaivam vidusha etâ

those (twenty-one verses). This, however, is mere speculation, for those (twenty-one verses) are not recited[1].

13. Thrice he should recite the first and thrice the last (verse), without drawing breath; for three are these worlds, so that he thereby spreads (santan) these worlds, gains these worlds. Also three breaths there are in man: this recitation thereby causes him (the sacrificer) to be extended (santata), not cut short (by death).

14. He (the Hot*ri*) should endeavour to recite this (uninterruptedly) as long as his strength lasts. If, on the other hand, he were to take breath in the middle (of the verse), it would be a slight on this very (sacrifice)[2]: by reciting this (holy) com-

anvâhu*h* so eshâ mîmâ*m*saiva na tv evaitâ anû*k*yante. Sâya*n*a seems to take it thus:—'He should recite them only for a gata*s*rî. A householder who desires neither an improvement nor a lowering of his position, is just such a one for whom the Hot*ri*s recite the sâmidhenîs in the appointed (niyatena) way. Further, for whomsoever, that thus knows the irregular (?aniyata, not regulated) way of recitation, they recite those twenty-one sâmidhenîs, he becomes either worse or better. What is set forth in the words from "A householder who desires neither an improvement" &c. is mere speculation; the recitation is not to be performed in this way.' The corresponding paragraph of the Kâ*n*va recension is much briefer and clearer:—Tad etad gata*s*rîr eva kurvîta na ha *s*reyân na pâpîyân bhavati yasyaivam anvâhu*h* saishâ mîmâ*m*saiva na tv anû*k*yante, 'only a gata*s*rî, however, should do this; for neither better nor worse becomes he for whom they recite thus. This is indeed speculation, but they (the twenty-one sâmidhenîs) are not recited.'

[1] In the Taitt. S. II, 5, 10, the number of verses (effected by the repetition) is given as varying, according to the special object in view, between fifteen and forty-eight.

[2] ? Or, it would be an act of neglect on his, the sacrificer's, part: by (the Hot*ri*) reciting without fetching breath, that act, that neglect would be avoided.

position without taking breath, that slight will be avoided.

15. If, however, he do not care to undertake this, he may also recite one (verse) at a time without drawing breath: he thereby spreads those worlds one by one, gains those worlds one by one. The reason why he takes breath, is that the gâyatrî is indeed breath; and that by reciting a complete gâyatrî verse, he accordingly bestows complete breathing (on the sacrificer): let him therefore recite one (verse) at a time without breathing.

16. He recites them in a continuous, uninterrupted way: thereby he makes the days and nights of the year continuous, and in a continuous, uninterrupted way revolve those days and nights of the year. And in this way he gives no access to the spiteful enemy; but access he would indeed give, if he were to recite them discontinuously: he therefore recites in a continuous, uninterrupted way.

Fourth Adhyâya. First Brâhmana.

1. He recites after uttering (the syllable) 'Hiṅ!' Sacrifice, they say, is not (performed) without the Sâman; and neither is the Sâman chanted without 'Hiṅ' having been uttered. By his uttering 'Hiṅ!' the peculiar nature (rûpam) of the word 'Hiṅ' is produced (in the sacrifice); and by the sacred syllable (om) it assumes the nature of the Sâman. By uttering 'Om! Om[1]!' this his entire sacrifice becomes endowed with the Sâman.

---

[1] That is, by uttering 'Om!' after each verse. The recitation of the first verse is preceded by the mystic words 'Hiṅ bhûr bhuvah svar om!' Âsv. S. I, 2, 3. Both syllables 'hiṅ' and 'om' are essential elements in the recitation of Sâman hymns. See II, 2, 4, 11 seq.

2. And (another reason) why he utters 'Hiṅ!' is this. The word 'Hiṅ' means breath, for the word 'Hiṅ' does indeed mean breath: he cannot therefore pronounce the word 'Hiṅ,' when he closes his nostrils. The *rik* (verse) he recites with his voice. Now, voice and breath are a pair, so that a productive union of the sâmidhenîs is thereby effected at the outset: for this reason he recites, after uttering 'Hiṅ!'

3. He utters the word 'Hiṅ' in a low voice. Were he, on the contrary, to pronounce 'Hiṅ' aloud, he would make 'voice' of both the one and the other: for this reason he utters the word 'Hiṅ' in a low voice.

4. He recites with 'â (hither)!' and 'pra (forth or thither)[1]!' He thereby joins a gâyatrî verse directed hitherward to one directed away from here: the one which tends from hence carries the sacrifice to the gods, and the one which tends hitherward pleases the men. For this reason he recites with 'â' and 'pra.'

5. And (another reason) why he recites with 'â' and 'pra,' is this. 'Pra (forth)' clearly means out-breathing, and 'â (hither)' means in-breathing: hence he thereby obtains out-breathing and in-breathing (for the sacrificer). For this reason he recites with 'â' and 'pra.'

---

[1] The particles pra and â were apparently used in phrases wishing one a safe journey and return (cf. Ait. Br. 3, 26, with Haug's note). The first sâmidhenî begins, 'prá vo vấgâ abhídyavah' (forth go your viands, heavenward); and the second 'ágna ấ yâhi vîtáye' (come hither, Agni, to the feast!). It is from these verses that the above symbolical explanation is derived. Cf. Taitt. S. II, 5, 7, 3 [prâkînam reto dhîyate—pratîkîh pragâ gâyante].

6. Yet (other reasons) why he recites with 'hither (â)' and 'thither (pra),' are these. 'Thither' the seed is cast, and 'hither' birth takes place. 'Thither' the cattle disperse (for grazing), 'hither' they return. Indeed, everything here (moves) 'hither' and 'thither:' for this reason he recites with 'â' and 'pra.'

7. He recites[1], 'Forth go your viands, heaven-

[1] The following is a connected translation (as literal as possible, if not elegant) of the eleven sâmidhenîs, or kindling verses, in the same octosyllabic metre as the original. The first and eleventh verses are recited three times; and when at the end of each verse the Hotri pronounces the syllable *om*, the Adhvaryu throws a stick (samidh) into the fire,—up to the eighth verse, at the end of which the tenth stick is thrown in. At the end of the ninth verse five of the remaining six sticks are thrown into the fire. The throwing of the first stick is accompanied by the sacrificer pronouncing the dedicatory formula (tyâga), 'For Agni this, not for me!'

1. Forth go your viands, heavenward,
In havis rich; with buttered (spoon)
He nears the gods, wishful of bliss.

2. Come hither, Agni, to the feast;
Invokèd for the offering-gift,
As Hotri on the barhis sit!

3. With samidhs thee, O Aṅgiras,
With butter we exhilarate:
Shine forth, O youngest, brilliantly!

4. Agni, do thou obtain for us
That region wide and glorious,
That great and mighty one, O God!

5. Praiseworthy he, adorable,
Visible through the veil of gloom,
Agni, the mighty one, is lit.

6. The mighty Agni is lit up,
Yea, as a horse that bears the gods:
With offerings him they glorify.

7. O mighty one! we mighty men
Do kindle thee, the mighty one,—
O Agni, thee that brightly shines.

ward!'—hereby, then, the 'thither' is (realised). And (in the second verse), 'Come hither, Agni, to expand[1]!'—by this, on the other hand, the 'hither' is (realised).

8. Now, in reference to this point, some people say, 'Both these (texts) surely result in a "thither[2]."' This, however, is beyond the ordinary understanding: the text, 'forth go your viands, heavenward!' is clearly (directed) away from (the sacrificer); and the text, 'Come hither, Agni, to expand!' is (directed) towards (him).

9. He recites (the first kindling verse), 'Forth go your viands, heavenward!' this, then, tends in a forward direction. 'Viands' (vâga)[3] he says, because viands mean food: hence food is obtained (for the sacrificer) by this recitation. 'Heavenward' he says, because those that tend heavenward are the half-

---

8. Agni we choose as messenger,
As Hotri the all-knowing,—him,
Performing well this sacrifice.

9. He who is kindled at the cult,
Agni, the bright, the laudable,
The flaming-locked, him we adore.

10. O Agni, worshipped, thou art lit:
Adore, good worshipper, the gods!
Oblation-bearer, sure, art thou.

11. Make offerings! do reverence!—
Him, Agni, while the cult proceeds,
For your oblation-bearer choose!

[1] See further on, par. 22 seq.

[2] Inasmuch as Agni, whilst coming to the sacrifice, goes away from the gods. Sây.

[3] In the Taitt. S. II, 5, 7, 3-4 also vâga is in the first place rendered by 'food,' while afterwards it is identified with the months (i.e. the coursers? gamanasîla, Sây.); as abhidyavah (in the sense of 'shining in both directions,' i.e. in the form of the waxing and waning moon, Sây.) is referred to the half-moons.

moons: it is, therefore, the half-moons which he obtains by this recitation. 'In havis rich' he further says, because those that are rich in havis (milk, butter) are the cattle; it is cattle, therefore, that he thereby obtains through the recitation.

10. 'With buttered (spoon)—' he adds. Now Mâthava, the (king of) Videgha[1], carried Agni Vaisvânara in his mouth. The *Ri*shi Gotama Râhûga*n*a was his family priest. When addressed (by the latter), he made no answer to him, fearing lest Agni might fall from his mouth.

11. He (the priest) began to invoke the latter with

[1] To this important legend attention was first drawn by Professor Weber, Ind. Stud. I, 170 seq. (cf. also Ind. Streifen, I, p. 13; J. Muir, Sanskrit Texts, II, p. 402). It was pointed out by Weber that this legend distinguishes three successive stages of the eastward migration of the Brâhmanical Hindus. In the first place the settlements of the Âryans had already been extended from the Pa*ñg*ab (where they were settled in the times of the hymns of the Rig-veda) as far as the Sarasvatî. They thence pushed forward, led by the Videgha Mâthava and his priest, according to our legend, as far east as the river Sadânîrâ (that is, 'she that is always filled with water'), which, according to Sâya*n*a, is another name for the Karatoyâ (the modern Kurattee, on which Bograh lies), which formed the eastern boundary of the Videhas; or more probably the Ga*nd*akî (the modern Gunduck, a noble river which falls into the Ganges opposite Patna, and) which formed the boundary between the Kosalas and the Videhas (cf. par. 17). It would appear from our legend, that for some time the Âryans did not venture to cross this river; but at the time of the author the country to the east of it had long been occupied by them. Sâya*n*a takes the hero of the legend to be Videgha, the Mâdhava or son of Madhu; but Videgha, an older form of Videha, is more probably intended here (as Weber takes it) for the name of that people and country (corresponding to the modern Tirhut). The Agni Vaisvânara (or Agni who is common to all men) of our legend Professor Weber considers a personification of Brâhmanical worship and civilisation and the destructive effects of their extension.

verses of the Rig-veda, 'We kindle thee at the sacrifice, O wise Agni, thee the radiant, the mighty caller to the sacrificial feast (Rig-veda V, 26, 3)!—O Videgha!'

12. He (the king) did not answer. (The priest went on), 'Upwards, O Agni, dart thy brilliant, shining rays, thy flames, thy beams (Rig-veda VIII, 44, 16)!—O Videgha-a-a!'

13. Still he did not answer. (The priest continued), 'Thee, O butter-sprinkled one, we invoke! (Rig-veda V, 26, 2);' so much he uttered, when at the very mentioning of butter, Agni Vaisvânara flashed forth from the (king's) mouth: he was unable to hold him back; he issued from his mouth, and fell down on this earth.

14. Mâthava, the Videgha, was at that time on the (river) Sarasvatî[1]. He (Agni) thence went burning along this earth towards the east; and Gotama Râhûgana and the Videgha Mâthava followed after him as he was burning along. He burnt over (dried up) all these rivers. Now that (river), which is called 'Sadânîrâ,' flows from the northern (Himâlaya) mountain: that one he did not burn over. That one the Brâhmans did not cross in former times, thinking, 'it has not been burnt over by Agni Vaisvânara.'

15. Now-a-days, however, there are many Brâhmans to the east of it. At that time it (the land east of the Sadânîrâ) was very uncultivated, very marshy, because it had not been tasted by Agni Vaisvânara.

16. Now-a-days, however, it is very cultivated, for the Brâhmans have caused (Agni) to taste it through

[1] Or, according to Sâyana, he was then in the Sarasvatî, plunged into the river in order to quench the heat produced by Agni.

sacrifices. Even in late summer that (river), as it were, rages along[1]: so cold is it, not having been burnt over by Agni Vai*s*vânara.

17. Mâthava, the Videgha, then said (to Agni), 'Where am I to abide?' 'To the east of this (river) be thy abode!' said he. Even now this (river) forms the boundary of the Kosalas and Videhas; for these are the Mâthavas (or descendants of Mâthava).

18. Gotama Râhûga*n*a then said (to Mâthava), 'Why didst thou not answer when addressed by us?' He replied, 'Agni Vai*s*vânara was in my mouth; I did not reply, lest he should escape from my mouth.'

19. 'How then did this happen?'—'At the moment when thou didst utter the words, "(Thee), O butter-sprinkled one, we invoke!" just then, at the mention of butter, Agni Vai*s*vânara flashed forth from my mouth; I was unable to hold him back, he issued from my mouth.'

20. That (word) in the sâmidhenîs, therefore, which contains butter (gh*ri*ta) is especially suitable for kindling (sam-indh); and by it he accordingly kindles him (Agni, the fire) and bestows vigour on this (sacrificer).

21. Now that (word) is gh*ri*tâ*k*yâ, 'with the buttered (spoon).'—'He nears[2] the gods, wishful of bliss.' Wishful of bliss, truly, is the sacrificer, since he wishes to approach the gods, to go to[3]

---

[1] That is to say, it is not affected by the heat of the summer, as the other rivers, but rushes along as rapidly and as well-filled as ever.

[2] *G*igâti is taken by Sâya*n*a in the sense of 'he sings, praises.' Our author, on the other hand, seems to interpret it by 'he conquers (*g*i);' see, however, next note.

[3] The text has, 'Sa hi devân *g*igîshati sa hi devân *g*igâ*m*sati.' The Kâ*n*va recension has the same reading, except that it omits 'hi'

the gods: therefore he says, 'he nears the gods, wishful of bliss.' This (verse), which is addressed to Agni, is undefined (vague); and undefined, doubtless, is the 'All;' he thus commences (this holy work) with the All.

22. [He recites the second sâmidhenî]: 'Come hither, Agni, to expand!'—'To expand' he says, because at the beginning these worlds were wellnigh contiguous to one another: at that time one could touch the sky thus[1].

23. The gods desired, 'How could these worlds of ours become farther apart from one another? How could there be more space for us?' They breathed through them (the worlds) with these three syllables (forming the word) vîtaye[2],' and these worlds became far apart from one another; and there was then ampler space for the gods: ample space, therefore, he will have for whom, knowing this, they recite this (verse) containing (the word) 'vîtaye.'

24. He proceeds, 'Invoked for the giver of oblations!' 'The giver of oblations[3],' of course, is the

in both cases. Instead of gigâmsati, however, some MSS., as well as Sâyana, read gighâmsati ('he wishes to conquer, or beat, the gods'), probably an old corruption, easily accounted for by the circumstance that gigîshati is the regular desiderative of gi, 'to conquer,' though it also occurs in some passages as the desiderative of gâ, 'to go.' Sâyana, however, though he reads gighâmsati, here allows to the root han (with Naigh. 2, 14) the meaning of 'to go.' Cf. Weber, Omina und Portenta, p. 406, note 4.

[1] Viz. by stretching the arms upwards. Sâyana.

[2] That is, vi-itaye, 'for going asunder,' a fanciful analysis of the word vîti; the correct rendering is 'for the meal or food,' 'for the feast.'

[3] Havyadâti, the correct meaning of the word is 'the giving of oblations.'

sacrificer: hence 'invoked for the sacrificer' is what he thereby means to say.—'As Hotri on the barhis sit!' Agni, indeed, is the Hotri, and the barhis (the covering of sacrificial grass on the altar) is this world: hence he thereby establishes Agni (the fire) in this world, as this fire is established (or, beneficial, hita) in this world. This (verse), then, is recited with reference to this world (the earth): through it this world is conquered by him for whom, knowing this, they recite this (verse).

25. [He recites the third sâmidhenî]: 'With samidhs thee, O Aṅgiras!'—with samidhs (kindling-sticks), indeed, the Aṅgiras kindled him. 'O Aṅgiras!' he says, for Agni is indeed Aṅgiras[1].—'With butter we exhilarate!' This (viz. ghritena, 'with butter') is a word which is especially suitable for the kindling of Agni: by it he kindles him, and bestows vigour on this (sacrificer).

26. 'Shine forth, O youngest, brilliantly!' he adds; for brilliantly he shines, when kindled; and 'O youngest!' he says, because he is really the youngest Agni[2]: therefore he says, 'O youngest!' This (verse) is recited with reference to yonder world, to wit, the aërial world; hence this (verse), which is addressed to Agni, is undefined, for undefined is yonder world: that world he thereby gains, for whom, knowing this, they recite this verse.

27. [He recites the fourth sâmidhenî]: 'Agni, do thou obtain for us that (region) wide and

---

[1] Rig-veda I, 31, 1, he is called the first of the Aṅgiras.

[2] The fire which has just been kindled is frequently called the youngest (yavishtha). Sâyana takes it as 'the ever young.' See also the legend regarding the three Agnis who preceded the present Agni in the office of divine Hotri, I, 2, 3, 1; 3, 3, 13.

glorious!' For wide, indeed, is yonder (region) wherein the gods (dwell), and glorious is that (region) wherein the gods (dwell). When he says, 'Do thou obtain for us[1],' he means to say, 'make us go to it!'

28. 'That great and mighty one, O God!' For great, indeed, is yonder (region) wherein the gods (dwell), and mighty[2] is that wherein the gods (dwell). This (verse), then, is recited with reference to yonder world: that heavenly world he thereby gains, for whom, knowing this, they recite this (verse).

29. He recites (the fifth sâmidhenî): 'Praiseworthy he, adorable,' for worthy of praise he is, and worthy of adoration;—'visible through the veil of gloom,' for when kindled he is seen right through the gloom;—'Agni, the mighty one (bull), is lit,' for he is indeed lit up, the mighty one.

[He recites the sixth sâmidhenî]: 'The mighty Agni is lit up,' for he is indeed lit up.

30. 'Yea[3], as a horse that bears the gods,' for having become a horse he does indeed carry the sacrifice to the gods: the (word) 'na' which occurs in this verse has the meaning of 'om' (verily); hence he says, 'Yea, as a horse that bears to the gods.'

---

[1] Vivâsasi, Sâya*n*a explains it by prakâsaya, 'illuminate it;' but cf. Sâya*n*a on Rig-veda VI, 16, asmân a*kkh*a abhigamaya, 'make it (dhanam) come to us.'

[2] Suvîrya is taken by our author as an adjective, co-ordinate with the others; but it is evidently a noun ('abundance of heroes' or 'manliness, manly power,' St. Petersburg Dictionary) qualified by the adjectives.

[3] Na is taken by our author as a particle of asseveration; though in reality it is a particle of comparison. In later Sanskrit na is only used as particle of negation.

31. 'With offerings him they glorify,' for with offerings men indeed glorify him; therefore he says, 'with offerings him they glorify.'

32. [He recites the seventh sâmidhenî): 'O mighty one[1]! we mighty men do kindle thee, the mighty one!' for they indeed kindle him;—'O Agni, thee that brightly shines!' for he indeed shone brightly when he was kindled.

33. He recites this tristich which contains the word (vrishan), 'mighty.' All these kindling verses, it is true, are addressed to Agni; Indra, however, is the deity of sacrifice, Indra is the mighty (hero); hence these his (the sacrificer's) kindling verses thereby become possessed of Indra: this is the reason why he recites the tristich containing the word 'mighty.'

34. He recites [the eighth sâmidhenî]: 'Agni we choose as messenger!' Now the gods and the Asuras, both of them sprang from Pragâpati, were contending for superiority. When they were thus contending, the gâyatrî stood between them. That gâyatrî was the same as this earth, and this earth indeed lay between them[2]. Now both of them knew that whichever she would side with, they would be victorious and the others would be defeated. Both parties then invited her secretly to come to them. Agni acted as messenger for the gods; and an Asura-Rakshas, named Sa-

---

[1] Vrishan, 'the male, the vigorous one, the bull;' cf. Max Müller, Translation of Rig-veda Sanhitâ, I, p. 121 seq.

[2] 'On the top of Mount Meru lies the city of Amarâvatî, wherein the gods dwell; and beneath Meru lies Irâvatî, the city of the Asuras: between these two lies the earth.' Sâyana.

harakshas[1], for the Asuras. She then followed Agni: he therefore recites, 'Agni we choose for messenger,' because he was the messenger of the gods.—'As Hotri the all-knowing, him!'

35. Here now some people recite, 'He who is the Hotri of the all-knowing[2];' lest (in saying 'for Hotri, the all-knowing, him') one should say to oneself 'enough (i.e. have done)!' This, however, he should not do; for by (doing) so they do at the sacrifice what is human; and what is human, is inauspicious at a sacrifice. Therefore, lest he should do what is inauspicious at the sacrifice, he should recite, just as it is recited by the *Rik*, 'for Hotri, the all-knowing, him!' [He continues], 'Performing well this sacrifice!' for he, Agni, is indeed a good performer of the sacrifice: for this reason he says, 'performing well this sacrifice.' She (gâyatrî, or the earth) sided with the gods, and the gods thereupon were victorious and the Asuras were defeated: and verily he for whom, knowing this, they recite this (verse), is himself victorious and his adversaries are defeated.

36. He therefore recites this, the eighth sâmidhenî). This, indeed, is peculiarly a gâyatrî verse, since it is of eight syllables that the gâyatrî (metre) consists: for this reason he recites the eighth (sâmidhenî).

---

[1] Cf. the corresponding passage in Taitt. S. II, 5, 11, 8, where Daivya is given as the name of the messenger of the Asuras.

[2] That is to say, instead of 'Hotâram visvavedasam,' they recite 'Hotâ yo visvavedasah;' for the reason that Hotâram (accusative of hotri) might be understood to be 'hotâ aram,' aram, 'enough,' being a particle implying a prohibition. Our author, however, promptly sets his face against this application of human reasoning to an inspired text.

37. Here now some people place the two (dhâyyâs) additional kindling verses before (the eighth sâmidhenî), arguing, 'The two dhâyyâs[1] mean food: this edible food we place in front (or, in the mouth, mukhata*h*).' But let him not do this: for with him who inserts the additional verses before (the eighth), the latter (the eighth) is clearly out of its place[2], since in that case it (and the succeeding verse) become the tenth and eleventh verses. With him, on the other hand, for whom they recite this as the eighth (kindling verse), it is indeed in its proper place: let him therefore insert the two additional verses after (the ninth).

38. [He recites the ninth kindling verse]: 'He who is kindled at the cult'—the cult (adhvara), doubtless, is the sacrifice: 'he who is kindled at the sacrifice' he thereby says;—'Agni, the bright, the laudable,' for he is both bright and laudable;—'the flaming-locked, him we adore!' for when he is kindled, his locks, as it were, flame. Previously to (the beginning of the tenth verse), 'O Agni, worshipped, thou art lit!' let him (the Adhvaryu) put on

---

[1] Whenever thirteen kindling verses are recited instead of eleven (or counting the repetitions of the first and last verses, seventeen instead of fifteen), the two verses Rig-veda III, 27, 5 and 6 are inserted according to our author after the ninth, and according to others before the eighth, sâmidhenî. They are called dhâyyâ, probably derived from dhâ, 'to put, add,' whilst those ritualists whose practice is here rejected apparently connect the word with the root dhâ (dhe), 'to suck.'

[2] According to Sâya*n*a, because it no longer occupies the eighth place for which it is specially appropriate on account of its being, according to our author, 'peculiarly a gâyatrî (eight-syllabled) verse.' This reasoning is far from satisfactory, since the two dhâyyâs (Rig-veda III, 27, 5 and 6) are also gâyatrî verses.

all the kindling-sticks with the exception of the one stick (which is to be put on at the after-offerings[1]); for it is now that the Hotri completes (the kindling); and what then is left of the kindling-sticks, other than the one stick, that is left (unused altogether); and what is left (unused) of the sacrifice, that is left for his (the sacrificer's) spiteful enemy: let him, therefore, previously to this (verse), put on all the samidhs, save one.

39. [He continues]: 'Adore, good worshipper, the gods!' worship (adhvara) doubtless means sacrifice: 'adore the gods, good sacrificer,' he thereby says;—'Oblation-bearer, sure, art thou!' for he, Agni, is indeed the bearer of oblations: for this reason he says 'oblation-bearer, sure, art thou.'

[He recites the last sâmidhenî]: 'Make offerings! do reverence! Him, Agni, while the cult proceeds, for your oblation-bearer choose!' by this (verse) he urges them on: 'make offerings and worship! do this for (the accomplishment) of whatever desire you kindled him!' this is what he thereby means to say. 'Him, Agni, while the cult proceeds,' he says, because cult means sacrifice: hence he thereby says, 'him, Agni, whilst the sacrifice proceeds;'—'for your oblation-bearer choose!' for he, Agni, is indeed the oblation-bearer, and for this reason he says 'for your oblation-bearer choose (him)!'

40. This tristich, containing (the word) 'cult (adhvara),' he thus recites. For once when the gods were engaged in sacrificing, their rivals, the Asuras, wished to injure (dhurv, dhvar) them; but, though desirous of injuring them, they were

[1] See I, 8, 2, 3.

unable to injure them and were foiled: for this reason the sacrifice is called adhvara ('not damaged, uninterrupted'); and for whomsoever, that knows this, they recite this tristich containing (the word) adhvara ('cult, sacrifice'), his rival, though desirous of injuring him, is foiled; and he, (the sacrificer), moreover, gains as much as one gains by offering a Soma-sacrifice[1].

Second Brâhmana.

1. Now in former times the gods appointed Agni to the chief (office), namely, that of Hotri; and having appointed him to the chief (office) saying 'do thou carry this our oblation!' they cheered him up, saying, 'Surely, thou art vigorous; surely, thou art equal to this!' thereby endowing him with vigour, even as in our own days, when they appoint any one from among their kinsmen to the chief (office), they cheer him up saying 'surely, thou art vigorous; surely, thou art equal to this!' thereby endowing him with vigour. By what, therefore, he recites after this, he eulogizes him, puts vigour into him[2].

2. 'O Agni, thou art great! O priest (brâhmana), O Bhârata!' for Agni, indeed, is the brahman

[1] Saumya adhvara is the common designation of the solemn Soma-sacrifice; hence, our author argues, the word adhvara is here used for sacrifice (yagña) with a view to insure to this offering the efficacy of a Soma-sacrifice.

[2] The invocations he now proceeds to recite, on the termination of the sâmidhenîs or kindling verses, belong to the class of formulas called nigada. In the present case, they consist of the pravara mantra—or formula by which Agni is invited to assist the sacrificer as Hotri or Invoker on the present occasion, as he has of old assisted his ancestors (cf. the following note)—and of short detached formulas called nivid. Sâyana on Taitt. S. II, 5, 8.

(sacerdotium): therefore he says 'O Brâhmana!'—'O Bhârata' he says, because he (Agni) bears (bhar) the oblation to the gods: therefore they say 'Agni is bhârata (the bearer).' Or, he, being the breath, sustains (bhar) these creatures: therefore he says 'O Bhârata (sustainer)!'

3. He now calls on (Agni as) the ancestral (Hotri priest)[1]. He thereby introduces him both to the Rishis and to the gods (as if he were to say), 'Of great vigour is he who has obtained the sacrifice!' This is the reason why he calls on (Agni as) the ancestral (Hotri).

4. He calls from the remote end (of the sacri-

---

[1] Ârsheyam pravrinîte, literally 'he chooses the ancestral' (rishi). I take 'ârsheyam' as a masculine adjective qualifying a supplied '(Agnim) hotâram.' In this way the formula is explained by Sâyana on I, 5, 1, 9 (rishînâm sambandhinam adhvaryur hotâram vrinîte), and this seems to me the most natural interpretation. It is true, however, that, as the formula ('he chooses the ancestral') became stereotyped, its exact import became forgotten, and ârsheya was generally taken as a neuter, either adjective (viz. 'nâmadheyam,' 'apatyam') or noun (ancestral lineage). Agni is invoked as the one who has of old officiated as the Hotri of the sacrificer's ancestors, three or five ancestral names being usually mentioned: thus, in the case of a sacrificer belonging to the Gâmadagna Vatsa family, claiming Bhrigu, Kyavana, Apnavâna, Aurva, and Gamadagni as its founders, Agni is invoked, on the present occasion, as 'Bhârgava Kyâvana Âpnavâna Aurva Gâmadagna!' (Âsval. Sr. 12, 10, 6; Sâyana on Taitt. S. II, 5, 8). If the sacrificer belongs to the Kshatriya or Vaisya castes, the priest substitutes for the sacrificer's ancestors those of his family priest (purohita) or his spiritual guide (guru); and in the case of kings the same course was adopted, or the names of their royal rishi ancestors (râgarshi) were chosen. As to the second pravara, or the election of the human Hotri, for the present sacrifice, see I, 5, 1, 1. Cf. Max Müller, History of Ancient Sanskrit Literature, p. 386 seq.; A. Weber, Ind. Stud. IX, 321 seq.; X, 78 seq.; M. Haug, Aitar. Br., Translation, p. 479.

ficer's ancestral line) downwards; for it is from the remote end downwards that a race is propagated. He (the Hotri) also thereby propitiates the lord of seniority for him (the Sacrificer); for here among men the father comes first, then the son, and then the grandson: this is the reason why he calls from the remote end downwards.

5. Having named (him as) the ancestral one, he says, '(thou wert) kindled by the gods, kindled by Manu;' for in olden times the gods did kindle him: for this reason he says 'kindled by the gods;' and 'kindled by Manu' he says, because in olden times Manu did kindle him: for this reason he says 'kindled by Manu.'

6. He continues, 'Praised by the *Ri*shis (wert thou);' for in olden times the *Ri*shis did praise him: for this reason he says 'praised by the *Ri*shis.'

7. Further, 'Gladdened by bards (vipra);' for those bards, the *Ri*shis, indeed gladdened him: for this reason he says 'gladdened by bards.'

8. Further, 'Celebrated by sages (kavi);' for those sages, the *Ri*shis, indeed celebrated him: this is why he says 'celebrated by sages.'

9. Further, 'Sharpened by the brahman (the Veda or vedic formulas),' for he is indeed sharpened by the brahman;—'the receiver of butter-offerings,' for he is indeed the receiver of butter-offerings.

10. Further, 'The leader of oblations (ya*gñ*a), the carrier of (Soma-)sacrifices (adhvara),' for through him they lead forward all oblations, both the domestic oblations and the others: this is why he says 'the leader of oblations.'

11. 'The carrier (rathî) of sacrifices;' for being a cart (as it were) he conveys the sacrifice to the

gods: this is the reason why he says 'the carrier of sacrifices.'

12. Further, 'The unsurpassed Hotri, the surpassing bearer of oblations;' for him the Rakshas do not surpass (tar): for this reason he says 'the unsurpassed (atûrta) Hotri.' 'The surpassing (tûrni, rather 'swift') bearer of oblations,' for he overcomes (tar) every evil: therefore he says 'the surpassing bearer of oblations[1].'

13. Further, 'The mouth-vessel[2], the offering-spoon of the gods;' for he, Agni, is indeed the vessel of the gods: therefore they make offerings in Agni to all the gods, he being the vessel of the gods. And, verily, whosoever knows this, obtains the vessel of him whose vessel he desires to obtain[3].

14. Further, 'The cup from which the gods drink;' for from him, being (as it were) a cup, the gods drink (the Soma-libations): for this reason he says 'the cup from which the gods drink.'

15. Further, 'Thou, O Agni! dost encompass the gods, as the felly the spokes;' 'in the same way in which the felly on all sides encompasses the spokes, so dost thou on all sides encompass the gods,' this is what he thereby says.

16. 'Bring hither the gods for the sacrificer!' this he says in order that he (Agni) may bring the gods

---

[1] At this point of the recitation a pause is made, during which (as already partly during the preceding recitation) the Adhvaryu and Âgnîdhra engage in the acts detailed in I, 4, 4, 13 seq. Cf. Hillebrandt, Neu und Vollm. p. 81.

[2] Âs-pâtram: the fire is, as it were, the vessel into which the sacrificial food is thrown and from which it is eaten by the gods.

[3] ? Sâyana supplies 'food:' he obtains the vessel of that food of which he wishes to obtain the vessel.

to this sacrifice[1].—'Bring Agni hither, O Agni!' this he says in order that he may bring Agni to the butter-portion intended for Agni.—'Bring Soma hither!' this he says in order that he may bring Soma to the butter-portion intended for Soma.—'Bring Agni hither!' this he says in order that he (Agni) may bring Agni hither to that indispensable[2] cake which is offered to Agni on both occasions (at the new- and the full-moon sacrifices).

17. And (in the same way) according to the respective deities[3]. He then continues, 'Bring hither the butter-drinking gods!' this he says in order that he may bring hither the prayâgas and anuyâgas (fore and after-offerings), for the prayâgas and anuyâgas (represent) indeed the butter-drinking gods.—'Bring Agni hither for the Hotriship!' this he says in order that he may bring Agni hither for the office of Hotri.'—'Your own greatness bring hither!' this he says in order that he (Agni) may

---

[1] Here begins what is called the devatânâm âvahanam, or invitation (lit. bringing) of the deities to the oblations. Whilst the Hotri recites these formulas, the Adhvaryu performs what is set forth in I, 4, 5, 2 seq.

[2] Akyuta, lit. 'not fallen,' i. e. immutable, invariable. For the legendary explanation of this epithet of Agni and his oblation, see I, 6, 1, 6; 2, 5–6.

[3] The three preceding invocations are used alike at the new- and full-moon sacrifices, but the subsequent ones differ according to the oblations that are made, viz. a rice-cake to Indra-Agni (or an oblation of mixed milk and butter to Indra) at the new-moon ceremony; and to Agni-Soma at the full-moon sacrifice. Previously to these an upâmsuyâga or 'low-voiced oblation' is made by some to Agni-Soma at the full moon, and one to Vishnu (or to Agni-Soma) at the new-moon sacrifice; according to others also one to Pragâpati,—the names of the gods being whispered in the respective formulas.

bring hither his own greatness; his own greatness, in truth, is his voice: hence he says it in order that he may bring hither his voice[1].—'Bring thou hither (the gods), O *G*âtavedas[2], and offer up a good offering!' what deities he bids him bring hither, with regard to those (deities) he thereby says 'bring them hither!' When he says, 'offer up a good offering!' he means to say, 'sacrifice in the proper order!'

18. He recites (the invitatory prayer)[3] while standing, since it is yonder (sky) which he thereby recites; for, indeed, the invitatory prayer (signifies) yonder (sky), and by it he recites that which is yonder (sky). This is the reason why he recites standing.

19. The offering-prayer[3] he pronounces while sitting, since the offering-prayer (represents) this (earth): hence no one pronounces the offering-prayer while standing; for the offering-prayer is

---

[1] Sâya*n*a on Taitt. S. II, 5, 9 explains the formula 'Bring hither the own greatness' by 'bring hither whatever greatness or power is peculiar to each of the havis-eating gods,' and he remarks expressly that it is not to be referred to Agni, as our author certainly appears to do. Cf. I, 7, 3, 13.

[2] *G*atavedas probably means 'he who knoweth (all) beings,' but it is more generally explained by 'he who possesseth riches (or wisdom),' not to mention other interpretations. According to Haug, Ait. Br. vol. ii. p. 224, the proper meaning of the term is 'having possession of all that is born, i. e. pervading it.' He further mentions that the *Ri*shis are quite familiar with the idea of the fire being an all-pervading power; and that by *G*âtavedas the 'animal fire' is particularly to be understood. Our present formula 'â *k*a vaha *g*âtaveda*h* suya*g*â *k*a ya*g*a' somewhat differs from the corresponding formula of the Taitt. S. II, 5, 9, 5, 'â *k*âgne devân vaha suya*g*â *k*a ya*g*a *g*âtaveda*h*.'

[3] For the anuvâkyâ or invitatory prayer, and the yâ*g*yâ or offering-prayer, see p. 135 note.

this earth, and by it he pronounces that which is this (earth). This is the reason why he pronounces the offering-prayer while sitting.

THIRD BRÂHMANA.

1. The fire that has been kindled by means of the kindling verses, assuredly, blazes more brightly than any other fire; for, indeed, it is unassailable, unapproachable.

2. And in like manner as the fire blazes when kindled by means of the kindling verses, so also blazes the priest (brâhmana) that knows and recites the kindling verses; for, indeed, he is unassailable, unapproachable.

3. He recites, 'Pra vah[1];' for the (word) prâna contains the syllable pra ('forwards;' or, is directed forwards): hence it is the prâna (out-breathing) which he kindles by this (the first sâmidhenî). [He further recites the second verse], 'Come hither, Agni, to expand!' the backward breathing (apâna)[2], doubtless, is of this nature: the backward breathing he accordingly kindles with this (verse). Further (in the third verse), 'Shine forth, O youngest, brilliantly!' the high-flaming one[3], indeed, is the upward breathing (udâna): the upward

[1] The first two words of the first sâmidhenî, cf. p. 101 note. A mystic meaning is obtained for them by our author combining them and identifying the form obtained with the adjective pravant, meaning both 'containing the syllable pra' and 'directed forwards,' both of which meanings apply to the breathing-forth or expiration (prâna, cf. I, 1, 3, 2).

[2] Bahir nirgatasya vâyor âtmâbhimukhî vrittir hy apânah, udânavâyur dehasyotkshepanâd adhikategoyuktah. Sâyana.

[3] The author apparently takes brihakkhokâ(h) as a compound.

breathing he accordingly kindles with this (the third verse).

4. Further, 'Sa na*h* pr*i*thu *s*ravâyyam[1],' the 'far-hearing one,' indeed, is the ear, for it is with the ear that one hears here far or widely: the ear he accordingly kindles with this (the fourth verse).

5. Further, 'Praiseworthy he, adorable;' the praiseworthy[2] one, doubtless, is the voice; for it is the voice which praises everything here; by the voice everything is praised here: he accordingly kindles the voice with this (the fifth verse).

6. Further, 'Yea, as a horse that bears (to) the gods;' that which conveys to the gods is indeed the mind, for it is the mind which chiefly conveys the wise man (to the gods): the mind he accordingly kindles with this (the sixth verse).

7. Further, 'O Agni, thee, that brightly shines!' the eye, assuredly, shines: the eye he accordingly kindles by this (the seventh verse).

8. Further, 'Agni we choose for messenger,'—what central breath there is (in the body), that he kindles with this (the eighth verse): that one indeed is the internal motive force of the breathings; from it (two) others tend upwards, and from it (two) others tend downwards, for it is indeed the internal motive force. And whosoever knows that internal motive force of the breathings, him they regard as the internal motive force.

---

[1] 'That (region) wide and glorious' (do thou obtain for us); but the author takes pr*i*thu *s*ravâyyam as 'that widely hearing one' or 'the wide hearing.' Sâya*n*a, on Taitt. S. II, 5, 8, interprets it by 'that (holy work) which is extended and worthy of being heard by the gods.'

[2] He apparently takes îdenya in an active sense.

9. Further, 'The flaming-locked, him we adore!' the flaming-locked, doubtless, is the sisna, for it is that organ which chiefly burns (torments) him who is endowed with it: the sisna he accordingly kindles by this (the ninth verse).

10. Further, 'O Agni, worshipped, thou art lit!' what downward breathing there is that he kindles with this (the tenth verse); 'make offerings, do reverence!' with this (the eleventh verse) he kindles the entire body from the nails to the hair.

11. And if any one were to curse this one (the Hotri) at the (recitation of the) first kindling verse, then he (the Hotri) should say to him, 'Thereby thou hast put thine own out-breathing into the fire: by that out-breathing of thine shalt thou undergo suffering!' for this is what would take place.

12. If any one were to curse him at the second (verse), he should say to him, 'Thereby thou hast put thine own in-breathing into the fire: by that in-breathing of thine shalt thou undergo suffering!' for this is what would take place.

13. If any one were to curse him at the third (verse), he should say to him, 'Thereby thou hast put thine own up-breathing into the fire: by that up-breathing of thine shalt thou undergo suffering!' for this is what would take place.

14. If any one were to curse him at the fourth (verse), he should say to him, 'Thereby thou hast put thine own ear into the fire: by that ear of thine shalt thou undergo suffering, thou shalt become deaf!' for this is what would take place.

15. If any one were to curse him at the fifth (verse), he should say to him, 'Thereby thou hast put thine own voice into the fire: by that voice of

thine shalt thou undergo suffering, thou shalt become dumb!' for this is what would take place.

16. If any one were to curse him at the sixth (verse), he should say to him, 'Thereby thou hast put thine own mind into the fire: by that mind of thine shalt thou undergo suffering, thou shalt move about as one possessed with the (demon) "mind-stealer," as one deranged in mind!' for this is what would take place.

17. If any one were to curse him at the seventh (verse), he should say to him, 'Thereby thou hast put thine own eye into the fire: by that eye of thine shalt thou undergo suffering, thou shalt become blind!' for this is what would take place.

18. If any one were to curse him at the eighth (verse), he should say to him, 'Thereby thou hast put thine own central breath into the fire: by that central breath of thine shalt thou undergo suffering, thou shalt expire and die!' for this is what would take place.

19. If any one were to curse him at the ninth (verse), he should say to him, 'Thereby thou hast put thine own organ into the fire: by that organ of thine shalt thou undergo suffering, thou shalt become emasculate!' for this is what would take place.

20. If any one were to curse him at the tenth (verse), he should say to him, 'Thereby thou hast put thine own down-breathing into the fire: by that down-breathing of thine shalt thou undergo suffering, thou shalt die from constipation!' for this is what would take place.

21. If any one were to curse him at the eleventh (verse), he should say to him, 'Thereby thou hast

put thine entire body into the fire: with that entire body of thine shalt thou undergo suffering, thou shalt swiftly pass to yonder world!' for this is what would take place.

22. For in like manner as one undergoes suffering on approaching the fire that has been kindled by means of the kindling verses, so also does one undergo suffering for cursing a priest (brâhmana) who knows and recites the kindling verses.

Fourth Brâhmana.

1. That same fire, then, they have kindled, (thinking), 'In it, when kindled, we will sacrifice to the gods.' In it, indeed, he makes these two first oblations[1] to Mind and Speech (or, Voice); for mind and speech, when yoked together, convey the sacrifice to the gods.

2. Now, what is performed (with formulas, pronounced) in a low voice, by that the mind conveys the sacrifice to the gods; and what is performed (with formulas) distinctly uttered by speech, by that the speech conveys the sacrifice to the gods. And thus takes place here a twofold performance, whereby

[1] Viz. the two âghâras, or pourings (libations) of butter. The first libation, which belongs to Pragâpati, is made by the Adhvaryu, while seated north of the fire, immediately after the commencement of the pravara, in a continuous line from west to east, on the north part of the fire. The second libation (cf. note on I, 4, 5, 3) is made by the Adhvaryu while standing on the south side, in the same way on the southern part of the fire. According to some authorities of the Black Yagus ritual (quoted by Hillebrandt, Neu und Vollm. pp. 80, 86) the sacrificer pronounces the anumantranas, 'For Pragâpati is this, not for me: thou art the mind of Pragâpati!' and 'Indra's voice (speech) art thou: enter into me with the voice, with Indra's power!' over the two libations respectively.

he gratifies these two, thinking, 'gratified and pleased, these two shall convey the sacrifice to the gods.'

3. With the dipping-spoon (sruva, m.) he makes that libation (of clarified butter) which he makes for the mind; for the mind (manas, n.!) is male, and male is the sruva.

4. With the offering-spoon (sruk, f.) he makes that libation which he makes for speech (vâk, f.); for speech is female, and female is the sruk.

5. Silently (without a formula) and even without 'svâhâ (hail)!' he makes that libation which he makes for the mind; for undefined (or indistinct) is the mind, and undefined is what takes place silently.

6. With a mantra he makes that libation which he makes for speech; for distinct is speech, and distinct is the formula.

7. Sitting he makes that libation which he makes for the mind, and standing that which he makes for speech. Mind and speech, when yoked together, assuredly convey the sacrifice to the gods. But when one of two yoke-fellows is smaller (than the other) they give him a shoulder-piece[1]. Now speech is indeed smaller than mind; for mind is by far the more unlimited, and speech is by far the more limited (of the two); hence he thereby (by standing) gives a shoulder-piece to speech, and as well-matched yoke-fellows these two now convey the sacrifice to the gods: for speech, therefore, he sprinkles while standing.

8. Now the gods, when they were performing sacrifice, were afraid of a disturbance on the part

[1] Upavaha (m.; upavahas, n., Kânva rec.), explained by Sâyana as a piece of wood inserted under the yoke (and on the neck of an ox) in order to make it level with the height of the yoke-fellow.

of the Asuras and Rakshas. They, therefore, stood up erect against them on the south side (of the sacrificial ground); for strength is, as it were, erect; hence he makes the (second) libation while standing to the south (of the fire). When he makes a libation on each side (of the fire, north and south), this (pair), mind and speech, though indeed joined together, become separate: for one of the two libations is the head of the sacrifice and the other is its root.

9. With the dipping-spoon (sruva) he makes that libation which is the root of the sacrifice, and with the offering-spoon (sruk) that which is the head of the sacrifice.

10. Silently he makes that libation which is the root of the sacrifice; for silent, as it were, is this root (of trees &c.), and in it the voice does not sound.

11. With a formula he makes that libation which is the head of the sacrifice; for the formula is speech, and from the head this speech sounds.

12. Sitting he makes that libation which is the root of the sacrifice; for seated, as it were, is this root. Standing he makes that libation which is the head of the sacrifice; for this head stands, as it were.

13. When he has made the first libation with the dipping-spoon, he says, 'Agnîdh, sweep (touch over) the fire[1]!' In like manner as one would lay the yoke on (the shoulders of the team), so also he makes that first libation; for after laying on the yoke they fasten (the team to it).

14. He (the Âgnîdhra) then sweeps (the fire with

[1] See I, 4, 2, 12, with note.

the band of the fire-wood): he thereby harnesses it, thinking, 'Now that it has been harnessed, may it convey the sacrifice to the gods!' for this reason he sweeps it. While sweeping it he moves around, since in harnessing they move around the team. He sweeps thrice each time (i.e. thrice along each of the three enclosing-sticks): threefold is the sacrifice.

15. He sweeps (once), with the text (Vâ*g*. S. II, 7 a), 'O Agni, food-gainer! I cleanse thee, the food-gainer, who art about to hasten to the food!' Whereby he says, 'I cleanse thee who art going to convey the sacrifice (to the gods), thee fit for the sacrifice!' He then sweeps thrice over (the fire) silently: for just as, after harnessing (the animal), one urges it on, saying, 'Go on! pull!' so does he thereby strike it with the lash[1], thinking, 'Go on and convey the sacrifice to the gods!' That is why he (sweeps) thrice over it silently; and in like manner as this act is performed between (the two sprinklings of butter), so this mind and speech, though forming one, thereby become, as it were, separate.

FIFTH BRÂHMA*N*A.

1. When he (the Adhvaryu) is about to make the second libation with the offering-spoon (sru*k*), he (twice) lays his joined hands (a*ñg*ali) on the ground before the two offering-spoons (*g*uhû and upabh*ri*t), with the formulas (Vâ*g*. S. II, 7 b), 'Adoration to the gods!' 'Svadhâ to the fathers!' Thereby he propitiates the gods and the fathers, now that

[1] The sweeping of the fire is performed with the straw-band with which the fire-wood was tied together (Kâty. III, 1, 13), and which is here compared with the lash of a whip.

he is about to perform the duties of the sacrificial priest. With the formula, 'May ye two be easy to manage for me!' he takes the two offering-spoons: he thereby means to say, 'May ye two be easy to handle for me; may I be able to handle you!'—He further says (Vâg. S. II. 8), 'May I this day offer up the butter to the gods unspilt!' whereby he means to say, 'May I to-day perform an undisturbed sacrifice to the gods!'

2. And again, 'May I not sin against thee with my foot, O Vishnu!' Vishnu, indeed, is the sacrifice: it is the latter therefore that he propitiates by saying, 'may I not sin against thee!' Further, 'May I step into thy wealth-abounding shade, O Agni!' whereby he says, 'may I step into thy auspicious shade, O Agni[1]!'

3. Further, 'Thou art the abode of Vishnu!' Vishnu, indeed, is the sacrifice, and near to this he now stands: this is why he says, 'thou art the abode of Vishnu!'—'Here Indra performed his heroic deed[2];' for it was while standing in this place that Indra drove off towards the south the evil spirits, the Rakshas: for this reason he says, 'here Indra performed his heroic deed.'—'Erect stood the cult;' cult,

---

[1] While he pronounces this formula (and while the Hotri recites the formula of invitation to the gods, cf. note on I, 4, 2, 16) the Adhvaryu steps to the south side of the altar (and Âhavanîya fire) and in so doing must take care always to keep the left foot before the right (Kâty. III. 1, 16, 18) and not to touch the top of the prastara, ib. 17, schol. In returning (par. 5) to his former position he has to keep the right foot before the left.

[2] With this and the succeeding formulas, the Adhvaryu makes the second libation (cf. note on I, 4, 4, 1). Before the butter is poured into the fire the sacrificer pronounces the dedicatory formula, 'Om! for Indra this, not for me!'

namely, means sacrifice, hence he thereby says 'erect stood the sacrifice.'

4. Further (Vâ*g*. S. II, 9): 'O Agni, take thou upon thyself the office of Hot*ri*, take thou upon thyself the part of messenger!' for Agni is both Hot*ri* and messenger to the gods: hence he thereby says, 'know thou[1] both (offices) which thou art (holding) for the gods!'—'May earth and heaven guard thee! Guard thou earth and heaven!' there is nothing obscure in this.—'Indra, by this butter-oblation, may be the maker of good offering (svish*t*ak*ri*t) for the gods! Svâhâ!' Indra, indeed, is the deity of sacrifice; therefore he says 'Indra, by this butter-oblation...' 'It is for speech that he makes this sprinkling, and Indra is speech' so say some; and for this reason also he says 'Indra, by this butter-oblation...'

5. Having then returned (to his former position behind the altar), without letting the two offering-spoons touch each other, he mixes (some of the butter left in the *g*uhû) with (that in) the dhruvâ. Now the second libation (which he has just offered) is the head of the sacrifice, and the dhruvâ is its body[2]: hence he thereby replaces the head on the body. And the second libation, moreover, is the head of the sacrifice, and the head (*s*iras) represents excellence (*s*rî), for the head does indeed represent excellence: hence, of one who is the most excellent (*s*resh*th*a) of a community, people say that he is 'the head of that community.'

---

[1] Ve*h*, in the formula, our author refers to vid, 'to know,' instead of to vî, 'to strive after, undertake.'

[2] Cf. I, 3, 2, 2, and Taitt. S. II, 5, 11, 7–8. The second libation (âghâra) has just been made with the *g*uhû.

6. The sacrificer, assuredly, stands behind the dhruvâ, and he who means evil to him stands behind the upabhrit[1]. Hence if he were to mix (the butter remaining in the guhû) with (that in) the upabhrit, he would bestow excellence on him who means evil to the sacrificer; but in this way he bestows that excellence on the sacrificer himself: for this reason he mixes (the butter in the guhû) with (that in) the dhruvâ.

7. He mixes it, with the text (Vâg. S. II, 9 h), 'Light with light!' for light (lustre), indeed, is the butter in the one (spoon) and light also is that in the other. Thereby these two lights unite with each other, and for this reason he mixes (the butter) in this manner.

8. Now a dispute once took place between Mind and Speech as to[2] which was the better of the two. Both Mind and Speech said, 'I am excellent!'

9. Mind said, 'Surely I am better than thou, for thou dost not speak anything that is not understood by me; and since thou art only an imitator of what is done by me and a follower in my wake, I am surely better than thou!'

10. Speech said, 'Surely I am better than thou, for what thou knowest I make known, I communicate.'

---

[1] The same idea has been expressed above, I, 3, 2, 11.

[2] Cf. Taitt. S. II, 5, 11, 4: 'Mind and Speech (or Voice) were contending against one another.' 'I will carry the oblation to the gods!' said Speech. 'I (will carry it) to the gods!' said the Mind. They went to Pragâpati to question him. Pragâpati said (to Speech), 'Thou art the handmaid (dûtî) of the mind, for what one thinks in one's mind that one speaks with one's speech.' [Speech replied], 'Then indeed they shall not offer to thee with speech!' For this reason they offer to Pragâpati with the mind; for Pragâpati, as it were, is the mind, &c.

11. They went to appeal to Pra*g*âpati for his decision. He, Pra*g*âpati, decided in favour of Mind, saying (to Speech), 'Mind is indeed better than thou, for thou art an imitator of its deeds and a follower in its wake; and inferior, surely, is he who imitates his better's deeds and follows in his wake.'

12. Then Speech (vâ*k*, fem.) being thus gainsaid, was dismayed and miscarried. She, Speech, then said to Pra*g*âpati, 'May I never be thy oblation-bearer, I whom thou hast gainsaid!' Hence whatever at the sacrifice is performed for Pra*g*âpati, that is performed in a low voice; for speech would not act as oblation-bearer for Pra*g*âpati.

13. That germ (retas) the gods then brought away in a skin or in some (vessel). They asked: 'Is it here (atra)?' and therefore it developed into Atri. For the same reason one becomes guilty by (intercourse) with a woman who has just miscarried (âtreyî); for it is from that woman, from the goddess Speech, that these (germs) originate[1].

FIFTH ADHYÂYA. FIRST BRÂHMA*N*A.

1. He (the Adhvaryu) now utters his call for the Pravara (choosing of the Hot*ri*)[2]. The reason why he utters his call, is that the (Adhvaryu's) call is

[1] 'Tasmâd apy âtreyyâ yoshitainasvy etasyai hi yoshâyai vâ*k*o devatâyâ ete sambhûtâ*h*,' [ete laukikâ*h* sarve garbhâ*h* sambhûtâ*h*, Sây.]—The Kâ*n*va text has, 'Tasmâd api striyâtreyyainasvîty âhur etasyâ hi sa yoshâyâ devatâyâ vâ*k*a*h* sambhûta iti' ['—for it is from that woman, from the goddess Speech, that he (Atri) originated'].

[2] The Hot*ri*, on concluding the invitation of the gods, sits down with raised knees in the same place where he has been standing (see p. 95, note 1), parts the sacrificial grass of the altar, and measures a span on the earth, with the text (Â*s*v. I, 3, 22), 'Aditi is his mother, do not cut him off from the air. With the aid of

the sacrifice: 'having bespoke the sacrifice, I will choose the Hotri,' thus (he thinks, and) for this reason he utters his call for the Pravara.

2. He utters his call after taking the fuel-band; for if the Adhvaryu were to utter his call without taking hold of the sacrifice, he would either be unsteady or meet with some other ailment.

3. Here now some utter the call after taking sacrificial grass (barhis) from the covered altar, or they utter the call after cutting off and taking a chip of fire-wood, arguing, 'this, surely, is something belonging to the sacrifice; after taking hold of this, the sacrifice, we will utter the call.' Let him, however, not do this; for that also wherewith the fire-wood was tied together and wherewith they sweep the fire[1] is, doubtless, something belonging to the sacrifice; and thus indeed he utters his call after taking hold of the sacrifice: for this reason let him utter the call after taking the fuel-band.

4. Having uttered the call, he in the first place chooses him who is the Hotri of the gods, that is, Agni. Thereby he propitiates both Agni and the gods: for by first choosing Agni, he propitiates Agni;

Agni, the god, the deity; with the threefold chant, with the râthantara-sâman, with the gâyatrî metre, with the agnishtoma sacrifice, with the vashat-call, the thunderbolt,—I here kill him who hates us, and whom we hate!' The Adhvaryu having thereupon walked round the Hotri from left to right, steps behind the utkara (heap of rubbish) with his face to the east and the fuel-band in his hand, and calls on (âsrâvayati) the Âgnîdhra, with Õ srâvaya (or Õm srâvaya, i.e. â srâvaya; or simply srâvaya;' cf. Sâyana on Taitt. S. I, 6, 11). The Âgnîdhra (whilst standing north of the Adhvaryu, with his face to the south, and taking the wooden sword and the fuel-band from the Adhvaryu) responds (pratyâsrâvayati) by 'astu sraushat.'

[1] See p. 127, note 1.

and by first choosing him who is the Hot*ri* of the gods, he propitiates the gods.

5. He says, 'Agni, the god, the divine Hot*ri*—,' for Agni is indeed the Hot*ri* of the gods, therefore he says 'Agni, the god, the divine Hot*ri*:' thereby he propitiates both Agni and the gods; for by his first mentioning Agni he propitiates Agni; and by his first mentioning him who is the Hot*ri* of the gods, he propitiates the gods.

6. 'May he worship, knowing the gods[1], he the thoughtful one,'—for he, Agni, indeed, knows the gods well: hence he thereby says 'may he who knows them well worship (them) in due form!'

7. 'Like as Manu (did), like as Bharata;'—Manu, indeed, worshipped with sacrifice in olden times, and doing as he did these descendants of his now sacrifice: therefore he says 'like as Manu.' Or, say they, (it means) 'at the sacrifice of Manu,' and therefore he says 'as (he did) with Manu.'

8. 'Like as (with) Bharata,'—for, say they, he bears (bhar) the oblation to the gods, hence Bharata (the bearer) is Agni; or, say they, he, having become the breath, supports (bhar) these creatures, and therefore he says 'like as Bharata.'

9. He then chooses (Agni as) the ancestral (Hot*ri*). He thus introduces him both to the (ancestral) *ri*shis and to the gods (as if he were saying), 'he is of mighty strength who obtained the sacrifice!' for this reason he chooses (him as) the ancestral one.

10. He chooses from the remote end (of the sacrificer's ancestral line)[2] downwards; for it is from the

[1] Thus our author. It should rather be 'May (he) worship the gods, he the wise, the considerate one.'

[2] Cf. p. 115, note 1.

remote end downwards that a race is propagated. Thereby he also propitiates the lord of seniority; for here among men the father comes first, then the son, and then the grandson: this is the reason why he chooses from the remote end downwards.

11. Having named the ancestral, he says, 'Like as Brahman;'—for Agni is the Brahman (the Veda, or the sacerdotium), and therefore he says 'like as Brahman;'—'may he bring (the gods) hither!' what deities he bids him bring hither, those he refers to in saying 'may he bring (them) hither.'

12. 'The Brâhmanas (priests) are the guardians of this sacrifice;' for guardians of the sacrifice, indeed, are those Brâhmanas who are versed in the sacred writ, because they spread it, they originate it: these he thereby propitiates; and for this reason he says, 'the Brâhmanas are the guardians of the sacrifice.'

13. 'N. N. is the man,' thereby he chooses this man for his Hotri; heretofore he was not a Hotri, but now he is a Hotri.

14. The chosen Hotri mutters,—has recourse to the deities: in order that he may give the vashat-call to the gods in its proper order, that he may convey the oblation to the gods in its proper order, that he may not stumble, he has thus recourse to the deities.

15. He mutters on this occasion[1], 'Thee, O divine Savitri, they now choose,'—thereby he has recourse to Savitri for his impulsion (prasava), for Savitri is the impeller (prasavitri) of the gods;—'(thee who art) Agni, for the Hotriship,' thereby he

[1] Except the beginning, these formulas are entirely different from those given by Âsv. S. I, 3, 23–24.

propitiates both Agni and the gods; for by first naming Agni, he propitiates Agni; and by first naming him who is the Hotri of the gods, he propitiates the gods.

16. 'Together with father Vaisvânara,'—for the father Vaisvânara ('common to all men'), doubtless, is the year, is Pragâpati (lord of creatures); hence he thereby propitiates the year and thus Pragâpati.—'O Agni! O Pûshan! O Brihaspati! speak forth and offer up sacrifice (pra-yag)!'—he (the Hotri), namely, will have to recite the anuvâkyâs and the yâgyâs [1]; he therefore now propitiates those gods: 'do ye recite, do ye offer!' thus (he thereby says).

17. 'May we partake of the bounty of the Vasus, of the wide sway of the Rudras! may we be beloved of the Âdityas for the sake of (aditi) security from injury, free from obstruction!'—these, to wit, the Vasus, Rudras, and Âdityas, namely, are three (classes of) gods: 'may we enjoy their protection' he thereby says.

18. 'May I this day utter speech that is agreeable to the gods;'—by this he means to say 'may I this day recite what is agreeable to the gods,' for auspicious it is when one recites what is agreeable to the gods.

19. 'Agreeable to the Brahmans,'—by this he means to say 'may I this day recite what is agreeable to the Brâhmanas (priests);' for auspicious it is when one recites what is agreeable to the Brâhmanas.

---

[1] The yâgyâs (offering-prayers) are the prayers which the Hotri pronounces when the offerings are poured into the fire (this being done simultaneously with, or immediately after, the vaushat, 'may he carry it,' with which the yâgyâ ends, is pronounced). At the chief oblations the offering-prayer is preceded by an anuvâkyâ or puro 'nuvâkyâ (invitatory prayer) by which the gods are invited to come to the offering, and which ends with 'om.'

20. 'Agreeable to Narâsamsa[1],'—man (nara), namely, is a creature: hence he says this for all the creatures; thereby it is auspicious, and whether or not he knows (forms of speech that are agreeable), they are uttered (and received with applause), 'well he has recited! well he has recited!'—'What at the Hotri choice may escape the crooked eye this day, that may Agni bring back here, he, the knower of beings (gâtavedas), the nimble one (vikarshani)!'—by this he means to say, 'even as those (three) Agnis, whom they first chose for the Hotriship, passed away[2], (but thou, the fourth Agni, wast then obtained,) so do thou make good for me whatever mistake may have been committed at my election!' and it is accordingly made good for him.

21. He now touches the Adhvaryu and the Âgnîdhra: for the Adhvaryu is the mind, and the Hotri is speech: thus he thereby brings mind and speech together.

22. At the same time he mutters[3], 'From anguish may the six spaces protect me, fire, earth, water, wind, day, and night[4]!'—'may these deities protect

[1] Narâsamsa ['the hope or desire (âsamsâ) of man (nara)'] is a mystical form of Agni, invoked chiefly in the Âprî-hymns at animal sacrifices. 'Yathâ sarve 'pi narâ â sarvatah samsanti tathâvidhâya.' Sâyana.

[2] See the legend I, 2, 3, 1 seq.

[3] This and the succeeding formulas also are entirely different from those given in Âsv. S. I, 3, 27 seq. The Sâṅkhây. S. I, 6 (Hillebrandt, Neu und Vollm. p. 91) seems to coincide, to some extent, with those given by our author.

[4] The six spaces or wide expanses (urvî) are several times referred to in Vedic texts, but the conception seems to have been very vague. They are generally supposed to include the space above, the space below, and the four quarters. In Rigveda VI, 47, 3-5 it is stated that they have been measured out

me from disease!' thus he thereby says; for he whom these deities protect from disease, will not stumble (or fail).

23. He steps beside the Hot*ri*'s seat, takes one stalk of (reed) grass from the Hot*ri*'s seat and casts it outside (the sacrificial ground), with the formula, 'Ejected is the wealth-clutcher (parâvasu, lit. "off-wealth")!' Formerly, namely, the Hot*ri* of the Asuras was one Parâvasu by name: him he thereby ejects from the Hot*ri*'s seat.

24. He then sits down on the Hot*ri*'s seat, with the formula, 'I here sit down on the seat of the wealth-bestower (arvâvasu, lit. "hither-wealth")!' for one Arvâvasu by name was the Hot*ri* of the gods [1], and on his seat he accordingly sits down.

25. At the same time he mutters, 'O All-maker, thou art the protector of lives! do not ye two (fires) scorch me away (from this) [2], injure me not! this

by Indra, and that outside of them there is no being (bhuvanam); and they are then enumerated thus: the expanse of the earth, the height (varshman, ? highest point or sphere) of the sky (div), the sap (pîyûsha) in the three elevations [? i.e. flowing, animating moisture, as rain, rivers, sap, &c.], the atmosphere, the ocean (? ar*n*as, ? of light, air), and the sky (div). The enumeration of six objects in Atharva-veda II, 12, 1 seems to refer to the same conception: heaven and earth (dyâvâp*ri*thivî), the wide atmospheric region, the genius (fem.) of the field (kshetrasya patnî), the far-strider (Sun, Light), the wide atmospheric region (uru-antariksham as before; cf. the double enumeration of div in the *Ri*k passage); and what has the Wind for its guardian (vâtagopa). Cf. Weber, Ind. Stud. XIII, p. 164. Sâṅkh. G*ri*hya-sûtra I, 6, 4 gives heaven and earth, day and night, water and plants (St. Petersburg Dictionary s.v.).

[1] According to the Kaushît. Br. VI, 10, Arvâvasu was the Brahman of the gods. Weber, Ind. Stud. II, 306.

[2] The Hot*ri*'s seat stands north of the north-west corner of the altar, the Âhavanîya and the Gârhapatya fires being about equidistant from it towards south-east and south-west respectively.

is your sphere;' with this he moves slightly northwards: by this (mantra, he indicates that) he sits midway between the Âhavanîya and the Gârhapatya, and thus he propitiates these two; and in accordance with what he says, 'do not scorch me away from this! injure me not!' they do not injure him.

26. He then mutters whilst looking at the (Âhavanîya) fire, 'All ye gods, instruct me, how and what I am to mind while seated here as the chosen Hotri! declare my share (of the sacrificial duties), how and by what road I am to convey the oblation to you!'—for as one says to those for whom food has been cooked, 'order me how I am to bring it you, how I am to serve it up for you!' in like manner he is desirous of directions regarding the gods, and for this reason he mutters thus, 'instruct me how I may utter the Vashat-call for you in its proper order, how I may bring you the oblation in its proper order!'

Second Brâhmana.

The Fore-offerings (Prayâgas).

1. [The Hotri continues], 'May Agni, the priest (hotri), know (undertake) Agni's priestly duty (hautram),'—thereby he says 'may Agni, as Hotri, know this!' 'Agni's priestly duty' he says, because it is his duty that he must know;—'that means of salvation [1],'—the means of salvation, assuredly, is the sacrifice: 'may he know the sacrifice' is what he thereby says.—'Favourable to thee, O Sacrificer, is

---

[1] Prâvitram, literally 'that which promotes, protects' ('unser Hort'). Sâyana on Taitt. S. II, 5, 9, 5 explains it by 'prakrishtam avitram phaladânarûpam asmadrakshanam yasmin homânushthâne tad idam prâvitram.' For this and the succeeding formulas, see Âsv. I, 4, 10–11.

the deity!' by this he says 'favourable is the deity to thee, O Sacrificer, whose Hotri is Agni[1]!'—'Take up[2] the spoon, O Adhvaryu, full of butter!' thereby he urges on the Adhvaryu. The reason why he mentions one (spoon) only (is this).

2. The Sacrificer, doubtless, stands behind the guhû, and he, who means evil to him, stands behind the upabhrit; and if he were to speak of two (spoons), he would cause the spiteful enemy to countervail the Sacrificer. Behind the guhû stands the eater, and behind the upabhrit the one to be eaten; and if he were to speak of two (spoons), he would make the one to be eaten countervail the eater. For these reasons he speaks of one (spoon) only.

3. [He continues], '—(the spoon which is) devoted to the gods, possessed of all boons,' he praises, he magnifies it when he says 'devoted to the gods, possessed of all boons.'—'Let us praise the gods, the praiseworthy! let us adore the adorable! let us worship the worshipful!' that is, 'let us praise those gods who are praiseworthy! let us adore those who are adorable! let us worship those who are worthy of worship!' the praiseworthy, to wit, are the men, the adorable the fathers, and the worshipful the gods.

4. For, indeed, the creatures that are not allowed to take part in the sacrifice are forlorn; and therefore

---

[1] Âsv. I, 4, 10, and Sânkh. I, 6 give as belonging to the text of the mantra: yo agnim hotâram avrithâh, 'thou who hast chosen Agni for thy Hotri;' the same reading is mentioned in Taitt. S. II, 5, 9, 5.

[2] Thus Sâyana (âsyasva=haste dhâraya); 'schöpfe ein (ladle in),' St. Petersburg Dictionary; 'pour into the fire,' Hillebrandt, p. 93.

he makes those creatures here on earth that are not forlorn, take part in the sacrifice: behind the men are the beasts, and behind the gods are the birds, the plants, and the trees; and thus all that here exists is made to take part in the sacrifice.

5. These same (preceding formulas) are nine utterances; for nine, in number, are those breaths (or vital airs) in man[1], and these he thereby puts into him (the sacrificer): for this reason there are nine utterances.

6. The sacrifice fled away from the gods. The gods called out after it, 'Listen (â-sru) to us[2]! come back to us!' It replied, 'So be it!' and returned to the gods; and with what had thus returned to them, the gods worshipped; and by worshipping with it they became the gods they now are.

7. Now when he (the Adhvaryu) calls (on the Âgnîdhra), he thereby calls after the sacrifice, 'Listen to us! come back to us!' and when he (the Âgnîdhra) responds, then the sacrifice comes back, saying 'so be it!' and with it, thus passing over to them, as with seed[3], the priests carry on the tradition, imperceptibly to the sacrificer; for even as people hand on from one to the other a full vessel[4], in

---

[1] See p. 20, note 1.

[2] The legend is intended to explain the origin and symbolical meaning of the call (âsrâvana) of the Adhvaryu (viz. O srâvaya! 'make listen!') and the response (pratyâsravana) of the Âgnîdhra (viz. astu sraushat!).

[3] The sacrifice is the seed (vîga) that produces heaven as its fruit. Sâyana.

[4] I. e. 'even as they pass on from hand to hand a pail (ghata) filled with water when a tub is to be filled inside the house.' Sâyana.

the same way they (the priests) hand down that (sacrifice) from one to the other. They hand it down by means of speech, for the sacrifice is speech (prayer), and speech is seed: therefore they keep up the tradition by means of it.

8. After he has said (to the Hotri), 'Recite!' the Adhvaryu must utter nothing improper (worldly); neither must the Hotri utter anything improper. The Adhvaryu[1] utters his call: thereby the sacrifice passes on to the Âgnîdhra.

9. The Âgnîdhra must utter nothing improper until his response. The Âgnîdhra responds: thereby the sacrifice passes back to the Adhvaryu.

10. The Adhvaryu must utter nothing improper until he pronounces (the word) 'yaga (recite the offering-prayer):' in saying 'yaga the Adhvaryu hands the sacrifice on to the Hotri.

11. The Hotri must utter nothing improper until his vashat-call. By the vashat-call he pours it (the sacrifice) into the fire, as seed into the womb; for the fire is indeed the womb of the sacrifice, from thence it is brought forth. So now at the havis-sacrifice. And at the Soma-cult,—

12. When he has drawn (the Soma), the Adhvaryu must not utter anything improper until his summons

[1] As soon as the Hotri has pronounced the formula 'O Adhvaryu, take up the spoon full of butter!' (par. 2 above), the Adhvaryu takes the two offering-spoons (guhû and upabhrit) and steps back (from the west side along the north side of the altar and the west side of the fire) to the south side of the altar and the fire (the yagati-sthâna), and (with his face to north-east) utters his call, and (having been responded to by the Âgnîdhra) calls on the Hotri: 'samidho yaga (pronounce the offering-prayer to the kindling-sticks)!' Kâty. III, 2, 16.

(for the chanting of the stotra[1]): with the call 'draw near!' the Adhvaryu hands the sacrifice on to the Udgâtris (chanters).

13. The Udgâtris must not utter anything improper until the last (stotra-verse): 'this is the last one,' thus thinking, the Udgâtris hand on the sacrifice to the Hotri.

14. The Hotri must utter nothing improper until the vashat-call. With the vashat-call he pours it (the sacrifice) into the fire, as seed into the womb; for the fire is indeed the womb of the sacrifice, since from thence it is brought forth.

15. If he whom the sacrifice approaches were to utter anything improper, he would waste the sacrifice, even as he might waste (water by spilling from) a full vessel. And where the officiating priests thus practice sacrifice with a perfect mutual understanding between them, there everything works regularly and no hitch occurs: therefore it is in this way that the sacrifice must be nursed.

16. Now there are here five utterances, viz. (1) 'Bid (him, Agni, or them) hear!' (2) 'Yea, may he (or, one) hear!' (3) 'Pronounce the prayer to the kindling-sticks!' (4) 'We who pronounce the prayer . . .' (5) 'May he bear (the sacrifice to the gods)[2]!' fivefold is the sacrifice, fivefold the animal victim, five are the seasons of the year: this is the one measure of the sacrifice, this its consummation.

---

[1] See IV, 2, 5, 7–8.

[2] (1) O srâvaya (for â srâvaya), the Adhvaryu's call; (2) astu sraushat, the Âgnîdhra's response; (3) (samidho) yaga, the Adhvaryu's summons to the Hotri; (4) ye yagâmahe, the beginning of the Hotri's yâgyâ, or offering-prayer (see p. 135 note); (5) vaushat, concluding formula of the yâgyâ.

17. These (five formulas) consist of seventeen syllables;—seventeenfold, indeed, is Pragâpati, and Pragâpati is the sacrifice: this is the one measure of the sacrifice, this its consummation.

18. With 'O srâvaya[1]!' the gods sent forth the east wind; with 'Astu sraushat[1]!' they caused the clouds to flow together; with 'Yaga (pronounce the yâgyâ)!' (they sent forth) the lightning; with 'Ye yagâmahe (we who pray),' the thunder; with the vashat-call they caused it to rain[2].

19. Should he (the sacrificer) be desirous of rain, or should he perform a special offering[3], or even at the new- and full-moon sacrifice itself, he may say, 'Verily, I am desirous of rain!'—and he may also say to the Adhvaryu, 'Ponder thou in thy mind the east wind and the lightning!'—to the Âgnîdhra, 'Ponder thou the clouds in thy mind!'—to the Hotri, 'Ponder thou in thy mind the thunder and rain!'—to the Brahman, 'Ponder thou all these in thy mind!'—for where the officiating priests thus practice sacrifice with a perfect mutual understanding between them, there it will indeed rain.

20. With 'O srâvaya!' the gods called the shining one (virâg, viz. cow), with 'Astu sraushat!' they untied the calf and let it go to her; with 'Yaga!' they raised (its head to the udder of the cow)[4]; with

---

[1] For âsrâvaya (cf. p. 131, note 2), i.e. 'bid (him, Agni, or them) hear!' but the author here makes srâvaya the causative of sru (sru), 'to flow;' hence â srâvaya, 'make flow;' and astu sraushat [properly 'Yea, may he (or one) hear!'] he makes 'Yea, may it flow!'

[2] A fanciful etymology of vashat from root vrish, 'to rain;' for the true derivation of the word, see p. 88, note 2.

[3] I. e. an offering made with a view to the obtainment of some special wish (kâmyeshti).

[4] Thus (or 'they led it up to the udder of the cow') Sâyana

'Ye yagâmahe!' they sat down by her (for milking); with the vashat-call they milked her. The shining one, doubtless, is this (earth), and of her this is the milking: and for him who knows this to be the milking of the shining one, this shining (earth-cow) thus milks out all his desires.

THIRD BRÂHMANA.

1. The fore-offerings (prayâga), assuredly, are the seasons: hence there are five of them, for there are five seasons.

2. The gods and the Asuras, both of them sprang from Pragâpati, were once contending for this sacrifice, (which is) their father Pragâpati, the year: 'Ours it (he) shall be!' 'Ours it (he) shall be!' they said.

3. Then the gods went on praising and toiling. They saw these fore-offerings and worshipped with them. By means of them they gained (pra-gi) the seasons, the year; they deprived their rivals of the seasons, of the year: hence (the fore-offerings are) victories (pragaya), for, assuredly, pragaya is the very same term as prayâga (fore-offering)[1]. And in the same way this one (the sacrificer) wins by means of them the seasons, the year; deprives his rivals of the seasons, of the year. This is the reason why he performs the fore-offerings.

4. The sacrificial food at these offerings consists of

explains udanayan. In his commentary on Taitt. S. I, 6, 11 he interprets the analogous udanaishît by 'he raises (or brings) the milk-pail;' where the St. Petersburg Dictionary apparently takes it in the sense of 'he led the calf away from the cow.'

[1] In reality prayâga (from yag, 'to sacrifice') has, of course, nothing to do with pragaya (from gi, 'to conquer').

clarified butter. Now the butter, indeed, is a thunderbolt, and with that thunderbolt, the butter, the gods gained the seasons, the year, and deprived their rivals of the seasons, of the year. And with that thunderbolt, the butter, he now, in the same way, gains the seasons, the year, and deprives his enemies of the seasons, of the year. For this reason clarified butter forms the sacrificial food at these (offerings).

5. Now this butter is the year's own liquor: hence the gods gained it (the year) by means of its own liquor; and in the same way he also now gains it by means of its own liquor. This is the reason why clarified butter forms the sacrificial food at these (fore-offerings).

6. Let him (the Adhvaryu) not move from that same spot where he may be standing when he calls for the fore-offerings. A battle, it is true, is witnessed whenever any one performs the fore-offerings, and whichever of the two combatants is worsted, that one, no doubt, retreats; and he who obtains the victory, advances still nearer: he (the Adhvaryu) might therefore (feel inclined to) step nearer and nearer (to the fire), and offer the oblations (while moving) nearer and nearer[1].

7. This, however, he should not do; he should not move from that same spot where he may be standing when he calls for the fore-offerings. Let

[1] Though the author does not state expressly that this change of position in performing the five fore-offerings is advocated by some other ritualists, he apparently argues in this passage against an actually adopted theory and practice, which the Sûtras also mention as optional. In the case of the Adhvaryu changing his position, he is at each successive fore-offering to pour the butter on a part of the fire east of the preceding one. Kâty. III, 2, 18-21.

him rather offer the (five) oblations in that part (of the fire) where he thinks there is the fiercest blaze; for only by being offered in blazing (fire), oblations are successful.

8. He (the Adhvaryu), having called (on, and having been responded to by, the Âgnîdhra), says (to the Hotri), 'Pronounce the offering-prayer (yâgyâ) to the Samidhs (kindling-sticks)!' Thereby he kindles the spring; the spring, when kindled, kindles the other seasons; the seasons, when kindled, generate the creatures and ripen the plants. In the same (formula) he also implies the (four) remaining seasons, and in order to avoid sameness, he introduces the others by merely saying each time, 'Pronounce the offering-prayer!' For were he to say, 'Pronounce the offering-prayer to Tanûnapât!' 'Pronounce the offering-prayer to the Ids!' and so on, he would commit (the fault of) repetition: hence he introduces the remaining (seasons or fore-offerings) by merely saying each time, 'Pronounce the offering-prayer[1]!'

9. He (the Hotri) now pronounces the offering-prayer (yâgyâ) to the Samidhs. The samidh (kindler), doubtless, is the spring. The gods, at that time, appropriated the spring, and deprived their rivals of the spring; and now this one (the

[1] On the necessity of avoiding sameness of ritualistic practices cf. note on I, 3, 2, 8. The five fore-offerings (prayâga, here identified with the five seasons) are addressed respectively to the kindling-sticks (samidh), to Tanûnapât (or Narâsamsa, both mystical forms of Agni), to the Ids (personifications of the forms of devotional feeling), to the sacrificial grass-covering of the altar (barhis), and to Agni and Soma (or other deities). Since, in introducing the first fore-offering, the Adhvaryu has mentioned its recipient, he is not to do so in the case of the remaining four.

sacrificer) also appropriates the spring, and deprives his rivals of the spring: this is the reason why he pronounces the offering-prayer to the Samidhs.

10. After that he pronounces the offering-prayer to Tanûnapât. Tanûnapât, doubtless, is the summer; for the summer burns the bodies (tanûn tapati) of these creatures. The gods, at that time, appropriated the summer, and deprived their rivals of the summer; and now this one also appropriates the summer, and deprives his rivals of the summer: this is the reason why he pronounces the offering-prayer to Tanûnapât.

11. He then pronounces the offering-prayer to the I*d*s. The I*d*s (praises), doubtless, are the rains; they are the rains, inasmuch as the vile, crawling (vermin)[1] which shrink during the summer and winter, then (in the rainy season) move about in quest of food, as it were, praising (î*d*) the rains: therefore the I*d*s are the rains. The gods, at that time, appropriated the rains, and deprived their rivals of the rains; and now this one also appropriates the rains, and deprives his rivals of the rains: this is the reason why he pronounces the offering-prayer to the I*d*s.

12. He then pronounces the offering-prayer to the Barhis (covering of sacrificial grass on the altar). The barhis, doubtless, is the autumn; the barhis is the autumn, inasmuch as these plants which shrink during the summer and winter grow by the rains, and in autumn lie spread open after the fashion of barhis: for this reason the barhis is the autumn. The gods, at that time, appropriated the autumn, and deprived their rivals of the autumn;

[1] Such as lizards, alligators. Sâya*n*a.

and now this one also appropriates the autumn, and deprives his rivals of the autumn: this is why he pronounces the prayer to the barhis.

13. He then pronounces the offering-prayer with 'Svâhâ! Svâhâ[1]!' The Svâhâ-call, namely, marks the end of the sacrifice, and the end of the year is the winter, since the winter is on the other (remoter) side of the spring. By the end (of the sacrifice) the gods, at that time, appropriated the end (of the year); by the end they deprived their rivals of the end; and by the end this one also now appropriates the end; by the end he deprives his rivals of the end: this is why he pronounces the offering-prayers with 'Svâhâ! Svâhâ!'

14. Now the spring, assuredly, comes into life again out of the winter, for out of the one the other is born again: therefore he who knows this, is indeed born again in this world.

15. In order to avoid sameness he prays (alternately) with 'may they accept!' and 'may he (or it) accept[2]!' for he would commit (the fault) of repe-

---

[1] See further on, par. 22. As to Svâhâ! marking the conclusion of the sacrifice, see the Samishtayagus I, 9, 2, 25–28.

[2] The first offering-prayer (to the logs) is 'yê yagâmahe samidhah, samidho agna âgyasya vyantû vâushat!' i.e. 'we who pronounce the offering-prayer to the Samidhs,—the Samidhs, O Agni, may accept the butter! vâushat!' Similarly at the other fore-offerings; but at the second and fourth, where the object of worship is a single one (viz. Tanûnapât and the Barhis respectively), 'may he (or it) accept (vetu)!' has to be substituted for 'may they accept (vyantu)!' The difference of number in these verbal forms is symbolically explained as implying a distinction of sex, for the reason that there may be more wives to one man, but only one husband to a woman. The elliptic expression ye yagâmahe is thus explained by Sâyana on Taitt. S. I, 6, 11: 'All we Hotri priests that are urged on by the Adhvaryu calling "Recite (thou)!" we do recite, we do pronounce

tition, if he were to pray with 'may they accept!' each time, or with 'may he accept!' each time. By 'may they accept!' doubtless, females (are implied); and by 'may he accept!' a male (is implied): thereby a productive union is effected, and for this reason he prays (alternately) with 'may they accept!' and 'may he (or it) accept!'

16. Now at the fourth fore-offering, to the barhis, he pours (butter) together (into the *g*uhû[1]). The barhis, namely, represents descendants, and the butter seed: hence seed is thereby infused into the descendants, and by that infused seed descendants are generated again and again. For this reason he pours together (butter) at the fourth fore-offering, that to the barhis.

17. Now, a battle, as it were, is going on here when any one performs the fore-offerings; and whichever of the two combatants a friend (an ally) joins, he obtains the victory: hence a friend thereby joins the *g*uhû from out of the upabh*ri*t, and by him it (or he) obtains the victory. This is why he pours together (butter) at the fourth fore-offering, that to the barhis.

18. The sacrificer, doubtless, (stands) behind the *g*uhû, and he who means evil to him, (stands)

---

the yâ*g*yâ.' This introductory part of the offering-formula is called âgur, 'acclamation, assent' (Âsv. I, 5, 4); it is alluded to in Mahâbhâr. Vanap. 12480 (cf. Muir, O. S. T. I, p. 135), and apparently by Pâ*n*. VIII, 2, 88 (cf. Haug, Ait. Br. II, p. 133 n.).

[1] In making the oblation, the Adhvaryu holds the *g*uhû over the upabh*ri*t and pours some of the butter from the *g*uhû over the spout of the upabh*ri*t into the fire. At the third prayâ*g*a he empties all the butter remaining in the *g*uhû into the fire, and thereupon, for the fourth oblation, replenishes the empty spoon with half the contents of the upabh*ri*t, after which he proceeds as before.

behind the upabhrit: hence he thereby makes the spiteful enemy pay tribute to the sacrificer. The consumer, doubtless, (stands) behind the guhû, and the one to be consumed behind the upabhrit: hence he thereby makes the one that is to be consumed pay tribute to the consumer. This is the reason why he pours (butter) together at the fourth fore-offering, that to the barhis.

19. He pours (the butter) together without (the two spoons) touching (each other). If he were to touch (the one spoon with the other) he would touch the sacrificer with his spiteful enemy, he would touch the consumer with the one to be consumed: for this reason he pours (the butter) together without touching.

20. He holds the guhû over the upabhrit). Thereby he keeps the sacrificer above his spiteful enemy, he keeps the consumer above the one to be consumed: for this reason he holds the guhû over (the upabhrit).

21. The gods once said, 'Well then, now that the battle has been won, let us establish the entire sacrifice on a firm basis; and should the Asuras and Rakshas (again) trouble us, our sacrifice will then be firmly established!'

22. At the last fore-offering they established the entire sacrifice by means of the Svâhâ ('hail!'). With 'Svâhâ Agni!' they established the butter-portion for Agni; with 'Svâhâ Soma!' they established the butter-portion for Soma; and with (the second) 'Svâhâ Agni!' they established that indispensable sacrificial cake which there is on both occasions (i.e. at the new- and full-moon sacrifices).

23. And so with the (other) deities respec-

tively[1]. With 'Svâhâ the butter-drinking gods!' they established the fore-offerings and the after-offerings (anuyâgas), for the fore-offerings and after-offerings, doubtless, represent the butter-drinking gods. With the formula 'May Agni graciously accept of the butter!' they established Agni as Svishtakrit ('maker of good offering'), for Agni is indeed the maker of good offering. And till this day that sacrifice stands as firm as the gods established it. This is the reason why at the last fore-offering he prays with 'Svâhâ! Svâhâ!' according to the number of oblations (there are at the chief sacrifice). After he (the sacrificer) has won his battle, he establishes the entire sacrifice on a firm basis, so that, if after this he should violate the proper order of the sacrifice, he need not heed it; for he will know that his sacrifice is firmly established. Now what with exclaiming 'Vashat,' with offering, and with calling out 'Svâhâ,' this same sacrifice was well-nigh exhausted.

24. The gods were anxious as to how they might replenish it, how they might again render it efficient and practise (worshipping) with it, when efficient.

25. Now what was left in the guhû of the butter wherewith they had established the sacrifice, with that they sprinkled the havis (dishes, or kinds, of sacrificial food) one after another, and thereby replenished them and again rendered them efficient, because the butter is indeed efficient. Hence after offering the last fore-offering, he sprinkles the havis one after another, and thereby replenishes them and again renders them efficient, because the butter is indeed efficient[2]. Hence also from whatever sacrificial

[1] Cf. p. 118, note 3. The words 'Svâhâ Agnim' &c. are preceded by 'ye yagâmahe,' see before, p. 148, note 2.

[2] After the Adhvaryu has performed the last fore-offering, he

food he (afterwards at the principal oblations) cuts off (a portion for a deity), that he again sprinkles (with butter), that he replenishes and renders efficient for the (Svishtakrit) maker of good offering. But when he cuts off the portion for the maker of good offering, then he does not again sprinkle (the sacrificial food out of which the portion has been cut), since after that he will not make any other oblation in the fire from the sacrificial food[1].

FOURTH BRÂHMANA.

1. He (accordingly) pronounces the offering-prayer to the Samidhs (kindling-sticks). The Samidhs (kindlers), doubtless, are the breaths (vital airs), and he thereby kindles the breaths; for this man (the sacrificer) is kindled (animated) by his breaths: hence if he (the sacrificer) be burning (with fever, &c.), he (the Adhvaryu) will say, 'Stroke (thyself)!' If he be hot, then one may feel confident, for then he is kindled; and if he be cold, then one need hope no longer. Thus he thereby puts the breaths into him: this is the reason why he pronounces the prayer to the Samidhs.

2. He then pronounces the offering-prayer to Tanûnapât. Tanûnapât, doubtless, is seed; hence he thereby casts seed: this is why he pronounces the prayer to Tanûnapât.

---

steps back behind the altar and sitting down beside the dishes of sacrificial food, anoints, with the butter remaining in the guhû, first the (butter in the) dhruvâ, then the several sacrificial dishes, and finally the (butter in the) upabhrit. Kâty. III, 3, 9.

[1] What remains of the dish of sacrificial food, after the oblation to Agni Svishtakrit (I, 7, 3, 1 seq.) has been made, is eaten by the priests and the sacrificer, and in their case the several portions are basted with butter, as they are cut off, but not the dish of food from which the portions have been taken.

3. He then pronounces the offering-prayer to the *Id*s. The *Id*s, doubtless, are offspring; when the seed thus cast springs into life, then it moves about in quest of food, as it were, praising (*îd*). Hence he thereby makes him (the sacrificer) propagate offspring: this is the reason why he pronounces the prayer to the *Id*s.

4. He then pronounces the offering-prayer to the Barhis. The barhis, doubtless, means abundance, hence he thereby produces an abundance: this is why he pronounces the prayer to the barhis.

5. He then pronounces the offering-prayer with 'Svâhâ! Svâhâ!' The Svâhâ-call, indeed, is what the winter is among the seasons; for the winter subjects these creatures to its will: hence in winter the plants wither, and the leaves fall off the trees; the birds retire more and more, and fly lower and lower; and the wicked man has his hair, as it were, falling off[1]; for the winter subjects these creatures to its will. And, verily, he who knows this, makes that locality wherein he lives, his own, for his own happiness and supply of food.

6. The gods and the Asuras, both of them sprung from Pra*g*âpati, were once contending for superiority. With staves and bows neither party were able to overcome the other. Neither of them having gained the victory, they (the Asuras) said, 'Well then, let us try to overcome one another by speech, by sacred writ (brahman)! He who cannot follow up our uttered speech by (making up) a pair, shall be defeated and lose everything, and the other party

[1] The Kâ*n*va recension has, 'the beasts retire more and more, and the birds fly lower and lower; and the vile-caste man (pâpavar*n*a*h* purusha*h*) has his hair, as it were, falling off.'

shall win everything!' The gods replied, 'So be it!' The gods said to Indra, 'Speak thou!'

7. Indra said, 'One (eka, m., unus) for me!' The others then said, 'One (ekâ, f., una) for us!' and thus found that (desired) pair, for eka (unus) and ekâ (una) make a pair.

8. Indra said, 'Two (dvau, m., duo) for me!' The others then said, 'Two (dve, f., duae) for us!' and thus found that pair, for dvau (duo) and dve (duae) make a pair.

9. Indra said, 'Three (trayah, m.) for me!' The others then said, 'Three (tisrah, f.) for us!' and thus found that pair, for trayah and tisrah make a pair.

10. Indra said, 'Four (katvârah, m.) for me!' The others then said, 'Four (katasrah, f.) for us!' and thus found that pair, for katvârah and katasrah make a pair.

11. Indra said, 'Five (pañka, m. f., quinque) for me!' Then the others found no pair, for after that (numeral four) there is no pair, for then both (masculine and feminine) are pañka. Thereupon the Asuras were defeated and lost everything, and the gods won everything from the Asuras, and stripped their rivals, the Asuras, of everything.

12. For this reason let him (the sacrificer) say[1], when the first fore-offering has been performed, 'One (eka) for me!' and 'One (ekâ) for him whom

[1] Viz. as anumantrana, or after-call, supplementary prayer, pronounced immediately after the oblation has been poured into the fire. According to Kâty. III, 3, 5, a second anumantrana has to be added each time, consisting of a single word, viz. 'brilliant,' 'respectable,' 'famous,' 'holy,' 'an eater of food' [suppl. 'may I become'] respectively. Differently the Black Yagus; cf. Hillebrandt, p. 96, note 6.

we hate!' And if he should not hate any one, let him say, 'who hates us and whom we hate!'

13. With the second fore-offering, 'Two (dvau) for me!' and 'Two (dve) for him who hates us and whom we hate!'

14. With the third fore-offering, 'Three (trayah) for me!' and 'Three (tisrah) for him who hates us and whom we hate!'

15. With the fourth fore-offering, 'Four (katvârah) for me!' and 'Four (katasrah) for him who hates us and whom we hate!'

16. With the fifth fore-offering, 'Five (pañka) for me!' and 'Nothing for him who hates us and whom we hate!' For, there being 'five' to 'five,' he (the enemy) is defeated, and whoever knows this, appropriates to himself everything that belongs to that (enemy of his), strips his enemies of everything.

SIXTH ADHYÂYA. FIRST BRÂHMANA.

1. Now the Seasons were desirous to have a share in the sacrifice among the gods, and said, 'Let us share in the sacrifice! Do not exclude us from the sacrifice! Let us have a share in the sacrifice!'

2. The gods, however, did not approve of this. The gods not approving, the Seasons went to the Asuras, the malignant, spiteful enemies of the gods.

3. Those (Asuras) then throve in such a manner that they (the gods) heard of it; for even while the foremost (of the Asuras) were still ploughing and sowing, those behind them were already engaged in reaping and threshing: indeed even without tilling the plants ripened forthwith for them.

4. This now caused anxiety to the gods: 'That owing to that (desertion of the Seasons), enemy

(viz. the Asuras) seeks to injure enemy (viz. us) is of little consequence; but this indeed goes too far: try to find out how henceforth this may be different[1]!'

5. They then said, 'Let us invite the Seasons!'—'How?'—'Let us offer prayer to them first of all at the sacrifice!'

6. Agni then said, 'But whereas hitherto you used to offer prayer to me in the first place, what is now to become of me?' 'We will not remove you from your place!' said they. And since, in inviting the Seasons, they did not remove Agni from his place, for that reason Agni is immutable[2]; and verily, he who knows that Agni to be immutable, does not move from the place where he bides.

7. The gods said to Agni, 'Go and invite them hither!' Agni went to them and said, 'O Seasons, I have obtained for you a share in the sacrifice among the gods.' They said, 'In what form hast thou obtained it for us?' He replied, 'They will offer prayer to you first at the sacrifice.'

8. The Seasons said to Agni, 'We will let thee share along with us in the sacrifice who hast obtained for us a share in the sacrifice among the gods!' And because Agni has been allowed a share along with the Seasons (the offering-prayers are): 'The Samidhs, O Agni, (may accept the butter)[3]...!'

---

[1] 'Kanîya in nv ato dvishan dvishate 'râtîyati kim v etâvanmâtram upagânîta yathedam ito 'nyathâsad iti.' The Kânva MS. has, 'tad u vai devânâm atathâsa kanîya in nu tato dvishan dvishate 'râtîyed atha kim tâvanmâtram. Te hokuh katham idam ito no 'nyathâ syâd iti.'

[2] Akyuta, literally 'not fallen,' hence invariable, indispensable is an epithet frequently applied to Agni's sacrificial cake; cf. I, 4, 2, 16; I, 6, 2, 5.

[3] See p. 148, note 2.

'Tanûnapât, O Agni . . . !' 'The Ids, O Agni . . . !' 'The Barhis, O Agni . . . !' 'Svâhâ Agni!' And verily, whosoever knows that Agni is thus allowed to share (in the sacrifice) along with the Seasons, he is allowed to participate in whatever auspicious rite is performed by one who professes to be equal (in that knowledge) to him;—for him, being possessed of Agni, the Seasons, themselves possessed of Agni, ripen the plants and everything here.

9. Now, as to this point, some raise the objection, 'But since they invite the fore-offerings last of all (at the two libations of butter)[1], why do they offer prayer to them first of all?'—Because they established them last of all in the sacrifice[2]; and because they said, 'we will offer prayer to you first:' for that reason they invite them last, and offer prayer to them first.

10. By the fourth fore-offering the gods, assuredly, obtained the sacrifice, and by the fifth they firmly established it; and by what part of the sacrifice after that remained unaccomplished they gained the world of heaven.

11. In going to heaven they were afraid of an attack from the Asuras and Rakshas. They placed Agni at their head, as the Rakshas-killer, the repeller of the Rakshas; they placed Agni in their midst, as the Rakshas-killer, the repeller of the Rakshas; they placed Agni in their rear, as the Rakshas-killer, the repeller of the Rakshas.

---

[1] In the devatânâm âvahanam or invitation of the deities, the last formula, addressed to the butter-drinking deities, is supposed to refer to the fore- and after-offerings. Cf. I, 4, 2, 16–17.

[2] See I, 5, 3, 23.

12. And if the Asuras and Rakshas wished to attack them in front, Agni repelled them, as the Rakshas-killer, the repeller of the Rakshas; if they wished to attack in the centre, Agni repelled them, as the Rakshas-killer, the repeller of the Rakshas; and if they wished to attack in the rear, Agni repelled them, as the Rakshas-killer, the repeller of the Rakshas: being thus guarded on all sides by Agnis, they reached the world of heaven.

13. And in the same way this one now obtains the sacrifice by means of the fourth fore-offering, and by means of the fifth he establishes it; and by what part of the sacrifice after that remains unaccomplished, he gains the world of heaven.

14. Now when he pronounces the offering-prayer over Agni's butter-portion, he thereby places Agni in front, as the Rakshas-killer, the repeller of the Rakshas; and when Agni's sacrificial cake is (offered), he thereby places Agni in the midst, as the Rakshas-killer, the repeller of the Rakshas; and when he pronounces the offering-prayer to Agni Svish*t*akr*i*t (the maker of good offering), he thereby places Agni in the rear, as the Rakshas-killer, the repeller of the Rakshas.

15. And if the Asuras and Rakshas try to attack him (the sacrificer) in front, Agni repels them, as the Rakshas-killer, the Repeller of the Rakshas: if they try to attack him in the centre, Agni repels them, as the Rakshas-killer, the repeller of the Rakshas; and if they try to attack him from behind, Agni repels them, as the Rakshas-killer, the repeller of the Rakshas: being thus guarded on every side by Agnis, he gains the world of heaven.

16. And if any one were to imprecate evil on him

previously to (or, in the fore-part of) the (chief) sacrifice, let him be thus spoken to, 'Thou shalt suffer some disease of the face! thou shalt become either blind or deaf!' for these, in truth, are diseases of the face: and thus it would indeed fare with him.

17. If any one were to imprecate evil on him in the middle of the sacrifice, let him be thus spoken to, 'Thou shalt be without offspring, without cattle!' for offspring and cattle, indeed, constitute the centre (i.e. the substantial possession of man): and thus it would indeed fare with him.

18. If any one were to imprecate evil on him after the completion of the (chief) sacrifice, let him be thus spoken to, 'Unstable and poor, thou shalt swiftly go to yonder world!' for thus it would indeed fare with him. One should not therefore utter imprecations: for whosoever thus understands this has the advantage.

19. He who gains by means of the fore-offerings, assuredly, gains the year[1]. But he alone gains it who knows its doors; for what were he to do with a house who cannot find his way inside? Even as those (fore-offerings) are (the doors) of this (sacrifice), so is the spring a door, and so is the winter a door, of that (year). This same year he enters, as the world of heaven; for, assuredly, the year is all, and the All (universe) is imperishable: his thereby becomes imperishable merit, the imperishable world.

THE TWO BUTTER-PORTIONS (ÂGYABHÂGA) TO AGNI AND SOMA.

20. Here now some say, 'To what deity belong the butter-portions?' Let him reply, 'To Pragâpati;'

---

[1] See I, 5, 3, 3.

for, assuredly, Pragâpati is undefined[1] (mysterious); and undefined are the butter-portions, because they have the sacrificer for their deity; for the sacrificer is Pragâpati at his own sacrifice, since it is by his order that the priests spread and produce it.

21. Having basted the havis with butter and made two cuttings from it, he pours some of the butter thereon: thus the oblation is offered combined with butter, and thereby indeed it is offered combined with the sacrificer; and for one who knows this,—whether he has a sacrifice performed for him while he is far away, or while he is near,—the sacrifice is performed in the same way as it would be performed if he were near; and he who knows this, even though he do much evil, is not shut out from the sacrifice.

SECOND BRÂHMANA.

1. Verily, by means of the sacrifice the gods made that conquest (of the world of heaven). When they had conquered, they said, 'How may this (celestial region) be made unattainable by men?' They then sipped the sap of the sacrifice, as bees would suck out honey; and having drained the sacrifice and effaced the traces of it with the (sacrificial) post[2], they

[1] Because he (? as lord of creatures) represents all the deities, and one cannot say 'he is such or such a one,' Sâyana. Cf. also I, 1, 1, 12.

[2] Yûpena yopâyitvâ, literally 'having made it level by means of the yûpa,'=yûpenâkkhâdya, 'having covered it over with the yûpa,' Sâyana (cf. also on Rig-veda I, 104, 4). For other versions of the same myth, cf. Ait. Br. II, 1 ['they debarred them (ayopayan, viz. the men and Rishis from the sacrificial knowledge) by means of the yûpa,' Haug]; Taitt. S. VI, 3, 4, 7;

concealed themselves: and because they effaced (ayopayan, viz. the sacrifice) with it, therefore it is called yûpa (sacrificial post). Now this was heard by the *Ri*shis:

2. 'Verily, by means of the sacrifice the gods gained this conquest. When they had conquered, they said, "How may this (celestial region) be made unattainable by men?" They then sipped the sap of the sacrifice, as bees would suck out honey; and having drained the sacrifice and effaced the traces of it with the (sacrificial) post, they concealed themselves.' They (the *Ri*shis) thereupon set about searching for it.

3. They went on praising and toiling; for by (religious) toil, the gods indeed gained what they wished to gain, and (so did) the *Ri*shis. Now whether it be that the gods caused it (the sacrifice) to attract (or, peep forth to) them, or whether they took to it of their own accord, they said, 'Come, let us go to the place whence the gods obtained possession of the world of heaven!' They went about saying (to one another), 'What attracts? What attracts[1]?' and came upon the sacrificial cake which had become a tortoise and was creeping about. Then they all thought, 'This surely must be the sacrifice!'

4. They said, 'Stand still for the A*s*vins! stand still for Sarasvatî! stand still for Indra!' still it

5, 3, 1. The legend is intended to supply, by means of a fanciful etymology, a symbolical meaning for the yûpa or sacrificial post to which the victim is tied.

[1] Kim prarokate='what thinkest thou?' Sâya*n*a. The primary meaning of pra-ru*k* is 'to shine forth.' Here it has apparently to be taken in the double sense of 'to peep forth, to appear,' and 'to please.' The German 'einleuchten' (St. Petersburg Dictionary) approaches more nearly to the original.

crept on;—'Stand still for Agni!' at this it stopped. Having then enveloped it in fire (Agni), knowing, as they did, that it had stopped for Agni, they offered it up entirely, for it was an oblation to the gods. Then the sacrifice pleased them[1]; they produced it, they spread it. And this same sacrifice is taught by the former to the later; the father (teaches it) to his son when he is a student (brahma*k*ârin).

5. Now that (cake), which caused the sacrifice to attract (or, appear to) them, first (puras) bestowed (dâ*s*) it upon them: hence it is (called) purodâ*s*a, for puro*d*â*s*a, doubtless, is the same as purodâ*s*a[2]. This same cake on eight potsherds for Agni is indispensable on both occasions (at the new- and full-moon ceremonies).

6. That (cake for Agni) does not constitute the (special) sacrificial food (havis) either at the full-moon, or at the new-moon, sacrifice; since the one for Agni and Soma constitutes the havis at the full-moon, and the Sânnâyya[3] at the new-moon sacrifice. That one (for Agni) constitutes rather the regular (or, corresponding) sacrifice on both occasions, and because of its fearing lest it should become detached from the sacrifice, it is offered up at the beginning of both the full-moon and the new-moon sacrifice: this is the reason why it is offered at this particular time.

---

[1] Or 'appeared to them, shone forth to them, prâro*k*ata; see preceding note.

[2] In the compound puro*d*âsa or puro*d*â*s* the original dental d has been changed to the lingual *d*, apparently through the influence of the preceding r.

[3] See I, 6, 4, 9. One would expect the Sânnâyya (to Indra) or the cake to Indra-Agni. The full-moon offering is sacred to Agni-Soma; and the new-moon offering to Indra-Agni; see I, 8, 3, 1 seq.

7. And if any one (householder) were to resort to him (the Adhvaryu) and say, 'Perform an ishti for me!' let him perform it. Whatever desire the *Ri*shis entertained when they performed that sacrifice, that desire of theirs was accomplished; and accordingly whatever desire he (the sacrificer) entertains in having this sacrifice performed, that desire of his is accomplished. For whatever deity sacrificial food is taken, to that deity they offer it up in the fire (Agni);—and if he is about to offer it up in the fire, why should he announce it to another deity? To Agni alone therefore (it is announced).

8. Agni (the fire), assuredly, represents all the deities, since it is in the fire that they make offering to all deities: to Agni alone therefore (he should announce it), since he thereby has recourse to all the deities.

9. Agni, assuredly, is the safest[1] among the gods: let him then have recourse to him whom he considers the safest among the gods, and therefore (announce the sacrifice) to Agni.

10. Agni, assuredly, is the most tender-hearted of gods: let him then have recourse to him whom he considers the most tender-hearted of gods, and therefore (announce the sacrifice) to Agni.

11. Agni, assuredly, is the nearest of the gods: let him then have recourse to him whom he considers as the nearest of those to be approached, and therefore (let him announce the sacrifice) to Agni.

12. If (beside the full-moon sacrifice) he perform an ishti (with a view to the accomplishment of some

[1] Addhâtamâm, adv., literally 'most surely;' according to Sâya*n*a =atiśayena pratyakshaphaladam, 'pre-eminently a giver of perceptible benefits.'

special desire)[1], let him recite seventeen kindling verses; (and in that case) he utters the offering-prayer (yâ*g*yâ) in a low voice, for this is the characteristic form of an ish*t*i; the yâ*g*yâ and the anuvâkyâ should contain the word 'head[2];' the two butter-portions should be offered to the V*ri*tra-slayer (Indra); and the two sa*m*yâ*g*yâs[3] should be in the virâ*g* metre.

THIRD BRÂHMA*N*A.

1. Tvash*tri* had a three-headed, six-eyed son. He had three mouths; and because he was thus shaped, his name was Vi*s*varûpa ('All-shape').

2. One of his mouths was Soma-drinking, one spirit-drinking, and one for other kinds of food. Indra hated him and cut off those heads of his.

3. Now from the one which was Soma-drinking, a hazel-cock (francoline partridge) sprang forth; whence the latter is of brownish colour, for king Soma is brown.

4. From the one which was spirit-drinking, further, a sparrow sprang; whence the latter talks as if stammering, for he who has drunk spirits, talks as if he stammered.

5. Then from the one which served for other kinds of food, a partridge sprang; whence the latter

[1] See I, 3, 5, 10.

[2] For these verses, the first of which begins 'Agni is the head of the sky,' see Vâ*g*. S. XIII, 14 and 15.

[3] That is, the yâ*g*yâ (offering-prayer) and puro'nuvâkyâ (invitatory prayer) at the Svish*t*akr*i*t, or oblation to Agni, as the maker of good offering, at the end of the chief oblations. The two virâ*g* formulas are Rig-veda VII, 1, 3 (Vâ*g*. XVII, 76; Taitt. S. I 4) preddho agne dîdihi, and Rig-veda VII, 1, 18 (Taitt. , 3, 13, 6) imo agne. Cf. Ait. Br. I, 5.

is much variegated in colour: on its wings, namely, butter-drops, as it were, have dropped in one place and honey- (or mead-) drops in another, for suchlike, as it were, was the food which he consumed with that (mouth).

6. Tvashtri was furious: 'Has he indeed slain my son?' he exclaimed. He brought Soma-juice from which Indra was excluded; and just as the Soma-juice on being produced had Indra excluded from it (apendra), so it remained (when it was offered up).

7. Indra thought with himself, 'They are now excluding me from Soma!' and though uninvited, he consumed what pure (Soma) there was in the tub, even as the stronger (consumes) that of a weaker. That (Soma) however, injured him; it flowed in all directions from (the openings of) his vital airs; from his mouth alone it did not flow, but from all the other (openings of the) vital airs it flowed; hence (was instituted) at that time the ishti, called Sautrâmanî: on the occasion of that (ceremony) it is explained how the gods healed him [1].

8. Tvashtri was furious, and exclaimed, 'Has he indeed consumed my Soma uninvited?' However, he himself desecrated the sacrifice, for what pure (Soma) there was left in the tub he let flow (into the fire), saying, 'Grow thou, having Indra for thy foe [2]!' The moment it reached the fire, it

[1] See V, 5, 4, 2 seq., where the whole legend is repeated; and Taitt. S. II, 4, 12, 1. One of the objects of the Sautrâmanî is the expiation of an immoderate consumption of Soma by a priest.

[2] According to Taitt. S. II, 4, 12, 1, also the fault committed by Tvashtri consisted in his faulty accentuation of the compound indrasatru in the formula. What he intended to say was that Agni, on drinking the Soma, should grow strong so as to be 'the foe (slayer) of Indra,' and the compound should therefore have been accented on the second member, viz. indrasátru (the foe of

developed (into human shape), or, as some say, it so developed whilst on its way (to the fire). It became possessed of[1] Agni and Soma, of all sciences, all glory, all nourishment, all prosperity.

9. And since it so developed whilst rolling onwards (v*ri*t), it became V*ri*tra; and since he sprang forth footless, therefore he was a serpent. Danu and Danâyû received him like mother and father[2], whence they call him Dânava.

10. And because he (Tvash*tri*) said, 'Grow thou, having Indra for thy foe!' therefore Indra slew him (V*ri*tra). Had he said, 'Grow thou, the foe (slayer) of Indra!' he (V*ri*tra) would certainly have forthwith slain Indra.

11. And because he (Tvash*tri*) said, 'Grow thou!' therefore he (V*ri*tra) grew an arrow's range sideways and an arrow's range forward: he forced back both the western ocean and the eastern one; and in proportion as he extended did he devour the food.

12. In the fore-noon the gods offered him food, at mid-day the men, and in the after-noon the Fathers.

13. Now while Indra was thus moving on (in pursuit of V*ri*tra), he addressed Agni and Soma, 'Ye belong to me and I belong to you! That one is nothing to you: why then do ye support that Dasyu against me? Come over to me!'

Indra); but by accenting it on the first member, índra*s*atru, he made it 'having Indra for his foe (slayer).' According to the version of the Taitt. S., Agni, the fire, on the Soma being poured into it, rose up (spirted) as if to execute Tvash*tri*'s wish; but immediately relapsed into its former state of inertness on hearing the mis-pronounced word.

[1] Abhisambabhûva, 'he grew by consuming,' &c. Sâya*n*a.

[2] The Kâ*n*va text has, 'Danu and Dânavî received him as mother and father.'

14. They replied, 'What is to be our reward in that case?' He offered them that Agni-Soma cake on eleven potsherds: this is the reason why there is a cake on eleven potsherds for Agni and Soma.

15. They went over to him, and after them went forth[1] all the gods, all the sciences, all glory, all nourishment, all prosperity: thus by offering that (cake to Agni and Soma) Indra became what Indra now is. Such then is the significance of the full-moon offering; and he who, knowing this, performs the full-moon offering in this wise, attains to the same state of prosperity, becomes thus endowed with glory, becomes such a consumer of food (as V*ri*tra).

16. Now V*ri*tra, on being struck, lay contracted like a leather bottle drained of its contents, like a skin bag with the barley-meal shaken out. Indra rushed at him, meaning to slay him.

17. He said, 'Do not hurl (thy thunderbolt) at me! thou art now what I (was before). Only cut me in twain; but do not let me be annihilated!' He (Indra) said, 'Thou shalt be my food!' He replied, 'So be it!' He accordingly cut him in twain; and from that (part) of his which was of the Soma nature[2], he made the moon, and that which was demoniacal (asurya) he made enter these creatures as their belly; hence people say[3]: 'V*ri*tra was then a consumer of food, and V*ri*tra is so now.' For even now, whenever that one (the moon) waxes fuller, it fills itself out of this world[4]; and when-

[1] Preyuh, 'the gods &c. that were in V*ri*tra's mouth went out,' Sâya*n*a; see preceding page, note 1.

[2] 'Yat saumyam nyaktam âsa' ['yat saumyo nyaṅga âsa,' Kâ*n*va rec.], 'what was imbued with Soma,' 'what had Soma inherent in it.' Cf. 'yat somasya nyaktam âsa,' I, 7, 1, 1.

[3] 'People say so when anybody eats much food.' Sâya*n*a.

[4] See I, 6, 4, 15.

ever these creatures crave for food, they pay tribute to this Vritra, the belly. Whosoever knows that Vritra as a consumer of food, becomes himself a consumer of food.

18. Those deities then said, 'Ye, Agni and Soma, whom we have followed hither, take the best part (of the sacrificial food): do let us share along with you in what ye have!'

19. They both said, 'What (share) shall then be ours?' They replied, 'For whatever deity they shall take out sacrificial food, they shall in the first place offer to you some clarified butter!' Whenever, therefore, they take out sacrificial food for any deity, they in the first place offer two butter-portions to Agni and Soma. This does not take place at the Soma-sacrifice, nor at the animal offering; for they said, 'for whatever deity they take out ...[1].'

20. Agni then said, 'In me they shall sacrifice for all of you, and thus I give you a share in me!' For this reason they sacrifice in Agni (the fire) to all the gods; and for this reason they say that Agni is all the deities.

21. Soma then said, 'Me they shall offer up to all of you, and thus I give you a share in me!' For this reason they offer up Soma to all the gods; and hence they say that Soma is all the deities.

22. And further, since all the gods were abiding in Indra, for that reason they say that Indra is all the deities, that the gods have Indra for their chief (sreshtha). Thus the gods came in a three-

[1] The nirvapanam, or taking out (literally throwing out) of (handfuls of) havis from the receptacle and putting it into the winnowing basket (or other vessels), does not apply to these two kinds of sacrifices. Cf. I, 1, 2, 5 seq.

fold way to consist of one deity; and he who knows this becomes individually the chief of his own (people).

23. Twofold, verily, is this, there is no third: to wit, the moist and the dry; and what is dry, that relates to Agni; and what is moist, that relates to Soma. But (it may be objected) if this is twofold only, why then this manifold performance:—the two butter-portions for Agni and Soma, the low-voiced offering to Agni and Soma, and the rice-cake for Agni and Soma,—when by means of any one of these he obtains all, why then this manifold performance? [The answer to this objection is that] so manifold is the power, the generative force of Agni and Soma.

24. The sun, indeed, relates to Agni, and the moon to Soma; the day relates to Agni, and the night to Soma; the waxing half-moon relates to Agni, and the waning one to Soma.

25. 'By means of the two butter-portions he obtains the sun and the moon; by means of the low-voiced offering he obtains the day and the night; and by means of the rice-cake he obtains the two half-moons,' thus say some.

26. Âsuri, on the other hand, said: 'By means of the two butter-portions he gains any two (of those objects[1]); by means of the low-voiced offering he obtains any (other) two; and by means of the rice-cake he obtains any (other) two: "all has been obtained, all has been conquered by me! with that All I will slay V*ri*tra; with the All I will slay the

[1] 'Yatame vâ yatame vâ dve âpnoti.' Sâya*n*a supplies vastunî, 'objects.' The Kâ*n*va recension, on the other hand, reads, 'Yatame vâ yatame vâ dve devate âpnoti.'

spiteful enemy!" thus he thinks, and for that reason there is this manifold performance.'

27. On this point it has also been remarked: 'Why this sameness (of performance)? By what is introduced between the butter(-offering) to Agni and Soma and the rice-cake to Agni and Soma, a repetition of performance (is committed)[1].' Sameness (of performance), nevertheless, is avoided in this way: the one (viz. the low-voiced offering) consists of butter, and the other of a rice-cake, hence the one is different from the other. Moreover, after reciting a *Ri*k-verse as anuvâkyâ, he pronounces the yâ*g*yâ with the word 'pleased' (in the case of the butter-portions to Agni and Soma); and after reciting a *Ri*k-verse as anuvâkyâ, he pronounces the yâ*g*yâ in the form of a *Ri*k-verse (in the case of the low-voiced offering to Agni and Soma), hence the one is (again) different from the other[2]. Sameness of performance is also avoided in this way: in a low voice (he utters the formulas when) he offers of the butter, and with a loud voice of the cake; and what is (uttered) in a low voice, that is the manner of Pra*g*âpati: hence he recites for that (low-

[1] See p. 80, note 2. The objection here raised is, that the low-voiced offering, which is intermediate between the two above-mentioned oblations to Agni-Soma, is made to the same two deities.

[2] When the two butter-portions to Agni and Soma are offered, the Hot*ri* recites the verses Rig-veda VI, 16, 34 (Vâ*g*. S. 33, 9), and Rig-veda I, 95, 5 (Vâ*g*. S. 19, 42) respectively, as anuvâkyâs, or invitatory prayers, each of which is followed by the yâ*g*yâ (offering-formula): 'We who pronounce the offering-prayer to Agni (or Soma respectively),—may Agni (Soma) pleased (*g*ushâ*n*a*h*) accept of the butter-oblation! Vausha*t*!' At the low-voiced offering (upâ*ms*uyâ*g*a) to Agni-Soma, on the other hand, he first utters (in a low voice) as anuvâkyâ the verse Rig-veda I, 93, 2, and thereupon as yâ*g*yâ Rig-veda I, 93, 6.

voiced offering) an anush*t*ubh-verse as the invitatory formula (anuvâkyâ), for the anush*t*ubh represents speech, and Pra*g*âpati also is speech.

28. By means of that low-voiced offering the gods stealing near slew, with that thunderbolt, the vasha*t*-call, whichever they wished of the Asuras; and so does this one, after stealing near by means of that low-voiced offering, slay with that thunderbolt, the vasha*t*-call, the wicked, spiteful enemy[1]. This is why he performs the low-voiced offering.

29. Having recited (at the butter-portions) a *Ri*k-verse as the anuvâkyâ, he recites the yâ*g*yâ with the word 'pleased:' in consequence of this, creatures are brought forth here with teeth on one side (in one jaw); for the *Ri*k means bone and the tooth also is bone, so that he thereby produces bone on one side.

30. Having recited (at the low-voiced offering) a *Ri*k-verse as the anuvâkyâ, he recites as the yâ*g*yâ a (second) *Ri*k-verse: in consequence of this, creatures with teeth on both sides are brought forth here; for the *Ri*k means bone and the tooth also is bone, so that he thereby produces bone on both sides. These creatures, indeed, are of two kinds, viz. such as have teeth on one side only, and such as have teeth on both sides[2]; and verily he who sacrifices, knowing

[1] The two prayers of the low-voiced offering are muttered in a low voice; but the 'Vâusha*t*!' at the end of the offering-prayer (as the 'Om!' at the end of the invitatory prayer) is uttered aloud. Hence the above symbolical explanation.

[2] The same distinction is made in Rig-veda X, 90, 10, where it is stated that from the Purusha sprang the horse and what other animals with two rows of teeth (viz. the ass and mule, according to Sâya*n*a) on the one hand, and cows, goats, and sheep on the other. In Taitt. II, 2, 6, 3, also the horse is mentioned along with man as belonging to the former class of living beings. Cf. also Taitt. V, 1, 2, 6; Ath.-veda V, 19, 2; 31, 3; Weber, Ind. Stud. X, 58.

thus the generative power of Agni and Soma, becomes rich in offspring and cattle.

31. When he (the sacrificer) is about to enter upon the fast of the full-moon ceremony, he may not be entirely sated. He therefore now compresses (that part of) his belly which relates to the Asuras; and next morning, by means of the oblations, that which relates to the gods. Now the practice regarding the full-moon ceremony is as follows:

32. One may (enter on the) fast at the very time (of full moon), thinking, 'Now I will slay V*ri*tra, now I will slay the spiteful enemy!'

33. One may also fast only on the following day. Now he who (enters on the) fast at the very time (of full moon), gets, as it were, into collision[1] (with some one); and when two come into collision with one another, it is indeed doubtful which of the two will get the better of the other. He, on the other hand, who prefers to fast on the second day (only), is as one who crushes from behind a retreating (enemy) before he is able to resist the attack: striking in one direction[2], in fact, is he who thus keeps the fast on the second day only.

34. Let him therefore enter on the fast at the very time (of full moon). He who keeps the fast on the following day only is as one who finally crushes one struck down by some one else; he only does what has been done before by some one else, he only

[1] Sam-kramate, literally 'comes together with, meets (somebody).' This symbolical explanation was probably suggested by the circumstance that the full moon marks the junction (sandhi) of the two pakshas or half months; whereas the new moon (amâvâsyâ, 'dwelling together') marks the point of least distance between sun and moon.

[2] Anyatoghâtin, ? thus St. Petersburg Dictionary.

follows another's lead; let him therefore enter on the fast at the very time (of full moon).

35. After Pra*g*âpati had created the living beings, his joints (parvan) were relaxed. Now Pra*g*âpati, doubtless, is the year, and his joints are the two junctions of day and night (i. e. the twilights), the full moon and new moon, and the beginnings of the seasons.

36. He was unable to rise with his relaxed joints; and the gods healed him by means of these havis-offerings: by means of the Agnihotra they healed that joint (which consists of) the two junctions of day and night, joined that together; by means of the full-moon and the new-moon sacrifice they healed that joint (which consists of) the full and new moon, joined that together; and by means of the (three) *K*âturmâsyas (seasonal offerings) they healed that joint (which consists of) the beginnings of the seasons, joined that together.

37. With his joints thus repaired he betook himself to this food,—to the food which is here (offered) to Pra*g*âpati; and he who, knowing this, enters upon the fast at the very time (of full moon), heals Pra*g*âpati's joint at the proper time, and Pra*g*âpati favours him. Thus he who, knowing this, enters upon the fast at the very time (of full moon) becomes a consumer of food: let him therefore enter on the fast at the very time (of full moon).

38. These two butter-portions (to Agni and Soma), truly, are the eyes of the sacrifice; he, therefore, offers them in front (of, or before, the havis), for these eyes are in the front (of the head). Hence he thereby places the eyes in the front; and for this reason these eyes are in the front (of the head).

39. Some people offer Agni's butter-portion in the north-eastern part (of the fire), and Soma's butter-portion in the south-eastern part, thinking, 'Thereby we place the eyes in the front (of the head).' This, however, is rather unintelligible; for the several dishes of sacrificial food (havis) represent the body of the sacrifice; when therefore he offers in front of (or before) the havis, he thereby places the eyes in the front. Let him rather make the offerings (in that part of the fire) where he thinks the fiercest blaze is; for only by being offered in blazing (fire) are oblations successful[1].

40. Having recited (at the butter-portions) a *Ri*k-verse as anuvâkyâ (invitatory formula), he recites by way of yâ*g*yâ (offering-prayer) the (formula containing the word) 'pleased;' thereby these boneless eyes are set in what is bone. If, on the other hand, after reciting a *Ri*k-verse as anuvâkyâ, he

---

[1] Kâty. III, 3, 20-22 admits either mode of offering the butter-portions. These oblations are effected in the following way:—The Adhvaryu, having called on the Hot*ri* to recite the anuvâkyâ, takes with the dipping-spoon (sruva) butter from the dhruvâ and puts it into the *g*uhû; he then draws some with the sruva from the butter-pot and replenishes the dhruvâ with it [according to the Kâ*n*vas, with the text 'May the dhruvâ fatten with the havis-butter, sacrifice after sacrifice, for those who go to the gods,—the udder of Sûryâ in the lap of Aditi: may the earth flow abundantly at this sacrifice!']. The same process is then repeated three (additional) times (with a *G*amadagni four times): hence the offering is said to consist of four (or five) cuttings. The Hot*ri* then recites the anuvâkyâ (see note on I, 6, 3, 27), which is followed by the Adhvaryu's call 'om *s*râvaya' and the Âgnidhra's response 'astu *s*raushat.' Thereupon the Hot*ri*, having been called upon by the Adhvaryu to give the offering-prayer to Agni (or Soma), recites the respective yâ*g*yâ, at the concluding vausha*t* of which the oblation is poured into the fire, (whilst the sacrificer utters the usual dedicatory formula, 'This for Agni (Soma), not for me!')

were to use a *Ri*k-verse as the yâ*g*yâ, he would make it bone instead of eye.

41. Those two (qualities), truly, are related to the natures of Agni and Soma: that which is white is related to Agni, and that which is black is related to Soma. If, however (it were asserted), on the contrary, that what is black is related to Agni, and what is white is related to Soma,—[the answer would be:—] what sees is of the nature of Agni, for dry, as it were, are the eyes of one who looks, and that which is dry relates to Agni;—and what sleeps is of the nature of Soma, for moist, as it were, are the eyes of one who is asleep, and moist also is Soma. And, verily, he who thus knows those two butter-portions to be eyes, remains endowed with eye-sight till old age in this world, and starts in yonder world possessed of eye-sight.

Fourth Brâhma*n*a.

Special Preliminary Rites of the New-moon Sacrifice.

1. When Indra had hurled the thunderbolt at V*ri*tra, thinking himself to be the weaker, and fearing lest he had not brought him down, he concealed himself and went to the farthest distances[1]. Now the gods knew that V*ri*tra had been slain and that Indra had concealed himself.

2. Agni of the deities, Hira*n*yastûpa[2] of the *Ri*shis, and the B*ri*hatî of the metres, set about searching for him. Agni discovered him and stayed

[1] Parâ*h* parâvata*h*, literally 'to the most distant distances,' 'zu den fernsten Fernen.'

[2] Hira*n*yastûpa, of the family of the Aṅgiras, is the reputed author (or seer) of the hymns Rig-veda I, 31–35; IX, 4; 69. Of these, I, 32 and 33, which celebrate the exploits of Indra, seem to have been especially prized.

with him (as a guest) that (day and) night. He (Indra), namely, is the Vasu[1] of the gods, for he is their hero.

3. The gods said, 'Our Vasu, who has gone to live away from us, is this day dwelling together (amâ vas, viz. with Agni[2]);' and as one would cook a dish of rice or a goat in common for two relatives or friends who have come to stay with him,—for such-like is human (fare), as the sacrificial food (havis) is that of the gods,—in like manner they offered to those two together that sacrificial food, the rice-cake on twelve potsherds for Indra and Agni. This is the reason why there is a rice-cake on twelve potsherds for Indra and Agni.

4. Indra said, 'When I had hurled the thunderbolt at Vritra, I was terrified, and (in consequence of this fright) I am much emaciated. This (cake) does not satiate me: prepare for me what will satiate me!' The gods replied, 'So be it!'

5. The gods said, 'Nothing but Soma will satiate him: let us prepare Soma for him!' They prepared Soma for him. Now this king Soma, the food of the gods, is no other than the moon[3]. When he

[1] That is, as would seem, the benefactor, or the treasure (dhanarûpa, Sâyana) of the gods. Indra is the chief of the Vasus. Indra being so beneficent and important a personage, it was, according to Sâyana, worth Agni's while to stay with him. Possibly also a play on the word Vasu, and vas, 'to dwell,' is intended here.

[2] Thus Sâyana; but it probably means, 'he is staying at a home, or at home (amâ) to-day.'

[3] The identification of the Soma (plant and juice) with the moon already occurs in some of the hymns of the Rig-veda, all of which, however, probably belong to the later ones. According to the St. Petersburg Dictionary, the identification was probably suggested by the circumstance that indu, 'drop, spark,' applies both to the Soma and the moon. Rig-veda X, 85, 3 says that 'of that Soma which the priests know, no one ever eats.'

(the moon, masc.) is not seen that night either in the east or in the west, then he visits this world; and here he enters into the waters (f.) and plants (f.). He is indeed a treasure for the gods, he is their food. And since during that night he here dwells together[1] (amâ vas), therefore that (night of new moon) is called amâvâsyâ (the dwelling together, or at home).

6. They prepared it[2] (Soma for Indra), after having it collected, part by part, by the cows: in eating plants (they collected it) from the plants, and in drinking water (they collected it) from the waters. Having prepared and coagulated it, and made it strong (pungent), they gave it to him[3].

7. He said, 'This does indeed satiate me, but it does not agree with me[4]: devise some means by which it may agree with me!' They made it agree with him by means of boiled (milk).

8. Now although this (mixture of sweet and sour milk) is, indeed, one and the same substance—it being milk (payas) and belonging to Indra—they,

[1] Viz. with the waters and plants (or, he stays at home).

[2] It should be borne in mind that Soma is masculine in Sanskrit.

[3] In Taitt. S. II, 5, 3, 2 seq. the corresponding story is applied directly to the Sânnâyya. In consequence of the struggle with Vritra, Indra lost his energy, which fell to the earth and produced plants and shrubs. He thereupon complained to Pragâpati, who bade the cattle collect (sam-nî) it again by browsing the plants and shrubs. It was then milked out from them, and as the milk did not agree with Indra, it was boiled, and as it still did not satisfy Indra, it was mixed with sour milk.

[4] Na mayi srayate, literally 'it does not stay in me' = na tishthati, na sâtmyam bhagate, Sâyana. The author here (as in I, 8, 1, 17) connects, or confounds, the verb sri with srâ, 'to cook, make done,'—hence, 'it does not boil in me;' the milk being warm, or, as it were, boiled, when it comes from the cow, see II, 2, 4, 15. Hence also boiled milk is mixed with the Soma.

nevertheless, declare it to be (two) different (substances). Since he said 'it satiates (dhî) me,' therefore it is sour milk (dadhi); and since they made it agree (sri) with him with boiled milk (or, by boiling), therefore it is (fresh) boiled milk (srita)[1].

9. In the same way as the Soma stalk becomes strong[2] (by being touched or sprinkled with water), so he (Indra) became strong (by the Soma being mixed with boiled milk) and overcame that evil, the jaundice[3]. Such is likewise the significance of the new-moon ceremony (and the Sânnâyya, or libation of sweet and sour milk offered to Indra thereat); and verily he who, knowing this, mixes (sweet and sour milk at the new-moon sacrifice) in like manner increases in offspring and cattle, and overcomes evil: let him therefore mix together (sweet and sour milk)[4].

---

[1] The author here endeavours to establish some connection between the Sânnâyya (or offering of sweet and sour milk to Indra, which may take the place of the second sacrificial cake offered, at the new-moon sacrifice, to Indra and Agni) and the Soma libations. Sâyana refers to the passage Taitt. Br. I, 4, 7, 6–7, where it is stated that for the morning libation the Soma is to be mixed with boiled milk, for the mid-day libation with sour milk, and for the third (or evening) libation with sour milk that is partly changed into butter (nîtamisra).

[2] Âpyâyeta. On the strengthening or increasing (âpyâyanam) of the Soma-plant by sprinkling it with water before the juice is extracted, see III, 4, 3, 12 seq. Sâyana seems to take the passage thus: 'In the same way as the Soma would make strong (? or become strong), so also the sânnâyyam destroys that evil, the jaundice, in those who drink it.'

[3] By the admixture of milk the Soma-juice loses its brownish colour, and is therefore apparently considered to produce the same effect in those who drink the mixture.

[4] The preparation of the sânnâyya, as it is now practised by priests in Western India, is thus described by Haug (Ait. Br. II, p.

10. In reference to this point they say, 'One who has not performed the Soma-sacrifice[1], must not offer the Sânnâyya; for, indeed, the Sânnâyya is (of the same significance as) a Soma libation, and the latter is not permitted to one who is not a Soma-sacrificer: hence he who has not performed the Soma-sacrifice, must not offer the Sânnâyya.'

11. He may nevertheless offer the Sânnâyya; for have we not heard within this place[2] that he (Indra) said, 'Do ye now offer Soma to me, and then ye will prepare for me that invigorating draught (âpyâyana, viz. the Sânnâyya)!' 'This does not satiate me, prepare for me what will satiate me!' That invigorating draught they indeed prepared for

---

443): 'The Adhvaryu takes the milk from three cows called Gaṅgâ, Yamunâ, and Sarasvatî, on the morning and evening, and gives it to the Âgnîdhra. Half the milk is first drawn from the udder of each of the three cows under the recital of mantras; then the same is done silently. The milk is taken from these cows on the evening of the new-moon day, and on the morning of the following day, the so-called Pratipad (the first day of the month). The milk drawn on the evening is made hot, and lime-juice poured over it to make it sour; whereupon it is hung up. The fresh milk of the following morning is then mixed with it, and both are sacrificed along with the Purodâsa. Only he who has already performed the Agnishtoma is allowed to sacrifice the Sânnâyya at the Darsapûrnima ishti. (Oral information.)' In Vâg. S. I, 4 (Sat. Br. I, 7, 1, 17; Kâty. IV, 2, 25, 26) the names of the three cows are given as Visvâyu, Visvakarman, and Visvadhâyus, unless these are intended merely for epithets or mystic names. Cf. p. 188 note; Weber, Ind. Stud. IX, 232. Instead of the lime-juice, mentioned by Haug as used for rennet, Kâty. IV, 2, 33 prescribes that the milk remaining from the Agnihotra of the preceding evening, and since become sour, should be used.

[1] Thus Taitt. S. II, 5, 5, 1.

[2] Atrântarena; atra vishaye antarena madhye, Sâyana; ? within this our range of hearing; or, in the course of the present ceremony.

him, and therefore even one who has not performed the Soma-sacrifice, may offer the Sânnâyya.

12. The full-moon oblation, assuredly, belongs to the Vritra-slayer, for by means of it Indra slew Vritra; and this new-moon oblation also represents the slaying of Vritra, since they prepared that invigorating draught for him who had slain Vritra.

13. An offering in honour of the Vritra-slayer, then, is the full-moon sacrifice. Vritra, assuredly, is no other than the moon[1]; and when during that night (of new moon) he is not seen either in the east or in the west, then he (Indra) completely destroys him by means of that (new-moon sacrifice), and leaves nothing remaining of him. And, verily, he who knows this, overcomes all evil and leaves nothing remaining of evil.

14. Here now some people enter upon the fast when they (still) see (the moon, on the fourteenth day of the half-month), thinking, 'To-morrow he will not rise: already, then, there is unfailing food for the gods in yonder heaven[2], and to this we will offer them more from hence (to-morrow)!'—He, indeed, is in a prosperous state with whom, while the old food is still unfailing, fresh food is accruing; for such a one has indeed abundant food. However, he is not now offering Soma, but he is offering milk (i.e. the Sânnâyya), and that (milk) becomes king Soma[3] (in yonder world):

---

[1] See I, 6, 3, 17.

[2] Viz. in the form of Soma, i.e. the moon, still shining in the heavens during the night preceding the new moon.

[3] Who, as we saw, resides in the plants and waters at the time of new moon and consequently in the milk used for the Sânnâyya. If, however, one were to enter upon the fast (and hence on the

15. But as they (the cows), previously (to the new moon), eat mere plants (not imbued with the moon or Soma), and drink mere water, and yield mere milk,—so that (milk which they offer on the day before new moon, is not imbued with Soma, is ordinary milk). For king Soma, the food of the gods, indeed, is no other than the moon. When he is not seen that night either in the east or in the west, then he visits this world, and here enters into the waters and plants. Having then collected him from the water and plants, he (the performer of the Sânnâyya) causes him to be reproduced from out of the libations; and he (Soma, the moon), being reproduced from the libations, becomes visible in the western sky.

16. Now it is only when that food of the gods is unfailing that it comes back (to men): for him, therefore, who knows this, there is unfailing food in this, and imperishable righteousness in yonder, world.

17. Thus during that night (of new moon) food moves away from the gods and comes to this world. Now the gods were desirous as to how that (food) might (be made to) come back to them; how it might not perish away from them. For this they put their trust in those who prepare the libation of sweet and sour milk (sânnâyya), thinking, 'when they have prepared it, they will offer it to us.' And, verily, in him, who knows this, both his own kin and strangers put their trust; for in him, who attains to the highest rank, people indeed put their trust.

18. Now the one that burns there (viz. the sun)

---

sacrifice) previously to the new moon, he would be offering mere milk, not imbued with, and not liable to change into, Soma, and therefore unfit for the gods.

is, assuredly, no other than Indra, and that moon is no other than Vritra. But the former is of a nature hostile to the latter, and for this reason, though this one (the moon, Vritra) had previously (to the night of new moon) risen at a great distance from him (the sun, Indra), he now swims towards him and enters into his open mouth.

19. Having swallowed him, he (the sun) rises; and that (other) one is not seen either in the east or in the west. And, verily, he who knows this, swallows his spiteful enemy, and of him they say, 'He alone exists, his enemies exist not[1].'

20. Having sucked him empty, he throws him out; and the latter, thus sucked out, is seen in the western sky, and again increases; he again increases to serve that (sun) as food: and verily if the spiteful enemy of one who knows this, thrives either by trade or in any other way, he thrives again and again in order to serve him as food.

21. Now some people offer (the Sânnâyya) to (Indra under the name of) 'Mahendra' (the great Indra), arguing, 'Before the slaying of Vritra he was Indra, it is true; but after slaying Vritra he became Mahendra, even as (a râgan, or king, becomes) a Mahârâga after obtaining the victory: hence (the Sânnâyya should be offered) to Mahendra.' Let him, nevertheless, offer it to 'Indra;' for Indra he was before the slaying of Vritra, and Indra he is after slaying Vritra: therefore let him offer it to 'Indra[2].'

---

[1] With this explanation of the disappearance of the moon may be compared the later notion of the sun and moon being swallowed by the demon Râhu, at the time of the eclipses.

[2] Kâty. IV, 2, 10 leaves it optional whether the libation of mixed

SEVENTH ADHYÂYA. FIRST BRÂHMANA.

1. He (the Adhvaryu) drives the calves away (from the cows) with a parna branch[1]. The reason why he drives the calves away with a parna branch is this. When the Gâyatrî flew towards Soma (the moon), a footless archer aiming at her while she was carrying him off, severed one of the feathers (parna) either of the Gâyatrî or of king Soma[2]; and on falling down it became a parna (palâsa) tree; whence its name parna. 'May that

sweet and sour milk is to be offered to Indra or to Mahendra. According to IV, 5, 25, however, such option seems to be permitted only so far as the first performance is concerned, after which one is apparently bound to go on offering during the rest of one's life to whichever deity one has chosen at the beginning. Taitt. S. II, 5, 4, 4, lays it down as the rule that only a gatasrî (one who has reached the highest grade of prosperity), viz. a brâhmana versed in the three Vedas (susruvân=vedatrayâbhigña, Sâyana), the head of a village (grâmanî), and a râganya, can make offering to Mahendra, since he is their special deity. Others, however, may do the same, after offering the sânnâyyam to Indra for a whole year, and on the expiration of it a rice-cake on eight potsherds to Agni, as the Keeper of Vows.

[1] Parna=palâsa, Butea Frondosa.

[2] Gâyatryai vâ somasya vâ='both of G. and of S.,' Sâyana. Apâd astâ, 'a footless shooter,' is a doubtful reading and perhaps an old corruption; Sâyana reads apâdhastâ (? adhastât); cf. Weber, various readings, p. 133. The Kânva MS. reads, 'devebhyas tasyâ âharantyâ avâdastâbhyâyatya parnam prakikkheda.' According to Rig-veda IV, 27, 3, it was the archer Krisânu, who hit the falcon when it was carrying off the Soma from heaven, and brought down one of its feathers. On the whole myth, see A. Kuhn, Herabkunft des Feuers und des Göttertranks, p. 137 seq. Cf. Taitt. S. III, 5, 7, 1; Taitt. Br. I, 1, 3, 10, 'Soma was in the third heaven from here; Gâyatrî fetched him away; one of his feathers was cut off, it became a parna (palâsa) tree.' Similarly Taitt. Br. I, 2, 1, 6; see also Sat. Br. I, 8, 2, 10.

which then was of the Soma nature[1] be here with us now!' so he thinks, and for this reason he drives away the calves with a parna branch.

2. That (branch) he cuts off[2], with the formula (Vâg. S. I, 1 a, b), 'For sap (I cut) thee! for pith thee!'—'for rain thee' he means to say, when he says 'for sap thee;' and when he says 'for pith thee' he means to say 'for that food-essence which springs from the rain.'

3. They then let the calves join their mothers. He thereupon touches (each) calf (in order to drive it away from the cow), with the formula (Vâg. S. I, 1 c), 'The winds are ye!'—for, indeed, it is this wind that here blows[3], it is this (wind) that makes swell all the rain that falls here; it is it that makes those (cows) swell; and for this reason he says 'the winds are ye!' Some people add here the formula[4], 'Going near are ye!' but let him not say this, because thereby another (an enemy) approaches (the sacrificer).

4. After separating one of the mothers from her calf, he touches her, with the text (Vâg. S. I, 1 d), 'May the divine Savitri animate you—' for Savitri, indeed, is the impeller (prasavitri) of the gods:

---

[1] 'Somasya nyaktam,' see p. 167, note 2.

[2] This act as well as that of letting the calves join the cows, of course, precedes the driving away of the calves. These proceedings take place on the day before the new moon, after the agnyanvâdhâna. According to Kâty., the sacrificer enters on the vow of abstinence, after the branch has been cut. Previously to these rites, however, the so-called Pinda-pitriyagña, or oblation of obsequial pindas (balls, dumplings) to the deceased ancestors, has to be performed; for which see II, 4, 2, 1 seq.

[3] Pavate, 'blows, purifies.'

[4] Thus Taitt. S. I, 1, 1, 1.

'may they, impelled by Savitri, prepare the sacrifice!' so he thinks, and for this reason he says, 'May the divine Savitri animate you!'

5. '—To the most glorious work!' for assuredly the sacrifice is the most glorious work: hence, when he says 'to the most glorious work!' he means to say 'to the sacrifice.'

6. 'Make swell, ye invincible (or inviolable) ones, the share for Indra!' In like manner as then[1], in taking the sacrificial food (rice), he announces it to the deity, so now also he announces that (libation of milk) to the deity when he says 'make swell, ye invincible ones, the share for Indra!'

7. 'Over you that are rich in offspring, over you that are free from suffering and disease—;' in this there is nothing that is obscure; '—no thief, no ill-wisher may lord it!'—he thereby means to say, 'may the evil spirits, the Rakshas, not lord it over you!'—'May ye be numerous and constant to this lord of cattle!'—thereby he means to say 'may ye be numerous with this sacrificer, and not abandon him.'

8. He then hides the branch on the front (eastern) side either of the Âhavanîya or the Gârhapatya house, with the formula (Vâg. S. I, 1 e), 'Protect the sacrificer's cattle!' he thus makes over the sacrificer's cattle to it for protection by means of the Brahman (sacred writ).

9. On it he fastens a strainer (pavitram)[2], with

---

[1] Viz. on the occasion of his taking from the cart the rice for the oblations, see I, 1, 2, 17–19.

[2] See p. 19, note 1. According to Karka this takes place before the hiding of the branch, Scholl. on Kâty. IV, 2, 15. According to Kâty. IV, 2, 12, 13, the upavesha (see I, 2, 1, 3) is cut at this juncture—with the text, 'Accomplishing (vesha) art thou'—from the bottom part of the palâsa branch on the remaining part

the formula (Vâg. S. I, 2 a), 'Vasu's means of purification (ventilator, strainer, pavitram) art thou!' Vasu, indeed, is the sacrifice: for this reason he says, 'Vasu's means of purification art thou!'

10. That night he performs the Agnihotra with rice-gruel (yavâgû). That milk, namely, (which he milks that night) has already been announced as sacrificial food to a (special) deity; hence, if he were to make the offering with milk, he would offer to one deity that which has been set apart as sacrificial food for another deity: this is the reason why on that night he performs the Agnihotra with rice-gruel. As soon as they have performed the Agnihotra, the pot is made ready. He (the Adhvaryu) thereupon says, 'Announce that she (the cow) has been let loose to (the calf)!' When he (or she, the milker[1]) announces, 'She has been let loose!'—

11. He puts the pot on (the Gârhapatya hearth), with the text (Vâg. S. I, 2 b, c): 'Thou art the sky! thou art the earth!'—he praises and eulogises her by thus saying, 'thou art the sky! thou art the earth!'—'Mâtarisvan's cauldron (gharma) art thou[2]!' he thereby makes it (a means of) sacrifice, and puts it on just as if he were putting on the

of which he thereupon fixes the strainer. When the sânnâyya oblation is not made (and consequently no palâsa branch is used), the upavesha is made of varana wood.

[1] The milker may be anybody except a Sûdra, Taitt. Br. III, 2, 3, 9; Kâty. IV, 2, 22; Âpast. I, 12, 15.

[2] Mâtarisvan's cauldron is identified in Taitt. Br. III, 2, 3, 2 with the atmosphere. Mâtarisvan, though sometimes identified with the wind, is more generally either a name of Agni, or the name of a mythic personage who (Prometheus-like) is supposed to have fetched the fire from heaven and brought it to the Bhrigus, who communicated it to man. See Roth, Nir. p. 111; Kuhn, Herabkunft des Feuers und des Göttertranks, p. 5 seq.

(pravargya-) cauldron (gharma)[1].—'All-holding art thou! stand firm by the highest law! do not waver!'—thereby he steadies it, renders it firm.—'May thy Lord of Sacrifice not waver!'—the Lord of Sacrifice, doubtless, is the sacrificer, hence it is for the sacrificer that he thereby prays for steadiness.

12. He then puts the strainer (on the pot). He puts it down with the top turned eastwards, for the east is the region of the gods; or with the top turned northwards, for the north is the region of the men; means of purification (pavitram) assuredly is that (wind) which here blows, it sweeps across these worlds: let him therefore put it down with the front northwards[2].

13. Just as then (i. e. at the Soma-sacrifice) they clarify king Soma with a strainer, in like manner he now clarifies (the milk); and since the strainer wherewith on that occasion they clarify king Soma has its fringe directed towards the north, therefore let him now also put it down with the top northward.

14. He puts it down, with the text (Vâ*g*. S. I, 3 a), 'Vasu's means of purification (pavitram) art thou!'—Vasu, indeed, is the sacrifice: for this reason he says, 'Vasu's means of purification art thou!'—'flowing in a hundred streams, flowing in a thousand streams!'—he praises and eulogises it when he says, 'flowing in a hundred streams, flowing in a thousand streams.'

---

[1] See I, 2, 2, 7, and note. Compare also the interesting introduction to Dr. Garbe's edition and translation of Âpastamba's aphorisms on the Pravargya ceremony, Zeitsch. der D. Morg. Ges. XXXIV, p. 319 seq.

[2] The direction from west to east is the chief one in all sacrificial arrangements: hence that from south to north is the one that lies across the former.

15. He now maintains silence as long as the milking of the three (cows) lasts, for the sacrifice, doubtless, is speech: 'May I perform the sacrifice undisturbed!' so he thinks.

16. When it (the milk of each of the three cows) is poured (by the milker from the wooden pail through the strainer into the pot), he (the Adhvaryu) consecrates it by (whispering each time) the formula (Vâg. S. I, 3 b), 'May the divine Savitri purify thee with Vasu's means of purification, well cleansing and flowing in a hundred streams!' for just as then (at the Soma-sacrifice) they clarify king Soma with a strainer, so he thereby clarifies (the milk).

17. He then says (Vâg. S. I, 3-4), 'Which didst thou milk?' 'Such and such a one,' (the milker replies.) 'This one is Visvâyu (containing all life),' he (the Adhvaryu) says. He then[1] asks regarding the second one, 'Which didst thou milk?' 'Such and such a one,' is the reply. 'This one is Visvakarman (all-doing),' he says. He then asks regarding the third, 'Which didst thou milk?' 'Such and such a one,' is the reply. 'This one is Visvadhâyas (all-sustaining),' he says. The reason why he thus asks is that he thereby bestows certain energies on them. Three (cows) he milks, for three are these worlds: he thereby renders them fit for these worlds. He is now at liberty to speak.

[1] That is, when the milk has been poured through the strainer as before. The Taittirîya school make the mystic names (or epithets) of the three cows Visvâyu, Visvavyakas (all-embracing), and Visvakarman, cf. Taitt. S. I, 1, 3; Taitt. Br. III, 2, 3, 7. In the latter passage these names are, as here, identified with the earth, atmosphere, and heavens respectively. The milker, in replying to the Adhvaryu, apparently calls the cows by their ordinary names. Cf. p. 178, note 4.

18. After having the last (cow) milked, and having poured a drop of water into the pail which he has made the milker use, and stirred it, he pours it to (the milk)[1], thinking 'what milk was left there, let that also be here!'—(he does so) for the completeness of the sap; for when it rains here, then plants spring up, and on the plants being eaten and the water drunk, thence is this juice produced: and therefore (the water is poured to the milk) for the completeness of the sap. Having then taken it off (the fire), he coagulates it[2]: he thereby makes it sharp (pungent); for this reason he coagulates it, after taking it off (the fire).

19. He coagulates it, with the formula (Vâg. S. I, 4 d), 'With Soma I coagulate thee, the portion of Indra!' Just as on a former occasion[3], when taking sacrificial food for a deity, he announces it (to that deity), in like manner he now announces it to the deity, saying, 'Thee, the portion of Indra!' By saying 'with Soma I coagulate thee,' he makes it palatable to the gods.

20. He then covers it over by a vessel[4], with the hollow part upwards and containing water, 'lest the evil spirits, the Rakshas, should touch it from above;' for water, indeed, is a thunderbolt; hence

---

[1] According to Taitt. S. I, 1, 3, Kâty. IV, 2, 32, &c., he, whilst doing so, pronounces the text, 'Unite, ye that follow the eternal law, ye waving ones (with the wave, Kâty.), ye sweetest,—[filling the milk with honey, Kâty.],—ye delightful ones, for the obtainment of wealth!'

[2] Viz. by adding to it the (sour) milk that is left from the performance of the Agnihotra.

[3] See I, 1, 2, 18.

[4] According to Taitt. Br. III, 2, 3, 11, it may be either a metal or wooden vessel, but not an earthen one (Kâty. IV, 2, 34).

he thus drives away from it the evil spirits, the Rakshas, with a thunderbolt: this is the reason why he covers it over by a vessel with the hollow part upwards and containing water.

21. He covers it over, with the formula (Vâg. S. I, 4 e), 'O Vishnu, protect the oblation!' for Vishnu, indeed, is the sacrifice; hence he thereby makes over this sacrificial food to the sacrifice for protection: for this reason he says, 'O Vishnu, protect the oblation!'

SECOND BRÂHMANA.

THE CHIEF OFFERINGS.

1. Verily, whoever exists, he, in being born, is born as (owing) a debt to the gods, to the *Ri*shis, to the fathers, and to men[1].

2. For, inasmuch as he is bound to sacrifice, for that reason he is born as (owing) a debt to the gods: hence when he sacrifices to them, when he makes

---

[1] The wording of this passage is very ambiguous; so much so indeed, that it could also be taken in the sense that 'whoever exists, is born as (one to whom) a debt (is owed) from the gods,' &c.; cf. I, 1, 2, 19: 'Whichever deities are chosen (for the oblations), they consider it as a debt (due from them), that they are bound to fulfil whatever wish he entertains while taking the oblation.' But see Taitt. Br. VI, 3, 10, 5: 'Verily, a Brâhmana who is born, is born as owing a debt in respect to three things: in the shape of sacred study (brahmakarya) to the *Ri*shis, in the shape of sacrifice to the gods, and in the shape of offspring to the fathers. Free from debt, verily, is he who has a son, who is a sacrificer, who lives (for a time with a guru) as a religious student.' Ath.-veda VI, 117, 3 (Taitt. Br. III, 7, 9, 8): 'May we be debtless in this, debtless in the other, debtless in the third, world! What worlds (paths, Taitt. Br.) there are trodden by the gods and trodden by the fathers,—may we abide debtless on all (those) paths!'

offerings to them, he does this (in discharge of his debt) to them.

3. And further, inasmuch as he is bound to study (the Veda), for that reason he is born as (owing) a debt to the *Ri*shis: hence it is to them that he does this; for one who has studied (the Veda) they call 'the *Ri*shis' treasure-warden.'

4. And further, inasmuch as he is bound to wish for offspring, for that reason he is born as (owing) a debt to the fathers: hence when there is (provided by him) a continued, uninterrupted lineage, it is for them that he does this.

5. And further, inasmuch as he is bound to practise hospitality, for that reason he is born as (owing) a debt to men: hence when he harbours them, when he offers food to them, it is (in discharge of his debt) to them that he does so. Whoever does all these things, has discharged his duties: by him all is obtained, all is conquered.

6. And, accordingly, in that he is born as (owing) a debt to the gods, in regard to that he satisfies (ava-day) them by sacrificing; and when he makes offerings in the fire, he thereby satisfies them in regard to that (debt): hence whatever they offer up in the fire, is called avadânam (sacrificial portion)[1].

7. Now this (oblation) consists of four cuttings; (the reason for this is, that) there is here first, the invitatory prayer (anuvâkyâ), then the offering-prayer (yâ*g*yâ), then the vasha*t*-call, and as the fourth, the deity for which the sacrificial food is

[1] The word is really derived from ava-dâ (do), 'to cut off.' The Taitt. Br. gives the same fanciful etymological explanation of the term as here.

(destined): for in this way the deities are dependent on the sacrificial portions, or the portions are dependent on the deities: hence what fifth cutting there is (made by some), that is redundant, for—for whom is he to cut it? For this reason it consists of four cuttings.

8. But a fivefold cutting also takes place (with some people): fivefold is the sacrifice, fivefold the animal victim, and five seasons there are in the year,—such is the perfection of the fivefold cutting; and he, assuredly, will have abundant offspring and cattle for whom, knowing this, the fivefold cutting is made. The fourfold cutting, however, is the approved (practice) among the Kuru-Pa*ñk*âlas, and for this reason a fourfold cutting takes place (with us[1]).

---

[1] The four 'cuttings' of which each oblation of rice-cake consists are made in the following way: first, some clarified butter, 'cut out' or drawn from the butter in the dhruvâ-spoon by means of the sruva (dipping-spoon) and poured into the *g*uhû (this is called the upastara*n*a or under-layer of butter); second and third, two pieces of the size of a thumb's joint, cut out from the centre and the fore-part of the rice-cake and laid on that butter; and fourth, some clarified butter poured on these pieces of cake (the technical name of this basting of butter being abhighâra*n*a). The family of the *G*amadagnis, which is mentioned as always making five cuttings (Kâty. I, 9, 3–4), take three pieces of cake instead of two, viz. an additional one from the back (or west) part of the cake. Yâ*gñ*ika Deva on Kâty. quotes a couplet from some Sm*ri*ti, in which the Vatsas, the Vidas, and the Ârsh*t*ishe*n*as are mentioned beside the *G*amadagnis, as pa*ñk*âvattina*h* or making five cuttings. At the Upâ*ms*uyâ*g*a (low-voiced offering),—which is performed between the cake-oblation to Agni and that to Agni-Soma at the full moon, and between the cake-oblation to Agni and that to Indra-Agni (or the sânnâyya, or oblation of sweet and sour milk, to Indra) at the new moon, and which consists entirely of butter,—the four cuttings are effected in the same way as described

9. Let him cut off only a moderate quantity; for were he to cut off a large quantity, he would make it human; and what is human is inauspicious at the sacrifice. Let him therefore cut off only a moderate quantity, lest he should do what is inauspicious at the sacrifice.

10. Having made an under-layer of butter (in the *g*uhû-spoon) and cut off twice from the havis, he then pours over it some butter. There are, indeed, two (kinds of) oblations; the oblation of Soma being one, and the oblation of (or rather, with) butter being the other. Now the one, viz. the Soma-oblation, is (an oblation) by itself; and the other, viz. the butter-oblation, is the same as the offering of havis (rice, milk, &c.) and the animal offering[1]; hence he thereby makes it (the cake) butter, and therefore butter is on both sides of it. Butter, doubtless, is palatable to the gods; hence he thereby renders it palatable to the gods: for this reason butter is on both sides of it.

11. The invitatory prayer (anuvâkyâ, f.), doubtless, is yonder (sky), and the offering-prayer (yâ*g*yâ, f.) is this (earth)—these two are females. With each of these two the vasha*t*-call (vasha*t*kâra, m.) makes up a pair[2]. Now the vasha*t*, indeed,

page 174 note. At the sânnâyya, two (or three) sruva-fuls of both the sweet and the sour milk take the place of the two (or three) pieces of cake.

[1] See page 26, note 1. The parts of the cakes or the sânnâyya, from which cuttings have been made, he bastes, each once, with butter taken with the sruva from the butter-pot; and whenever butter is ladled with the sruva from the dhruvâ into the *g*uhû, the former is replenished from the butter-pot.

[2] Tayor mithunam asti vasha*t*kâra eva, 'to these two the vasha*t*-call is the complement in forming a pair.' On the vasha*t* (vausha*t*) and the other two formulas, see note on I, 5, 2, 16.

is no other than that scorching one (the sun). When he rises he approaches yonder (sky); and when he sets he approaches this (earth): hence whatever is brought forth here by these two, that they bring forth through that male.

12. Having recited the invitatory prayer and pronounced the offering-prayer[1], he afterwards (paskât) utters the vashat formula; for from behind (paskât) the male approaches the female: hence, after placing those two in front, he causes them to be approached by that male, the vashat. For the same reason let him make the offering either simultaneously with the vashat or (immediately) after the vashat has been pronounced.

13. A vessel of the gods, doubtless, is that vashat. Even as, after ladling, one would mete out (food) into a vessel, so here. If, on the other hand, he were to make the offering before the vashat, it would be lost, as would be that (food) falling to the ground: for this reason also let him make the offering either simultaneously with the vashat or after it has been pronounced.

14. As seed is poured into the womb, so here. If, on the other hand, he were to make the offering before the vashat, it would be lost, as would be the seed poured not into the womb: for this reason also let him make the offering either simultaneously with the vashat or after it has been pronounced.

15. The invitatory formula, doubtless, is yonder (sky), and the offering-formula is this (earth). The gâyatrî metre also is this (earth), and the trishtubh

[1] The usual formalities, which have been detailed before (see page 174 note), have, of course, to be gone through at each oblation.

is yonder (sky)[1]. He recites the gâyatrî verse, thereby reciting yonder (sky), for the invitatory formula (anuvâkyâ) is yonder (sky). He recites this (earth), for the gâyatrî verse (viz. the offering-formula) is this (earth).

16. He then presents the offering with a trish-tubh verse[2], thereby presenting it by means of this

[1] In this passage the invitatory formula (anuvâkyâ or puro-'nuvâkyâ), which is in the gâyatrî metre, is identified with the sky, and the offering-formula (yâgyâ), which is in the trishtubh metre, with the earth. On the other hand, the gâyatrî also is the earth (cf. I, 4, 1, 34), and the trishtubh the sky; so that, according to this mode of reasoning, there is not only an intimate connection between the two metres, but actual identity. The gâyatrî verse, used as invitatory formula, on the occasion of the rice-cake offering to Agni, is Rig-veda VIII, 44, 16 [agnir mûrdhâ divah kakut, 'Agni, the head and summit of the sky,' &c.]; with that to Agni and Soma, at the full-moon sacrifice, Rig-veda I, 93, 3 [agnîshomau savedasau, sahûtî vanatam girah, 'O Agni and Soma, of self-same wealth and invocation, accept this song!' &c.]; and to Indra and Agni, at the new moon, Rig-veda VII, 94, 7 [indrâgnî avasâ gatam, 'O Indra and Agni, come to us with favour!' &c.]; or with the (optional) milk-offering (sânnâyyam), at the new moon, Rig-veda I, 8, 1 [endra sânasim rayim, 'hither, O Indra, bring abundant treasure!' &c.], if to Indra; or Rig-veda VIII, 6, 1 [mahâñ indro ya ogasâ parganyo vrishtimâñ iva, 'the Great Indra, who in might is equal to the rainy thunder-cloud,' &c.], if to Mahendra.

[2] The trishtubh verse, used as offering-formula with the oblation of cake to Agni, both at the new and full moon, is Rig-veda X, 8, 6 [bhuvo yagñasya ragasas ka netâ . . . agne . . . , 'be thou the leader of the sacrifice and welkin, . . . O Agni!' &c.]; with that to Agni and Soma, at the full moon, Rig-veda I, 93, 5 [yuvam etâni divi rokanâni . . . agnîshomau . . . , 'you, O Agni and Soma, (fixed) those lights in the heaven,' &c.]; with that to Indra and Agni, at the new moon, Rig-veda VII, 93, 4 [gîrbhir viprah pramatim ikkha-mâna . . . indrâgnî . . . , 'the bard, seeking your grace by songs . . . , O Indra and Agni,' &c.]; and with the milk-offering, at the same sacrifice, if to Indra, Rig-veda X, 180, 1 [pra sasâhishe puruhûta satrûn . . . indrâ . . . , 'thou, O Indra, the much-invoked, hast vanquished the enemies!' &c.]; or, if to Mahendra, Rig-veda X, 50, 4 [bhuvas

(earth), for the offering-formula (yâgyâ) is this (earth). Over yonder (sky) he places the vashat, for yonder (sky) also is the trishtubh. Thereby he makes those two (sky and earth) yoke-fellows; and as such they feed together; and after their common meal all these creatures get food[1].

17. Let him pronounce the invitatory formula lingering, as it were: the invitatory formula, namely, is yonder (sky), and the brihat(-sâman) also is yonder (sky), since its form is that of the brihat. With the offering-formula let him, as it were, hurry on fast: the offering-formula, doubtless, is this (earth), and the rathantara(-sâman) also is this (earth), since its form is that of the rathantara[2]. With the invitatory formula he calls (the gods), and with the

tvam indra brahmanâ mahân, 'mighty, O Indra, mayest thou be through (our) prayer!' &c.].

[1] For the notion that there is rain (and consequently food) when heaven and earth are on friendly terms with each other, see I, 8, 3, 12. The rain is the food of the earth; and the food, produced thereby, in its turn furnishes food for the sky (or the gods) in the form of oblations.

[2] The brihat-sâman (tvâm id dhi havâmahe, 'on thee, indeed, we call,' &c., Sâma-veda II, 159–160=Rig-veda VI, 46, 1–2) and the rathantara-sâman (abhi tvâ sûra nonumah, 'to thee, O Hero, we call,' &c., Sâma-veda II, 30–31=Rig-veda VII, 32, 22–23) are two of the most highly prized Sâma-hymns, which are especially used in forming the so-called prishthas, or combinations of two hymns in such a way that one of them (being a mystic representation of the embryo) is enclosed in the other, which is supposed to represent the womb. In these symbolical combinations the brihat and rathantara, which must never be used together, are often employed as the enclosing chants, representative of the womb. They are already mentioned in Rig-veda X, 181. See also Sat. Br. IX, 1, 2, 36–37. Taitt. S. VII, 1, 1, 4, Pragâpati is said to have first created from his mouth Agni together with the Gâyatrî, the Rathantara-sâman, the Brâhmana, and the goat; and then from his chest and arms Indra, the Trishtubh, the Brihat-sâman, the Râganya, and the ram.

offering-formula he presents (food to them): hence the invitatory formula (anuvâkyâ) has some such form as 'I call,' 'We call,' 'Come hither!' 'Sit on the barhis!' for with it he calls. With the offering-formula (yâgyâ) he offers: hence the offering-formula has some such form as, 'Accept the sacrificial food!' 'Relish the sacrificial food!' 'Accept the potation (âvrishâyasva)!' 'Eat! Drink! There[1]!' for by it he offers that which (is indicated by) 'there!'

18. Let the invitatory formula be one that has its distinctive indication (in the form of the name of the respective deity) at the beginning (in front): for the invitatory formula is yonder (sky); and that (sky) yonder has the moon, the stars, and the sun for its mark below[2].

19. The offering-formula then should be one that has its characteristic indication (further) back[3]; for the offering-formula is this (earth), and this same (earth) has plants, trees, waters, fire, and these creatures for its mark above.

20. Verily, that invitatory formula alone is auspicious, in the first word of which he utters the (name of the) deity; and that offering-formula alone is auspicious in the last word of which he pronounces the vashat upon the deity[4]; for the (name

[1] Literally, 'forwards, thither (pra).'

[2] Avastâllakshma, 'the sign below or on this (the, to us, nearest or front) side.' See the formulas above, p. 195, note 1.

[3] Or upwards, on the upper side, uparishtâllakshanam. See the offering-formulas above, p. 195, note 2.

[4] Vashat, or rather vaushat ['may he (Agni) carry it (to the gods)!'], is pronounced after each yâgyâ or offering-formula, which contains the name of the deity towards the end, or at least not at the very beginning.

of the) deity constitutes the vigour of the *Rik* (verse): hence after thus enclosing it[1] on both sides with vigour, he offers the sacrificial food to that deity for which it is intended.

21. He pronounces (the syllable) vauk[2]; for, assuredly, the vasha*t*-call is speech; and speech means seed: hence he thereby casts seed. 'Sha*t*' (he pronounces), because there are six seasons: he thereby casts that seed into the seasons, and the seasons cause that seed so cast to spring up here as creatures. This is the reason why he pronounces the vasha*t*.

22. Now the gods and the Asuras, both of them sprung from Pra*g*âpati, entered upon their father Pra*g*âpati's inheritance[3], to wit, these two half-moons. The gods entered upon the one which waxes, and the Asuras on the one which wanes.

23. The gods were desirous as to how they might appropriate also the one that had fallen to the Asuras. They went on worshipping and toiling. They saw this haviryag*ñ*a, to wit, the new- and full-moon sacrifices, and performed them; and by performing them they likewise appropriated the one—

24. Which belonged to the Asuras. Now when these two revolve, then the month is produced; and month (revolving) after month, the year (is produced). But the year, doubtless, means all; hence the gods thereby appropriated all that belonged to

---

[1] Viz. the invitatory and offering-formulas.

[2] The sacrificial call vausha*t* (for vasha*t*, irregular aorist of vah, 'to bear,' cf. p. 88, note 2) is here fancifully explained as composed of vauk, for vâk, 'speech,' + sha*t*, 'six.'

[3] Pra*g*âpati, or Lord of Creatures, is here, as often (cf. I, 2, 5, 13), taken as representing the year, or Time.

the Asuras, they deprived their enemies, the Asuras, of all. And in the same way he (the sacrificer) who knows this appropriates all that belongs to his enemies, deprives his enemies of all.

25. That (half-moon) which belonged to the gods is (called) yavan, for the gods possessed themselves (yu, 'to join') of it; and that which belonged to the Asuras is ayavan, because the Asuras did not possess themselves of it.

26. But they also say contrariwise:—That which belonged to the gods is (called) ayavan, because the Asuras did not get possession of it; and that which belonged to the Asuras is yavan, because the gods did get possession of it. The day is (called) sabda, the night sagarâ, the months yavya, the year sumeka[1]: sveka ('eminently one'), doubtless, is the same as sumeka. And since the Hot*ri* is concerned with these—to wit, the yavan and the ayavan, which (according to some) is yavan—they call (his office) yâvihotram[2].

THIRD BRÂHMANA.

OBLATION TO AGNI SVISHTAKRIT, [AND THE BRAHMAN'S PORTIONS.]

1. Now by means of the sacrifice the gods ascended to heaven. But the god who rules over

[1] Sumeka is taken by the St. Petersburg Dictionary to mean 'firmly established;' by Grassmann, 'bountiful,' literally 'well-showering.' Our author identifies it with su-eka. The words sabdam (*s*abdam, Kâ*n*va rec., ?=the sounding one) and sagarâ are obscure; yavya here apparently means, 'consisting of the yavas or half-months.'

[2] The term yâvihotram is obscure, and does not seem to occur anywhere else. The Kâ*n*va MS. reads yâmihotram (? = *g*âmihotram). Sâya*n*a's comment is corrupt in several places and affords little help.

the cattle was left behind here: hence they call him Vâstavya, for he was then left behind on the (sacrificial) site[1] (vâstu).

2. The gods went on worshipping and toiling with the same (sacrifice) by which they had ascended to heaven. Now the god who rules over the cattle, and who was left behind here,—

3. He saw (what occurred, and said), 'I have been left behind: they are excluding me from the sacrifice!' He went up after them, and with his raised (weapon)[2] rose up on the north—the time (when this happened) was that of the (performance of the) Svishtakrit.

4. The gods said, 'Do not hurl!' He said, 'Do not ye exclude me from the sacrifice! Set apart an oblation for me!' They replied, 'So be it!' He withdrew (his weapon), and did not hurl it; nor did he injure any one.

5. The gods said (to one another), 'Whatever portions of sacrificial food have been taken out by us, they have all been offered up. Try to discover

---

[1] Or perhaps, 'he was left behind with, or in, the remains (of the sacrifice);' vâstu being evidently also taken in this sense by our author, in par. 7.

[2] The text has âyatayâ merely, which, to become intelligible, clearly requires some noun, which may have been lost here. Sâyana is silent on this point. In Dr. Muir's version of the legend, Original Sanskrit Texts, IV, p. 202, the word is left untranslated. I am inclined to supply some such noun as heti, 'weapon;' cf. XII, 7, 3, 20, where this very word is used in connection with Rudra: in later times it is also specially applied to Agni's weapon or flame (gihvâ, 'tongue'). It is not impossible, however, that we have to supply tanvâ ('with his raised body, or self'). To mâ vi srâkshîh (for which the Kânva recension reads mâ 'sthâh), 'do not hurl,' and to samvivarha ('he drew back'), Sâyana supplies yagñam, 'sacrifice:' hence he apparently takes it thus,—'do not scatter (the sacrifice),'—'he kept (the sacrifice) together and did not injure it in any way.'

some means by which we may set apart an oblation for him!'

6. They said to the Adhvaryu priest, 'Sprinkle the sacrificial dishes (with butter) in proper succession; and replenish them for the sake of one (additional) portion, and again render them fit for use; and then cut off one portion for each!'

7. The Adhvaryu accordingly sprinkled the sacrificial dishes in proper succession, and replenished them for the sake of one (additional) portion, and again rendered them fit for use, and cut off one portion for each. This then is the reason why he (Rudra) is called Vâstavya[1], for a remainder (vâstu) is that part of the sacrifice which (is left) after the oblations have been made: hence, if sacrificial food is offered to any deity, the Svish*t*ak*ri*t (Agni, 'the maker of good offering') is afterwards invariably offered a share of it; because the gods invariably gave him a share after themselves.

8. That (offering) then is certainly made to 'Agni,' for, indeed, Agni is that god;—his are these names: *S*arva, as the eastern people call him; Bhava, as the Bâhîkas (call him); Pa*s*ûnâm pati ('lord of beasts,' Pa*s*upati), Rudra, Agni[2]. The name Agni, doubtless, is the most auspicious

[1] On the identification of Agni with Rudra, see also VI, 1, 3, 7; and Muir, Original Sanskrit Texts, IV, p. 339 seq.

[2] Passages such as this and VI, 1, 3, 7 seq. are of considerable interest, as showing, on the one hand, the tendency towards identifying and blending originally distinct and apparently local Vedic gods, especially Rudra, with the person of Agni, the representative of the divine power on earth in the later Vedic triad; and, on the other hand, the origin of the conception of *S*iva, in the pantheistic system of the post-Vedic period. On our passage, see also Weber, Ind. Stud. II, p. 37; I, p. 189; Muir, Original Sanskrit Texts, IV, p. 328.

(sânta), and the other names of his are inauspicious: hence it is offered to (him under the name of) 'Agni,' and to (him as) the Svishtakrit.

9. They (the gods) said, 'What we have offered unto thee who art in yonder place[1], do thou render that well-offered (svishta) for us!' He made it well-offered for them; and this is the reason why (it is offered) to (Agni as) the Svishtakrit.

10. Having recited the invitatory formula[2], he (the Hotri) enumerates (those deities) which (have received oblations at the fore-offerings, butter-portions, &c.), as well as Agni Svishtakrit:—'May Agni offer Agni's favourite dainties!' thereby he refers to Agni's butter-portion[3].—'May he offer Soma's favourite dainties!' thereby he refers to Soma's butter-portion.—'May he offer Agni's favourite dainties!' thereby he refers to that indispensable cake for Agni which is (offered) on both occasions (at the new- and full-moon sacrifices).

11. And so with the several deities. 'May he offer the favourite dainties of butter-drinking gods!' thereby he refers to the fore-offerings (prayâga) and after-offerings (anuyâga), for, assuredly, the butter-drinking gods (represent) the fore-offerings and after-offerings.—'May he offer Agni the Hotri's

[1] That is, according to Sâyana, on the Âhavanîya fire-place.

[2] The anuvâkyâ for the Svishtakrit is Rig-veda X, 2, 1: piprîhi devâñ usato yavishtha ('gladden thou the longing gods, O youngest!') &c. Âsv. S. I, 6, 2.

[3] See I, 4, 2, 16–17. These formulas (nigada) of enumeration (ayâd agnir agneh priyâ dhâmâni, &c.—yakshad agner hotuh priyâ dhâmâni, &c.) form part of the offering-formula. The yâgyâ proper, however, which they precede is Rig-veda VI, 15, 14, agne yad adya viso adhvarasya hotah ['O Agni, Hotri of the cult! when this day (thou comest) to the men'], &c.

favourite dainties!' thereby he refers to Agni as Hot*ri*; for after the gods had set apart this oblation for him, they still further propitiated him by this (formula), and invited him to his favourite dainty[1]: this is the reason why he thus enumerates.

12. Here now some make (the name of) the deity precede the 'may he offer (ayâ*t*)!' thus—'Of Agni may he offer (the favourite dainties)!' 'Of Soma may he offer!' But let him not do this; for those who make the deity precede the 'may he offer!' violate the proper order at the sacrifice, since it is by pronouncing the 'may he offer,' that he pronounces what comes first here: let him therefore place the 'may he offer' first.

13. [The Hot*ri* continues to recite]: 'May he sacrifice to his own greatness!' When, on that occasion[2], he asks him (Agni) to bring hither the deities, he also makes him bring hither his own greatness; but before this no worship of any kind has been offered to 'his (Agni's) own greatness:' and he therefore now gratifies him, and thus that (fire) has been established so as to prevent failure on his (the sacrificer's) part. This is the reason why he says 'may he sacrifice to his own greatness.'

14. 'By sacrifice may he obtain for himself food worthy of sacrifice[3]!' the food, doubtless, is these creatures: he thereby makes them eager to sacrifice, and these creatures go on sacrificing, worshipping and performing austerities.

---

[1] Or, resort, abode, dhâman.

[2] Viz. at the 'devatânâm âvahanam,' cf. I, 4, 2, 17; p. 118, n. 1.

[3] 'Âya*g*atâm e*g*yâ isha*h*.' Mahîdhara, on Vâ*g*. S. XXI, 47, interprets it thus: 'May these (isha*h*) desirous (creatures), fit for sacrifice, sacrifice properly!' Similarly perhaps Sâya*n*a on our passage.

15. 'May he, the knower of beings, (perform)[1] the sacred cult; may he graciously accept the sacrificial food!' Thereby he prays for success to this sacrifice; for when the gods graciously accept the sacrificial food, then he (the sacrificer) gains great things[2]: for this reason he says 'may he graciously accept the sacrificial food!'

16. The reason why on this occasion the invitatory and offering-formulas are made closely to correspond to each other (avakliptatama), is that the svishtakrit (is equivalent to) the evening libation, and the evening libation, doubtless, belongs to the Visve Devâh (the 'All-gods')[3]. 'Gladden thou the longing gods, O youngest!' this much in the invitatory formula refers to the Visve Devâh[4]. 'O Agni, Hotri of the cult! when this day (thou comest) to the men[5];' this much in the offering-formula refers to the Visve Devâh. And because such is the form of these two (formulas), therefore they are of

[1] Here krinotu is omitted in the text, but cf. Vâg. S. XXI, 47; Taitt. Br. III, 5, 7, 6; Âsv. S. I, 6, 5. Dr. Hillebrandt, Altind. Neu- und Vollmondsopfer, p. 11 onstrues it with the preceding formula: 'er mache darbringungswerth die Speisen; er, der Wesenkenner, nehme beim Opfer das havis an.' (?)

[2] Mahat, 'grosses.'

[3] See Vâg. S. XIX, 26. Here the author, as usual (cf. p. 5 note), attempts to enhance the solemnity of the ceremony by identifying it with the tritîya-savana, or evening libation at the Soma-sacrifice, both offerings constituting the final ceremonies in the main performance of the respective sacrifices. We shall, however, see (cf. I, 8, 3, 25) that as at the evening libation the remains of the Soma are offered up, so also are the remains of havis offered to the visve devâh at the conclusion of the present sacrifice. At IV, 4, 5, 17 it is more especially the offering of rice-cake to Agni and Varuna, at the evening libation, which is identified with the svishtakrit.

[4] See p. 202, note 2.

[5] See p. 202, note 3.

the form of the evening libation; and this is why the invitatory and offering-formulas on this occasion are made closely to correspond to each other.

17. They are both trishtubh verses; for the svishtakrit is, as it were, the residue (or site, vâstu) of the sacrifice, and the residue (or, a vacant site) is without energy[1]. Now the trishtubh means manly power[2], energy: hence he thereby imparts manly power, energy to that residue, the svishtakrit. This is why they are both trishtubh verses.

18. Or they are both anushtubh verses. The anushtubh is residue (or site, vâstu), and the svishtakrit also is residue: hence he thereby puts a residue to a residue[3]. And, verily, one who knows this, and whose (invitatory and offering-formulas) are two anushtubh verses, his homestead (vâstu) is prosperous, and he himself prospers in regard to progeny and cattle.

---

[1] Avîryam; cf. II, 1, 2, 9, where the (sarîra) empty body (of Pragâpati) is called a vâstu ayagñiyam avîryam. See also above, I, 7, 3, 7, where we met with vâstu in the sense of 'remainder, that which remains,' as Sâyana also seems to take it here.

[2] Indriyam, literally 'Indra's power.' The trishtubh often (e.g. Rig-veda X, 130, 5) appears specially related to Indra; and the hymns addressed to him are almost entirely in this metre. Taitt. S. VII, 1, 1, 4 it is said to have been created by Pragâpati from his own chest and arms, immediately after Indra, and together with the Brihat-sâman, the Râganya, and the ram; and that these are therefore vîryâvant, having been created out of vîrya (i.e. the seats of 'manly power').

[3] For this symbolical explanation see Taitt. S. VII, 1, 1, 5, where the anushtubh is said to have been created by Pragâpati, by his fourth and last creative act, from his feet, together with the Vairâga-sâman, the Sûdra, and the horse; the two last named being, therefore, styled 'bhûta-sankrâmin (? subservient to creatures).' I do not find it stated anywhere, what anushtubh verses may optionally be taken for the anuvâkyâ and yâgyâ of the svishtakrit.

19. Now here Bhâllabeya[1] made the invitatory formula (consist of) an anushtubh verse, and the offering-formula of a trishtubh verse, thinking, 'I thus obtain (the benefits of) both.' He fell from the cart, and in falling, broke his arm. He reflected: 'This has befallen because of something or other I have done.' He then bethought himself of this: '(It has befallen) because of some violation, on my part, of the proper course of the sacrifice.' Hence one must not violate the proper course (of sacrificial performance); but let both (formulas) be verses of the same metre, either both anushtubh verses, or both trishtubh verses.

20. He cuts (the portions for Agni Svishtakrit) from the north part (of the sacrificial dishes)[2], and offers them up on the north part (of the fire): for this is the region of that god, and therefore he cuts from the north part and offers on the north part. From that side, indeed, he arose[3], and there they (the gods) appeased him: for this reason he cuts from the north part, and offers on the north part.

21. He offers on this side (in front), as it were, of the other oblations. Following the other oblations cattle are produced, and the Svishtakrit represents Rudra's power: he would impose Rudra's power on

[1] That is, Indradyumna Bhâllabeya, as the Kânva recension reads here and II, 1, 4, 6. Cf. X, 6, 1, 1.

[2] He makes, as usual, an under-layer (upastarana) of butter in the guhû; cuts a piece from the north part of each of the two cakes (or of the one cake and of both the sweet and the sour milk constituting the sânnâyya); and thereupon bastes the pieces twice (not once) with butter.

[3] See above, par. 3. The same quarter is assigned to Rudra. IX, 1, 1, 10. See also Weber, Ind. Stud. I, p. 225.

the cattle if he were to bring it (the Svishtakrit) into contact with the other oblations; and his (the sacrificer's) household and cattle would be destroyed. For this reason he offers on this side, as it were, of the other oblations.

22. That (fire)—to wit, the Âhavanîya—is, indeed, that sacrifice by which the gods then ascended to heaven; and that (other fire) which was left behind here, is the Gârhapatya: hence they take out the former from the Gârhapatya, (so as to be) before (east) of it.

23. He may lay it (the Âhavanîya) down at the distance of eight steps (from the Gârhapatya); for of eight syllables, doubtless, consists the gâyatrî: hence he thereby ascends to heaven by means of the gâyatrî.

24. Or he may lay it down at the distance of eleven steps[1]; for of eleven syllables, indeed, consists the trishtubh: hence he thereby ascends to heaven by means of the trishtubh.

25. Or he may lay it down at the distance of twelve steps; for of twelve syllables, indeed, consists the gagatî: hence he thereby ascends to heaven by means of the gagatî. Here, however, there is no (fixed) measure: let him, therefore, lay it down where in his own mind he may think proper[2]. If he takes it ever so little east (of the Gârhapatya), he ascends to heaven by it.

26. Here now they say, 'Let them cook the sacri-

[1] The Baudhây. Sulvas. (66) lays it down as the rule that the Brâhmana has to construct his Âhavanîya fire at the distance of eight prakramas (step of two padas or feet each) to the east of the Gârhapatya, the Râganya at the distance of eleven, and the Vaisya at the distance of twelve, steps. Thibaut, Pandit X, p. 22.

[2] See I, 2, 5, 14.

ficial dishes on the Âhavanîya; for thence, assuredly, the gods ascended to heaven, and therewith they went on worshipping and toiling: therein we will cook the sacrificial dishes; therein we will perform the sacrifice! For, as it were, a displacement[1] of the sacrificial dishes would take place, if they were to cook them on the Gârhapatya. The Âhavanîya is the sacrifice: we will perform the sacrifice in the sacrifice!'

27. However, they also do cook on the Gârhapatya, arguing, 'The former is indeed âhavanîya (i.e. "suitable for a burnt-offering"); but that one, surely, is not (intended) for this,—viz. that they should cook uncooked (food) on it; but it is (intended) for this,—viz. that they should offer up cooked (food) on it.' He may therefore do it on whichever (fire) he pleases.

28. That sacrifice spake, 'I dread nakedness.' 'What is unnakedness for thee?' 'Let them strew (sacrificial grass) all round me!' For this reason they strew (sacrificial grass) all round the fire. 'I dread thirst.' 'How art thou to be satiated?' 'May I satiate myself after the priest has been satisfied!' Let him therefore, on the completion of the sacrifice, order that the priest be satisfied; for then he satisfies the sacrifice.

FOURTH BRÂHMAṆA.

1. Pragâpati conceived a passion for his own

[1] Apaskhala. Sâyaṇa takes skhala to mean winnowing- (or threshing-) floor (? khala): hence apaskhala would mean 'the leaping (of the husk, &c.) out of the winnowing-floor.' The Kâṇva MS. reads, 'apaskhala iva sa havishâm yad gârhapatyaḥ' (? 'the Gârhapatya is to the sacrificial food the outside of a winnowing-floor, as it were.')

daughter,—either the Sky or the Dawn[1]. 'May I pair with her!' thus (thinking) he united with her.

2. This, assuredly, was a sin in the eyes of the gods. 'He who acts thus towards his own daughter, our sister, [commits a sin],' they thought.

3. The gods then said to this god who rules over the beasts (Rudra)[2], 'This one, surely, commits a sin who acts thus towards his own daughter, our sister. Pierce him!' Rudra, taking aim, pierced him. Half of his seed fell to the ground. And thus it came to pass.

4. Accordingly it has been said by the *Ri*shi[3] with reference to that (incident), 'When the father embraced his daughter, uniting with her, he dropped his seed on the earth.' This (became) the chant (uktha) called âgnimâruta[4]; in (connection with)

[1] For other versions of this legend about Pra*g*âpati (Brahman)'s illicit passion for his daughter, which, as Dr. Muir suggests, probably refers to some atmospheric phenomenon, see Ait. Br. III, 33, and Tâ*nd*ya Br. VIII, 2, 10; cf. Muir, Original Sanskrit Texts, IV, p. 45; I, p. 107. See also *S*at. Br. II, 1, 2, 9, with note.

[2] The construction here is irregular. Perhaps this is part of the speech of the gods, being a kind of indirect address to Rudra in order to avoid naming the terrible god. Dr. Muir translates: 'The gods said, "This god, who rules over the beasts, commits a transgression in that he acts thus to his own daughter, our sister: pierce him through."' In the Kâ*n*va MS. some words seem to have been omitted at this particular place. According to the Ait. Br., the gods created a god Bhûtavat, composed of the most fearful forms of theirs. After piercing the incarnation of Pra*g*âpati's sin, he asked, and obtained, the boon that he should henceforth be the ruler of cattle.

[3] Viz., Rig-veda X, 61, 7, where verses 5–7 contain the first allusion to this legend.

[4] The âgnimâruta is one of the *s*âstras recited at the evening libation of the Soma-sacrifice; and made up chiefly of a hymn addressed to Agni Vai*s*vânara and one to the Maruts; and [following the stotriya and anurûpa pragâtha] a hymn to *G*âtavedas; [and one to the Âpas, followed by various detailed

this it is set forth how the gods caused that seed to spring[1]. When the anger of the gods subsided, they cured Pragâpati and cut out that dart of this (Rudra); for Pragâpati, doubtless, is this sacrifice.

5. They said (to one another), 'Think of some means by which that (part of the sacrifice torn out with the dart) may not be lost, and how it may be but a small portion of the offering itself!'

6. They said, 'Take it round to Bhaga (Savitri, the Patron), who sits on the south side (of the sacrificial ground): Bhaga will eat it by way of fore-portion[2], so that it may be as though it were offered. They accordingly took it round to Bhaga, who sat on the south side. Bhaga (Savitri) looked at it: it burnt out his eyes[3]. And thus it came to pass. Hence they say, 'Bhaga is blind.'

7. They said, 'It has not yet become appeased here: take it round to Pûshan!' They accordingly

verses or couplets]; viz., Rig-veda III, 3, 'vaisvânarâya prithupâgase,' &c., and I, 87, 'pratvakshasah pratavaso,' &c.; [Rig-veda I, 168, 1–2, stotriya; VII, 16, 11–12, anurûpa]; and Rig-veda I, 143, 'pratavyasîm navyasîm,' &c. (and X, 9, 'âpo hi shthâ mayobhuvas,' &c.) respectively, at the Agnishtoma (and first day of the dvâdasâha). See Âsv. Sr. V, 20, 5; Ait. Br. III, 35; IV, 30.

[1] According to Ait. Br. III, 35, where this legend is also given in connection with the âgnimâruta sâstra, Agni Vaisvânara, aided by the Maruts, stirred (and heated) the seed; and out of it sprang successively Âditya (the sun), Bhrigu, and the Âdityas; whilst the coals (angâra) remaining behind became the Angiras, and Brihaspati, and the coal dust, the burnt earth and ashes were changed into various kinds of animals. According to Harisvâmin it would seem that our passage has to be understood to the effect that the composition of the âgnimâruta sâstra shows the order of beings which the gods caused to spring forth from the seed. See also IV, 5, 1, 8.

[2] See note on I, 7, 4, 18.

[3] 'Nirdadâha.' The Kaushît. Br. VI, 10 (Ind. Stud. II, 306) and Yâska Nir. 12, 14 have nirghaghâna, 'it knocked out his eyes.' The Kaushît. Br. also makes them first take the prâsitra to Savitri, and when it cut his hands, they gave him two golden ones.

took it round to Pûshan. Pûshan tasted it: it knocked out his teeth. And thus it came to pass. Hence they say, 'Pûshan is toothless;' and therefore, when they prepare a mess of boiled rice (*k*aru)[1] for Pûshan, they prepare it from ground rice, as is done for one toothless.

8. They said, 'It has not yet become appeased here: take it round to B*ri*haspati[2]!' They accordingly took it round to B*ri*haspati. B*ri*haspati hasted to Savit*ri* for his impulsion (influence, prasava[3]), for assuredly Savit*ri* is the impeller (prasavit*ri*) of the gods. 'Impel (influence) this for me!' he said. Savit*ri*, as the impeller, accordingly impelled it for him, and being thus impelled by Savit*ri*, it did not injure him: and thus it was henceforth appeased. This, then, is essentially the same as the fore-portion.

9. Now when he cuts off the fore-portion, he cuts out what is injured in the sacrifice,—what belongs to Rudra. Thereupon he touches water: water is (a means) of lustration, hence he lustrates by means of water[4]. He now cuts off piece by piece the i*d*â[5], (which represents) cattle.

[1] *K*aru, in the ordinary sense of the word, is a potful of rice (barley, &c.) grains boiled, or rather steamed (antarûshmapakva), so as to remain whole, as in Indian curry. Cf. Weber, Ind. Stud. IX, p. 216.

[2] According to Kaushît. Br. VI, 10, they took it from Pûshan to Indra, as the mightiest and strongest of the gods; and he appeased it with prayer (brahman); whence the Brahman (in taking the prâ*s*itra) says, 'Indra is Brahman.' Weber, Ind. Stud. II, p. 307.

[3] The consistent use of derivations from one and the same root (pra-su) in this and similar passages is, of course, quite as artificial in Sanskrit as must be any imitation of it in English.

[4] He thereby averts the evil effects of the act which is connected with Rudra, 'the terrible god;' see p. 2, note 2. Besides, the i*d*â with which he now proceeds representing the cattle, he thereby guards the cattle from the rudriya, cf. above I, 7, 3, 21.

[5] See I, 8, 1, 12, 13.

10. Let him cut off (for the fore-portion) ever so small a piece[1]: thus the dart comes out; let him therefore cut off ever so small a piece. He should (according to some) put clarified butter on one side only, either below or above: thus that which is hard becomes soft and flows forth; and for this reason he should put butter on one side only, either below or above.

11. Having (nevertheless[2]) made an underlayer of butter[3] and a double cutting from the oblation (havis), he pours butter on the upper side of it; for it is only in this way that this becomes part of the sacrifice.

12. Let him not carry it (to the Brahman) along the front (east) side of the Âhavanîya fire); (though) some, it is true, do carry it along the front side. For on the front side stand the cattle facing the sacrificer: hence he would impose the power of Rudra on the cattle, if he were to carry it along the front side, and his (the sacrificer's) household and cattle would be overwhelmed. Let him therefore cross over in this way (behind the paridhis); for thus he does not impose Rudra's power on the cattle and he removes that (dart) sideways[4].

---

[1] According to Kâty. III, 4, 7, the prâsitra, or (Brahman's) fore-portion, is to be of the size of a barley-corn or a pippala (Ficus Religiosa) berry.

[2] There is no indication in the text of two different practices being here referred to. The Kânva recension, however, puts in here, 'but let him not do so,' which is evidently understood in our text also.

[3] Viz. in the prâsitraharana, or pan which is to receive the Brahman's portion. The hollow part of the vessel is to be either of the shape of a (hand-)mirror, i.e. with a round bowl, or of that of a kamasa or jug, i.e. with a square bowl (p. 7, note 1). Kâty. I, 3, 40, 41. On the 'underlayer' of butter, see I, 7, 2, 8.

[4] 'Tiryag evainam nirmimîte.' I am in doubt as to whether

13. He (the Brahman) receives[1] it, with the text (Vâg. S. II, 11 b, c), 'At the impulse (prasava) of the divine Savitri I receive thee with the arms of the Asvins, with the hands of Pûshan!'

14. And in like manner as Brihaspati then hasted to Savitri for his impulsion,—for, assuredly, Savitri is the impeller of the gods,—and said, 'Impel this for me!' and Savitri, the impeller, impelled it for him; and, impelled by Savitri, it did not injure him; so now also this one (the Brahman) hastes to Savitri for his impulsion,—for, assuredly, Savitri is the impeller of the gods,—and says 'impel this for me!' and Savitri, the impeller, impels it for him; and, impelled by Savitri, it does not injure him.

15. He eats[2] the fore-portion, with the text (Vâg. S. II, 11 d), 'With Agni's mouth I eat thee!' for Agni, assuredly, it does not injure in any way; and so neither does it injure him (the Brahman).

16. He must not chew it with his teeth: 'lest this power of Rudra should injure my teeth!' so (he thinks), and therefore he must not chew it with his teeth.

17. He then rinses his mouth with water;—water is (a means of) purification: hence he purifies himself with water, (that is, a means of) purification. After he has rinsed the vessel[3],—

enam (which is omitted in the Kânva text) really refers to Rudra's dart. Cf. par. 9.

[1] According to Kâty. II, 2, 15, he first looks at it, with the text (Vâg. S. p. 58): 'With Mitra's eye I look on thee!'

[2] According to Kâty. II, 2, 17, he previously puts it down on the shoulder of the altar, with the text (Vâg. S. p. 58), 'I put you down on the navel of the earth, in the lap of Aditi!' According to 19, however, this is optional (except when the Brahman does not eat the prâsitra immediately).

[3] According to Kâty. II, 2, 20, the Brahman, having rinsed the

18. They bring him the Brahman's portion[1]. The Brahman, in truth, sits south of the sacrifice, as its guardian. He sits facing that portion. As regards the fore-portion, that they have already brought to him and he has eaten it. In the Brahman's portion which they now bring to him, he obtains his own share; and henceforth he watches what remains incomplete of the sacrifice: for this reason they bring him the Brahman's portion.

19. He (the Brahman) must maintain silence (from the time he takes his seat on being elected)[2] up to that speech (of the Adhvaryu), 'Brahman, shall I step forward?' Those (priests) who, in the midst of the sacrifice, perform the i*d*â, which represents the domestic offerings (pâkaya*g*ña)[3], tear the sacrifice to pieces, injure it. Now the Brahman, assuredly, is the best physician: hence the Brahman thereby restores the sacrifice; but, if he were to sit there talking, he would not restore it: he must therefore maintain silence.

20. If he should utter any human sound before that time, let him there and then mutter some *Rik* or Ya*g*us-text addressed to Vish*n*u; for Vish*n*u is

vessel [or, according to the comment, the two prâsitraharana, one of which is used as lid to the other], touches his navel, with the text (Vâ*g*. S. p. 58), 'May the deities there are in the waters purify this! Enter the stomach of Indra, being offered with "Hail!" Mix not with my food! Settle down above my navel! In Indra's stomach I make thee settle!'

[1] The Brahman's regular portion (brahmabhâga) of the sacrificial food is cut, like the prâsitra or fore-portion (which apparently he receives as the representative of B*ri*haspati), from Agni's cake.

[2] See I, 1, 4, 9.

[3] According to the scholiast, it represents the pâkaya*g*ña or domestic (cooked) offerings, because at the latter, as in the i*d*â, the remains of the offerings are eaten.

the sacrifice, so that he thereby again obtains a hold on the sacrifice: and this is the expiation of that (breach of silence).

21. When he (the Adhvaryu) says, 'Brahman, shall I step forward?' the Brahman mutters thus (Vâ*g*. S. II, 12), 'This thy sacrifice, O divine Savit*ri*, they have announced . . . ,'—thereby he has recourse to Savit*ri* for his impulsion (prasava), for he is the impeller (prasavit*ri*) of the gods;—'to B*ri*haspati, the Brahman,'—for B*ri*haspati, assuredly, is the Brahman of the gods: hence he announces that (sacrifice) to him who is the Brahman of the gods; and accordingly he says, 'to B*ri*haspati, the Brahman.'—'Therefore prosper the sacrifice, prosper the lord of sacrifice, prosper me!' In this there is nothing that requires explanation.

22. [He continues, Vâ*g*. S. II, 13]: 'May his mind delight in the gushing (of the) butter[1]!' By the mind, assuredly, all this (universe) is obtained (or pervaded, âptam): hence he thereby obtains this All by the mind.—'May B*ri*haspati spread (carry through) this sacrifice! May he restore the sacrifice uninjured!'—he thereby restores what was torn asunder.—'May all the gods rejoice here!'—'all the gods,' doubtless, means the All: hence he thereby restores (the sacrifice) by means of the All. He may add, 'Step forward!' if he choose; or, if he choose, he may omit it.

---

[1] ? 'Mano *g*ûtir [*g*yotir, Kâ*n*va rec.] *g*ushatâm â*g*yasya.' I am inclined to read *g*ûter [cf. Ath.-veda XIX, 58, 1: gh*ri*tasya *g*ûti*h* samânâ]. Mahîdhara interprets: 'May the rushing (eager) mind devote itself to the butter!' Hillebrandt, Neu- und Vollmondsopfer, p. 135, apparently proposes to combine mano*g*ûtir 'des Geistes Schnelligkeit.' Perhaps *g*ushatâm has to be taken in a transitive sense: 'May the gushing of the butter delight the mind.'

EIGHTH ADHYÂYA. FIRST BRÂHMANA.

THE IDÂ.

1. In the morning they brought to Manu[1] water for washing, just as now also they (are wont to) bring (water) for washing the hands. When he was washing himself, a fish came into his hands.

2. It spake to him the word, 'Rear me, I will save thee!' 'Wherefrom wilt thou save me?' 'A flood will carry away all these creatures[2]: from that I will save thee!' 'How am I to rear thee?'

3. It said, 'As long as we are small, there is great destruction for us: fish devours fish. Thou wilt first keep me in a jar. When I outgrow that, thou wilt dig a pit and keep me in it. When I outgrow that, thou wilt take me down to the sea, for then I shall be beyond destruction.'

4. It soon became a *ghasha* (a large fish); for that grows largest (of all fish)[3]. Thereupon it said, 'In such and such a year that flood will come. Thou

---

[1] For other translations of this important legend of the deluge, see A. Weber, Ind. Streifen, I, p. 9 (Ind. Stud. I, 161 seq.); Max Müller, History of Ancient Sanskrit Literature, p. 425; J. Muir, Original Sanskrit Texts, I, p. 182. For the later versions of the same legend, especially the one from the Mahâbhârata (Vanaparvan 12747–12802), see Original Sanskrit Texts, I, p. 196 seq.

[2] According to the scholiast, 'it will carry away all these creatures that live in Bharatavarsha to some other country.'

[3] ? *S*asvad dha *gh*asha âsa, sa hi *gy*esh*th*am vardhate 'thetithî*m* samâ*m* tad augha âgantâ. 'Bald war er ein Grossfisch (*gh*asha), denn er wuchs gewaltig,' Weber. 'He became soon a large fish. He said to Manu, "When I am full-grown, in the same year the flood will come,"' Max Müller. 'Straightway he became a large fish; for he waxes to the utmost,' Muir. Perhaps *gh*asha is here intended for the name of some fabulous horned fish (cf. *sri*ṅgi, *sri*ṅgî). In the Black Yagur-veda (Taitt. S. I, 7, 1; II, 6, 7) the

shalt then attend to me (i.e. to my advice) by preparing a ship[1]; and when the flood has risen thou shalt enter into the ship, and I will save thee from it.'

5. After he had reared it in this way, he took it down to the sea. And in the same year which the fish had indicated to him, he attended to (the advice of the fish) by preparing a ship; and when the flood had risen, he entered into the ship. The fish then swam up to him, and to its horn he tied the rope of the ship, and by that means he[2] passed swiftly up to yonder northern mountain.

6. It then said, 'I have saved thee. Fasten the ship to a tree; but let not the water cut thee off[3], whilst thou art on the mountain. As the water

---

i*d*â is represented as a cow, produced by Mitra and Varu*n*a (see below, par. 24). Perhaps it was this version and the symbolical representation of the i*d*â as meaning cattle, which suggested the notion of a horned fish, in adapting an older legend.

[1] I adopt here, though not without hesitation, the interpretation proposed in the St. Petersb. Dict. (s.v. upa-âs), which the separation of mâm from the verb favours. Professor Max Müller translates: 'Build a ship then, and worship me.' Dr. Muir: 'Thou shalt, therefore, construct a ship, and resort to me.' The Mahâbhârata has: 'When standing on the ship, thou shalt look out for me: I shall be recognisable (by my being) furnished with a horn,' which, after all, may furnish the correct explanation of our passage.

[2] Or, 'it,' that is, either the ship, or the fish. That abhi-dudrâva, the reading of the Kâ*n*va school, is the right one, seems to follow from the next paragraph. Professor Weber's edition has ati-dudrâva, as read by his best MS., 'it (or he) sailed across the mountain.' The reading of the other MSS. adhi-dudrâva must be a clerical error, most likely for abhi-dudrâva. Professor Müller translates: 'The fish carried him by it over the northern mountain.' Dr. Muir: 'By this means he passed over (or, he hastened to) this northern mountain.'

[3] Anta*sk*h*aitsît, ? 'cut thee asunder,' Max Müller; 'wash thee away;' 'fortspült,' Weber; 'abschneiden, intercludere,' St. Petersb. Dict. I adopt this last meaning, = 'leave thee stranded.'

subsides, thou mayest gradually descend!' Accordingly he gradually descended, and hence that (slope) of the northern mountain is called 'Manu's descent[1].' The flood then swept away all these creatures, and Manu alone remained here.

7. Being desirous of offspring, he engaged in worshipping and austerities. During this time he also performed a pâka-sacrifice: he offered up in the waters clarified butter, sour milk, whey, and curds. Thence a woman was produced in a year: becoming quite solid[2] she rose; clarified butter gathered in her footprint. Mitra and Varuna met her.

8. They said to her, 'Who art thou?' 'Manu's daughter,' she replied. 'Say (thou art) ours,' they said. 'No,' she said, 'I am (the daughter) of him who begat me.' They desired to have a share in her. She either agreed or did not agree[3], but passed by them. She came to Manu.

9. Manu said to her, 'Who art thou?' 'Thy daughter,' she replied. 'How, illustrious one, (art thou) my daughter?' he asked. She replied,

---

[1] According to the version of the Mahâbhârata, 'the peak of the Himâlaya to which the ship was tied, was afterwards called naubandhana, 'the tying of the ship.' Professor Weber also draws attention to Ath.-veda XIX, 39, 8, where the term nâvaprabhramsana or 'gliding down of the ship' is used in connection with the summit of the Himavat.

[2] Pibdamânâ-iva, as taken by the St. Petersb. Dict. The meaning 'dripping with fat, unctuous,' offered by the commentator, was probably suggested to him by what follows in the text; and by the cow-version (p. 216, note 3), Taitt. Br. II, 6, 7, 1.

[3] Or, as the commentator takes it, 'she both promised and did not promise it;' that is to say, she promised, inasmuch as she (Idâ) is called maitrâvarunî (belonging to, or the daughter of, Mitra or Varuna; see XIV, 9, 4, 27), but refused, inasmuch as Mitra and Varuna have no share in the idâ portions.

'Those offerings (of) clarified butter, sour milk, whey, and curds, which thou madest in the waters, with them thou hast begotten me. I am the blessing (benediction): make use of me at the sacrifice! If thou wilt make use of me at the sacrifice, thou wilt become rich in offspring and cattle. Whatever blessing thou shalt invoke through me, all that shall be granted to thee!' He accordingly made use of her (as the benediction) in the middle of the sacrifice; for what is intermediate between the fore-offerings and the after-offerings, is the middle of the sacrifice.

10. With her he went on worshipping and performing austerities, wishing for offspring. Through her he generated this race, which is this race of Manu; and whatever blessing he invoked through her, all that was granted to him.

11. Now this (daughter of Manu) is essentially the same as the I*d*â; and whosoever, knowing this, performs with (the) I*d*â[1], he propagates this race which Manu generated; and whatever blessing he invokes through it (or her), all that is granted to him.

12. It (the i*d*â) consists of a fivefold cutting; for the i*d*â, doubtless, means cattle, and cattle consist of five parts[2]: for this reason it (the i*d*â) consists of a fivefold cutting.

13. When he (the Adhvaryu) has cut off the i*d*â piece by piece[3], and broken off the fore-part of the

[1] I*d*ayâ *k*arati has the double meaning 'lives with I*d*â (the woman)' and 'practices sacrificial rites with the i*d*â-ceremony.'

[2] See p. 16, note 1.

[3] The technical expression used for this fivefold cutting of the i*d*â is sam-ava-do, 'to cut off completely (or together),' or, according to the St. Petersb. Dict., 'to divide and collect the

cake (for the sacrificer's portion), he puts it (the latter) down (on the barhis) before the dhruvâ-spoon. Having then handed over the former (the idâ) to the Hotri[1], he passes by him towards the south.

14. He anoints the Hotri here[2] (with clarified butter taken from the idâ); and with it the Hotri anoints his lips, with the text, 'Of thee, offered by the lord of the mind, I eat for sap, for out-breathing!'

15. He then anoints the Hotri here[2]; and with it the Hotri anoints his lips, with the text, 'Of thee, offered by the lord of speech, I eat for strength, for in-breathing!'

16. At that time, namely, Manu became apprehensive (thinking), 'This (part) of my sacrifice—that is, this idâ representing the domestic offering—is certainly the weakest: the Rakshas must not

---

pieces.' The five cuttings of the idâ consist of the upastarana, or underlayer of butter in the idâpâtrî; of two cuttings of each of the havis (or dishes of sacrificial food) from their southern and central parts respectively; and of two drippings (or bastings, abhighârana) of butter, as in the case of the svishtakrit (see Kâty. III, 4, 6, and note on I, 7, 3, 20). According to some authorities, the idâ consists of four cuttings only (cf. Hillebrandt, Neu- und Vollm. p. 122).

[1] According to Kâty. III, 4, 8, 9, he does so without quitting his hold of the idâ; and he withdraws the latter from the Hotri, when he anoints him.

[2] A gesture here indicates the two middle joints (or, according to Harisvâmin, the intermediate links) of the Hotri's right fore-finger, viz. first the lower joint, and afterwards (par. 15) the upper joint; whereupon the Hotri applies the respective joints to his lips and smears the butter on them, cf. Âsv. S. I, 7, 1; Kâty. III, 4, 9; Hillebrandt, op. cit., p. 124. In Sat. Br. XII, 2, 4, 5 the fore-finger is called annâditamâ, or the finger 'which eats most food;' cf. Weber, Pratigñâsûtra, p. 97.

injure my sacrifice at this place.' Accordingly by that (butter, taken from the i*d*â, and smeared on his lips) he promoted it (the i*d*â to a safe place, thinking), 'Before the Rakshas (come)! before the Rakshas (come)!' And in like manner this one also thereby promotes (the i*d*â to a safe place, thinking), 'Before the Rakshas (come)! before the Rakshas (come)!' And though he does not (at present) eat (the i*d*â) visibly, lest he should eat it before it is invoked, he nevertheless promotes it (to a safe place), when he smears the (butter) on his lips.

17. He now cuts off piece by piece (the avântare*d*â) in (or, into) the Hot*ri*'s hand. That which is cut up piece by piece he thus makes visibly enter [1] the Hot*ri*; and through that which has entered (or is cooked in) his own self, the Hot*ri* invokes a blessing on the sacrificer: for this reason he cuts it off piece by piece in the Hot*ri*'s hand [2].

18. He now calls [3] (the i*d*â) in a low voice. At that time, namely, Manu became apprehensive (thinking), 'This (part) of my sacrifice—that is, this i*d*â

---

[1] Enâm hotari *s*rayati, literally 'he makes it enter into, remain in, the Hot*ri*.' The author, however, here, as in I, 6, 4, 7, mixes up the verb *s*ri with *s*râ, 'to cook.' The reason for this see p. 177, note 4.

[2] This, according to Â*s*v. *S*r. I, 7, 3, and comm., is effected in the following way: the Hot*ri* takes the i*d*â with his joined hands (a*ñg*ali) and makes it lie in his left hand; whereupon the Adhvaryu cuts the (fivefold cut) avântare*d*â from the i*d*â into the Hot*ri*'s right hand, the fingers of which point northwards; the five cuttings apparently consist of the 'underlayer' of butter, two pieces cut from the i*d*â, and drippings of butter on them. Cf. Hillebrandt, op. cit., p. 125.

[3] During the invocation of the i*d*â the Hot*ri* holds the butter (as well as the avântare*d*â), and the other priests (except the Brahman) and the sacrificer touch the i*d*â (or, according to Karka, the Hot*ri*). Kâty. III, 4, 11, 12.

representing the domestic offerings—is certainly the weakest: the Rakshas must not injure my sacrifice at this place.' He accordingly called it to him in a low voice (thinking), 'Before the Rakshas (come)! before the Rakshas (come)!' And in like manner this one (the Hotri) thereby calls it (thinking), 'Before the Rakshas (come)! before the Rakshas (come)!'

19. He calls thus (in a low voice)[1], 'Hither is called the Rathantara (chant), together with the earth: may the Rathantara, together with the earth, call me[2]! Hither is called the Vâmadevya (chant), together with the atmosphere: may the Vâmadevya, together with the atmosphere, call me! Hither is called the Brihat (chant), together with the sky: may the Brihat, together with the sky, call me!' In thus calling her (the Idâ) to him, he calls to him both these (three) worlds and those chants[3].

20. 'Hither are called the cows[4], together with the

---

[1] There are considerable differences between the text of the Hotri's call to the idâ as here given and that given in Âsv. S. I, 7, 7. The text of the Black Yagur-veda (Taitt. Br. III, 5, 8; Taitt. S. II, 6, 7; I, 7, 1), on the other hand, only differs from ours in one or two points. According to Âsv. S. I, 5, 28, the calls are to be uttered in the highest pitch (cf. Hillebrandt, Neu- und Vollmondsopfer, p. 126, note).

[2] Viz. the Hotri, as the representative of the officiating priests. Schol.

[3] On the rathantara and brihat sâmans, see p. 196, note 2. The vâmadevya sâman is Sâma-veda II, 32–34: kayâ nas kitra â bhuvad ûtî sadâvridhah sakhâ, 'with what favour will he assist us, the wonderful, ever-gladdening, friend,' &c. Cf. Haug, Ait. Br. II, 246.

[4] For upahûtâ gâvah, the Taitt. reads upahûtâ dhenuh, 'called hither is the cow.' Âsval. Sr. has upahûtâ gâvah sahâsirah—upahûtâ dhenuh saharishabhâ. Here and after the succeeding calls we have apparently to supply the inverse formulas, 'May

bull!'—the idâ, assuredly, means cattle: hence it is her he thereby calls in an indirect (mystic) way; (and in saying), 'together with the bull,' he calls her together with her mate.

21. 'Hither is called (Idâ) by that (sacrifice) which is performed by the seven Hotris!'—he thereby calls her by the Soma-sacrifice performed by the seven Hotris[1].

22. 'Hither is called Idâ, the conquering!'—he thereby calls her directly. 'Conquering' he says, because she overcomes evil, and for that reason he calls her 'the conquering.'

23. 'Hither is called the friend, the food[2]!'—the friend, the food, doubtless, means breath: hence he thereby calls hither the breath. 'Hither is called the Hek[3]!'—he thereby calls hither the (body of idâ), he thereby calls hither the entire (idâ).

24. He now intones (in a loud voice): 'Idâ is called hither! Hither (thither) is called Idâ! May Idâ also call us to her!' In saying, 'Idâ is called

the cows together with the bull call us,' &c., as in Taitt. Br., they being likewise omitted in Taitt. S. II, 6, 7.

[1] The seven Hotris comprise the Hotri with his assistants, the Maitrâvaruna (or Prasâstri), and Akkhâvâka; and the chief assistants of the Brahman, viz. the Brâhmanâkkhamsin, Âgnîdhra, Potri, and Neshtri. The Grâvastut, another assistant of the Hotri, is often added as eighth Hotri. Cf. Haug, Ait. Br. II, p. 147. Instead of upahûtâ saptahotrâ in our text, the Kânva text and the Black Yagur-veda read upahûtâh saptahotrâh, 'called hither are the seven Hotriships;' Âsval. Sr. upahûtâ divyâ sapta hotârah, 'called hither are the seven divine Hotris.'

[2] Bhaksha, 'the eating, enjoying;' perhaps the author here takes it in the sense of 'feeder,' in that of 'eater, quaffer;' Sâyana, on Taitt. S. II, 6, 7, 3, takes it as Soma-drink (somapîtha).

[3] Apparently, like hikkâ (verb hikk), imitative of the internal sound of the hiccough. The Kânva MS. has harik instead; and the Black Yagus ho, which it identifies with the self (âtman).

hither,' he, in a direct way, calls her, who is thereby called hither, as being what she really was: a cow, assuredly, she was, and a cow is four-footed; and therefore he calls her four times[1].

25. But in calling her four times, he calls her in different ways, in order to avoid repetition (of sacrificial performance); for, if he were to call, 'I*d*â is called hither! I*d*â is called hither!' or 'Hither is called I*d*â! hither is called I*d*â!' he would indeed commit the (fault of) repetition. By saying, 'I*d*â is called hither!' he calls her hitherwards; and by 'Hither (or thither, lit. called to somebody) is called I*d*â!' he calls her thitherwards. By saying, 'May I*d*â also call us to her,' he does not omit himself, and, besides, it (the formula) is changed. By (the second), 'I*d*â is called hither!' he again calls her hitherwards; so that he thereby (and by the second, 'Hither is called I*d*â,' again) calls her hitherwards and thitherwards.

26. 'Manu's daughter, the butter-pathed (ghr*i*ta-padî);'—Manu, indeed, begat her of old: for this reason he says, 'Manu's daughter.' 'The butter-pathed' he says, because butter gathered in her foot-print: therefore he calls her 'butter-pathed.'

27. And further, 'She who belongs to Mitra and Varu*n*a;'—this 'Maitrâvaru*n*a nature' (is hers), because she met Mitra and Varu*n*a[2].—'She, the god-fashioned one, is called hither as the Brahman[3];'

---

[1] After 'May I*d*â also call us to her,' he repeats 'I*d*â is called hither! Called hither (thither) is Idâ!'

[2] See I, 8, 1, 7–8, with note 3.

[3] Brahmâ devakr*i*topahûtâ; the Black Yagur-veda and Âsval. *S*r. read 'brahma devakr*i*tam upahûtam.' Cf. Taitt. S. I, 7, 1, 5, brahma vai devânâm br*i*haspati*h*.

for she, the god-fashioned one, is indeed called hither as their Brahman.—'Hither are called the divine Adhvaryus, called hither the human!'—he thereby calls both the divine Adhvaryus and those that are human: the divine Adhvaryus indeed are the calves[1] (vatsâh), and what others there are, are the human ones.

28. '—They who are to prosper this sacrifice, they who are to prosper the lord of sacrifice.' Those Brâhmanas, who have studied and teach the Veda, assuredly prosper the sacrifice, since they spread (perform) and produce it: these he thereby propitiates. And the calves also assuredly make the lord of sacrifice prosper; for the lord of sacrifice who possesses abundance of them, does indeed prosper; for this reason he says, 'They who are to prosper the lord of sacrifice.'

29. 'Hither are called the primeval, law-abiding, divine (fem.) heaven and earth, whose sons are gods.' He thereby calls to him those two, heaven and earth, within which all this (universe) is embraced.—'Hither is called this sacrificer:' thereby he calls the sacrificer to him. Why he does not mention his name on this occasion, is that this is a mysterious benediction on the idâ. Were he, on the contrary, to mention the name, he would do what is human, and the human certainly is inauspicious at the sacrifice: hence he does not mention

---

[1] ? The commentator remarks: 'He says, The divine Adhvaryus assuredly are the calves,' because, in his opinion, the sânnâyya constitutes the sacrificial food which contains the Adhvaryus (havis—adhvaryuvat). In I, 1, 2, 17 we met with the Asvins as the two divine Adhvaryus.

the name, lest he should do what is inauspicious at the sacrifice[1].

30. 'Hither (he is) called for future worship of the gods;' he thereby in a mysterious manner invokes the blessing of life on this (sacrificer); for as he sacrificed heretofore, so, while living, he will sacrifice hereafter.

31. Moreover, he thereby in a mysterious manner invokes the blessing of offspring for him; for whosoever has offspring,—while he, on his part, goes to yonder world, his offspring sacrifice in this world: hence future worship of the gods means offspring.

32. Moreover, he thereby in a mysterious manner invokes the blessing of cattle for him; for whosoever has cattle, will sacrifice hereafter, as he has sacrificed heretofore.

33. 'Hither (he is) called for more abundant havis-offering;' he thereby in a mysterious manner invokes the blessing of life on him; for as he has sacrificed heretofore, so while living will he hereafter again and again make offerings.

34. Moreover, he thereby in a mysterious manner invokes the blessing of offspring for this (sacrificer); for whosoever possesses offspring,—though he, of his own self, be one only, yet that offering is made tenfold by his offspring: hence offspring means more abundant offering.

35. Moreover, he thereby in a mysterious manner invokes the blessing of cattle for him; for whosoever possesses cattle, will make offering again and again, as he has sacrificed heretofore.

36. This then is the benediction (implied in these formulas), 'May I live, may I have offspring, may

[1] With this and the following paragraphs cf. I, 9, 1, 12 seq.

I obtain prosperity!' Now in praying for the blessing of cattle, he prays for prosperity; for cattle means prosperity: hence through these two benedictions everything is obtained; and therefore these two benedictions are here pronounced.

37. [He continues to call], 'Hither (he is) called to this (sacrifice, for the prayer[1]), "May the gods graciously accept this my offering (havis)!"' he thereby invokes complete success on the sacrifice; for what offering the gods graciously accept, by that one gains great things: for this reason he says, 'may they graciously accept[2].'

38. They (the priests and sacrificer) eat it (the idâ), and do not offer it up in the fire; for assuredly the idâ means cattle: hence they do not offer it in the fire, lest they should throw the cattle into the fire.

39. In the vital airs rather it is offered, partly in the Hotri, partly in the Sacrificer, partly in the Adhvaryu. Now, when he has broken off the forepart of the (Agni) cake, he places it before the dhruvâ-spoon. But the dhruvâ represents the sacrificer: hence this will be eaten by the sacrificer. And if he does not now visibly eat it, lest he should eat before the sacrifice is completed, it nevertheless is now (symbolically) eaten by him. All of them

---

[1] See Sâyana's comm. on Taitt. S. II, 6, 7, 6.

[2] Before this formula the Black Yagur-veda inserts, 'Called (he is) to the heavenly abode!' and after it as the final formula, 'All that is dear to him (the sacrificer) is called! Called (he is) of (? by) everything dear that is called!' Taitt. Br. III, 5, 9, 3. For the modifications of the concluding mantras in the case of the idâ being invoked for the mistress of the house (Sat. Br. I, 9, 2, 5), see Taitt. Br. III, 5, 13.

eat (of the idâ): 'May it be offered for me in all!' thus (he thinks). Five eat of it,—the idâ indeed means cattle, and cattle are fivefold: hence five eat of it.

40. Now when he (the Hotri) intones (in a loud voice)[1], he (the Adhvaryu) divides the (Agni) cake into four parts, and lays it on the barhis (the sacrificial grass covering the altar). Here it lies in place of the fathers; for there are four intermediate quarters, and the intermediate quarters represent the fathers: for this reason he divides the cake into four parts, and lays it on the barhis[2].

[1] Viz. 'Idâ is called hither!' see par. 24. According to Kâty. III, 4, 12, all (the other priests and the sacrificer, probably with the exception of the Brahman) touch the idâ (or, according to Karka, they touch the Hotri who holds the idâ) whilst the invocation of the ida takes place. The quartering of the cake, according to ib. 13, is done with the text, 'Make swell, O ruddy one! milk me life; milk me offspring; milk me cattle; milk me brahmahood; milk me kshatriyahood; milk me people! Fatten through the progeny, through the cattle of him who hates us, whom we hate!'

[2] According to Kâty. III, 4, 14, the Adhvaryu puts the four parts on the barhis and assigns one to each priest. But according to the commentary and to other Sûtras, it is the sacrificer who allocates the portions by laying them down so as to correspond with the four intermediate regions, commencing in the south-east (or Agni's) region, and saying, 'This for the Brahman,' 'This for the Hotri,' 'This for the Adhvaryu,' 'This for the Agnîdh.' The sacrificer then shifts his Brâhmanical cord from the right to the left shoulder, and while touching the four portions, and looking towards the south (the region of the fathers), murmurs (Vâg. S. II, 31), 'Here, O fathers, regale yourselves! Like bulls come hither (âvrishâyadhvam) each to his own share!' He then quits his hold of the portions, and murmurs, 'The fathers have regaled themselves: like bulls they came each to his own share!' See Sat. Br. II, 4, 2, 20 seq.; Vâg. S. p. 57. [The Kânva text of the Brâhmana does not mention the formulas here any more than does our author.] He then shifts the cord back on his left shoulder, touches water, and hands the portions to the priests for them to eat. Kâty. III, 4, 16–18.

41. And when he recites, 'Hither are called heaven and earth,' he hands it (the sha*d*avatta[1]) to the Âgnîdhra. The Âgnîdhra eats (the two pieces), with the respective texts (Vâ*g*. S. II, 10–11), 'Hither is called mother Earth; may mother Earth call me to her! Agni (am I) by virtue of my Âgnîdhraship. Hail!' 'Hither is called father Heaven; may father Heaven call me to him! Agni (am I) by virtue of my Âgnîdhraship. Hail!' He, the Âgnîdhra, truly is the representative of heaven and earth, and therefore he eats (the sha*d*avatta) in this manner.

42. And when (the Hot*ri*) pronounces the benediction[2], then (the sacrificer) mutters (Vâ*g*. S. II, 10 a), 'May Indra bestow on me that power of his! may abundant riches accrue to us! may there be blessings for us! may there be true blessings for us!' For indeed this is a receiving of blessings: hence what blessings the priests on this occasion invoke on him, those he thereby receives and makes his own.

43. [On the conclusion of the invocation and the eating[3]] they cleanse themselves (with water poured)

---

[1] Kâty. *S*r. III, 4, 19. There is some uncertainty as to the particular time when the Adhvaryu cuts the sha*d*avatta; cf. Hillebrandt, p. 123. Mahîdhara on Vâ*g*. S. II, 10 remarks: When the Hot*ri* pronounces the call to heaven and earth, then he (the Adhvaryu), having put one piece of each of the two cakes in (the two bowls of) the Sha*d*avatta (vessel), gives it to the Agnîdh; and the latter eats it with the formulas 'Hither is called (the mother Earth),' &c. The 'six cuttings' of the Sha*d*avatta consist of a piece of the Agni cake with an 'underlayer' and a dripping of butter for each of the two bowls of the Sha*d*avatta dish.

[2] That is, the formula 'Hither is called the sacrificer,' see par. 29.

[3] The priests eat first their quarter of the cake and then, with the sacrificer, their share of the i*d*â. The Hot*ri* eats also the avântare*d*â, with the text (Â*s*v. *S*. I, 7, 8), 'O I*d*â, accept graciously our share!' &c.

through the two strainers (pavitra, 'purifier'). For they have now performed the idâ, which represents the domestic offerings; and thinking, 'Purified by the purifiers we will now perform what part of the sacrifice remains still unaccomplished,' they cleanse themselves with the strainers.

44. He (the Adhvaryu) then throws the two strainers on the prastara[1]. The prastara, doubtless, represents the sacrificer, and the two strainers the out-breathing and in-breathing: hence he thereby invokes out-breathing and in-breathing on the sacrificer; and for this reason he throws the strainers on the prastara.

Second Brâhmana.

The After-Offerings (Anuyâgas).

1. They now remove two burning samidhs (from the Âhavanîya fire). That fire, indeed, is now worn out, (and therefore useless) for the after-offerings, since it has been carrying the sacrifice to the gods: 'Let us perform the after-offerings in such (fire) as is not out-worn!' thus they think, and for this reason they remove those two burning samidhs (from the fire).

2. Thereupon they again move them close (to the fire). Thereby they cause the fire to increase again and to be no longer out-worn: 'Let us perform what part of the sacrifice remains still unaccomplished in such (fire) as is not out-worn!' so think they, and for this reason they again move them close (to the fire).

3. He (the Âgnîdhra) then puts on the kindling-

[1] See I, 3, 2, 5 seq. The Kânva text omits this paragraph.

stick (which was reserved at the time of kindling)[1]. He thereby kindles that (fire): 'Let us perform in the well-kindled (fire) what part of the sacrifice remains unaccomplished!' thus he thinks, and for this reason he puts on the samidh.

4. The Hotri consecrates it (the kindling-stick), with the formula (Vâg. S. II, 14 a), 'This, O Agni, is thy kindler; mayest thou grow and increase by it; and may we also grow and increase!' for even as before he recited over the fire when it was being kindled, so also now he recites. This is the Hotri's duty; but the sacrificer himself may pronounce the consecratory formula, if he think that the Hotri does not know it[2].

5. He (the Âgnîdhra) then sweeps (the fire) together. He thereby harnesses it: 'Thus harnessed, may it convey (to the gods) what part of the sacrifice still remains unaccomplished!' thus he thinks, and for this reason he sweeps it together. He sweeps

---

[1] See I, 4, 1, 38. The Adhvaryu takes the fresh stick (samidh), asks the permission of the Brahman to step forward for the after-offerings; and orders the Âgnîdhra to put the stick on, and trim, the fire. Whilst the Brahman mutters his formula (Vâg. S. II, 12–13), 'This thy sacrifice, O divine Savitri, they proclaimed to Brihaspati, the Brahman,' &c. (see I, 7, 4, 21), the Âgnîdhra executes the Adhvaryu's orders. Kâty. III, 5, 1; II, 2, 21.

[2] That is to say (as would appear), if the Hotri follows a school which does not recognise this particular ceremony as belonging to the Hotri's ritual. Thus the Âsval. Sr. makes no mention of it, and hence a Hotri belonging to the Sâkala or Bâshkala sâkhâs would not undertake the recitation of this consecratory formula. The Sâṅkhây. Sr., on the other hand, does prescribe it (cf. Hillebrandt, Neu- und Vollm. p. 135, note 4), and a Hotri of the Kaushîtaki-sâkhâ would accordingly claim it as his privilege or duty to consecrate the samidh. For a somewhat different view, cf. Weber, Ind. Stud. X, 155; V, 408.

once (with the band of the fire-wood along each of the three enclosing-sticks); for thrice each time they swept for the gods on the former occasion[1]: 'Lest we should do it in the same way as for the gods;' thus he thinks, and accordingly he sweeps once each time in order to avoid repetition (of sacrificial performance). Repetition he would undoubtedly commit, if he were to sweep thrice the first time and thrice the second: for this reason he sweeps once (along each stick).

6. He sweeps (each time), with the formula (Vâg. S. II, 14 b), 'O Agni, food-gainer, I cleanse thee, the food-gainer, who hast hastened to the food!' On the former occasion he said, 'thee who art about to hasten (to the food),' for on that occasion he was indeed about to hasten thither; now, however, he says, who hast hastened (to the food),' for now he has indeed hastened thither: for this reason he says 'thee who hast hastened.'

7. He now makes the after-offerings. Whatever gods he invokes by means of this sacrifice, and for whichever of them this sacrifice is performed, to all offering has now been made; and to all those to whom offering has been made, he now, after that, offers once more: hence the name 'after-offerings.'

8. Now this is why he makes the after-offerings. The after-offerings assuredly are the metres[2], and the metres are the cattle of the gods: hence as cattle, when harnessed, here convey (burdens) for men, so in like manner the metres, being harnessed,

[1] See I, 4, 4, 14. While, on the former occasion, the Âgnîdhra in sweeping moved round the fire, on the present occasion he remains standing on the north side of it. Kâty. III, 5, 4.

[2] See I, 3, 2, 8, 9.

convey the sacrifice to the gods. Now the occasion on which the metres gratified the gods, and for which the gods, in their turn, then gratified the metres, was when before this the metres, on being harnessed, conveyed the sacrifice to the gods and thereby gratified them.

9. And this again is why he makes the after-offerings. The after-offerings are the metres: hence he thereby gratifies the metres, and for this reason also he makes the after-offerings. By whatever team, therefore, he has himself drawn, that (team) he would thereby unyoke, saying, 'Give it to drink, feed it well!' and thus his team is propitiated.

10. In the first place he makes offering to the Barhis (sacrificial-grass covering). Though the smallest metre, the gâyatrî is yoked first of the metres [1]; and this on account of its strength, since, having become a falcon, it carried off the Soma from heaven [2]. They consider it unseemly, however, that the gâyatrî, being the smallest metre, should be yoked first of the metres; and the gods accordingly arranged the metres here, at the after-offerings, so as it ought to be, 'lest there should be a confusion.'

11. In the first place, then, he offers to the Barhis. The Barhis indeed is this world; the Barhis is the plants: hence he thereby bestows plants on this world, and these plants are firmly rooted in this world. Now this entire universe (*g*agat) is contained in this (metre), and therefore the latter is (called) *g*agatî: this is why they have placed the *g*agatî metre first.

12. In the second place he offers to Narâ*s*a*m*sa.

[1] See, for instance, I, 3, 4, 6.

[2] For this myth, see I, 7, 1, 1.

Now, Narâsamsa is the air. Man (nara), namely, means (human) being; and these same beings move about in the air speaking aloud. And when he (man) speaks, they say 'he chants (sams);' and therefore Narâsamsa is the air[1]. But the trishtubh also is the air[2], and for this reason they have placed the trishtubh second.

13. Then Agni is the last (to whom offering is made). Agni assuredly is the gâyatrî; and therefore they placed the gâyatrî last. In this way they established the metres in complete and proper order; and hence no confusion here takes place.

14. The Adhvaryu[3] says (to the Hotri), 'Pronounce the offering-prayer (yâgyâ) to the gods!' and the Hotri (begins his prayer) at all (the three offerings) with 'The divine....' For the metres assuredly are the gods of the gods, since they are their cattle, and cattle means a home, and a home is a safe resting-place. The after-offerings, doubtless, are the metres: therefore the Adhvaryu says, 'Pronounce the offering-prayer to the gods!' and at all of them the Hotri begins with 'The divine . . .[4].'

[1] That is, because man (nara) speaks, chants, (samsati) in it.

[2] Either because both are in the middle (viz. the trishtubh of the three chief metres, and the air between heaven and earth), or because they consist of eleven parts (viz. the trishtubh of eleven syllables, and the air having ten directions, Sat. Br. VI, 2, 2, 34; VIII, 4; 2, 13, with itself as the eleventh), or because they are both connected with Rudra. Comm.

[3] As on previous occasions, the Adhvaryu first calls on the Âgnîdhra, 'Bid (Agni) hear (o srâvaya)!' and the latter responds by 'Yea, may (he) hear (astu sraushat)!' This is repeated before each of the two other after-offerings. See I, 5, 2, 16.

[4] The drift of the argument of this paragraph is not quite clear to me. The after-offerings have for their deities the metres, and hence the latter are apparently called the deities of the deities, that is, of the

15. ['The divine Barhis (or Narâsamsa) may accept (the offering)] for abundant obtainment of abundant gift! [Vaushat!]' For a deity only the vashat-call is pronounced, to a deity only offering is made; but here at the after-offerings there is no (proper) deity[1]. When he says 'The divine Barhis,' in this there is neither Agni, nor Indra, nor Soma; when he says 'The divine Narâsamsa,' neither is there in this anything whatever (of the nature of a god); and what Agni there is (in the third offering-prayer), he indeed is virtually the gâyatrî.

16. The reason, then, why he offers with the formula 'for abundant obtainment of abundant gift[2],'

---

recipients of the offerings. The difference between the fore-offerings and after-offerings in regard to the offering-formula lies in this, that at the first fore-offering the Adhvaryu, in calling on the Hotri, names the particular object of the offering, viz. 'Pronounce the offering-prayer to the samidhs!' while for the remaining prayâgas he merely calls 'Pronounce the offering-prayer!' and the Hotri begins all his prayers (after the introductory âgur-formula) with the name of the respective recipient of the oblation. At the after-offering, on the other hand, the Adhvaryu calls each time, 'Pronounce the offering-prayer to the gods' (or, according to Kâty. III, 5, 8, optionally without 'to the gods,' the second and third times), and the Hotri's prayers begin with 'The divine (Barhis, or Narâsamsa, or Agni Svishtakrit) . . . .' See I, 5, 3, 8 seq.

[1] Agni Svishtakrit, the recipient of the third after-offering, is, as we saw, regarded as representing the gâyatrî metre.

[2] Vasuvane vasudheyasya (vetu); perhaps better, as Sâyana, on Taitt. S. II, 6, 9, takes it, 'May he partake of the gift of wealth for the (sacrificer's) obtainment of wealth.' 'For the wealth-desirer of wealth-gift'='for the desirer of wealth-possession,' St. Petersb. Dict. Our author apparently takes it in the sense of 'for the obtainer of wealth and for the receiver of wealth;' and Mahîdhara (Vâg. S. XXII, 48; XXVIII, 12) interprets it 'for the giving (or obtainment) of wealth and for the depositing of treasure (i.e. for burying a treasure in the sacrificer's house!)' Harisvâmin takes vasuvane as vocative; but the accent is against his view.

is that Agni is the obtainer of wealth, and Indra is the recipient of wealth; and Indra and Agni are indeed the (joint) divinity of the metres: and in this way it is for a deity that the vashat is pronounced, and to a deity that the offering is made.

17. After he has made the last after-offering, he pours together (the butter which remains in the upabhrit with that which attaches to the guhû), and offers it (by pouring it from the guhû in a line from west to east into the fire). For doubtless these are the after-offerings to the fore-offerings: hence even as there, at the fore-offerings[1], he makes the spiteful enemy pay tribute to the sacrificer, and the one to be consumed pay tribute to the consumer; so now he makes him pay tribute at the after-offerings.

Third Brâhmana.

Sûktavâka, Samyuvâka, and Offering of Remains[2].

1. He now separates the two spoons (guhû and upabhrit), with the text (Vâg. S. II, 15 a), 'May I be victorious after the victory of Agni and Soma! with the impetus of the (sacrificial) food I urge myself on.' With his right hand he moves the guhû eastwards (from its usual place on the prastara-bunch upon the altar), with the text (ib. b), 'May Agni and Soma drive him away who hates us, and whom

[1] See I, 5, 3, 18.

[2] The whole of the third Brâhmana is taken up with the duties of the Adhvaryu and Âgnîdhra at the three ceremonies: paragraphs 1–19 with those at the sûktavâka; pars. 20–22 with those at the samyuvâka; and pars. 23–27 with those at the offering of the remains (samsrava) of butter. The duties of the Hotri are then detailed in the fourth Brâhmana.

we hate! with the impetus of the (sacrificial) food I drive him away.' With his left hand he moves the upabh*ri*t westwards (from its place on the barhis to outside the altar):—Thus, if the sacrificer himself (does it)[1].

2. And if the Adhvaryu (does it, he says), 'May this sacrificer be victorious after the victory of Agni and Soma! with the impetus of the food I urge him on;' and, 'May Agni and Soma drive him away whom this sacrificer hates, and who hates him! with the impetus of the food I drive him away.' Thus he does at the full-moon sacrifice, because the full-moon offering belongs to Agni and Soma.

3. At the new-moon sacrifice, on the other hand, he uses the texts (ib. c, d), 'May I be victorious after the victory of Indra and Agni[2]! with the impetus of the food I urge myself on;' and, 'May Indra and Agni drive him away who hates us, and whom we hate! with the impetus of the food I drive him away:'—Thus, if the sacrificer himself does it.

4. And if the Adhvaryu (does it, he says), 'May this sacrificer be victorious after the victory of Indra and Agni! with the impetus of the food I urge him on;' and, 'May Indra and Agni drive him away whom this sacrificer hates, and who hates him! with the impetus of the food I drive him away.' Thus he says at the new-moon sacrifice, because the new-

---

[1] In Taitt. Br. III, 3, 9 a different symbolical explanation is given of the separation of the spoons: it is said there that by shifting the *g*uhû eastwards, he drives away the enemies that have been born; and by shifting the upabh*ri*t towards the west, he drives away those that will be born hereafter; and the sacrificer then stands firmly established in this world.

[2] See p. 162, note 3.

moon offering belongs to Indra and Agni. And in this manner he separates (the spoons) according to the respective deities. This is why he thus separates them:

5. Behind the *g*uhû stands the sacrificer, and behind the upabh*ri*t stands he who means evil to him: hereby, then, he brings the sacrificer forward to the front (or east), and the one who means evil him he drives back (or towards the west). Behind the *g*uhû stands the eater (enjoyer), and behind the upabh*ri*t the one to be eaten (enjoyed): thus he now brings the eater (enjoyer) to the front, and the one to be eaten (enjoyed) he drives back.

6. Thus the separation (of the eater and the eaten) is effected in one and the same act; and hence from one and the same man spring both the enjoyer (the husband), and the one to be enjoyed (the wife): for now kinsfolk (*g*âtyâ*h*) live sporting and rejoicing together, saying, 'In the fourth (or) third man (i.e. generation) we unite[1].' And this is so in accordance with that (separation of the spoons).

---

[1] This passage is of considerable importance, as showing that the prohibition of intermarriage between near blood-relations,—so rigidly enforced in later times, and already formulated in passages such as Âpast. Dharm. II, 5, 15, 16, 'One must not give one's daughter to a man belonging to the same gotra. Nor to one related (within six degrees) on the mother's (or father's) side.' Gobh. III, 4, 3-5, 'One must take for one's wife one who is not of the same gotra, or one who is not sapi*nd*a to one's mother,'—was not as yet firmly established in our author's time. Harisvâmin remarks on our text, that the Kâ*n*vas allow intermarriage in such cases from the third generation—(the Kâ*n*va text of the *S*at. Br. reads, 'In the third man we unite, in the fourth man we unite')—and the Saurâsh*t*ras from the fourth generation; and that the Dâkshi*n*âtyas allow marriage with daughters of the mother's brother,

7. Thereupon (the Adhvaryu) anoints the enclosing-sticks (paridhi) with (the butter attaching to) the *g*uhû. With that (spoon) with which he has made offering to the gods, with which he has concluded the sacrifice, he thus gratifies the enclosing-sticks: this is why he anoints them with the *g*uhû.

8. He anoints them (successively)[1], with the texts (Vâ*g*. S. II, 16 a–c), 'For the Vasus thee!' 'For the Rudras thee!' 'For the Âdityas thee!' For these—to wit, the Vasus, Rudras, and Âdityas—are three (classes of) gods: 'for them (I anoint) thee,' he thereby says.

9. Thereupon, taking hold of the (middle) enclosing-stick, he calls (on the Âgnîdhra) to bid (them) listen[2]: thus (i. e. by touching the paridhi) it is for the enclosing-sticks that he calls for the *s*rausha*t*. The *s*rausha*t*-call assuredly is the sacrifice: hence he thereby expressly gladdens the enclosing-sticks by means of the sacrifice: for this reason he calls for the *s*rausha*t*, while taking hold of the enclosing-stick.

10. Having called for the *s*rausha*t* (and been responded to by the Âgnîdhra), he thus addresses (the Hot*ri*), 'The divine Hot*ri*s[3] are summoned—,' the divine Hot*ri*s, namely, are (represented by) these

and with sons of the father's sister. See Weber, Ind. Stud. X, p. 75; Max Müller, History of Ancient Sanskrit Literature, p. 387; Bühler, Sacred Laws of the Âryas, I, p. 126.

[1] Viz. in the order in which they were laid around, i.e. first the middle one, then the southern, and lastly the northern one. Kâty. III, 5, 24.

[2] The Adhvaryu calls on the Âgnîdhra with 'Make listen (o *s*râvaya); and the latter responds with 'Yea, may (one) listen! (astu *s*rausha*t*). See I, 5, 2, 18 seq.

[3] Sâya*n*a on Taitt. S. I, 1, 13 explains this by 'Impelled are the divine Hot*ri*s by the highest Lord (parame*s*vara).'

enclosing-sticks, since these are Agnis (fires)[1]. When he says, 'the divine Hotris are summoned (ishita),' he means to say, 'the divine Hotris are wished for (ishta).' [He continues], '—for the proclamation of success[2],'—for on this the gods themselves are indeed intent, to wit, that they should speak what is favourable (conducive to success, sâdhu), that they should do what is favourable: hence he says 'for the proclamation of success.'—'The human one is called upon for the song of praise (sûktavâka)[3]!' by these words he urges on this human Hotri to singing praises.

11. He now takes the prastara-bunch[4]. The prastara assuredly is the sacrificer: hence whithersoever his sacrifice went, thither he thereby wishes him good-speed[5]! Now it is to the world of the gods that his sacrifice went; and to the world of the gods accordingly he thereby takes the sacrificer.

---

[1] On the Agnis officiating as Hotri, I, 2, 3, 1.

[2] Thus Sâyana explains bhadravâkyâya on Taitt. S. I, 1, 13 (vol. i. p. 233). For the Hotri's formula itself, see Sat. Br. I, 9, 1, 4.

[3] According to Kâty. III, 6, 1, and the other Sûtras, the Adhvaryu adds here sûktâ brûhi, 'recite the praises (hymns)!' which Sâyana on Taitt. Br. III, 6, 15 combines with the preceding sûktavâkâya, and explains thus: 'hotâ tvam sûktasya vâko vakanam yasya so 'yam devah sûktavâkah (? i.e. Agni, cf. Sat. Br. I, 9, 1, 4) tasmai sûktavâkâya devâya sûktâ brûhi, idam dyâvâprithivîm anuvâkoktâni sobhanâni vakanâni kathaya (!);' but differently on Taitt. S. I, 1, 13, 'idam dyâvâprithivî bhadram abhûd (Taitt. Br. III, 5, 10) ityâdy-anuvâkah sûktam, tasya vâko vakanam, tadartham mânusho hotâ preshitah; ato hetoh, he hotas tat sûktam brûhi.'

[4] The two stalks, called vidhriti (separation), separating the prastara-bunch from the barhis or grass-covering of the altar (cf. I, 3, 4, 10), he puts back in the place whence they were taken. Kâty. III, 6, 4.

[5] Svagâ. ? literally 'self-go,' i.e. 'success to him!'

12. Should he desire rain, let him take up (the prastara), with this text (Vâg. S. II, 16 d), 'Be ye in harmony with each other, O heaven and earth!' for when heaven and earth are in harmony with each other, then indeed it rains[1]: for this reason he says, 'be ye in harmony with each other, O heaven and earth!'—'May Mitra and Varuna favour thee with rain!' whereby he says, 'may he who rules over the rain favour thee with rain!' Now he that rules over the rain is undoubtedly that blowing one (Vâyu, the wind); and he, it is true, blows as one only; but, on entering into man, he becomes a forward and a backward moving one; and they are these two, the out-breathing and the in-breathing. And Mitra and Varuna assuredly are the out-breathing and in-breathing; and hence he says by that (prayer), 'may he who rules over the rain favour thee with rain!' Let him then take it up, with this text, for then the rain will at all times be propitious. He anoints it (the prastara): thereby he makes him (the sacrificer) an oblation, thinking, 'May he, as an oblation, go to the world of the gods!'

13. He anoints the top (of the prastara with the butter) in the guhû, the middle part (with that) in the upabhrit, and the lower end (with that) in the dhruvâ; for the guhû is, as it were, the top, the upabhrit the middle, and the dhruvâ the root.

---

[1] Cf. Ait. Âr. III, 1, 2, 2-4 (Max Müller, Up. I, p. 249): 'The first half (of a samhitâ or combination of final and initial letters) is the earth, the second half heaven, their uniting the rain, the uniter Parganya. And so it is when he (Parganya) rains thus strongly, without ceasing, day and night; then they say also (in ordinary language), "Heaven and earth have come together." See also Sat. Br. I, 7, 2, 16.

14. He anoints (each time), with the text (Vâg. S. II, 16 e), 'May (the gods) eat, licking the anointed bird[1]!' He thereby causes it (the prastara and hence symbolically the sacrificer) to be a bird and fly up from this world of men to the world of the gods. He then draws it twice (towards the Âhavanîya) alow (near the ground). The reason why he must draw it alow (is this): the prastara is the sacrificer; and in this way he does not remove him from this firm footing of his; and he, moreover, secures rain for this locality.

15. He draws it along, with the text (Vâg. S. II, 16 f), 'Go to the spotted (mares) of the Maruts!' He means to say, 'Go to the world of the gods,' when he says, 'Go to the spotted (mares) of the Maruts[2]!'—'Having become a spotted cow, go to the sky and thence bring us rain hither!' The spotted cow, doubtless, is this (earth): whatever rooted and rootless food is here on this (earth), by that this (earth) is a spotted cow. 'Having become

[1] Vyantu vayo 'ktam rihânâh. Mahîdhara interprets it, 'May the birds (i. e. the metres) go (? to heaven,—taking and) licking the anointed (prastara).' The Kânvas read, 'vyantu vayo ripto rihânâh.' The Black Yagus (Taitt. S. I, 1, 13, 1) has 'aktam rihânâ viyantu vayah, pragâm yonim mâ nirmriksham, âpyâyantâm âpa oshadhayah,' which Sâyana explains by 'May the birds having licked the anointed (top) go their several ways,' &c.; and the Taitt. Br. III, 3, 9, 3 remarks to viyantu vayah, 'Having made him birds, he makes him go to the heavenly world.' According to Sâyana, the three above formulas are by Âpastamba referred to the three acts of anointing, whereas the others, he says, divide the first formula into two, and use the second one (pragâm, &c.) while the lower part of the prastara is anointed. See, however, Hillebrandt, Neu- und Vollm. p. 142, note 3.

[2] The Black Yagus (Taitt. S. I, 1, 13) has, 'The spotted (mares) of the Maruts are ye (O plants)!'

this (earth), go thou to the sky!' this is what he thereby says. 'Thence bring us rain hither!' From rain certainly spring vigour, sap, well-being: for this reason he says, 'thence bring us rain hither!'

16. He then takes a single stalk from it. The prastara-bunch is the sacrificer; and therefore, if he were to throw the whole prastara (at once) into the fire, the sacrificer would speedily go to yonder world. In this way, however, the sacrificer will live long; and what the full measure of human life here on earth is, for that he takes this (single stalk) therefrom.

17. Having held (the prastara) for a moment, he throws it into the fire: whither his (the sacrificer's) one (part of) self (or, body)[1] went, thither he thereby causes it to go[2]. But were he not to throw it into the fire, he would cut off the sacrificer from (yonder) world. In this way, however, he does not cut off the sacrificer from (yonder) world.

18. He throws it (with its top) to the east, for the east is the region of the gods; or to the north, for the north is the region of man. With the fingers only they should smooth it down, not with pieces of wood; since it is with sticks that they pierce any other corpse. Fearing, lest they should treat it in the same way as any other corpse, they should smooth it down with the fingers only, not with pieces of wood. When the Hotri recites the song of praise,—

19. The Âgnîdhra says (to the Adhvaryu), 'Throw

[1] The itara âtmâ in pars. 17 and 19 have to be taken correlatively.

[2] That is to say, he makes sure that the sacrificer has really obtained the object for which the sacrifice was undertaken,—the right to go to the heavenly world after his death.

(the single stalk) after (the prastara)!'—'whither his (the sacrificer's) other self went, thither make it now go,' this is what he thereby says. [The Adhvaryu] having thrown it silently after, touches himself[1], with the text (Vâg. S. II, 16 f): 'Guardian of the eye art thou, O Agni; guard mine eye!' In this way also he does not throw himself into the fire after (the prastara or sacrificer).

20. He (the Âgnîdhra) then says[2] (to the Adhvaryu), 'Discourse together!'—he thereby says, 'Make him (the sacrificer) discourse with the gods.' [The Adhvaryu asks], 'Has he gone (to the gods), Agnîdh?' whereby he says, 'Has he really gone?'—'He has gone!' replies the other.—'Bid (the gods) hear!' by these words he (the Adhvaryu) means to say, 'Make him (the sacrificer) be heard, make him be noticed by the gods!'—'May (one or they) hear (srausha*t*)!' thereby he (the Âgnîdhra) means to say, 'They know him, they have recognised him.' Thus the Adhvaryu and the Âgnîdhra lead the sacrificer to the world of the gods.

21. He (the Adhvaryu) then says, 'Good-speed to the divine Hot*ri*s[3]!' The divine Hot*ri*s assuredly are these enclosing-sticks, since these are Agnis (fires): it is to them that he thereby bids good-speed, and therefore he says, 'good-speed to the

---

[1] He touches himself near the heart, or, according to Vaidyanâtha, he touches his eyes. After this he has, as usual, to touch the lustral water. See p. 2, note 2.

[2] Here begins the sa*m*yuvâka; see p. 241, note 1.

[3] 'Svagấ daívyâ hót*ri*bhya*h*.' The form daivyâ seems to have become fixed before hot*ri*, in consequence of its frequent use, especially in the Âprî hymns, as nom. acc. dual daívyâ hótârâ; and in the invocation of the I*d*â, as nom. plur. daívyâ hótâra*h*.

divine Hot*ri*s!'—'Success (svasti) to the human!' thereby he desires that this human Hot*ri* may not fail.

22. He now throws the enclosing-sticks into the fire. The middle enclosing-stick he throws first, with the text (Vâ*g*. S. II, 17 a), 'The stick which thou laidst around thee, O divine Agni, when thou wert concealed by the Pa*n*is, I bring thee for thy pleasure; may it not prove faithless to thee!'—With (ib. b), 'Approach ye the place beloved of Agni!' he throws the two others after it.

23. He then[1] seizes the *g*uhû and the upabh*ri*t at the same time. For on the former occasion[2], when he anoints (the prastara—sacrificer), he makes him an oblation, thinking, 'May he, as an oblation, go to the world of the gods!' for this reason he seizes the *g*uhû and the upabh*ri*t at the same time.

24. He seizes them for the Vi*s*ve Devâ*h* (the All-gods). For, assuredly, when any sacrificial food is taken without being announced to any one deity, then all the gods think that they have a share in it. Now when he takes that sacrificial food, the (residue of) butter, he does not announce it to any one deity; and hence he takes up (the two spoons) for the Vi*s*ve Devâ*h*, and thus makes that (residue of butter) the vai*s*vadeva[3] at the haviryag*ñ*a.

25. He seizes them, with the text (Vâ*g*. S. II, 18),

---

[1] Here begins the offering of the remains (sa*m*srava) of butter; see p. 236, note 2.

[2] See par. 14 above.

[3] The author again connects the havis-offering with the more solemn Soma-sacrifice; the third, or evening, libation of Soma being supposed to belong to the Vi*s*ve Devâ*h*; cf. Vâ*g*. S. XIX, 26; Ait. Br. VI, 4.

'The residue (of the butter) ye have for your share, ye, mighty by (this) food!' the residue, of course, is that which remains;—'O ye gods, staying on the prastara, and representing the enclosing-sticks[1];' for both the prastara and the enclosing-sticks have been thrown into the fire;—'All of you, applauding this speech,' thereby he makes it the vaisvadeva (belonging to the Visve Devâh);—'Be seated on this couch of grass (barhis) and enjoy yourselves! Svâhâ! Vât[2]!' as one offers what has been consecrated by 'vashat,' this (residue) thereby becomes such for him (the sacrificer).

26. For whomsoever they take the sacrificial food from a cart, for him they unyoke (the spoons, by placing them) on the yoke of that cart, thinking, 'Where we yoke, there we also unyoke[3];' for from the same place where they yoke, they also unyoke. For him, on the other hand, for whom they take it from a jar, (they unyoke the spoons, by placing them) on the wooden sword, thinking, 'Where we yoke, there we also unyoke;' for from the same place where they yoke, they also unyoke.

27. Yoke-fellows, indeed, are these two spoons for the sacrifice: he yokes them when he starts[4] (or,

[1] Paridheyâh, literally 'ye who are to be laid around;' according to Mahîdhara = paridhibhavâh. The Kânva text has paridhayah, 'enclosing-sticks.' The Black Yagus (Taitt. S. I, 1, 13, 2) has 'barhishadah (sitting on the barhis)' instead.

[2] The original meaning of this sacrificial call, as of the apparently allied vashat, vaushat, appears to be, 'May he (Agni) carry it (the oblation to the deity)!' Cf. p. 88, note 2.

[3] See I, 1, 2, 8.

[4] This seems to refer to the time when he gets the spoons ready for their sacred use. He then wipes them with sacrificial grass; that is, he, as it were, rubs down the horses before starting on his journey to the world of the gods. See p. 68, note 1.

first uses them). Now, were he only to release (unyoke) either of them after putting it down, it would fall down just as a draught animal[1] (would, if made to lie down before being unyoked). At the Svishtakrit these two undergo an unyoking: he then lays them down, and so unyokes them. He then yokes them again, at the after-offerings. Having performed the after-offerings, he effects another unyoking: he lays them down, and so unyokes them. Thereupon he yokes them again when he seizes them both at the same time; and when he has travelled over the way for which he has yoked them, he unyokes them. After the sacrifice offspring (is produced). Hence this man yokes (unites), and then unyokes, and again yokes them; and when he has travelled over the way for which he yoked them, he finally unyokes them. He lays (the spoons) down, with the text (Vâg. S. II, 19 a), 'Fond of butter are ye; protect the two yoke-fellows! gracious are ye: lead me to grace!' whereby he says, 'good are ye: lead me to goodness!'

NINTH ADHYÂYA. FIRST BRÂHMANA.

1. Now[2] when (the Adhvaryu) says, 'The divine Hotris are summoned for the proclamation of success,

[1] I adopt the interpretation of Harisvâmin, who translates avârkhet by adhah patet. The St. Petersb. Dict. apparently proposes, 'he would unharness them, as he would unharness a horse (or team).' According to Harisvâmin, the author here controverts the view of the Karakas (karakasruti), who apparently taught that the (symbolical) unharnessing of the spoons should succeed their being laid down on the yoke; while our author maintains that the unharnessing should precede the laying down.

[2] The author now proceeds to give in detail the formulas to be recited by the Hotri during the ceremonies treated in the preceding Brâhmana (see p. 236, note 2); pars. 1–23 treating of the sûktavâka; pars. 24–29 of the samyuvâka.

the human one is called upon for the song of praise (sûkta-vâka);' and when the Hotri thereupon recites, he recites good words only[1]: he thereby invokes a blessing on the sacrificer. It is indeed after the sacrifice that he thus invokes a blessing. A twofold reason there is for his invoking the blessing after the sacrifice.

2. He who sacrifices, assuredly, is the producer of the sacrifice, since it is by his order that the priests spread it, that they produce it. He (the Hotri) now invokes a blessing; and that blessing invoked by him, the sacrifice, on its part, realises for this (sacrificer), knowing as it does that he has produced it. For this reason he invokes a blessing after the sacrifice.

3. He who sacrifices, assuredly, pleases the gods. Having pleased the gods by that sacrifice,—that is, partly by Rik-verses, partly by Yagus-formulas, and partly by oblations,—he obtains a share among them. When he has obtained a share among them, then (the Hotri) invokes a blessing (on him); and that blessing, invoked by him, the gods realise for this (sacrificer), knowing as they do that he has pleased them. For this reason also he invokes a blessing after the sacrifice.

4. He intones[2],—'Successful this has turned out, O heaven and earth—,' for successful indeed it has turned out, when one has completed the sacrifice.—'We have completed the song of praise, and the

[1] Sûktaiva tad âha, which the commentator paraphrases by sûktâny âha. It is apparently intended as an explanation of the term sûktavâka. The word sûkta here has exceptionally the accent on the penultimate.

[2] See p. 240, note 2. The formulas are given Taitt. Br. III, 5, 10; Âsv. S. I, 9, 1.

utterance of worship[1],' for indeed these two, the singing of praises and the utterance of worship, form the sacrifice: and accordingly he thereby says, 'We have accomplished the sacrifice, we have obtained possession of the sacrifice.'—'Thou, O Agni, art the voice of praise at the listening[2] of heaven and earth,' he thereby says to Agni, 'Thou art the voice of praise, while heaven and earth listen.'—'May heaven and earth be propitious to thee, O sacrificer, at this sacrifice!' whereby he says, 'May heaven and earth abound in food for thee, O sacrificer, at this sacrifice.'

5. 'They, propitious to the cattle[3], profuse in gifts,' he thereby says, 'May they both be propitious to the cattle, and profuse in gifts.'—'They, the fearless and inscrutable[4];' he thereby says, 'Mayest thou not be afraid of anybody; may no one obtain before thee this thy wealth!'

---

[1] 'Sûktavâkam uta namovâkam.' Our author seems to refer these terms to the *Ri*k-verses and the Ya*g*us-formulas used during the sacrifice. Sâya*n*a, on Taitt. S. II, 6, 9, takes 'namovâka' in a more restricted sense, viz. as referring to the formula 'namo devebhya*h*.' Both the Black Ya*g*ur-veda and Âsv. *S*. add '*ri*dhyâsma sûkto*k*yam,' which has probably to be taken in the sense of 'May we accomplish that which is expressed in the sûktas.' [Sâya*n*a, 'May we succeed with the sûkta yet to be pronounced.']

[2] For upa*s*rutî the Black Ya*g*ur-veda has upa*s*rito, which Sâya*n*a explains, 'Since thou art established in heaven and earth, thou art able to recite the sûkta.'

[3] *S*a*m*gavî seems to be a corruption of *S*a*m*gayî (propitious to the household), which is the reading of the Black Ya*g*ur-veda and Â*s*v. *S*. (cf. Rig-veda IX, 97, 17).

[4] ? Apravede, according to Sâya*n*a, on Taitt. S. I, 1, 13, in an active sense, 'they who do not tell of, do not betray, our faults' (hence 'verschwiegen,' reticent, discreet, St. Petersb. Dict.) 'Difficult to obtain,' Harisvâmin. Our author apparently takes it in the sense of 'not obtained before.'

6. 'They, of wide abode, the afforders of safety;' he thereby says, 'May they both be possessed of wide abodes and exempt from danger.'—'They, the rain-skied, the water-pouring,' he thereby says, 'May they both be possessed of rain.'

7. 'They, the genial and beneficent;' he thereby says, 'May they both be genial and beneficent.'—'They, the rich in sap and substance;' he thereby says, 'May they both abound in moisture and afford the means of subsistence.'

8. 'They, of easy access and good abode;' he thereby says, 'May yonder (sky), which thou approachest from below, afford thee easy access; may this (earth) on which thou abidest (or movest) afford thee good abode.'—'With their knowledge—,' thereby he says, 'Both of these approving—'

9. 'Agni has graciously accepted this oblation, he has grown in strength, he has acquired greater power,' he thereby refers to Agni's butter-portion.—'Soma has graciously accepted this oblation, he has grown in strength, he has acquired greater power,' he thereby refers to Soma's butter-portion.—'Agni has graciously accepted this oblation, he has grown in strength, he has acquired greater power,' he thereby refers to the indispensable cake which is (offered) on both occasions (the new- and full-moon sacrifice).

10. And in the same way according to the respective deities. 'The butter-drinking gods have graciously accepted the butter, they have grown in strength, they have acquired greater power;' thereby he refers to the fore-offerings and after-offerings; for the butter-drinking gods truly are the fore-offerings and after-offerings.—'Agni, by virtue of his Hot*ri*-ship, has graciously accepted this oblation, he has

grown in strength, he has acquired greater power;' thereby he refers to Agni, in virtue of his Hot*ri*ship. With 'has graciously accepted' he thus enumerates those deities to whom offering has been made: in saying 'Such a one has graciously accepted the oblation, such a one has graciously accepted the oblation,' he accordingly prays for the accomplishment of the sacrifice; for whatever oblation the gods graciously accept, by that he gains great things: hence he says, '(he) has graciously accepted it.' And '(he) has grown in strength' he says, because what the gods delight in, they make mountain high: for this reason he says '(he) has increased.'

11. '(He) has acquired (lit. made for himself) greater power' he says; for assuredly the power of the gods is the sacrifice: it is the latter therefore which they make still greater; and for this reason he says '(he) has acquired greater power.'

12. 'May he prosper in this sacrifice which goes to the gods!' he thereby says, 'May he be successful in this sacrifice which goes to the gods.'—'Thus prays this sacrificer, N. N.[1];' here he gives the name, and thereby makes him directly successful in his prayer.

13. 'He prays for long life,' what there (viz. at the invocation of the i*d*â)[2] was (called implicitly) 'future worship of the gods,' that is here (called) expressly 'long life.'

---

[1] Â*s*v. *S*. reads twice asau 'N.N., N.N.;' and the commentary remarks that the Hot*ri* has here to pronounce both the ordinary name of the sacrificer, and his nâkshatra name (i.e. the mystic name given him for the duration of the sacrifice, and derived from the respective lunar mansion, or its tutelary deity). This practice was probably not yet in vogue in the time of our author. Cf. Weber, Nakshatra II, p. 316 seq.

[2] See I, 8, 1, 30 seq.

14. 'He prays for abundant offspring,'—what then was 'more abundant offering,' that is here expressly 'abundant offspring.' He who proceeds in this way will ensure dominion. He may, however, say, 'He prays for future worship of the gods,' for thereby (he ensures) long life, offspring, cattle[1].

15. 'He prays for more abundant offering,' thereby (he prays for) that same object. 'He prays for dominion over his co-evals (or countrymen);'—his co-evals, doubtless, are his vital airs, for he is born along with his vital airs: hence he thereby prays for vital airs.

16. 'He prays for a heavenly abode;'—he who sacrifices assuredly sacrifices with the desire that there may be for him also (a place) in the world of the gods: he thereby confers on him a share in the world of the gods[2]. 'May he obtain, may he accomplish what he prays for through this offering!' he thereby says, 'May all, that he prays for through this offering, be fulfilled to him!'

17. These five prayers for blessings he offers now, and three (he offered) at the *idâ*, these are eight. Of eight syllables, truly, consists the gâyatrî metre, and the gâyatrî means vigour: hence he thereby imparts vigour to the prayers.

18. Let him not offer more than these; for if he offered more, he would do what is in excess; and what is in excess at the sacrifice, that remains over

---

[1] The ritual of the Black Yagur-veda (Taitt. Br. III, 5, 10; Taitt. S. II, 6, 9, 7) and the Âsv. *S*. prescribe both these formulas. The order of formulas also, as there given, differs somewhat from that of our work.

[2] The Black Yagur-veda and Âsv. *S*. insert here, 'He prays for all that is dear to him.'

for the benefit of his spiteful enemy: hence he should not offer more (prayers) than these.

19. Even less,—seven (he may offer)[1].—'May the gods vouchsafe him that!' he thereby says, 'May the gods grant him that.'—'May the god Agni solicit that from the gods, we men from Agni—,' he thereby says, 'May the god Agni solicit that from the gods, and we will then solicit it for this (sacrificer) from Agni—'

20. '—What was searched for and found[2];' they indeed searched for the sacrifice, and found it: therefore he says, 'what was searched for and found.'—And 'may both heaven and earth guard this one (enam) from anxiety!' he thereby says, 'may both heaven and earth protect him from suffering.'

21. Here now some say, 'And may both heaven and earth guard me (mâ[3]) . . . ,' arguing that in this way the Hot*ri* does not exclude himself from the benediction. Let him not, however, say this; for, surely, the benediction at the sacrifice is for the sacrificer: what then have the officiating priests to do with it? Whatever blessing the officiating priests invoke at the sacrifice, that is for the sacrificer only. On the other hand, whoever says, 'and may both heaven and earth guard me . . . ,' does not establish

---

[1] That is, if he chooses to omit the second formula mentioned in par. 14.

[2] 'Ish*t*a*m* *k*a vitta*m* *k*a.' This is also the reading of the Â*s*v. *S*. (? 'What was wished for and obtained'). The Kâ*n*va text reads 'ish*t*a*m* *k*a vitta*m* *k*âbhût.' Our author seems here to refer to the legend in I, 5, 2, 6 seq., or to that in I, 6, 2, 1 seq. The reading of the Black Yagus, ish*t*a*m* *k*a vîta*m* *k*a, 'what has been offered up and accepted (eaten by the gods),' is probably the original and correct one.

[3] The Kâ*n*va recension, the Black Yagur-veda, and Â*s*v. *S*. read no, 'us.'

that blessing anywhere: let him therefore say, 'and may both heaven and earth guard this one. . . .'

22. 'Hither lies the course of any boon;' he thereby makes over to this (sacrificer) whatever is excellent in the sacrifice: for this reason he says, 'hither lies the course of any boon.'

23. 'And this adoration (shall be offered) to the gods!' having attained the completion of the sacrifice, he thereby renders adoration to the gods: for this reason he says, 'and this adoration to the gods!'

24. Thereupon he pronounces the 'All-hail and blessing' (sam-yos)[1]. Now it was Samyu Bârhaspatya who perceived, in its true nature, the consummation of the sacrifice. He went to share in the world of the gods. Thereupon that (knowledge) was entirely lost to men.

25. It then became known to the *Ri*shis, that Samyu Bârhaspatya had perceived, in its true nature, the consummation of the sacrifice, and had gone to share in the world of the gods. By pronouncing the sam-yo*h*, they attained to that same consummation of the sacrifice which Samyu Bârhaspatya had perceived; and to that same consummation of the sacrifice, which Samyu Bârhaspatya had perceived, this (Hot*ri*)

[1] See p. 247, note 2. The original meaning of the terms sam yos, as they occur in the Rig-veda, is happily rendered by Professor Max Müller (Translation of the Rig-veda, I, p. 182) by 'health and wealth.' In the sacrificial ceremonial a deeper significance has come to be attached to this benedictory formula, for which it is difficult to find an exact equivalent. The entire samyuvâka, as here given, forms part of a khila to the last book of the *Ri*k-Sa*m*hitâ; cf. Max Müller's edition, vol. vi. p. 32; A. Weber, Ind. Stud. IV, p. 431. The Black Yagus version of the legend regarding Samyu Bârhaspatya (Taitt. S. II, 6, 10) is quite different from ours; they were both invented to explain sam yos.

attains by pronouncing the *s*am-yo*h*. For this reason he pronounces the 'All-hail and blessing.'

26. He intones, 'We long for that All-hail and blessing (*s*am-yo*h*);' whereby he says, 'We long for that consummation of the sacrifice which *S*amyu Bârhaspatya perceived.

27. 'Success to the sacrifice, success to the lord of sacrifice!' he who wishes for the consummation of the sacrifice, thereby wishes success to the sacrifice and success to the lord of sacrifice.—'Bliss (svasti) to us, bliss to men!' he thereby says, 'May we enjoy bliss among the gods, bliss among men!'—'May the means of salvation ascend on high!' he thereby says, 'May this sacrifice secure for us the world of the gods!'

28. 'All-hail, for us, to the two-footed, all-hail to the four-footed[1]!' for so far as the two-footed and the four-footed (extend), so far does this universe (extend). Having now attained the consummation of the sacrifice, he bids All-hail to this (sacrificer), and for this reason he says, 'All-hail, for us, to the two-footed, all-hail to the four-footed!'

29. He then touches (the earth) thus with this (finger)[2]. Non-human, verily, he becomes at the

[1] This formula occurs almost identically in Rig-veda VI, 74, 1; VII, 54, 1; (IX, 69, 7.) Cf. Max Müller, Translation of the Rig-veda, I, p. 180, where attention is drawn to a somewhat similar phrase in the Umbric prayers of the Eugubian tables.

[2] In Kâty. III, 6, 21 the touching of the altar is prescribed, with the text Vâ*g*. S. II, 19 b; the commentators differ as to whether the sacrificer or the Adhvaryu is to do this. The Kâ*n*va Sa*m*hitâ omits that formula, and hence assigns this touching to the Hot*ri*. Harisvâmin remarks that the Hot*ri* touches the earth with the little finger of his right hand, as stated in the Kâ*n*va recension. The latter reads 'with the little finger.' No mention is made in the Â*s*v. *S*. of this touching of the earth on the part of the Hot*ri*.

time when he is chosen for the office of sacrificial priest; and, this earth being a safe standing-place, he thereby (viz. by touching the earth) stands on this safe standing-place; and he thereby also again becomes human: for this reason he thus touches (the earth) with this (finger).

SECOND BRÂHMANA.

THE PATNÎSAMYÂGAS.

1. Being about to perform the patnîsamyâgas[1], they betake themselves back to the Gârhapatya fire. The Adhvaryu takes the guhû and sruva, the Hotri the veda, and the Âgnîdhra the butter-(melting) pot.

2. Here now the Adhvaryu, according to some, passes the Âhavanîya on the east side. Let him not, however, do this; for were he to walk on that side, he would be outside the sacrifice.

3. According to others, the Adhvaryu walks (so as to pass) behind the (sacrificer's) wife[2]. Let him not, however, do this either; for verily the Adhvaryu is the fore-part, and the wife is the hind-part of the sacrifice: hence, if he were to pass so, it would be as if one were to put his head behind; and he (the Adhvaryu) would be outside the sacrifice.

---

[1] The meaning of the term seems to be 'offerings made (to some deities) along with the wives (of the gods);' the deities to whom the four offerings are made, being Soma, Tvashtri, the Devapatnyah (wives of the gods), and Agni Grihapati.

[2] The lady of the house occupies a seat south-west of the Gârhapatya fire. See I, 3, 1, 12. The Adhvaryu now sits down with raised knees (south of her, with his face to the north-east). Kâty. III, 7, 5. The Âgnîdhra sits down in the same way north of the fire, with his face to the south, and the Hotri in the middle; cf. Hillebrandt, Neu- und Vollm. p. 151.

4. According to others, the Adhvaryu passes between the wife (and the Gârhapatya fire). Let him not, however, do this either; for were he to pass that way, he would cut off the wife from the sacrifice. Along the east side of the Gârhapatya and the inner side of the Âhavanîya (he passes); for thus he is not outside the sacrifice; and as before, in walking forward (to the Âhavanîya), he passed along the inner side, so he now also takes that path.

5. They now perform the patnîsamyâgas. From the sacrifice offspring is assuredly produced; and (that offspring) produced from the sacrifice is produced from union; and (the offspring) produced from union is produced after (in consequence of) the completion [1] of the sacrifice: hence one thereby (i.e. by the patnîsamyâgas) causes that (offspring) to be produced by means of a productive union after the completion of the sacrifice. And so now also offspring is produced by means of a productive union after the completion of the sacrifice. This is why they now perform the patnîsamyâgas.

6. He makes offering to four deities. Four doubtless means a couple; for a couple means a pair (dvandva, lit. two and two), and two and two indeed they are: thus a productive union is thereby effected; and accordingly he makes offering to four deities.

7. He makes (the offerings) of butter for sacrificial food. Butter indeed means seed: hence he thereby scatters seed, and therefore makes them of butter for sacrificial food.

---

[1] Or, 'is produced from the hind-part of the sacrifice,' i.e. from the sacrificer's wife, seated behind the altar, see par. 3.

8. In a low voice they engage in this (performance)[1]. Secretly, doubtless, union takes place; and secretly also (takes place) what (is spoken) in a low voice: this is why they perform in a low voice.

9. He first makes offering to Soma. Soma indeed means seed; hence he thereby scatters seed: this is why he makes offering to Soma.

10. He then makes offering to Tvash*tri*. Now, it is Tvash*tri* who transforms seed which is scattered. Accordingly it is he who transforms the seed now scattered[2]: this is why he makes offering to Tvash*tri*.

11. He then makes offering to the wives of the gods. In the wives, in the womb, the seed assuredly is planted, and thence it is produced; hence he thereby plants the seed in the wives, in the womb; and thence it is produced: for this reason he makes offering to the wives of the gods.

12. When he offers to the wives of the gods, he shuts (the fire) out from view on the eastern side; for, up to the time when they offer to the samish*t*a-ya*g*us, the deities continue waiting, thinking, 'This

[1] The Adhvaryu calls on the Hot*ri*: 'For Soma (Tvash*tri*, &c. respectively)' (in a low voice)—'recite!' (aloud). The Hot*ri* then recites the invitatory prayer (anuvâkyâ, for which see Âsv. Sr. I, 10, 5) in a low voice, except the concluding 'om!' which he pronounces aloud. The Adhvaryu now calls on the Âgnîdhra, who responds with 'Astu srausha*t*.' Thereupon the Adhvaryu calls on the Hot*ri*, 'For Soma,' &c. (in a low voice),—'pronounce the offering prayer!' (aloud); and the Hot*ri* recites the yâ*g*yâ, in a low voice, except the concluding 'Vausha*t*,' which is pronounced aloud, and simultaneously with which the Adhvaryu pours the oblation (consisting of four ladlings of butter from the butter-pot into the *g*uhû, by means of the sruva) into the fire.

[2] He does so in his capacity of divine artificer and architect.

he must offer up to us!' He thereby conceals (this offering) from them; and accordingly Yâ*gñ*avalkya says, 'Whenever human women here eat[1] (they do so) apart from men.'

13. He then makes offering to Agni, the householder. Agni, indeed, is this world: hence it is for this world that he thereby produces offspring and that this offspring is produced: this is why he makes offering to Agni, the householder.

14. This (ceremony) concludes with the i*d*â[2]; for here are neither enclosing-sticks nor the prastara-bunch. For on that occasion when he wishes the sacrificer good-speed (svagâ)[3] by (offering) the prastara, good-speed is at the same time wished to his consort also, since the wife comes (immediately) after the husband. But were he to use a substitute for the prastara-bunch, he would produce lassitude (in the wife): for this reason this (ceremony) should conclude with the i*d*â. Nevertheless a substitute for the prastara is (optionally) made.

15. If he choose to use a substitute for the prastara, he thereby wishes the wife good-speed just as

---

[1] *G*ighatsanti, 'eat greedily, swallow their food.' The Kâ*n*va text does not mention Yâ*gñ*avalkya, but merely says, 'hence women also here swallow their food apart from men.'

[2] The i*d*â-ceremony (I, 8, 1, 18) is repeated after the patnîsa*m*yâ*g*as, together with the *S*a*m*yuvâka and the offering of remains, but with special reference to the mistress of the house. Since the prastara-bunch and the enclosing-sticks have already been consumed by the fire, the Sûktavâka is omitted on the present occasion; the Adhvaryu merely throwing a stalk of the reed-grass of the veda into the fire, as a substitute for the stalk of the prastara (representing the sacrificer).

[3] See I, 8, 3, 11 seq.

he wishes the sacrificer good-speed by means of the prastara.

16. If he choose to use a substitute for the prastara, he plucks out one stalk from the veda, and anoints its top in the *g*uhû, its middle part in the aruva, and its lower end in the butter-pan.

17. The Âgnîdhra then says, 'Throw (it) after[1]!' [The Adhvaryu] having thrown it silently after (the prastara into the fire), touches himself, with the text (Vâ*g*. S. II, 16 f), 'Guardian of the eye art thou, O Agni, guard mine eye!' and in this way he avoids throwing himself after (the prastara into the fire).

18. He (the Âgnîdhra) then says (to the Adhvaryu), 'Discourse together!' (The Adhvaryu says), 'Has he gone (to the gods), Agnîdh?' 'He has gone!' 'Bid (the gods) hear!' 'May (one or they) hear!' 'Good-speed to the divine Hot*ri*s! Success to the human!' [Then the Adhvaryu to the Hot*ri*], 'Pronounce the "All-hail and blessing!"'

19. Thereupon[2] he (the Adhvaryu) seizes at the same time the *g*uhû and sruva. On the former occasion[3] indeed, by anointing (the prastara), he

---

[1] See I, 8, 3, 19 seq.

[2] That is, after the Hot*ri* has again recited the Sa*m*yuvâka, in the same way as above, I, 9, 1, 26–29.

[3] Viz. at the offering of the remains of butter (I, 8, 3, 23), of which the present ceremony is the counterpart. Dr. Hillebrandt, Neu- und Vollm. p. 160, (after a scholiast) calls this modification Pragrahahoma (offered to Agni adabdhâyu a*s*îtama). According to Kâty. III, 7, 18; 19, this ceremony is followed by the performance, in the Dakshi*n*a fire, of two (*g*uhoti) oblations of butter, to Agni sa*m*ve*s*apati and Sarasvatî respectively (see the formulas Vâ*g*. S. II, 20, b, c); and the pish*t*alepa-âhuti to the Vi*s*ve Devâ*h*, being an offering of the remnants of dough, left from the preparation of the sacrificial cakes. These offerings would then be succeeded by the ceremonies treated in par. 21 seq.

made (the sacrificer) an oblation, thus thinking, 'May he go to the world of the gods as an oblation!' For this reason he now seizes the *g*uhû and sruva at the same time.

20. He seizes them for Agni, with the text (Vâ*g*. S. II, 20 a), 'O Agni, unimpaired in vigour, far-reacher!' because Agni is immortal, he says, 'unimpaired in vigour:' and because Agni is farthest-reaching, he says, 'far-reacher[1].'—'Guard me from the thunderbolt! guard me from bonds! guard me from defective sacrifice! guard me from noxious food!' he thereby says, 'Protect me from all kinds of injury!'—'Make our nourishment free from poison!'—nourishment means food: 'make our food wholesome, faultless!' this is what he thereby says.—'In the lap, pleasant to sit in;' he thereby says, 'in thyself.'—'Svâhâ! Vâ*t*!' since one offers what has been consecrated by 'vasha*t*,' this (residue of butter) thereby becomes such for him.

21. The mistress then unties the veda-bunch. The altar (vedi) assuredly is female and the veda is male. For union the veda was made: and accordingly when he touches (the altar) with it during the sacrifice, a union productive of offspring is thereby effected.

22. And (the reason) why it is the mistress who unties the veda (is this): the mistress is female and the veda is male; consequently a union productive of offspring is thereby effected: this is why the mistress unties the veda.

23. She unties it. Should she wish to do so

[1] Harisvâmin derives a*s*îtama and a*s*ish*th*a from a*s*, 'to eat' (instead of from a*s*, 'to reach, penetrate'), hence 'the greatest eater.' Mahîdhara gives both derivations.

with a Yagus-text, let her do so with this one (Vâg. S. II, 21 a), 'The Veda art thou: whereby thou, O divine Veda, hast become Veda for the gods, thereby mayest thou become Veda for me[1]!'

24. (The Hotri) strews it (from the Gârhapatya) as far as (the east end of) the altar[2]; for the altar is female and the veda is male; and from behind the male approaches the female: from behind (i.e. west) he accordingly causes it (the altar) to be approached by that male, the veda. For this reason he strews (the grass of the veda) as far as (the east end of) the altar.

Concluding Ceremonies.

25. He (the Adhvaryu) now makes the samishtayagus-oblation, thinking, 'In the east my sacrifice shall be completed!' Were he to perform the samishtayagus-oblation first and then the patnîsamyâgas, that sacrifice of his would be completed in the west (behind the sacrificer)[3]: hence he makes

---

[1] According to Kâty. III, 8, 2, the lady thereupon unties the grass-cord with which she was girt (see I, 3, 1, 12), with the text, 'I free myself from Varuna's noose wherewith the gracious Savitri bound me; place me unscathed, together with my husband, in the lap of eternal law, in the world of righteousness!' Âsv. I, 11, 3, however, assigns this ceremony to the Hotri; and no doubt rightly, since it is not mentioned by our author, and the Vâg. S. does not give the formula. Thereby also the original form of the text (Rig-veda X, 85, 24), 'I free thee,' &c., is preserved. Mahîdhara on Vâg. S. here takes 'veda' either in the sense of 'the Veda (*Rik*, &c.),' or as 'the knower.' Perhaps it should rather be taken as 'the obtainer.'

[2] Thus â vedeh is explained by Harisvâmin (according to comm. on Kâty. III, 8, 3). Others take it in the sense of 'up to where the barhis begins.'

[3] The patnîsamyâgas were performed in the Gârhapatya fire, and therefore west of the altar; and on their completion, the priests betake themselves back to the Âhavanîya.

the samishtayagus-oblation at this particular time, thinking, 'In the east my sacrifice shall be completed!'

26. Now as to why it is called samishtayagus[1]: whatever deities he invites through this (new or full-moon) sacrifice, and for whichever deities this sacrifice is performed, all those are thereby 'sacrificed to together' (sam-ishta); and because he now makes a (butter) oblation[2] to all those deities, who have been 'sacrificed to together,' therefore this (oblation) is called samishtayagus.

27. And again as to why he performs the samishtayagus: whatever deities he invites through this sacrifice, and for whichever deities this sacrifice is performed, they continue waiting until the samishtayagus is performed, thinking, 'This he must offer to us!' These same (deities) he thereby dismisses in due form; and whatever be the practice in their case in accordance with that he has, in thus performing it, produced the sacrifice, and having thus produced it he now establishes it safely where there is a safe basis for it: this is why he performs the samishtayagus.

28. He makes the offering, with the text (Vâg. S. II, 21 b), 'Ye path-finding gods,'—for the gods

---

[1] The real original meaning of the term would rather seem to have been 'the formula marking the completion of the sacrifice,' it having afterwards come to be applied to the oblation (to the wind-god) itself. Cf. par. 30 and Weber, Ind. Stud. IX, 232.

[2] Or rather, 'because to all those deities to whom an ishti (or yagati-offering, made by the Adhvaryu standing south of the altar; and followed or accompanied by the vashat-call) has been offered in common, he now makes an âhuti (or guhoti-offering, made by him whilst standing north of the altar, with the svâhâ-call).'

are indeed the finders of the path[1];—'Having found the path—,' thereby he says, 'having found the sacrifice;'—'Walk in the path!' thereby he dismisses them in due form;—'O divine Lord of mind, this sacrifice—Svâhâ!—give to the wind!' for the sacrifice, indeed, is that blowing one (the wind). Having accordingly prepared this (special) sacrifice, he thereby establishes it safely in that (chief, full or new-moon) sacrifice, and thus unites sacrifice with sacrifice: for this reason he says, 'Svâhâ! give (it) to the wind!'

29. He then offers up the barhis. The barhis, truly, is this world, and the barhis (consists of) plants: hence he thereby bestows plants on this world, and these plants are safely established in this world: for this reason he offers up the barhis.

30. This offering he makes as an additional one, since the samishtayagus is the end of the sacrifice, and consequently what comes after the samishtayagus is additional; and because, in performing the samishtayagus, he offers to those (deities[2]), and thence additional unlimited plants are here produced.

31. He offers it, with the text (Vâg. S. II, 22), 'May the barhis combine with the sacrificial food, with the butter! May Indra combine with the Âdityas, the Vasus, the Maruts, and the Visve Devâh! May what (has been offered with) "Svâhâ" go up to the heavenly ether[3]!'

32. Having thereupon walked round (from the

[1] Mahîdhara refers gâtu-vidah and vittvâ to vid, 'to know.'

[2] According to Harisvâmin, he does so, since that offering is made for the sake of dismissing (satisfying) the deities.

[3] Mahîdhara interprets, 'May Indra—together with the Âdityas, the Vasus, the Maruts, and the Visve Devâh—anoint the barhis thoroughly with the havis-like ghee,' &c.

north side of the Âhavanîya fire) to the south, he pours the pranîtâ-water[1] out (on the altar). Now, when he spreads the sacrifice, he yokes it. But were he not to pour out (the pranîtâ-water), the sacrifice, being unyoked, would, in moving backward, injure the sacrificer. In this way, however, the sacrifice does not injure the sacrificer; and for this reason he pours out the pranîtâ-water, after walking round to the south.

33. He pours it out, with the text (Vâg. S. II, 23 a), 'Who[2] unyokes thee? He unyokes thee! For whom does he unyoke thee? For him he unyokes thee! For plenty!' He thereby announces to the sacrificer the highest prosperity. He pours it out with the same (vessel) with which he brings it forward; for wherewith they yoke the team, therewith they also unyoke it: with the yoke-tie they yoke it, and with the yoke-tie they unyoke it. By means of a potsherd he now throws the refuse from the cleaning of the rice[3] right under the black antelope skin; with the text (Vâg. S. II, 23 b), 'The Rakshas' share art thou!'

34. Now the gods and the Asuras, both of them sprung from Pragâpati, were contending about this sacrifice, (that is, their) father Pragâpati, the year. 'Ours it (he) shall be! ours it shall be,' they said.

35. Thereupon the gods obtained possession of the whole of the sacrifice, and dispossessed those

---

[1] See p. 9, note 1.

[2] Or, Pragâpati..., see I, 1, 1, 13, with note.

[3] See I, 1, 4, 23–24. According to the Paddhati on Kâty. III, 8, the Adhvaryu holds the deer-skin with his left hand over the utkara, or heap of rubbish, and pours the refuse under the skin on the utkara.

(Asuras) of it by (giving them) what was the worst part of the sacrifice, to wit, with the blood of the victim (they dispossessed them) of the animal sacrifice, and with the refuse of the rice of the haviryagña. 'May they be duly dispossessed of the sacrifice,' they thought for he indeed is duly dispossessed, who is dispossessed even while obtaining a (worthless) share. He, on the other hand, who is dispossessed without any share whatever, hopes for a while, and when it occurs to him, he says, 'What share hast thou given me?' Hence what share the gods set apart for those (Asuras), that same share he now makes over to them in pouring (the refuse of the rice) right under the black antelope skin. He thereby casts it into blind darkness, where there is no (sacrificial) fire. And in the same way he casts the blood of the victim into blind darkness, where there is no fire; thinking, 'Thou art the Rakshas' share!' For this reason they use not the gore of the victim (for sacrificial purposes), since it is the Rakshas' share.

THIRD BRÂHMANA.

1. The sacrifice being now complete, he (the Adhvaryu) walks round (the fire) to the south, and pours out a vessel (of water); for thus it is (poured out) towards north: therefore he pours it out after walking round to the south. He who sacrifices, doubtless, sacrifices with a desire that he also may obtain a place in the world of the gods. That sacrifice of his then goes forth towards the world of the gods: after it follows the fee which he gives (to the priests), and holding on to the priests' fee (follows) the sacrificer.

2. That same path leads either to the gods or to the fathers[1]. On both sides two flames are ever burning: they scorch him who deserves to be scorched, and allow him to pass who deserves to pass[2]. Now, water is (a means of) lustration: hence he thereby lustrates that path.

3. A full (vessel) he pours out, because full means all: hence he thereby lustrates that (path) by means of the All. He pours it out continuously, uninterruptedly: hence he thereby lustrates that (path) in a continuous, uninterrupted manner.

4. And again why he pours out a vessel (of water) is: where anything is done wrongly at the sacrifice, there they tear or wound it; and—water being (a means of) lustration—he lustrates it by that (means of) lustration, water; he heals it with water.

5. A full (vessel) he pours out, because full means all: hence he thereby heals it by means of the All. Continuously, uninterruptedly he pours it out: hence he thereby heals it in a continuous (lasting), uninterrupted manner.

6. He (the sacrificer) intercepts it with his open hands held together, while reciting the text (Vâg.

---

[1] Cf. Mahâbh. XII, 525, 'Two paths are known, one leading to the gods, and one leading to the fathers;' and ib. XIII, 1082, 'That sun is said to be the gate of the paths leading to the gods; and that moon is said to be the gate of the paths leading to the fathers.' See also *Kh*and. Up. V, 3. In *S*at. Br. VI, 6, 2, 4 the gate of the heavenly world is said to be situated in the north-east; whilst that of the world of the fathers, according to XIII, 8, 1, 5, lies in the south-east. Cf. Kaushît. Up. I, 2 seq. (Max Müller, Up. I, p. 274), 'Verily, the moon is the door of the heavenly world,' &c.

[2] According to Harisvâmin, they scorch him who has not fulfilled his duties, and allow him to pass who has done so.

S. II, 24), 'We have united with lustre, with vigour, with the bodies[1], with the happy spirit. May Tvashtri, the dispenser of boons, grant us riches, and make even what was injured in our body!' What was torn, that he thereby heals.

7. He then touches his face (with the water in his hands). The reason why he thus touches his face is twofold: water means ambrosia, and with ambrosia he accordingly touches himself; also he thereby transfers to himself that sacred work (the sacrifice): for these reasons he touches his face.

8. He now strides the (three) Vishnu-strides. He who sacrifices assuredly gratifies the gods. In gratifying the gods by that sacrifice—partly by riks, partly by yagus, partly by oblations—he acquires a share among them; and having acquired a share among them, he goes to them.

9. And again why he strides the Vishnu-strides, is: Vishnu, truly, is the sacrifice, by striding (vi-kram) he obtained for the gods that all-pervading power (vikrânti) which now belongs to them. By his first step he gained this same (earth), by the second this aërial expanse, and by his last (step) the sky. And this same pervading power Vishnu, as the sacrifice, obtains by his strides for him (the sacrificer): for this reason he strides

[1] That is, with the departed persons, the fathers; or, more probably, with new bodies (?), cf. the funereal hymns, Rig-veda X, 14–18; especially X, 15, 14; 16, 5; 14, 8. Perhaps, however, it would be better to construe, 'by (our) bodies we have united with lustre and vigour; by (our) mind with bliss.' In IV, 6, 1, 1 it is said, that the sacrificer is born in the next world with his entire body; similarly XI, 1, 8, 6; XII, 8, 3, 31. For further quotations regarding the views on future existence, see A. Weber, Ind. Streifen, I, p. 20 seq.; J. Muir, Original Sanskrit Texts, V, p. 314 seq.

the Vishnu-strides. Now it is indeed from this (earth) that most (beings) go (upwards).

10. Hence (he strides thrice) with the texts (Vâg. S. II, 25 a–c), 'On the earth Vishnu strode by means of the gâyatrî metre: excluded therefrom is he who hates us, and whom we hate!' 'In the air Vishnu strode by means of the trishtubh metre: excluded therefrom is he who hates us, and whom we hate!' 'In the sky Vishnu strode by means of the gagatî metre: excluded therefrom is he who hates us, and whom we hate!' When one has thus ascended these worlds, that is the goal, that the safe refuge: the rays of him (the sun) who burns there, are the righteous (departed)[1]; and what highest light there is[2], that is Pragâpati or the heavenly world. Having then in this way ascended these worlds, he reaches that goal, that safe refuge. Now he who wishes to give instructions from hence, should come hitherwards from above. Twofold is the reason why he should come hitherwards from above:

11. By (or, from) the escape (of the enemies)[3] indeed the conquering gods formerly gained first the sky, and then this aërial expanse; and there-

[1] In VI, 5, 4, 8 we shall meet with the statement, that 'the stars (nakshatra) are the lights of righteous men who go to the heavenly world.' In the same passage, however (as in others), the nakshatras (lunar mansions) are represented as divine female beings (with unclipped wings; cf. Vâg. S. XI, 61), with whom, in IX, 4, 1, 9, the moon is said to live together, as the Gandharvas with the Apsaras.

[2] See par. 16 with note. The Kânva text reads, 'yat param bhâti.'

[3] Apasaranatah; i.e. by allowing the enemies to escape, viz. first from the sky to the air, and then from the air to the earth. It also, however, has the meaning of 'from escape;' that is, the gods drove the enemies to the earth, whence there was no escape for them.

upon they drove their enemies away from this (earth), whence there was no escape. And in like manner he (the priest) also by the escape (of the enemies) gains first the sky, and then this aërial expanse; and thereupon he drives his enemies away from this (earth), whence there is no escape. This earth indeed is a firm footing: hence he thereby stands firm on this firm footing.

12. And in this way also (he may stride)[1]: 'In the sky Vishnu strode by means of the gagatî metre: excluded therefrom is he who hates us, and whom we hate!' 'In the air Vishnu strode by means of the trishtubh metre: excluded therefrom is he who hates us, and whom we hate!' 'On the earth Vishnu strode by means of the gâyatrî metre: excluded therefrom is he who hates us, and whom we hate!'—With the texts (Vâg. S. II, 25 d, e), '(Excluded) from this food! from this resort!' (pratishthâ, he looks down upon his portion and the altar respectively.) For on this (earth) all this food is safely established (pratishthita): for this reason he says, 'From this food! from this resort!'

13. He then looks towards the east. The east, indeed, is the region of the gods: for this reason he looks towards the east.

14. He looks, with the text (Vâg. S. II, 25 f), 'We have gone to the realm of light (svar).' The

[1] The sacrificer in making the strides of Vishnu, may begin either with the stride on earth or with that in the sky (Kâty. III, 8, 11, 12). He begins from the southern hip (or south-west corner) of the altar, and makes three strides eastward with his right foot in front, reciting one formula with each stride, along the south side of the altar up to the Âhavanîya fire.

realm of light assuredly means the gods: hence he thereby says, 'We have gone to the gods.'—With (ib. g), 'We have united with splendour' (he looks on the Âhavanîya fire): he thereby says, 'We have united with the gods.'

15. He then looks up to the sun, for that is the final goal, that the safe resort. To that final goal, to that resort he thereby goes: for this reason he looks up to the sun.

16. He looks up, with the text (Vâ*g*. S. II, 26 a), 'Self-existent art thou, the best ray of light!' The sun is indeed the best ray of light[1], and therefore he says, 'Self-existent art thou, the best ray of light.' '"Light-bestowing art thou: give me light (var*k*as)!" so say I,' said Yâ*gñ*avalkya, 'for at this indeed the Brâhma*n*a should strive, that he be brahmavar*k*asin (illumed by the brahma, or sacred writ).' Aupoditeya[2], on the other hand, said, 'He indeed will give me cows[3]: (therefore I say), "Cow-giving art thou, give me cows!"' Thus whatever wish he (the sacrificer) entertains (and expresses), that wish is granted to him.

17. He then turns (from left to right), with the text (Vâ*g*. S. II, 26 b), 'I move along the course of

---

[1] Seven rays of the sun are mentioned, Rig-veda I, 105, 9; II, 5, 2; Âth.-veda VII, 107, 1. Mahîdhara remarks that four of them lie in, or point to, the four quarters; one pointing upwards and another downwards; and the seventh, and best, being the disc of the sun itself, called Hira*n*yagarbha. This apparently is the param bhâs, or most excellent light, which in par. 10 is identified with Pra*g*âpati, or the heavenly world.

[2] That is, Tumi*ñg*a Aupoditeya Vaiyâghrapadya, as the Kâ*n*va text reads; cf. Taitt. S. I, 7, 2, 1.

[3] The heavenly rays of light are regarded as the heavenly cows, Naigh. I, 5; Nir. II, 6.

the sun;' having reached that final goal, that safe resort, he now moves along the course of that (sun)[1].

18. Thereupon he steps to (upa-sthâ) the Gârhapatya fire. Twofold is the reason why he steps to the Gârhapatya: the Gârhapatya is a house, and a house is a safe resort, hence he thereby stays in a house, that is, in a safe resort. And, besides, what full measure of human life there is for him here, that he thereby attains (upa-sthâ). This is why he steps to the Gârhapatya fire.

19. He steps to it, with the text (Vâg. S. II, 27 a), 'O householder Agni, may I become a good householder through thee, O Agni, the householder! Mayest thou, O Agni, become a good householder through me, the householder!' there is nothing in this requiring explanation.—'May our household matters be unlike a cart with only one bullock,' he thereby says, 'may our household matters be free from calamities;'—'for a hundred winters!' he thereby says, 'may I live a hundred years.' He need not, however, say this; for man lives even longer than a hundred years: hence he need not say this.

20. He then turns (from left to right), with the text (Vâg. S. II, 27 b), 'I move along the course of the sun:' having reached that final goal, that safe resort, he now moves along the course of that (sun).

21. Now (in pronouncing the following text) he

[1] When he has executed the pradakshina movement, he has to repeat the movement in the opposite direction, in accordance with the general rule, Kâty. I, 8, 24. The same applies to par. 20. On the sun-wise circumambulation, with and without fire, see p. 37 note, p. 45 note; also Martin, Western Isles, pp. 16–20, 85, 97, 116–119, 241, 277; Forbes Leslie, Early Races of Scotland, index, s. v. deisiol.

inserts his son's name: 'May this son (N. N.) carry on this manly deed of mine[1]!' Should he have no son, let him insert his own name.

22. He then steps up to the Âhavanîya fire. Silently he steps to it, thinking, 'In the east my sacrifice shall be completed!'

23. Thereupon he divests himself of the vow, with the text (Vâg. S. II, 28 b), 'Now am I he that I really am.' For, in entering upon the vow, he becomes, as it were, non-human; and as it would not be becoming for him to say, 'I enter from truth into untruth;' and as, in fact, he now again becomes man, let him therefore divest himself of the vow, with the text, 'Now am I he that I really am[2].'

---

[1] The Mâdhyandina text of the Vâg. S. does not give this formula. The Kânva text of the Samhitâ has the following (Weber's edition, p. 59), 'Woven art thou, a web art thou: weave me along (? extend my life) at this sacrifice, at this holy deed, in this food, in this world!' 'May my son weave on (continue) this work, this manly deed of mine!' Thus also Kâty. III, 8, 25. The Kânva text of the Brâhmana, however, mentions only the formula given above. According to Laugâkshi he names his favourite son; according to Sâṅkhâyana, his eldest son, or as many sons as he has. See comm. on Kâty. IV, 12, 11.

[2] See I, 1, 1, 6. For another mode of divesting oneself of the vow, see I, 1, 1, 3.

SECOND KÂNDA.

THE AGNYÂDHÂNA, THE AGNIHOTRA, THE PINDAPITRIYAGÑA, THE ÂGRAYANESHTI, AND THE KÂTURMÂSYÂNI.

I. THE AGNYÂDHÂNA OR ESTABLISHMENT OF THE SACRED FIRES.

First Adhyâya. First Brâhmana.

The Agny-âdhâna (or Agny-âdheya), or ceremony of establishing a set of sacrificial fires, on the part of a young householder, is, as a rule, performed on the first day of the waxing moon. Some authorities also allow the performance to take place at full moon, probably in order to enable the newly-married couple to enter on their sacred duties with as little delay as possible. Moreover, special benefits are supposed to accrue to the performer of the ceremony from the conjunction of the new moon with certain lunar asterisms; though the author of our work, at any rate, does not seem greatly to encourage this practice, but rather to urge the pious householder to set up fires of his own, whenever he feels a longing for the sacrifice.

The normal performance of the Agnyâdhâna, as that of the full and new-moon offerings, requires two days; the first of which is taken up with preliminary rites, while the second—that is, the first day of the respective half-moon—is devoted to the chief ceremonies, beginning with the production of the sacred fire by friction. (See II, 1, 4, 8 seq.)

After the sacrificer has chosen his four officiating priests—viz. the Brahman, Hotri, Adhvaryu, and Âgnîdhra (or Agnîdh)—he proceeds, together with them, to erect the two sheds or 'fire-houses.' In order to determine their exact sites, the Adhvaryu first draws from west to east the so-called 'easterly' line (cf. I, 2, 5, 14), and on it marks, at 8, 11, or 12 prakramas or steps from each other, the centres of the Gârhapatya and Âhavanîya fire-places, the outlines of which he then traces, making each a square aratni or cubit in area, the former circular, the latter square. The Dakshi-

*n*âgni or Anvâhârya-pa*k*ana, if it is required at all, is of the same area, but of semicircular form, and lies south of the space between the altar and the Gârhapatya fire. The Gârhapatya fire-house is constructed with its laths running either from west to east, or from south to north, and a door on the south side; and so as to enclose both the Gârhapatya and Dakshi*n*a fires. The Âhavanîya fire-house, on the other hand, with its laths necessarily running from west to east, and an entrance from the east, contains the Âhavanîya fire and the altar (vedi) adjoining it on the west, and partly enclosing it with its 'shoulders' on the north and south sides. The two houses are also open to each other on the inner side; and sufficient space is left on all sides for freely moving around the fires.

The Adhvaryu then procures a temporary fire,—either producing it by friction, or obtaining it from certain specified sources in the village,—and after the usual fivefold lustration of the Gârhapatya fire-place (cf. p. 2), he lays down the fire thereon. Towards sunset the sacrificer [while seated east of the Âhavanîya house] invokes the gods and manes with 'Gods, fathers! fathers, gods! I sacrifice, being who I am; neither will I exclude him whose I am: mine own shall be the offering, mine own the toiling, mine own the sacrifice!' He then enters the Âhavanîya house from the east, passes through it to the Gârhapatya, and sits down behind (west of) the fire; his wife at the same time entering the Gârhapatya house from the south and seating herself south of him,—both facing the east. Thereupon the Adhvaryu hands to the sacrificer two pieces of wood (ara*n*i),—if possible, of a*s*vattha, grown out of a *s*amî tree,—to be used next morning for the production (or 'churning') of the sacred fire by one of them (the upper ara*n*i) being rapidly drilled in a hole in the other (or lower ara*n*i). [The sacrificer and his wife then lay the upper and lower sticks respectively on their laps; whereupon certain propitiatory ceremonies are performed by them, and honours are paid to the priests and the sticks; and the latter are finally deposited on a seat.] In the house of the Gârhapatya a he-goat may then be tied up for the night, which, if it belong to the sacrificer, is to be presented by him to the Âgnîdhra on the completion of the sacrifice.

After sunset the Adhvaryu measures out four vessels of husked rice grains—each containing three handfuls, which quantity is considered sufficient to furnish a meal for one man—on an ox-hide died red [and spread out with the hairy side upwards and the neck-part to the east]. With this rice the (odana) *k*âtushprâ*s*ya, or '(pap) to be eaten by the four (priests),' is prepared on the provisional Gârhapatya fire. When it is ready, the Adhvaryu makes a hollow in the pap and pours clarified butter into it. He then takes three kindling-sticks (samidh), anoints them with some of that ghee, and puts them on the fire one after another, with texts (cf. note on II, 1, 4, 5). Thereupon the sacrificer [having paid due honours to the priests by washing their feet and giving them perfumes and wreaths, &c., and assigned to each his share] bids them eat.

During the night the sacrificer and his wife have to remain awake and keep up the fire. When the night clears up, the Adhvaryu extinguishes the fire, or, if there is to be a Dakshinâgni, he takes it southwards and keeps it in a safe place till that fire is made up. He then draws with the wooden sword three lines across the fire-place and proceeds with the preparation of the hearth-mounds in the way set forth in the first Brâhmana of this Book.

1. Now when he equips (Agni, the fire) from this and that quarter, that is the equipping (of the fire) with its equipments[1]. In whatever (objects) some of (the nature of) Agni is inherent, therewith he equips (the fire); and in thus equipping it he supplies it partly with splendour, partly with cattle, partly with a mate.

2. In the first place he (the Adhvaryu) draws (three) lines (with the wooden sword on the Gârhapatya fire-place[2]). Whatever part of this earth

---

[1] The verb here translated by 'to equip,' is sam-bhri, 'to carry, or bring, together, to collect;' and then 'to make the necessary preparations, to prepare;' hence sambhâra, 'the preparation, outfit,' the technical term for the objects employed in the preparation of the fire-place, with the view of symbolically ensuring success to the fire. In paragraphs 3 seq. the primary meaning 'to bring (together)' has been used, except where it seemed desirable to preserve its technical sense.

[2] The three lines drawn across the fire-place form a necessary part of its lustration; see p. 2. According to the Paddhati on Kâty. IV, 8, the Adhvaryu first makes the fivefold lustration of the hearth, and thereupon again draws the mystic lines (? or draws the outline of the fire-place, cf. Kâty. IV, 8, 16) and proceeds with the sambhâras; viz. he sprinkles the lines with water, while the sacrificer takes hold of him from behind; then puts down a piece of gold, and on it throws salt soil and the mould of a mole-hill, with which he forms the hearth-mound (khara)—circular in

is either trodden or spit upon, that he thereby removes from it; and he thus establishes his fire on earth that is entirely proper for the sacrifice: this is why he draws lines (across the fire-place).

3. He then sprinkles (the lines) with water. When he thus sprinkles (the fire-place) with water, that is the equipment (of the fire) with water. The reason why he brings water is that water is food; for water is indeed food: hence when water comes to this world, food is produced here. Thus he thereby supplies it (the fire) with food.

4. Water (ap, fem.), moreover, is female, and fire (agni, masc.) is male; so that he thereby supplies the latter with a productive mate. And since all this (universe) is pervaded (or obtained, âpta) by water, he sets up the fire, after he has obtained it by means of water[1]. This is why he brings water.

5. He then brings (a piece of) gold. Now Agni at one time cast his eyes on the waters[2]: 'May I pair with them,' he thought. He came together with them; and his seed became gold[3]. For this reason the latter shines like fire, it being Agni's

the case of the Gârhapatya, square the Âhavanîya, and semicircular the Dakshinâgni; but each equal in area to a square aratni or cubit. Along the edge of the mound he then lays pebbles close to each other [50 on the Gârhapatya, 73 on the Âhavanîya, and 22 on the Dakshinâgni, according to the Schol. on Kâty. IV, 8, 16]. According to some authorities, the piece of gold is laid on the top of the mound. He thus prepares successively the Gârhapatya, Âhavanîya, and Dakshina hearths; afterwards, if required, those of the Sabhya and Avasathya fires, which are, like the Gârhapatya, of circular form.

[1] An etymological play on the word ap, âpah, 'water,' and the verb âp, 'to obtain, pervade.'

[2] In the version of this myth given Taitt. Br. I, 1, 3, 8, the waters courted by Agni are called Varuna's wives.

[3] Tâh sambabhûva tâsu retah prâsiñkat tad hiranyam abhavat.

seed. Hence it (gold) is found in water, for he (Agni) poured it into the water. Hence also one does not cleanse oneself with it[1], nor does one do anything else with it. Now there is splendour (for the fire): for he thereby makes it to be possessed of divine seed, bestows splendour on it; and sets up a fire completely endowed with seed. That is why he brings gold.

6. He then brings salt. Yonder sky assuredly bestowed that (salt as) cattle on this earth : hence they say that salt soil is suitable for cattle. That (salt), therefore, means cattle ; and thus he thereby visibly supplies it (the fire) with cattle; and the latter having come from yonder (sky) is securely established on this earth. Moreover, that (salt) is believed to be the savour (rasa) of those two, the sky and the earth[2]: so that he thereby supplies it (the fire) with the savour of those two, the sky and the earth. That is why he brings salt.

7. He then brings (the earth of) a mole-hill (âkhu-karîsha)[3]. The moles certainly know the

[1] Sâyana interprets enena na dhâvayati by 'he does not clean (his teeth) with it;'—the St. Petersb. Dict. by 'he does not get himself conveyed (driven) by it.' The Kânva text has: Tasmâd enad apsv evânuvindanty apsu punanty apsu hy enat prâsiñkan nainena dhâvayanti na kim kana kurvanti.

[2] Cf. Taitt. Br. I, 1, 3, 2: 'The sky and the earth were (originally) close together. On being separated they said to each other, "Let there be a common sacrificial essence (yagñiyam) for us!" What sacrificial essence there was belonging to yonder sky, that it bestowed on this earth, that became the salt (in the earth); and what sacrificial essence there was belonging to this earth, that it bestowed on yonder sky, that became the black (spots) in the moon. When he throws salt (on the fire-place), let him think it to be that (viz. the black in the moon): it is on the sacrificial essence of the sky and the earth that he sets up his fire.'

[3] On the mythic connection of (the white, sharp teeth of) the

savour of this earth: hence, by entering deeper and deeper into this earth, they (grow) very fat, knowing, as they do, its savour; and wherever they know the savour of this earth to be, there they cast it up. Hence he thereby supplies it (the fire) with the savour of this earth: that is why he brings a mole-hill. Moreover, they say of one who has attained prosperity (or splendour, *s*rî) that he is purîshya; and purîsha and karîsha[1] doubtless mean one and the same thing: it is, therefore, for his (Agni's or the sacrificer's) attainment of splendour (*s*rî) that he brings a mole-hill.

8. He then brings pebbles. Now the gods and the Asuras, both of them sprung from Pra*g*âpati, once contended for superiority. This earth was then trembling like a lotus-leaf; for the wind was tossing it hither and thither: now it came near the gods, now it came near the Asuras. When it came near the gods,—

9. They said, 'Come, let us steady this resting-place; and when firm and steady, let us set up

âkhu (mole, mouse, rat), as of that of the boar, with the thunderbolt, see Dr. A. Kuhn's ingenious remarks, 'Herabkunft des Feuers und des Göttertranks,' p. 202. According to Taitt. Br. I, 1, 3, 3, Agni at one time concealed himself from the gods, and having become a mole, dug himself into the earth; so that the mole-hills thrown up by him, have some of Agni's nature attaching to them. The Taittirîyas also put on the hearth the earth of an ant-hill, which the Brâhma*n*a (in the same way as our author does of the mole-hill) represents as the savour (or marrow, essence) of the earth.

[1] The primary meaning of karîsha is 'that which is scattered, or strewn about,' hence 'refuse, rubbish' (and âkhu-karîsha, 'mole-cast'). Its secondary meaning, as is that of purîsha, is 'manure' (or perhaps also 'soft, rich mould'), an article naturally valued by an agricultural population. See I, 2, 5, 17, where purîsha is taken symbolically to represent cattle.

the two fires on it; whereupon we will exclude our enemies from any share in it.'

10. Accordingly, in like manner as one would stretch a skin by means of wooden pins, they fastened down this resting-place; and it formed a firm and steady resting-place. And when it was firm and steady, they set up the two fires on it; and thereupon they excluded their enemies from any share in it[1].

11. And in like manner that one (the Adhvaryu) now fastens down that resting-place by means of pebbles; and on it, when firm and steady, he sets up the two fires; whereupon he excludes the (sacrificer's) enemies from any share in it. This is the reason why he brings pebbles.

12. These then are the five equipments[2]: for fivefold is the sacrifice, fivefold the animal victim; and five seasons there are in the year.

[1] The corresponding myth of Taitt. Br. I, 1, 3, 5, though very different from ours, yet presents one or two points of resemblance. According to it, nothing was to be seen in the beginning except water and a lotus-leaf standing out above it. Pragâpati (being bent on creating the firm ground) bethought himself that the lotus-stalk must rest on something; and having assumed the form of a boar, he dived and brought up some of the earth. This he spread out (prath) on the lotus-leaf, whence originated the earth (prithivî), which he then fastened down by means of pebbles. Hence the latter are put on the hearth in order to afford a firm foundation for the fire.

[2] According to the authorities of the Black Yagur-veda there are not five, but fourteen sambhâras, seven of which are taken from the earth, viz. sand, salt, a mole-hill, an ant-hill, mire from a dried-up pool, pebbles, and gold; while the remaining seven consist of pieces of wood from the asvattha, udumbara, palâsa (? two pieces), samî, and vikankata trees, and from some tree that has been struck by lightning. The sprinkling of water about the fire-place is not counted by them as a sambhâra, but as one of the usual acts of lustration. Taitt. Br. I, 1, 3 seq.

13. Now, as to this, they say, 'Six seasons there are in the year.' And in that case the very deficiency (nyûna) itself is rendered a productive union[1], since it is from the lower part (nyûna, i.e. of the body) that offspring is here brought forth. Thus also a progressive improvement[2] (is assured to the sacrificer): for this reason there are five equipments. And when (it is nevertheless insisted on that) there are six seasons in the year, then Agni is the sixth of them, and thus there is no deficiency.

14. Here also they say, 'He should not equip it even with a single equipment!' For (they argue) all those (objects) are on this earth, and hence, when he establishes the fire on this earth, the latter of itself obtains all those equipments: he need not, therefore, equip it with a single equipment. But let him nevertheless bring (those objects) together; for when he establishes the fire on this (earth), then it obtains all the equipments: and what (benefit) accrues from the equipments being brought together, that also accrues to it[3]. Let him for that reason bring (the objects) together.

---

[1] Or, a deficient pairing is effected (on account of the uneven number). I do not quite understand Sâya*n*a's interpretation of the passage, the published text of the commentary being apparently corrupt in one or two places. The Kâ*n*va text reads: Tad âhu*h* sha*d* vâ *ri*tava*h* sa*m*vatsarasyeti yadi vai sha*l* *ri*tava*h* sa*m*vatsarasya nyûnam u vai pra*g*anana*m* nyûnâd vâ imâh pra*g*â*h* pra*g*âyante, &c.

[2] Literally, 'a prevailing (or advancing) better-to-morrow,' *s*va*h*-*s*reyasam uttarâvat.

[3] The drift of the author's reasoning evidently is that it is safer, by putting those objects on the fire-place, to make sure of the magic benefits of those symbols being really secured to the fire, and thereby to the sacrificer. The Kâ*n*va text of this paragraph, though differently worded, yields the same sense; except that it refers to

SECOND BRÂHMANA.

1. He may set up the two fires[1] under the Krittikâs; for they, the Krittikâs, are doubtless Agni's asterism, so that if he sets up his fires under Agni's asterism, (he will bring about) a correspondence (between his fires and the asterism): for this reason he may set up his fires under the Krittikâs.

2. Moreover, the other lunar asterisms (consist of) one, two, three or four (stars), so that the Krittikâs are the most numerous (of asterisms)[2]: hence he thereby obtains an abundance. For this reason he may set up his fires under the Krittikâs.

3. And again, they do not move away from the eastern quarter, whilst the other asterisms do move from the eastern quarter. Thus his (two fires) are established in the eastern quarter: for this reason he may set up his fires under the Krittikâs.

4. On the other hand (it is argued) why he should not set up the fires under the Krittikâs. Originally, namely, the latter were the wives of the Bears (riksha); for the seven Rishis[3] were in former times

---

the sacrificer himself and to the wishes he entertains in collecting the objects.

[1] That is, the Gârhapatya and Âhavanîya, the two principal fires.

[2] Whilst the Krittikâs, or Pleiades, are supposed to consist of seven (or, according to others, of six) stars, the remaining twenty-six nakshatras or lunar mansions, according to our author, vary between one and four stars. Hence the Krittikâs are also called Bahulâs, 'the numerous.' In the later accounts, however, a larger number of stars is attributed to several nakshatras. Cf. Weber, Nakshatra, II, pp. 368, 381. The Kânva text has: 'Other nakshatras are (i. e. consist of) four; and there is here an abundance, so that he thereby obtains abundance.'

[3] Saptarshi, or the seven Rishis, is the designation of the

called the *Ri*kshas (bears). They were, however, precluded from intercourse (with their husbands), for the latter, the seven *Ri*shis, rise in the north, and they (the K*ri*ttikâs) in the east. Now it is a misfortune for one to be precluded from intercourse (with his wife): he should therefore not set up his fires under the K*ri*ttikâs, lest he should thereby be precluded from intercourse.

5. But he may nevertheless set up (his fire under the K*ri*ttikâs); for Agni doubtless is their mate, and it is with Agni that they have intercourse: for this reason he may set up (the fire under the K*ri*ttikâs).

6. He may also set up his fires under (the asterism of Rohi*n*î. For under Rohi*n*î it was that Pra*g*âpati, when desirous of progeny (or creatures), set up his fires. He created beings, and the creatures produced by him remained invariable and constant[1], like (red) cows (rohi*n*î): hence the cow-like nature of Rohi*n*î. Rich in cattle and offspring therefore he becomes whosoever, knowing this, sets up his fires under Rohi*n*î.

7. Under Rohi*n*î, indeed, the cattle set up their fires, thinking that they might attain to (ruh) the desire (or love) of men. They did attain to the

constellation of Ursa Major, or the Wain. In the Rig-veda, *ri*kshâ*h* (bears) occurs once (I, 24, 10), either in the same restricted sense, or in that of stars generally.

[1] 'Tâ asya pra*g*â*h* s*ri*sh*t*â ekarûpâ upastabdhâs tasthû rohi*n*ya iva.' The Kâ*n*va text reads: Tam imâ*h* pra*g*â*h* s*ri*sh*t*â rohi*n*ya ivopastabdhâs tasthur ekarûpâ iva. Sâya*n*a interprets upastabdhâ*h* ('propped up, erect,' established) by 'pratibaddhaga*g*âtaya*h* (of continuous lineage),' and ekarûpâ*h* ('uniform') by 'avi*kkh*innapravâhâ*h* (of uninterrupted flow or succession).' In Taitt. Br. I, 1, 2, 2, it is stated that Pra*g*âpati created Agni under (the asterism) Rohi*n*î, and that the gods then set up that fire under the same asterism.

desire of men; and whatever desire the cattle then obtained in regard to men, that same desire he obtains, in regard to cattle, whosoever, knowing this, sets up his fire under Rohi*n*î.

8. He may also set up his fires under (the asterism of) M*ri*ga*s*îrsha. For M*ri*ga*s*îrsha, indeed, is the head of Pra*g*âpati [1]; and the head (*s*iras) means excellence (*s*rî), for the head does indeed mean excellence: hence they say of him who is the most excellent (*s*resh*th*a) of a community, that he is the head of that community. Excellence therefore he attains whosoever, knowing this, sets up his fire under M*ri*ga*s*îrsha.

9. On the other hand (it is argued) why one should not set up his fire under M*ri*ga*s*îrsha [2]. The latter, indeed, is Pra*g*âpati's body. Now, when they (the gods) on that occasion pierced him [3] with what is called 'the three-knotted arrow,' he abandoned that

---

[1] For the mythical allusions in this and the succeeding paragraphs, we have to compare *S*at. Br. I, 7, 4, 1; Ait. Br. III, 33. According to the version of the myth given in the latter work, Pra*g*âpati transformed himself into a roe-buck (*ri*sya) and approached his own daughter (either the sky, or the dawn), who had assumed the shape of a doe (rohit). Out of their most fearful forms the gods then fashioned a divine being called Bhûtavat (i. e. Rudra), in order to punish Pra*g*âpati for his incestuous deed. The latter was accordingly pierced by Bhûtavat's arrow and bounded up to the sky, where he became the constellation called M*ri*ga (i. e. M*ri*ga*s*îrsha), while his daughter became the asterism Rohi*n*î. The arrow on the other hand, with which Pra*g*âpati was pierced, became the constellation called 'the three-knotted arrow (perhaps the girdle of Orion).'

[2] The Black Ya*g*us does not recommend this asterism for the performance of agnyâdheya.

[3] The Kâ*n*va text reads, 'When, on that occasion, that god (viz. Rudra) pierced him with the three-knotted arrow.'

body, for the body is a mere relic (or dwelling, vâstu), unholy and sapless. He should therefore not set up his fires under M*ri*ga*s*îrsha.

10. But he may, nevertheless, set them up (under M*ri*ga*s*îrsha). For, assuredly, the body of that god, Pra*g*âpati, is neither a relic nor unholy[1]: he may therefore set up (his fires under M*ri*ga*s*îrsha). 'Under the Punarvasû he should perform the Punarâdheya[2],' thus (it is prescribed).

11. He may also set up his fires under the Phalgunîs. They, the Phalgunîs, are Indra's asterism[3], and even correspond to him in name; for indeed Indra is also called Ar*g*una, this being his mystic name; and they (the Phalgunîs) are also called Ar*g*unîs. Hence he overtly calls them Phalgunîs, for who dares to use his (the god's) mystic name? Moreover, the sacrificer himself is Indra, so that he in that case sets up his fires under his own asterism. Indra is the deity of the sacrifice; and accordingly his Agnyâdheya is thereby brought

---

[1] Na vâ etasya devasya vâstu nâya*g*ñiya*m* na *s*arîram asti.—Na vai tasya vâstu na nivîrya*m* nâya*g*ñiyam asti, 'for the relic of that (god) is neither sapless nor impure.' Kâ*n*va recension.

[2] I.e. the repetition of the âdheya, or setting up of his fires, a ceremony which has to be performed in the event of the âdheya having proved unsuccessful; that is, in case he should not have prospered or even sustained losses. The direction has been inserted in this place on account of the position of Punarvasû, as the fifth mansion, between M*ri*ga*s*îrsha, the third, and (Pûrva and Uttara) Phalgunîs, the ninth and tenth mansions, in the original order of the nakshatras.

[3] In Taitt. Br. I, 1, 2, 4, the Pûrve Phalgunî are assigned to Aryaman, and the Uttare Phalgunî to Bhaga. While, however, both these asterisms are there recommended for the agnyâdheya, the Pûrve Phalgunî are rejected as unsuitable further on, in par. 8 (? a later addition).

into relation with Indra. He may set up the fires under the first (Pûrva-phalgunîs)—whereby an advancing (successful) sacrifice accrues to him; or he may set them up under the second (Uttara-phalgunîs)—whereby a progressive (uttarâvat) improvement accrues to him.

12. Let him set up his fires under the asterism Hasta[1], whosoever should wish that (presents) should be offered him: then indeed (that will take place) forthwith; for whatever is offered with the hand (hasta), that indeed is given to him.

13. He may also set up his fires under *K*itrâ. Now the gods and the Asuras, both of them sprung from Pra*g*âpati, were contending for superiority. Both parties were desirous of rising to yonder world, the sky. The Asuras then constructed the fire (altar) called rauhi*n*a (fit to ascend by), thinking, 'Thereby we shall ascend (â-ruh) to the sky[2].'

---

[1] In the Taitt. Br. this asterism is not mentioned as suitable for the agnyâdheya. The Âsv. S. II, 1, 10 omits both Hasta and *K*itrâ; but permits the asterisms Visâkhe and Uttare Prosh*th*apade.

[2] In Taitt. Br. I, 1, 2, 4–6 this myth is related as follows: 'There were Asuras, named Kâlaka*ñg*as. They constructed a fire (altar) with a view to (gaining) the world of heaven. They put, every man of them, a brick to it. Indra, passing himself off for a Brâhman, put a brick on for himself, saying, "This one, *K*îtra (the wonderful or bright one) by name, is for me!" They climbed up to heaven; Indra, however, pulled out his brick, and they tumbled down. And they who tumbled down, became spiders: two of them flew up, and they became the two heavenly dogs.' On this myth, Dr. A. Kuhn, 'Über entwickelungsstufen der mythenbildung,' p. 129, remarks: 'The myth given in Homer's Od. xi, 305–325, of Otos and Ephialtes, who, in order to fight the immortal gods, piled Ossa on Olympos, and Pelion on Ossa, ἵν' οὐρανὸς ἄμβατος εἴη, and who are destroyed by Apollon, shows an obvious resemblance to these Indian myths; the more so, if we divest the latter of their Brâhmanical form, by which altar-bricks are sub-

14. Indra then considered[1], 'If they construct that (fire-altar), they will certainly prevail over us.' He secured a brick and proceeded thither, passing himself off for a Brâhman.

15. 'Hark ye!' he said, 'I, too, will put on this (brick) for myself!' 'Very well,' they replied. He put it on. That fire (altar) of theirs wanted but very little to be completely built up,—

16. When he said, 'I shall take back this (brick) which belongs to me.' He took hold of it and pulled it out; and on its being pulled out, the fire-altar fell down; and along with the falling fire-altar the Asuras fell down. He then converted those bricks into thunderbolts and clove the (Asuras') necks.

17. Thereupon the gods assembled and said, 'Wonderfully (*k*itram) indeed it has fared with us who have slain so many enemies!' Hence the wonderful nature (*k*itrâtva)[2] of the asterism

stituted for mountains; and if we bear in mind that the later versions of the myth, e.g. in the well-known passage of Ovid, put the Gigantes in the place of the Aloades.' See also Weber, Nakshatra, II, p. 372.

[1] The Kâ*n*va text here proceeds thus: The gods then were afraid and said, 'If those (Asuras) complete (samâsyanti) that (fire-altar), they will prevail over us.' Then Indra having fastened a brick with the lightning-band (ârke*n*a dâmnâ) went thither passing himself off for a Brâhman. He said, 'I, too, will put on this (brick) for myself.' They said, 'On then (upa hi)!' He put it on. That (fire-altar) wanted but very little to be built up, when he said, 'I shall take this (brick) which is mine.' 'Take it then (â hi)!' they said. Then seizing it (tâm abhihâya) he pulled it out. On its being pulled out the fire-altar tumbled down. On the fire-altar having tumbled down he made thunderbolts with those bricks and smote those (Asuras). Then the gods prevailed and the Asuras were worsted, &c.

[2] Or, perhaps, its identity with (Indra's brick) *K*itrâ; cf. preceding note.

Kitrâ; and verily wonderfully it fares with him, and he slays his rivals, his spiteful enemy, whosoever, knowing this, sets up his fires under Kitrâ. A Kshatriya, therefore, should especially desire to take advantage of this asterism; since such a one is anxious to strike, to vanquish his enemies.

18. Originally these (nakshatras) were so many different powers (kshatra), just as that sun yonder. But as soon as he rose, he took from them (â-dâ) their energy, their power; therefore he (the sun) is called Âditya, because he took from them their energy, their power[1].

19. The gods then said, 'They who have been powers, shall no longer (na) be powers (kshatra)[2]!' Hence the powerlessness (na-kshatratvam) of the nakshatras. For this reason also one need only take the sun for one's nakshatra (star), since he took away from them their energy, their power. But if he (the sacrificer) should nevertheless be desirous of having a nakshatra (under which to set up his fires), then assuredly that sun is a faultless nakshatra for him; and through that auspicious day (marked by the rising and setting of the sun) he should endeavour to obtain the benefits of whichever of those asterisms he might desire. Let him therefore take the sun alone for his nakshatra[3].

---

[1] The Kânva text reads: Tâni ha vâ etâni kshatrâni nânaiva tepur yathâsau vâ sûryas kandramâ vâ; teshâm hodyann evâdityah kshatram vîryam tegah pralulopa, tad vaishâm âdade.

[2] This etymology of nakshatra is of course quite fanciful. For Aufrecht's probably correct derivation of the word from nakta-tra, 'night-protector,' cf. Zeitschrift für vergl. Sprachf., VIII, pp. 71, 72. See also Weber, Nakshatra, II, p. 268.

[3] The Kânva text reads: Tasmân na nakshatram âdriyeta yadaivaisha kadâ kodîyâd apy âdadhîtaisha hi sarvâni kshatrâni;

THIRD BRÂHMANA.

1. The spring, the summer, and the rains, these seasons (represent) the gods; and the autumn, the winter, and the dewy season represent the fathers. That half-moon which increases represents the gods, and that which decreases represents the fathers. The day represents the gods, and the night represents the fathers. And, further, the forenoon represents the gods, and the afternoon the fathers.

2. Those seasons, then, are the gods and the fathers; and whosoever, knowing this, invokes them as the gods and fathers, with his invocation of the gods the gods comply, and with his invocation of the fathers the fathers comply. Him the gods favour at his invocation of the gods, and him the fathers favour at his invocation of the fathers, whosoever, knowing this, invokes (the seasons) as the gods and fathers.

3. Now when he (the sun) moves northwards, then he is among the gods, then he guards the gods; and when he moves southwards, then he is among the fathers, then he guards the fathers [1].

4. When he (the sun) moves northwards, then one may set up his fires;—the gods have the evil dis-

---

yadyu nakshatrakâma*h* syâd upo âsîta nakshatram ahâsya bhavati no etasyânudayo 'sti tasmâd v apy upaina(m â)sîta, 'he need therefore not attend to any nakshatra; but may set up his fires at any time when that (sun) rises, for he (the sun) is all the kshatras. Should he nevertheless be desirous of a nakshatra, let him approach (the sun) with veneration; for then there is a nakshatra for him, and that (sun) does not fail to rise: for this reason let him approach (the sun) with veneration.'

[1] According to the Kâ*n*va text, it is the rising sun, that guards the god-seasons and father-seasons respectively.

pelled from them (by the sun): he (the sacrificer) therefore dispels the evil from himself;—the gods are immortal: he therefore, though there is for him no prospect of immortality, attains the (full measure of) life, whosoever sets up his fires during that time. Whosoever, on the other hand, sets up his fires when (the sun) moves southwards, he does not dispel the evil from him,—since the fathers have not the evil dispelled from them (by the sun). The fathers are mortal: hence he dies before (he has attained the full measure of) life, whosoever sets up his fires during that time.

5. The spring is the priesthood, the summer the nobility, and the rainy season the common people (*vis*): a Brâhman therefore should set up his fires in spring, since the spring is the priesthood; and a Kshatriya should set them up in summer, since the summer is the nobility; and a Vaisya should set them up in the rainy season, since the rainy season is the common people.

6. And whosoever[1] desires to become endowed with holy lustre (brahmavarkasin), let him set up his fires in spring,—for the spring is the priesthood,—and he will certainly become endowed with holy lustre.

7. And whosoever desires to become a power (kshatra)[2] in prosperity and renown, let him set up his fires in summer,—for the summer is the nobility (kshatra),—and he will certainly become a power in prosperity and renown.

8. And whosoever may desire to be rich in pro-

[1] I. e. whatsoever Brâhman, as the Kânva text reads.

[2] Kshatram sriyâ yasasâ syâm iti. The Kânva text reads: Kshatrasya pratimâ syâm sriyâ yasaseti, 'whosoever should wish to be an image of the kshatra in wealth and glory.'

geny and cattle, let him set up his fires in the rainy season[1],—for the rainy season is the common people, and the people means food,—and he certainly becomes rich in progeny and cattle, whosoever, knowing this, sets up his fires in the rainy season.

9. [In the opinion of others] both these (classes of) seasons have the evil dispelled from them, for the sun is the dispeller of their evil, and as soon as he rises he dispels the evil from both these (classes of seasons). He should therefore set up his fires at any time, when he feels called upon to sacrifice; and should not put it off from one day to the morrow: for who knows the morrow of man[2]?

FOURTH BRÂHMANA.

1. On the day preceding his Agnyâdheya, he (the sacrificer with his wife) should take his food in the day-time. For the gods know the minds of man: they are, therefore, aware that his Agnyâdheya is to take place on the morrow; and all the gods betake themselves to his house and stay (upa-vas) in his house; whence this day is called upavasatha (fast-day)[3].

2. Now, as it would be unbecoming for him to take food before men (who are staying with him as his guests) have eaten; how much more would it be so, if he were to take food before the gods have eaten: let him therefore take his food in the day-time. However, he may also, if he choose, take food at night,

---

[1] The Black Yagus recommends *s*arad, autumn, for the Agnyâdheya in the case of a Vai*s*ya.

[2] Ko hi manushyasya *s*vo veda. The Kâ*n*va text has: Na vai manushya*h* *s*vastanam veda (veda) ko hi (!) tasmai manushyo ya*h* *s*vastana*m* vidyât, 'in truth no man knows the morrow, for what man, that knows the morrow, is there for him?'

[3] See I, 1, 1, 7 seq.

since the observance of the vow is not necessary for him who has not performed Agnyâdheya. For so long as he has not set up a (sacrificial) fire of his own, he is merely a man, and may therefore, if he choose, take food at night.

3. Here now some tie up a he-goat[1], arguing that the goat is sacred to Agni and that (this is done) for the completeness of the fire. But he need not do this. Should he possess a he-goat, let him present it to the Âgnîdhra on the next morning; for it is thereby that he obtains the object he desires. He need, therefore, take no notice of that (practice).

4. They[2] then cook a rice-pap sufficient for (the) four (priests) to eat. 'Hereby we gratify the metres,' so they say, arguing that this is done in the same way as if one were to order a team, which he is going to use for driving, to be well fed. He need not, however, do this: for indeed that same wish (which he entertains in so doing) he obtains by the very fact that Brâhmans, be they sacrificial priests or not, are residing in his family (kula)[3]: he need, therefore, take no notice of that (practice).

5. Having then made a hollow in it (the pap) for

---

[1] This practice is perhaps the remnant of a former animal offering. See I, 2, 3, 6, where the goat is mentioned as the last of the animals meet for sacrifice.

[2] That is, as would seem, those ritualists who maintain that a goat should be tied up for that night. The Kânva text reads, 'Here some cook that night that kâtuhprâsya rice-pap, saying (vadantah), "Hereby we gratify the metres."' According to the Paddhati on Kâty IV, 8, the quotation 'Hereby we gratify the metres' seems to form the last of the formulas pronounced by the sacrificer, while washing the feet of the priests and offering them food.

[3] 'The fulfilment of that wish he obtains through Brahmans, whether officiating priests or not, staying in his house (kula) and taking food there.' Kânva text.

clarified butter to be poured in, and having poured clarified butter into it, they anoint three sticks of asvattha wood with this butter and put them on the fire with the (three) *Ri*k-verses containing the words 'kindling-stick (samidh)' and 'butter (ghrita)[1];' arguing that thereby they obtain what has grown out of a samî[2]. It is, however, only by (daily) putting (three kindling-sticks) on the fire for a whole year previous (to the Âdhâna) that one obtains that object: let him therefore take no notice of that (practice).

6. And on this point Bhâllabeya remarked, 'If he were to cook that rice-pap, this would assuredly

[1] The three verses containing the words samidh and ghrita are Vâg. S. III, 1, 3, 4. Taitt. Br. I, 2, 1, 9–10 has them in the order 1, 4, 3; and does not give the verse Vâg. S. III, 2 (Rig-veda V, 5, 1). As neither version of our Brâhmana makes any mention of this verse, it may be doubted whether originally it formed part of the Samhitâ. According to Kâty. IV, 8, 5–6 he (? the Adhvaryu) is to put on (the three kindling-sticks) with Vâg. S. III, 1, &c., one verse with each stick; whereupon he, (the sacrificer, according to the commentary,) is to mutter III, 4; and according to ib. 7 'the Adhvaryu optionally mutters the second.' The Paddhati reconciles the different statements thus: he takes the sticks, rises and puts the first on the fire with III, 1; then sitting down he mutters III, 2; thereupon he again rises and puts on the second with III, 3, and the third with III, 4. The commentator, however, alludes to differences of practice in different schools as to this point.

[2] The sacrificial fire, to be set up at the Âdheya, should probably be produced by means of two pieces of asvattha wood which has grown out of a samî tree. Sâyana remarks that the ritualists referred to in our passage consider that the cooking of the rice-pap takes place, not with the view of the latter being eaten by the priests, but merely to afford an opportunity for putting the kindling-sticks on the fire, and thereby securing to the sacrificer the benefits that would have accrued to him from the above mode of ignition. This view, however, is not countenanced by our author, who, on the contrary, favours the daily cooking of a mess of rice-pap for the four priests for a twelvemonth preceding the Agnyâdheya, as a substitute for the production of the fire by friction. See Kâty. IV, 8, 11 (and Paddhati).

be a mistake, just as if one were to do one thing, while intending to do another; or if one were to say one thing, while intending to say another; or if one were to go one way, while intending to go another.' And, indeed, it is not proper that they should either carry to the south, or extinguish, that fire on which a kindling-stick is put, or an oblation made, with a *rik* or a sâman or a ya*g*us. Now they do indeed either take it to the south with the view of its becoming the Anvâhâryapa*k*ana (or Dakshi*n*âgni), or (if there is to be no Dakshi*n*âgni) they extinguish it[1].

7. Thereupon they[2] remain awake (during that night). The gods are awake: so that he thereby draws nigh to the gods, and sets up his fires as one more godly, more subdued, more endowed with holy fervour (tapas). He may, however, sleep, if he choose, since the observance of the vow is not necessary for him who has not performed Agnyâdheya. For so long as he has not set up a (sacrificial) fire of his own, he is a mere man; and he may, therefore, sleep, if he choose.

8. Now some churn (the fire)[3] before sunrise and

[1] His argument seems to be that, since the cooking of the rice-pap involves the putting on of consecrated sticks with sacrificial formulas, one is not to cook the pap because that same fire will afterwards have to be extinguished or to be taken to the Dakshi*n*âgni hearth. The passage is, however, far from clear to me.

[2] Viz. the ritualists referred to; that is to say, they make the sacrificer and his wife remain awake all night. Sâya*n*a takes *g*âgrati to stand for *g*âgarti, 'he, the sacrificer, remains awake.' The Kâ*n*va text, however, has, 'Here now they say, he should remain awake that night.'

[3] The production of the sacred fire by means of two sticks (ara*n*i) of the a*s*vattha (Ficus Religiosa) is thus described by Stevenson, 'Translation of the Sâma Veda,' pref. p. vii: 'The process by which fire is obtained from wood is called churning, as it resembles

take it eastwards (from the Gârhapatya to the Âhavanîya) after sunrise, arguing that thereby they secure both the day and the night for the obtainment of out-breathing and in-breathing, of mind and speech. But let him not do so; for when they thus churn (the fire) before sunrise, and take it eastwards after sunrise, both his (fires) are in reality set up before sunrise. By churning the Âhavanîya after sunrise he will obtain that (combination of blessings).

9. The gods, assuredly, are the day. The fathers have not the evil dispelled from them (by the sun); (and accordingly) he (the sacrificer) does not dispel the evil (if he churns the fire before sunrise). The fathers are mortal; and verily he who churns the fire before the rising of the sun, dies before (he has attained his full measure of) life. The gods have the evil dispelled from them (by the sun): hence he (the sacrificer) dispels the evil (from himself, if he churn after sunrise). The gods are immortal; and—though there is for him no prospect of immortality—he attains (the full measure of life). The gods are bliss, and bliss he obtains; the gods are glorious, and glorious he will be, whosoever, knowing this, churns (the fire) after the rising of the sun.

---

that by which butter in India is separated from milk. The New-Hollanders obtain fire from a similar process. It consists in drilling one piece of arani wood into another by pulling a string tied to it with a jerk with the one hand, while the other is slackened, and so alternately till the wood takes fire. The fire is received on cotton or flax held in the hand of an assistant Brahman.' On the mythological associations of the agni-manthana, especially with the Teutonic need-fire and the myth of Prometheus; and those of the asvattha tree, grown out of a samî, with the mountain-ash (roun-tree, rowan-tree, witch-elm, witchen, witch-hazel, witch-wood; eber-esche), see A. Kuhn's epoch-making essay, 'Ueber die Herabkunft des Feuers und des Göttertranks.'

10. Here now they say, 'If the fire is not set up with either a *ri*k-verse, or a sâman, or a ya*g*us, wherewith then is it set up?' Verily, that (fire) is of the brahman: with the brahman it is set up. The brahman is speech: of that speech it is. The brahman is the truth, and the truth consists in those same (three) mystic utterances: hence his (fire) is established by means of the truth.

11. Verily, with 'bhû*h* (earth)!' Pra*g*âpati generated this (earth)[1]; with 'bhuva*h* (ether)!' the ether; with 'sva*h* (heaven)!' the sky. As far as these (three) worlds extend, so far extends this universe: with the universe it (the fire) is accordingly established.

12. With 'bhû*h*!' Pra*g*âpati generated the Brahman (priesthood); with 'bhuva*h*!' the Kshatra (nobility); with '*s*va*h*!' the Vi*s* (the common people). As much as are the Brahman, the Kshatra, and the Vi*s*, so much is this universe: with the universe it (the fire) is accordingly established.

13. With 'bhû*h*!' Pra*g*âpati generated the Self; with 'bhuva*h*!' the (human) race; with 'sva*h*!' the animals (pa*s*u). As much as are the Self, the (human) race, and the animals, so much is this universe: with the universe it (the fire) is accordingly established.

14. 'Bhûr bhuva*h*!' this much he utters while laying down the Gârhapatya fire; for if he were to lay it down with all (three words), wherewith should he lay down the Ahavanîya? Two syllables[2]

[1] Compare XI, 1, 6, 3.

[2] Viz. sva*h*, pronounced su-va*h*. In laying down the Gârhapatya he utters the first two words, consisting of three syllables; and in laying down the Âhavanîya he pronounces all three words, consisting of five syllables.

he leaves over, and thereby those (five syllables) become of renewed efficacy; and with all the five syllables—'Bhûr bhuva*h* sva*h*'—he lays down the Âhavanîya. Thus result eight syllables; for of eight syllables consists the gâyatrî, and the gâyatrî is Agni's metre: he thus establishes that (fire) by means of its own metre.

15. Now when the gods were about to set up their fires, the Asuras and Rakshas forbade them, saying, 'The fire shall not be produced; ye shall not set up your fires!' and because they thus forbade (raksh) them, they are called Rakshas.

16. The gods then perceived this thunderbolt, to wit, the horse. They made it stand before them, and in its safe and foeless shelter the fire was produced. For this reason let him (the Adhvaryu) direct (the Âgnîdhra) to lead the horse to where he is about to churn the fire. It stands in front of him[1]: he thus raises the thunderbolt, and in its safe and foeless shelter the fire is produced.

17. Let it be one used as a leader[2]; for such a one possesses unlimited strength. Should he be unable to obtain a leader, it may be any kind of horse. Should he be unable to obtain a horse, it may also be an ox, since that (fire) is related (bandhu) to the ox[3].

18. And when they carry that (fire) eastward[4],

---

[1] The horse is to stand east of the Gârhapatya fire-place, with its head to the west, where, behind the khara, the Adhvaryu is about to produce the fire.

[2] Pûrvavah, 'drawing in front,' i.e. a young (newly-harnessed) horse. The term may also mean 'conveying eastwards,' whence it is probably used here; cf. Taitt. Br. I, 1, 5, 6.

[3] See XIII, 8, 4, 6, where the ox is said to be sacred to Agni (âgneya). See also p. 292, note 1; and I, 2, 3, 6.

[4] The following particulars, not alluded to by our author, have

they lead the horse in front of it; so that, in proceeding in front of it, it wards off from it the evil spirits, the Rakshas; and they carry it (to the Âhavanîya) safely and unmolested by evil spirits.

19. Let them carry it (the fire) in such wise that it turns back towards him (the sacrificer); for, assuredly, that fire is the (means of) sacrifice, and it is in the direction of him (the sacrificer) that the sacrifice enters him, that the sacrifice readily inclines to him. And, verily, from whomsoever it (the fire) turns away, from him the sacrifice also turns away; and if any one were to curse him, saying, 'May the sacrifice turn away from him!' then he would indeed be liable to fare thus.

20. Moreover, that (fire) is the (sacrificer's) breath: let them therefore carry it in such wise that it turns

---

to be supplied here from Kâty. IV, 8, 29 seq., and the commentaries: As soon as fire has been obtained from the two pieces of wood, [it is placed in a pan and covered with dry, powdered gomaya; and] the sacrificer blows it with 'Breath I bestow on the immortal;' and the well-kindled flame he inhales with 'The immortal I bestow on the breath' (see II, 2, 2, 15). The fire is then set ablaze with fire-wood and laid down on the newly-made Gârhapatya hearth-mound with '[Om!] Bhûr bhuva*h* sva*h*!' (Vâ*g*. S. III, 5); and with 'I lay thee down, O Lord of Vows (vratapati), with the law (vrata) of N. N?'—the gotra-name being inserted in the case of the Bh*ri*gus and Aṅgiras; and those of different *Ri*shis or gods and divine beings in that of others. At the sacrificer's bidding the Brahman or Adhvaryu then chants the Rathantara-sâman (cf. p. 196, note 2). Then follows the uddhara*n*a or taking out fire from the Gârhapatya for the Âhavanîya. A bundle of wood is lighted at the lower ends on the Gârhapatya and placed in a pan on an underlayer of clay. It is then carried eastwards in such a way that the smoke is directed towards the sacrificer following it; the horse being led in front of the fire. At the starting of the procession the Brahman, at the Adhvaryu's call, chants the Vâmadevya-sâman.

back towards him; for it is in the direction of him that the breath enters into him. And, verily, from whomsoever it (the fire) turns away, from him the breath also turns away; and if in that case any one were to curse him, saying, 'May the breath turn away from him!' then he would indeed be liable to fare thus.

21. And, verily, the sacrifice is yonder blowing (wind). Let them, therefore, carry it in such wise that it[1] turns towards him; for it is in the direction of him that the sacrifice enters him, that the sacrifice readily inclines to him. And from whomsoever it turns away, from him the sacrifice also turns away; and if any one were to curse him, saying, 'May the sacrifice turn away from him!' then he would indeed be liable to fare thus.

22. And, verily, that (fire) is the (sacrificer's) breath. Let them, therefore, carry it in such wise that it turns towards him; for it is in the direction of him that the breath enters into him. And from whomsoever it (the fire) turns away; from him the breath also turns away; and if any one were to curse him, saying, 'May the breath turn away from him!' he would indeed be liable to fare thus.

23. He (the Adhvaryu) then makes the horse step on (the Âhavanîya fire-place)[2]. When he has made it step on it, he leads it out towards the east, makes it turn round again (from left to right) and lets it

[1] Viz. the wind indicated by the backward-turned flame of the fire, as it is carried eastwards to the Âhavanîya.

[2] The Adhvaryu sits down and makes the horse put its right fore-foot on the recently prepared hearth-mound. Having then led it eastwards and turned it round, he calls on the Brahman to chant the B*ri*hat-sâman (see p. 196, note 2).

stand there facing the west. The horse doubtless represents strength: hence he makes it turn round again in order that this strength shall not turn away from him (the sacrificer).

24. He lays that (fire) down on the horse's foot-print[1]; for the horse represents strength, so that he thereby lays it down on strength: for this reason he lays it down on the horse's foot-print.

25. In the first place he silently touches (the foot-print with the burning fire-wood). He then lifts it up and touches once more with it; and at the third time he lays it down with (Vâg. S. III, 5), 'Earth! ether! heaven!' For there are three worlds indeed; so that he thereby obtains these (three) worlds. This now is one (mode of laying down the fire).

26. Then there is this other. Silently he touches (the foot-print with it) in the first place; he then lifts it up, and at the second time lays it down with 'Earth! ether! heaven!' For he who wants to lift a load without having a firm footing on this (earth), cannot lift it; nay, it crushes him.

27. Now, when he touches it silently he thereby takes a firm footing on this resting-place: and having obtained a firm footing on it, he lays down (the fire): and thus he wavers not. Here now Âsuri, Pâñki, and Mâdhuki held it (the fire) slightly to the back (or west of the fire-place)[2]. 'For,' they argued, 'everything else (that is on the hearth)

---

[1] Taitt. Br. I, 1, 5, 9, on the contrary, forbids the fire to be laid down on the horse's foot-print, as the sacrificer's cattle is thereby surrendered to Rudra. Moreover, the horse is there made to step beside, not upon, the hearth-mound.

[2] The Kânva text reads: Tad v Âsurih Pâñkir Mâdhukir iti dadhrire, 'here now they held it thus.'

becomes, as it were, relaxed (on being touched by the fire): he should therefore, after holding it up, lay it down at the first (touching) with "Earth! ether! heaven!" for thus no relaxation takes place.' Let him then do this in whichever way he may deem proper.

28. He (the sacrificer) then goes round to the east side (of the fire), and taking hold of the top part of the burning sticks he mutters (Vâg. S. III, 5): 'Like unto the sky in plenty, like unto the earth in greatness!' When he says, 'Like unto the sky in plenty,' he means to say, 'Like as yonder sky is plenteous with stars, so may I become plenteous!' and when he says, 'Like unto the earth in greatness,' he means to say, 'As great as this earth is so great may I become!'—'On that back of thine, O Earth, that art meet for the worship of the gods'—for on her back he lays down that (fire)—'I lay down Agni, the eater of food, for the obtainment of food.' Agni is an eater of food: 'May I become an eater of food,' this is what he thereby says. This is a prayer for blessing,—he may mutter it, if he choose; or, if he choose, he may omit it.

29. He stands worshipping by (the fire) while muttering the (three) *Ri*k-verses of the queen of serpents (Vâg. S. III, 6-8)[1],—'Hither has come that spotted bull and has settled down before the mother; and before the father on going up to heaven.—She moves along through the luminous spheres, breathing forth from his breath: the mighty (bull) has illumined

[1] These verses form the hymn Rig-veda X, 189, the authorship of which is ascribed to the queen of serpents (either Kadrû, or the earth, according to Mahîdhara).

the sky.—He rules over the thirty domains; and song is bestowed on the winged one, yea, with the light at the break of day!' Thus he recites; and whatever (benefit) has not been obtained by him either through the equipments, or through the asterisms, or through the seasons, or through the laying down of the fire, all that is thereby obtained by him; and for this reason he stands worshipping by (the fire), while muttering the verses of the queen of serpents.

30. They say, however, that one need not stand by (the fire) worshipping with the verses of the queen of serpents. For the queen of serpents, they argue, is this earth; and accordingly when he lays down the fire on her, he thereby obtains all his desires: hence he need not stand by (the fire) worshipping with the verses of the queen of serpents.

SECOND ADHYÂYA. FIRST BRÂHMANA.

THE OBLATIONS.

1. When he has taken out the Âhavanîya fire[1], he performs the Full-offering[2]. The reason why

[1] Previously to the performance of the full-offering, the other fires (if there are any more) are laid down. An integral part of the laying down of the Sabhya, or hall-fire, which seems to have been kept up only by Kshatriyas, is a game of dice, played by the priests, with a cow, offered by the sacrificer, for the stake. On an ox-hide, spread north of the sacrificial ground, they place a brass vessel upside down, and on it throw four times five cowries (or, if such are not to be had, five sticks) with 'Even I win, uneven thou art won (or defeated)!'

[2] The pûrnâhuti, or 'full-offering,' is an oblation of a spoonful of clarified butter. Kâty. IV. 10, 5, and comm., supply the following particulars, applying to all ordinary guhoti-offerings: He puts butter into the butter-pot and places it on the Gârhapatya to

he performs the full-offering is that he thereby causes that Agni to become an eater of food for his own self; that he thereby offers food to him. Even as (a mother or cow) would offer the breast to a new-born child or calf, so does he thereby offer food to him.

2. And having been appeased by that food, he (Agni) waits patiently for the other oblations to be cooked. If, on the other hand, that oblation were not to be offered up in him, he would ere long burn either the Adhvaryu or the sacrificer, for these two pass nearest by him. This is the reason why he makes this offering.

3. He offers it (with a) full (spoon); for the full doubtless means the All (universe), so that he thereby appeases him with the All. He offers it with 'Svâhâ!' for the Svâhâ is undefined, and undefined also is the All, so that he thereby appeases him by means of the All.

4. The first offering which Pra*g*âpati made, he made with 'Svâhâ!' Now that (offering) indeed is virtually the same as this one; and hence he (the sacrificer) also makes it with 'Svâhâ!' At this (offering) he grants a boon (to the priests)[1]; but

melt. Having then wiped the dipping-spoon (sruva) and offering-spoon (*g*uhû) with sacrificial grass in the manner described at I, 3, 1, 6 seq., and taken the butter-pot off the fire, and strained the butter with the two stalks of darbha serving as strainers, he fills the *g*uhu with the sruva. He now takes one stick, steps over to the north side of the Âhavanîya fire, strews grass around it, and puts the stick on the fire. He then sits down with bent right knee, and, while the sacrificer takes hold of him from behind, he pours the spoonful of butter into the fire with 'Svâhâ!' the sacrificer pronouncing the dedicatory formula (tyâga), 'This to Agni!'

[1] After the full-offering the sacrificer breaks the silence, imposed on him, by the words, 'I give a boon,' Kâty. IV, 10, 6; presents,

a boon (may mean) everything, so that he thereby appeases him (Agni) with everything.

5. Here now they say, 'When he has made this offering, he need not attend to the subsequent oblations; for by this offering he obtains that wish for which he takes out the subsequent oblations.'

6. He takes out (material for an oblation)[1] to Agni Pavamâna (the Blowing)[2]. Now the blowing one is the breath, so that he thereby puts breath into him (the sacrificer). And this he puts into him by means of this (offering); for breath means food, and this offering also is food.

---

according to the commentary, being then made to the Adhvaryu and the Brahman. This ceremony is succeeded by the silent performance of the Agnihotra.

[1] The pûrnâhuti, which marks the close of the Agnyâdheya proper, is followed by the Agnihotra, performed with the texts pronounced in a low voice. Not less than twelve days after the Agnyâdheya (if at all)—the three fires being kept up during the interval—the young householder has to get performed for him (on the model of the new and full-moon offering, mutatis mutandis, there being neither the uddharana, or taking out of fire from the Gârhapatya, nor the choosing of a Brahman, &c.) the three ishtis mentioned above. At the first ishti, the special havis (sacrificial dish) consists of a rice-cake on eight potsherds for Agni Pavamâna;—at the second of two such cakes for Agni Pâvaka and Agni Suki respectively;—at the third of a potful of boiled rice for Aditi. The three havis of the first two ishtis being (according to Taitt. Br. I, 1, 6, 3) considered as representing the three bodies (tanu) of Agni; these offerings are called tanûhavir-ishtis. They are, however, also called Pavamâneshtis. At these the name of the recipient (Agni Pavamâna, &c.) has to be pronounced in a low voice in the formulas used at the chief offering. The Taitt. Br. mentions, besides, the usual Indrâgni cake (of the new-moon sacrifice) which is to be offered before the offering to Aditi.

[2] Sâyana, on Taitt. Br. I, 1, 5, 10, takes pavamâna as 'pure' or 'purified by himself' (svayam sriddha); pâvaka as 'purifying (others);' and suki as 'shining.'

7. He then makes offering to Agni Pâvaka (the Purifying). Now the purifying one means food, so that he thereby puts food into him (Agni, or the sacrificer). And this he puts into him by means of this (offering), for this offering is indeed food.

8. He then makes offering to Agni *Suki* (the Bright). Now brightness means vigour, so that he thereby puts vigour into him. And this he puts into him by means of this (offering); for when he offers up that oblation in him (Agni), then that vigour, that brightness of his blazes up.

9. For this reason they say, 'When he has made that (full) offering, he need not attend to any further oblations; for by this offering he obtains that wish for which he takes out the subsequent oblations.' But let him nevertheless take out the subsequent oblations; for what invisible (blessing, or meaning) there was in that (full-offering) that now becomes thus (visible).

10. Now the reason why he makes offering to Agni Pavamâna, is that the blowing one is the breath. When (the child) is born, then there is breath. And as long as it is not born, it breathes in accord with the mother's breath; but when it is born, then he thereby puts breath into it.

11. And the reason why he makes offering to Agni Pâvaka, is that the purifying one means food: hence he thereby puts food into (the child) when it is born.

12. And the reason why he makes offering to Agni *Suki*, is that brightness means vigour. Now when it (the child) grows by means of food, then there is vigour; and hence, when he has made it grow by means of food, he thereby puts into it that vigour, that brightness. This is why (he offers) to Agni *Suki*.

13. That other (practice) then is altogether erroneous[1]. For when Agni passed over from the gods to men, he bethought him, 'I must not pass over to men with my whole body!'

14. He then laid down in these (three) worlds those three bodies of his. That 'blowing (pavamâna)' form of his he laid down on this earth, that 'purifying (pâvaka)' one in the ether, and that 'bright (suki)' one in the sky. Now the *Ri*shis then existing became aware of this: 'Agni has not come to us with his whole body,' they said. They then prepared those oblations for him.

15. Now when he makes offering to Agni Pavamâna, he thereby obtains that form of his (Agni's) which he laid down on this earth; and when he makes offering to Agni Pâvaka, he thereby obtains that form of his which he laid down in the ether; and when he makes offering to Agni *S*u*k*i, he thereby obtains that form of his which he laid down in the sky: and thus he lays down the entire Agni unmutilated. For this reason also he should take out the oblations subsequent (to the full-offering).

16. The first oblation has a barhis (altar-covering of sacrificial grass) to itself; the two following ones have one barhis in common. Now the first oblation represents this world, the second one that ether, and the third one the sky. But this earth is compact; and the ether and yonder sky are, as it were, trembling: and in order that these two may counterbalance that (earth), the (last) two (oblations) have one barhis in common.

[1] Viz. the practice of performing the full-offering only, see par. 5. The Kâ*n*va text reads: Tad vâ etat samânam eva sad viparyastam iva.

17. All these sacrificial cakes (for Agni) are on eight potsherds; for of eight syllables consists the (pâda of the) gâyatrî, and the gâyatrî is Agni's metre[1]: with its own metre he accordingly establishes that fire. In all, these potsherds amount to twenty-four; for of twenty-four syllables consists the gâyatrî (stanza), and the gâyatrî is Agni's metre: with its own metre he accordingly establishes that fire.

18. He then offers a potful of boiled rice to Aditi. For he who performs those (preceding) oblations moves away, as it were, from this world, since he moves in the ascent of these worlds[2].

19. Now when he offers a potful of boiled rice to Aditi,—Aditi being this earth, and this earth being a firm resting-place,—he thereby again takes his stand on this firm resting-place. This is why he offers a potful of boiled rice to Aditi.

20. For her, they say, the two samyâgyâs[3] should be virâg verses; for the virâg is this (earth); or

---

[1] The Kânva text remarks that the anuvâkyâs (invitatory prayers) and yâgyâs (offering prayers) at the three offerings of cake are in the gâyatrî metre; and such indeed is the case. The anuvâkyâs of the oblations to Agni Pavamâna, Agni Pâvaka, and Agni Suki are Rig-veda IX, 66, 19; I, 12, 10; and VIII, 44, 21 respectively: and the yâgyâs are IX, 66, 21; V, 26, 1; and VIII, 44, 17 respectively; all of which are gâyatrî stanzas. See Âsv. Sr. II, 1, 20-25. Cf. also I, 7, 2, 15, with note. At the Svishtakrit of these two ishtis also both formulas are in the gâyatrî metre: the puro'nuvâkyâs being Rig-veda III, 11, 2, and III, 11, 6; and the yâgyâs III, 11, 1, and I, 1, 1 respectively.

[2] Prakyavata iva vâ esho 'smâl lokât . . . imân hi lokân samârohann eti. The Kânva text has: 'For he who takes out these oblations makes his self, as it were, depart from this world of men for the world of the gods, since he, as it were, moves rising upwards (ûrdhva iva hi samârohann eti).' Cf. paragraphs 14-16.

[3] For these (virâg) samyâgye, or invitatory and offering prayers at the Svishtakrit, see p. 164, note 2.—Âsv. Sr. II, 1, 29.

trishtubh verses, for the trishtubh is this (earth); or gagatî verses, for the gagatî is this (earth). Still, however, they should be virâg verses.

21. The priests' fee for (offering to) her consists of a cow; for this (earth) is, as it were, a cow: she milks out for men all their desires. The cow is a mother, and this (earth) also is a mother, for she bears the men: for this reason the priests' fee is a cow. This is one mode (of performing those offerings).

22. Then there is this other. He simply offers a cake on eight potsherds to Agni, and thereby, implicitly, to Agni Pavamâna, Agni Pâvaka, and Agni Suki; and immediately after he visibly sets him up (as Agni). For this reason he offers (a cake) to Agni[1], and then a potful of boiled rice to Aditi. The treatment of the potful of rice (in that case) is the same (as before).

SECOND BRÂHMANA.

1. Now, in performing that sacrifice, they slay it; and in pressing out the king (Soma), they slay him; and in quieting and immolating the victim, they slay it. The haviryagña they slay with the mortar and pestle, and with the two mill-stones.

2. When slain, that sacrifice was no longer vigorous. By means of dakshinâs (gifts to the priests) the gods again invigorated it: hence the name dakshinâ, because thereby they invigorated (dakshay) that

---

[1] According to the Kânva recension, the anuvâkyâ and yâgyâ, in that case, should consist of the verses containing the word mûrdhan ('head'), viz. Vâg. S. XIII, 14, 15; cf. Sat. Br. I, 6, 2, 12.

(sacrifice). Whatever, therefore, fails in this sacrifice when slain, that he now again invigorates by means of gifts to the priests; whereupon the sacrifice becomes successful: for this reason he makes gifts to the priests.

3. He may give six (cows)[1]; for six seasons, indeed, there are in the year, and the sacrifice, Pragâpati, is the year: thus as great as the sacrifice is, as large as its extent is, by so many (gifts, dakshinâs) does he thereby invigorate it.

4. He may give twelve; for twelve months there are in the year, and the sacrifice, Pragâpati, is the year: thus as great as the sacrifice is, as large as its extent is, by so many (gifts) does he thereby invigorate it.

5. He may give twenty-four; for twenty-four half-moons there are in the year, and the sacrifice, Pragâpati, is the year: thus as great as the sacrifice is, as large as its extent is, by so many (gifts) does he thereby invigorate it. Such is the measure of the priests' fees; but he may give more, according to (the depth of) his faith. The reason why he gives fees to the priests is this.

6. Verily, there are two kinds of gods; for, indeed, the gods are the gods; and the Brâhmans who have studied and teach sacred lore are the human gods. The sacrifice of these is divided into two kinds: oblations constitute the sacrifice to the gods; and gifts to the priests that to the human gods,

---

[1] Viz. at the tanûhavir-ishtis together, or at least three cows at each ishti if there are two ishtis. The greater the gift, the greater the merit. According to the Paddhati on Kâty. IV, 10, he is also to entertain a hundred Brâhmans at the end of the performance. See also Taitt. Br. I, 1, 7, 9–11.

the Brâhmans who have studied and teach sacred lore. With oblations one gratifies the gods, and with gifts to the priests the human gods, the Brâhmans who have studied and teach sacred lore. Both these kinds of gods, when gratified, place him in a state of bliss (sudhâ)[1].

7. Even as seed is poured into the womb, so the officiating priests place the sacrificer in the (heavenly) world[2], when he now makes gifts to those who, he hopes, will make him go thither. Such, then, (is the manner) of gifts to priests.

8. Now the gods and the Asuras, both of them sprung from Pragâpati, were contending with each other. They were both soulless, for they were mortal, and he who is mortal is soulless. Among these two (classes of beings) who were mortal, Agni alone was immortal; and it was through him, the immortal, that they both lived. Now whichsoever (of the gods) they (the Asuras) slew, he, indeed, was so (slain).

9. Thereupon the gods were left inferior. They went on praising and practising austerities, hoping that they might be able to overcome their enemies, the mortal Asuras. They beheld this immortal Agnyâdheya (consecrated fire).

10. They said, 'Come, let us place that immortal element in our innermost soul! When we have placed that immortal element in our innermost soul, and become immortal and unconquerable, we shall overcome our conquerable, mortal enemies.'

---

[1] That is, 'they convey him to the celestial world,' as reads the otherwise identical passage in IV, 3, 4, 4.

[2] The Kânva text has 'svarge loke.'

11. They said, 'With both of us is this fire (Agni): let us then treat openly with the Asuras[1].'

12. They said, 'We shall set up (or, establish within ourselves, â-dhâ) the two fires,—what will ye do then?'

13. They replied, 'Then we shall lay it down (ni-dhâ), saying, Eat grass here! eat wood here! cook pap here! cook meat here!' Now that fire, which the Asuras thus laid down, is this same (fire) wherewith men prepare their food.

14. The gods then established that (fire) in their innermost soul; and having established that immortal element in their innermost soul, and become immortal and unconquerable, they overcame their mortal, conquerable enemies. And so this one now establishes that immortal element in his innermost soul; and—though there is for him no hope of immortality—he obtains the full measure of life; for, indeed, he becomes unconquerable, and his enemy, though striving to conquer, conquers him not. And, accordingly, when one who has established his fires and one who has not established his fires, vie with each other, he who has established his fires overcomes the other, for, verily, he thereby becomes unconquerable, he thereby becomes immortal.

15. Now, when, on that occasion, they produce that (fire) by churning, then he (the sacrificer) breathes (blows) upon it, when produced; for fire indeed is breath: he thereby produces the one thus produced. He again draws in his breath: thereby he establishes that (fire) in his innermost soul; and that fire thus becomes established in his innermost soul[2].

[1] 'Pra tv evâsurebhyo bravâmeti.'—'Hantâsurebhyah pratiprabravâmeti,' Kânva text. ? 'Let us talk them out of it!'

[2] See p. 297, note 4.

16. Having kindled it, he makes it blaze, thinking, 'Herein I will worship, herein I will perform the sacred work!' Thereby he makes blaze that fire which has been established in his innermost soul.

17. 'It (or some one) might come between,—it might go away!' so (fear some)[1]; but, surely, as long as he lives no one comes between him and that fire which has been established in his innermost soul: let him, therefore, not heed this. And as to its becoming extinguished:—surely, as long as he lives, that fire which has been established in his innermost soul, does not become extinct in him.

18. The (sacrificial) fires, assuredly, are those breaths: the Âhavanîya and Gârhapatya are the out-breathing and the in-breathing; and the Anvâhârya-pa*k*ana is the through-breathing.

19. Now, attendance on (or, the worship of) that consecrated fire (agnyâdheya) means (speaking) the truth. Whosoever speaks the truth, acts as if he sprinkled that lighted fire with ghee; for even so does he enkindle it: and ever the more increases his own vital energy, and day by day does he become better. And whosoever speaks the untruth, acts as

---

[1] This paragraph is somewhat obscure. The Kâ*n*va recension has the following more explicit paragraphs instead:—As to this, there is a source of anxiety (âgas) to some, fearing that 'it (that fire) might go out (anvagan).' But let him not heed this, for, assuredly, that fire of his, which has been established in his innermost soul, does not go out. 'The carriage might pass through (vyayâsît), the cart might pass through;—it (or some one) may come between (me and the fire)!' such is another source of anxiety to some; but let him not heed this either; for, assuredly, the carriage does not pass through, the cart does not pass through that fire of his which has been established in his innermost soul. Cf. XII, 4, 1, 2–3.

if he sprinkled that lighted fire with water; for even so does he enfeeble it: and ever the less becomes his own vital energy, and day by day does he become more wicked. Let him, therefore, speak nothing but the truth.

20. Now the kinsmen spake unto Aru*n*a Aupave*s*i, 'Thou art advanced in years: establish thou the two fires!' He replied, 'Speak ye not thus! be thou a restrainer of speech[1]; for he who has established the fires must not speak an untruth: let him rather not speak at all, but let him not speak an untruth. Worship, above all, is truthfulness.'

THIRD BRÂHMA*N*A.

THE PUNARÂDHEYA OR RE-ESTABLISHMENT OF THE SACRED FIRES[2].

1. Now Varu*n*a established this (fire), being desirous of sovereignty. He obtained sovereignty; and, accordingly, whether one (who has established the fires) knows (this) or not, they call him 'king Varu*n*a.' Soma (established the fire), being desirous of glory. He became glorious, and, accordingly, whether one obtains a hold on Soma, or whether

---

[1] The Kâ*n*va text has: He said, 'Speak ye not thus; be thou a restrainer of speech!'—'Speak ye not,' so (he said); for, having established the two fires, one should not speak untruthfully (m*ri*shâ), nor should he who utters speech speak untruthfully. He should, therefore, strive to speak nothing but the truth.

[2] If the householder who has set up his fires, finds, after a year or more, that he does not prosper in his undertakings, or if he has otherwise met with misfortunes, and thus his âdheya has not proved successful, he should set up his fires a second time. The old fires have to be put out, either early in the day on which the performance is to take place, or from three nights to a whole year previous to the ceremony. With the exceptions noticed in the sequel, the performance is the same as that of the âdhâna.

one does not, they both obtain (glory),—for it is glory that people thereby get to see. Glorious therefore he becomes, and sovereignty he obtains, whosoever, knowing this, establishes a sacrificial fire of his own.

2. Now once upon a time the gods deposited with Agni all forms (rûpa)[1], both domestic and wild; either because they were about to engage in battle, or from a desire of free scope, or because they thought that he (Agni) would protect them as the best protector.

3. But Agni coveted them, and seizing them he entered the seasons with them. 'Let us go back thither,' said the gods, and betook themselves to (the place where) Agni (was) concealed. They were disheartened and said, 'What is here to be done? what counsel is there?'

4. Then Tvash*tri* beheld that re-consecrated fire (Punar-âdheya). He established it and thereby gained an entrance to Agni's beloved abode. He (Agni) gave up to him both kinds of forms, domestic and wild: hence they call them Tvash*tri*'s forms; since it is from Tvash*tri* that all form proceeds[2]; but all other creatures of whatever kind undergo it.

5. It is for him (Tvash*tri*), then, that one must re-establish the fire: for thus he enters Agni's

[1] Compare the corresponding legend Taitt. S. I, 5, 1; according to which the gods deposited their precious goods (vâma*m* vasu) with Agni; and Pûshan and Tvash*tri*, on performing sacrifice to Agni exclusively (the punarâdhyeya), became possessed of the cattle, whence the latter are said to belong to Pûshan (paush*n*a) and to Tvash*tri* (tvâsh*t*ra). Afterwards Manu and Dhât*ri* (here identified with the year) also performed the ceremony. See also *S*at. Br. II, 3, 4, 1 seq.

[2] Or, since it is to Tvash*tri* that all form belongs.

beloved abode, and the latter gives up to him both kinds of forms, domestic and wild. In that (fire) those two kinds of forms are seen: such is the ascendancy (which one obtains by the punarâdhyeya),—people, indeed, envy him; thus he thrives, and a conspicuous position (is obtained by him).

6. To Agni belongs this sacrifice. Agni is the light, the burner of evil: he burns away the evil of this (sacrificer): and the latter becomes a light of prosperity and glory in this, and a light of bliss[1] in yonder, world. This, then, is the reason why he should establish the fires (a second time).

7. Let him establish the fires (the second time) in the rainy season. The rains are all the seasons, for the rains are indeed all the seasons: hence, in counting over years, people say, 'In such and such a year (or rain, varsha) we did it; in such and such a year (or rain) we did it.' The rains, then, are one of the forms of manifestation (rûpa) of all seasons[2]; and when people say, 'To-day it is as if in summer,' then that is in the rainy season; and when they say, 'To-day it is as if in spring,' then that, too, is in the rainy season. From the year (or rain, varsha), indeed, (is named) the rainy season (varshâh).

8. There is, moreover, an occult form (through which the rains manifest themselves in the seasons)[3]. When it blows from the east, then that is the characteristic sign of spring:—when it thunders, it is that of

---

[1] *G*yotir amutra pu*n*yalokatvâ, lit. 'a light by (way of) blissful state.' The Kâ*n*va text has the same reading.

[2] This speculation is based on the identity of the words for year (varsha; also 'rain') and the rains, or rainy season (varshâ*h*).

[3] The characteristics of the seasons here selected are supposed to have a special connection with the rain and rainy season.

summer;—when it rains, it is that of the rainy season; when it lightens, it is that of autumn[1];—when it ceases to rain, it is that of winter. The rains are all the seasons. The seasons he (Agni) entered: from out of the seasons, therefore, he now produces him.

9. But the sun also is all the seasons: when he rises, then it is spring;—when the cows are driven together (for milking), then it is summer;—when it is mid-day, then is the rainy season;—when it is afternoon, then it is autumn;—when he sets, then it is winter. At mid-day (madhyandina), therefore, he should establish his fires, for then that (sun) is nearest to this world, and hence he produces that (fire) from the nearest centre (madhya).

10. Verily, this man is affected with evil, as with a shadow. But then (at mid-day) that (evil) of his (like his shadow) is smallest, and shrinks, as it were, beneath his foot: hence he thereby crushes that evil, when it is smallest. For this reason also he should establish his fires (the second time) at mid-day.

11. He takes it out (from the Gârhapatya) by means of sacrificial grass. By means of fire-wood, indeed, he takes it out the first time; and (were he to take it out) with fire-wood the first time, and with fire-wood the second time, he would commit a repetition, and raise a conflict. Now sacrificial grass means water, and the rainy season also means water. He (Agni) entered the seasons: with water he accordingly produces him from out of the waters; this is why he takes it (the fire) out by means of sacrificial grass.

12. Having prepared an (ordinary) rice cake on

[1] During the autumn, or sultry season succeeding the rains, there are frequent displays of sheet-lightning along the horizon at night.

two arka[1] leaves, he puts it in the place where he is about to establish the Gârhapatya fire, and thereon lays down the Gârhapatya.

13. Having prepared a (second) barley cake on two arka leaves, he puts it in the place where he is about to establish the Âhavanîya fire, and thereon lays down the Âhavanîya. [Some do so] arguing, 'Thereby we cover them with the first two fires;' but let him not do so, for it is by the nights that they come to be covered.

14. He then offers to Agni a sacrificial cake (purodâsa) on five potsherds[2]. Its offering prayers and invitatory prayers consist of pańkti strophes of five pâdas each[3]; for there are five seasons, and the seasons he (Agni) entered: from the seasons he accordingly produces him.

15. The whole (sacrifice) belongs to Agni; for it was thereby that Tvash*tri* entered Agni's beloved abode, and therefore the whole (sacrifice) belongs to Agni[4].

---

[1] Calotropis Gigantea. These cakes (apûpa, not puro*d*â*s*a, have first to be cooked either on the Avasathya, or on a secular fire. Before the cakes are then put on the Gârhapatya and Âhavanîya fire-places, the latter have to be consecrated in the usual way (cf. p. 2); and, after the putting on of the cakes, the fire-places are sprinkled by the Adhvaryu, while the sacrificer holds on to him from behind. Kâty. IV, 11, 8, Schol.

[2] Viz. he performs an ish*t*i with such a rice-cake for the havis, as a substitute for the tanûhavir-ish*t*is, offered after the full-offering, at the âdhâna. See II, 2, 1, 6, and note.

[3] The pańkti consists of five octosyllabic pâdas. The anuvâkyâ and yâ*g*yâ at the chief offering are Rig-veda IV, 10, 2 and 4; those of the svish*t*akr*i*t, ib., verses 4 and 1.—Â*s*v. II, 8, 14.

[4] The offering prayers of all libations and offerings at this ish*t*i must therefore contain Agni's name. At each of the fore-offerings and after-offerings a different case-form of agni is added after the respective objects of those offerings,—thus, '... samidho agne

16. They perform it (with the formulas pronounced) in a low voice; for if one wishes to prepare anything specially for a relative or friend, one must take care to keep it secret. Now the other sacrifice belongs to all the deities, but this belongs specially to Agni; and what is (kept) secret, that is (spoken of) in a low voice: this is why they perform it in a low voice.

17. The last after-offering he performs aloud; for then he has completed his work, and every one becomes aware of what has been done.

18. Having uttered his call (and having been responded to by the Âgnîdhra)[1], he says (to the Hotri), 'Pronounce the offering-prayer to the Samidhs (kindling-sticks)!'—the latter being one of Agni's mystic forms of manifestation (rûpa); but he may also say, 'Pronounce the offering-prayer to the fires!'—that being Agni's real (exoteric) form[2].

'gna âgyasya vyantu,' 'tanûnapâd agnim agna . . . ,' 'ido agninâgne . . . ,' &c. See par. 19; also p. 148, n. 2; I, 5, 4, 1 seq.; I, 8, 2, 1 seq. The two butter-portions otherwise offered to Agni or Soma respectively (cf. I, 6, 1, 20 seq.) are in this case offered to Agni; the anuvâkyâs, according to Âsv. II, 8, 7, being Rig-veda VIII, 44, 1, and VI, 16, 16 respectively. See, however, paragraphs 21 seq.

[1] Viz. the Adhvaryu calls, Õ srâvaya, 'cause (him or one) to hear!' and the Âgnîdhra responds by Astu sraushat, 'yea, may he (or one) hear!'

[2] Here, at the first fore-offering, an option is apparently left between the former, regular summons (see I, 5, 3, 8), and the latter, modified so as to make it apply directly to Agni. Kâty. IV, 11, 11 allows the same option for the first prayâga and anuyâga. For the latter, however, see further on, par. 24. The Kânva recension has as follows:—Now when the Adhvaryu, on stepping over (to the south side) and uttering his call (for the Agnîdhra) to bid attention, says, 'Pronounce the offering-prayer to the Samidhs!' then that, indeed, is one of Agni's forms of manifestation (âgneyam eva tad rûpam); but here let him say, as it were,

19. He (the Hotri) recites[1], '. . . They (the Samidhs), O Agni, may accept of the butter! Vaughak[2]!' '. . . He (Tanûnapât) may accept the fire of the butter! Vaughak!' '. . . . They (the Ids) may, through Agni, accept of the butter! Vaughak!' '. . . It (the barhis), the fire, may accept of the butter! Vaughak!'

20. He then says[3], 'Svâhâ Agnim!' with reference to Agni's butter-portion;—'Svâhâ Agnim Pavamânam!' if they determine upon (offering to) Agni, the blowing[4]; or 'Svâhâ Agnim Indumantam!' if they determine upon Agni, the drop-abounding[5];—'Svâhâ Agnim!'—'Svâhâ, the butter-drinking Agnis! May Agni graciously accept of the butter!'—this is the offering-prayer he (the Hotri) pronounces.

21. He (the Adhvaryu) then says, with regard to Agni's (first) butter-portion, 'Pronounce the invitatory prayer to Agni!' He (the Hotri) recites[6], 'Awake Agni with praise, enkindling the immortal, that he may take our offerings to the gods!' For, indeed, when Agni is removed (from the hearth)[7], he, as it were, sleeps: he (the priest) now awakens, rouses

in a mystic way, 'Pronounce the offering-prayer to the Agnis!' (paroksham iva tv agnîn yageti haiva tatra brûyât.)

[1] See p. 317, note 4.

[2] A modification of the ordinary vaushat. The Kânva text has here and in par. 25, as usual, vaushal.

[3] At the fifth fore-offering; see I, 5, 3, 22 seq.

[4] See II, 2, 1, 6, and note; also II, 2, 1, 22.

[5] This points forward to the second butter-portion, which is offered to Agni Pavamâna or Agni Indumat, instead of Soma; the first being offered to Agni simply. Kâty. IV, 11, 12.

[6] Rig-veda V, 14, 1. See, however, the formulas prescribed by Âsvalâyana, p. 317, note 4.

[7] The fire laid down at the âdheya is removed when the punarâdheya is to be performed.

him. For the offering-prayer he recites, 'May Agni graciously accept of the butter!'

22. And, if they determine upon (offering the second butter-portion to (Agni Pavamâna, let him then say, 'Pronounce the invitatory prayer to Agni Pavamâna; and he (the Hotri) recites (Rig-veda IX, 16, 19), 'O Agni, thou breathest forth life; produce thou food and sap for us! drive far away misfortune!' For thus, indeed, it becomes of the nature of Agni. Pavamâna (the one that becomes purified) means the Soma; but this (Soma-element) they eliminate from the butter-portion of Soma[1]. For the offering-prayer he recites, 'May Agni Pavamâna graciously accept of the butter!'

23. If, on the other hand, they determine upon (offering to) Agni Indumat, let him say, 'Pronounce the invitatory prayer to Agni Indumat!' He (the Hotri) recites (Rig-veda VI, 16, 16), 'Come hither, I will gladly sing to thee yet other songs, O Agni! mayest thou grow strong by these draughts (indu, drop).' Thus, indeed, it becomes of the nature of Agni: the draught doubtless means Soma, but this (Soma-element) they eliminate from the butter-portion of Soma. For the offering-prayer he recites, 'May Agni, the drop-abounding, graciously accept of the butter!' And thus he makes it all of the nature of Agni.

24. He then says, as to the chief offering (havis), 'Pronounce the invitatory prayer to Agni!' 'Pronounce the offering-prayer to Agni!' 'Pronounce the invitatory prayer to Agni Svishtakrit (the maker of good offerings)!' 'Pronounce the offering-

[1] Viz. that second butter-portion which by right belongs to Soma (see I, 6, 1, 20 seq.), but is here offered to Agni.

prayer to Agni Svish*t*ak*ri*t[1]!' Then where (otherwise) he would say, 'Pronounce the offering-prayer to the gods[2]!' he now says, 'Pronounce the offering-prayer to the Agnis!'

25. He recites[3], '[The divine Barhis] may accept (the offering) for Agni's abundant obtainment of abundant gift! Vau*g*h*ak!'—'[The divine Narâ*s*a*m*sa] may accept (the offering) for abundant obtainment, in Agni, of abundant gift! Vau*g*h*ak!'—'The divine Agni Svish*t*ak*ri*t....' this third (after-offering) is already in itself of the nature of Agni; and thus he makes the after-offerings relate to Agni.

26. Those same case-forms (of agni)[4], which he recites in the offering-prayers, are six; namely, four at the fore-offerings, and two at the after-offerings. Now there are six seasons; and the seasons he (Agni) entered: out of the seasons he accordingly thereby produces him.

27. There are either twelve or thirteen syllables (in these six case-forms)[5]. Now there are either twelve or thirteen months in a year[6]; and the

---

[1] For the formulas of the chief offering and Svish*t*ak*ri*t, see p. 317, note 3.

[2] That is, at the altar-offerings; see I, 8, 2, 14. Cf. also p. 318, note 2.

[3] See I, 8, 2, 15. Here a different case-form of the word agni (viz. agne*h* and agnau) is inserted in the offering-formulas of the first two anuyâ*g*as, immediately after the word indicating the object of the offering; the formula of the third and last anuyâ*g*a already containing the nominative agni*h* in the same place.

[4] See p. 317, note 4.

[5] The locative case agnau, inserted in the offering-prayer of the second after-offering, is optionally made trisyllabic by being written and pronounced agnâ-u.

[6] For other allusions to intercalary months in the Vedic texts, see Weber, Naxatra, II, p. 336.

year, the seasons, he (Agni) entered: out of the seasons he accordingly thereby produces him. In order to avoid sameness, no two (of these forms) are alike; but (the fault of) sameness he would undoubtedly commit, were any two of them alike. The characteristic form of the fore-offerings is (alternately), 'May they accept,' 'May it (or he) accept[1];' and that of the after-offerings is, 'For the abundant obtainment of abundant gift.'

28. The priests' fee for this (sacrifice) consists of gold[2]. This sacrifice belongs to Agni, and gold is Agni's seed[3]: this is why the priests' fee consists of gold. Or it may be an ox; for the latter is of the nature of Agni as far as its shoulder is concerned, since its shoulder (by carrying the yoke) is as if burnt by fire. Moreover, Agni is oblation-bearer to the gods, and that (ox) bears (or draws, loads) for men: this is why an ox may be given as the priests' fee.

Fourth Brâhmana.

II. THE AGNIHOTRA OR MORNING AND EVENING LIBATIONS; AND THE AGNY-UPASTHÂNA OR HOMAGE TO THE FIRES.

1. Pragâpati alone, indeed, existed here in the beginning. He considered, 'How may I be repro-

[1] See I, 5, 3, 15.

[2] See also II, 2, 4, 15. In Taitt. S. I, 5, 12 (referred to Kâty. XI, 2, 37) 'white gold' (ragatam hiranyam), i.e. silver, is expressly mentioned as unsuitable for the dakshinâ. The reason adduced is that, when the gods claimed back the goods deposited with Agni, he wept, and the tears he shed became silver; and hence, if one were to give silver as a dakshinâ, there would be weeping in his house before a year had passed.

[3] See II, 1, 1, 5.

duced?' He toiled and performed acts of penance. He generated Agni from his mouth; and because he generated him from his mouth, therefore Agni is a consumer of food: and, verily, he who thus knows Agni to be a consumer of food, becomes himself a consumer of food.

2. He thus generated him first (agre) of the gods; and therefore (he is called) Agni, for agni (they say) is the same as agri. He, being generated, went forth as the first (pûrva); for of him who goes first, they say that he goes at the head (agre). Such, then, is the origin and nature of that Agni.

3. Pragâpati then considered, 'In that Agni I have generated a food-eater for myself; but, indeed, there is no other food here but myself, whom, surely, he would not eat.' At that time this earth had, indeed, been rendered quite bald; there were neither plants nor trees. This, then, weighed on his mind.

4. Thereupon Agni turned towards him with open mouth; and he (Pragâpati) being terrified, his own greatness departed from him. Now his own greatness is his speech: that speech of his departed from him. He desired an offering in his own self, and rubbed (his hands); and because he rubbed (his hands), therefore both this and this (palm) are hairless. He then obtained either a butter-offering or a milk-offering;—but, indeed, they are both milk.

5. This (offering), however, did not satisfy him, because it had hairs mixed with it. He poured it away (into the fire), saying, 'Drink, while burning (osham dhaya)!' From it plants sprang: hence their name 'plants (oshadhayah).' He rubbed (his hands) a second time, and thereby obtained another

offering, either a butter-offering or a milk-offering;—but, indeed, they are both milk.

6. This (offering) then satisfied him. He hesitated: 'Shall I offer it up? shall I not offer it up?' he thought. His own greatness said to him, 'Offer it up!' Pragâpati was aware that it was his own (sva) greatness that had spoken (âha) to him; and offered it up with 'Svâhâ!' This is why offerings are made with 'Svâhâ!' Thereupon that burning one (viz. the sun) rose; and then that blowing one (viz. the wind) sprang up; whereupon, indeed, Agni turned away.

7. And Pragâpati, having performed offering, reproduced himself, and saved himself from Agni, Death, as he was about to devour him. And, verily, whosoever, knowing this, offers the Agnihotra, reproduces himself by offspring even as Pragâpati reproduced himself; and saves himself from Agni, Death, when he is about to devour him.

8. And when he dies, and when they place him on the fire, then he is born (again) out of the fire, and the fire only consumes his body. Even as he is born from his father and mother, so is he born from the fire. But he who offers not the Agnihotra, verily, he does not come into life at all: therefore the Agnihotra should by all means be offered.

9. And as to that same birth from out of doubt,—when Pragâpati doubted, he, while doubting, remained steadfast on the better (side), insomuch that he reproduced himself and saved himself from Agni, Death, when he was about to devour him: so he also who knows that birth from out of doubt, when he doubts about anything, still remains on the better (side).

10. Having offered, he rubbed (his hands). Thence

a Vikankata[1] tree sprung forth; and therefore that tree is suitable for the sacrifice, and proper for sacrificial vessels. Thereupon those (three) heroes among the gods were born, viz. Agni, that blower (Vâyu), and Sûrya: and, verily, whosoever thus knows those heroes among the gods, to him a hero is born.

11. They then said, 'We come after our father Pragâpati: let us then create what shall come after us!' Having enclosed (a piece of ground), they sang praises with the gâyatrî stanza without the 'Hin[2]:' and that (with) which they enclosed was the ocean; and this earth was the praising-ground (âstâva).

12. When they had sung praises, they went out towards the east, saying, 'We (will) go back thither!' The gods came upon a cow which had sprung into existence. Looking up at them, she uttered the sound 'hin.' The gods perceived that this was the 'Hin' of the Sâman (melodious sacrificial chant); for heretofore (their song was) without the 'Hin,' but after that it was the (real) Sâman. And as this same sound 'Hin' of the Sâman was in the cow, therefore the latter affords the means of subsistence; and so does he afford the means of subsistence whosoever thus knows that 'Hin' of the Sâman in the cow.

13. They said, 'Auspicious, indeed, is what we have produced here, who have produced the cow: for, truly, she is the sacrifice, and without her no sacrifice is performed; she is also the food, for the cow, indeed, is all food.'

14. This (word 'go'), then, is a name of those

---

[1] The sruva, or dipping-spoon, and the Agnihotra ladle, for instance, are made of this wood; see p. 331, note 2.

[2] On 'hin' as an essential element in the recitation of Sâma-chants, see I, 4, 1, 1 seq.

(cows), and so it is of the sacrifice: let him, therefore, repeat[1] it, (as it were) saying, 'Good, excellent!' and, verily, whosoever, knowing this, repeats it, (as it were) saying, 'Good, excellent!' with him those (cows) multiply, and the sacrifice will incline to him.

15. Now, Agni coveted her: 'May I pair with her,' he thought. He united with her, and his seed became that milk of hers: hence, while the cow is raw, that milk in her is cooked (warm); for it is Agni's seed; and therefore also, whether it be in a black or in a red (cow), it is ever white, and shining like fire, it being Agni's seed. Hence it is warm when first milked; for it is Agni's seed.

16. They (the men) said, 'Come, let us offer this up!'—'To whom of us shall they first offer this?' (said those gods).—'To me!' said Agni.—'To me!' said that blower (Vâyu).—'To me!' said Sûrya. They did not come to an agreement; and not being agreed, they said, 'Let us go to our father Pragâpati; and to whichever of us he says it shall be offered first, to him they shall first offer this.' They went to their father Pragâpati, and said, 'To whom of us shall they offer this first?'

17. He replied, 'To Agni: Agni will forthwith cause his own seed to be reproduced, and so you will be reproduced.' 'Then to thee,' he said to Sûrya; 'and what of the offered (milk) he then is still possessed of, that shall belong to that blower

[1] Pariharet [? 'let him avoid it (the term go in the sense of sacrifice), thinking that it is too holy']. Sâyana merely remarks, that both the cow and the sacrifice are here represented as extremely auspicious (utkrishtam punyam). Perhaps we have here a play on the words upanâma, 'a by-name,' and upanâmuka, 'inclining to (him).' 'Go' (for go-shtoma) is the designation of one of the days of the Abhiplava at the Gavâmayana.

(Vâyu)!' And, accordingly, they in the same way offer this (milk) to them till this day: in the evening to Agni, and in the morning to Sûrya; and what of the offered (milk) he then is still possessed of, that, indeed, belongs to that blower.

18. By offering, those gods were produced in the way in which they were produced, by it they gained that victory which they did gain: Agni conquered this world, Vâyu the air, and Sûrya the sky. And whosoever, knowing this, offers the Agnihotra, he, indeed, is produced in the same way in which they were then produced, he gains that same victory which they then gained;—indeed, he shares the same world with them, whosoever, knowing this, offers the Agnihotra. Therefore the Agnihotra should certainly be performed.

Third Adhyâya. First Brâhmana.

1. The Agnihotra, doubtless, is the Sun. It is because he rose in front (agre) of that offering[1], that the Agnihotra is the Sun.

2. When he offers in the evening after sunset, he does so thinking, 'I will offer, while he is here, who is this (offering);' and when he offers in the morning before sunrise, he does so thinking, 'I will offer, while he is here, who is this (offering):' and for this reason, they say, the Agnihotra is the Sun.

3. And when he sets, then he, as an embryo, enters that womb, the fire; and along with him thus becoming an embryo, all these creatures become embryos; for, being coaxed, they lie down contented[2].

---

[1] Apparently an etymological play on the word agnihotra = agre hotrasya, cf. II, 2, 4, 2.

[2] Îlitâ hi sere (serate, Kânva rec.) samgânânâh.

The reason, then, why the night envelops that (sun), is that embryos also are, as it were, enveloped.

4. Now when he offers in the evening after sunset, he offers for the good of that (sun) in the embryo state, he benefits that embryo; and since he offers for the good of that (sun) in the embryo state, therefore embryos here live without taking food.

5. And when he offers in the morning before sunrise, then he produces that (sun-child) and, having become a light, it rises shining. But, assuredly, it would not rise, were he not to make that offering: this is why he performs that offering.

6. Even as a snake frees itself from its skin, so does it (the sun-child) free itself from the night, from evil: and, verily, whosoever, knowing this, offers the Agnihotra, he frees himself from all evil, even as a snake frees itself from its skin; and after his birth all these creatures are born; for they are set free according to their inclination.

7. Then, as to his taking out the Âhavanîya (from the Gârhapatya) before the setting of the sun;—the rays, doubtless, are all those gods; and what highest light there is, that, indeed, is either Pra*g*âpati or Indra. Now all the gods approach the house of him who performs the Agnihotra: but whosesoever (offering) they approach before the fire has been taken out, from that the gods turn away, and he fails in it; and after the failure of that (offering) from which the gods turn away, people say, that, whether one knows it or not, the sun went down on account of that (fire) not having been taken out.

8. And another reason why he takes out the Âhavanîya before the setting of the sun, is this. In like manner as, when one's better comes to visit

one, he would honour him by trimming his house, so here: for whosesoever (offering) they approach, after the fire has been taken out, his Âhavanîya (house) they enter, in his Âhavanîya they repose.

9. Now when he offers in the evening after the sun has set, he thereby offers to them after they have entered his fire-house; and when he offers in the morning before sunrise, he offers to them before they go away. Therefore Âsuri said, 'The Agnihotra of those who offer after sunrise we regard as useless[1]: it is as if one were to take food to an empty dwelling.'

10. That which affords (the means of) subsistence is of two kinds; namely, either rooted or rootless. On both of these, which belong to the gods, men subsist. Now cattle are rootless and plants are rooted. From the rootless cattle eating the rooted plants and drinking water, that juice is produced.

11. Now when he offers in the evening after sunset, he does so thinking, 'I will offer to the gods of this life-giving juice: we subsist on this which belongs to them.' And when he afterwards takes his evening meal, he eats what remains of the offering, and whereof oblative portions (bali) have been distributed all round[2]; for he who performs the Agnihotra eats only what remains of the offering.

12. And when he offers in the morning before sunrise, he does so thinking, 'I will offer to the gods of this life-giving juice: we subsist on this which belongs to them.' And when he afterwards takes his meal in the day-time, he eats what remains of the

---

[1] V*ikkh*inna, ? lit. 'cut off (from its recipient).'

[2] Bali is the technical term of the portions of the daily food that have to be assigned to all creatures.

offering, and whereof oblative portions have been distributed all round; for he who performs the Agnihotra eats only what remains of the offering.

13. Here now they say,—All other sacrifices come to an end, but the Agnihotra does not come to an end. Although that which lasts for twelve years is indeed limited, this (Agnihotra) is nevertheless unlimited, since, when one has offered in the evening, he knows that he will offer in the morning; and when one has offered in the morning, he knows that he will again offer in the evening. Hence that Agnihotra is unlimited, and in consequence of this its unlimitedness, creatures are here born unlimited. And, verily, he who thus knows the unlimitedness of the Agnihotra, is himself born unlimited in prosperity and offspring.

14. Having milked[1] he puts that (milk) on (the Gârhapatya fire), because it has to be cooked. Here now they say, 'When it rises to the brim, then we shall offer it!' He must not however let it rise to the brim, since he would burn it, if he were to let it rise to the brim; and unproductive indeed is burnt seed: he must not, therefore, let it rise to the brim.

15. He should not offer it without having put it on the fire; for since this is Agni's seed, therefore it is hot (*srita*, 'cooked'); and by putting it on the

[1] For other ceremonies preceding those above, see I, 3, 3, 13 seq. According to Kâty. IV, 14, 1 he has the Agnihotra cow —standing south of the sacrificial ground and facing the east or north—milked by anybody except a *S*ûdra. The vessel to be used is of earthenware, and must have been made by an Ârya. The Adhvaryu then takes the vessel, and having entered the Âhavanîya house by the east door and passed over to the Gârhapatya, puts it there on coals previously shifted northwards from the fire.

fire, it is indeed heated: let him, therefore, offer (of the milk) only after he has put it on the fire.

16. He illumines it (with a burning straw)[1] in order that he may know when it is done. He then pours some water to it (with the sruva), both for the sake of appeasement, and in order to supplement the juice. For when it rains here, then plants spring up; and in consequence of the plants being eaten and the water drunk, this juice is produced: hence it is in order to supplement the juice (that he pours water to it); and therefore, if it should happen to him to have to drink pure milk, let him have one drop of water poured into it, both for the sake of appeasement, and in order to supplement the juice.

17. Thereupon he ladles four times (milk with the sruva into the Agnihotra ladle[2]), for in a fourfold way was that milk supplied[3]. He then takes a kindling-stick (samidh), and hastes up (to the Âhavanîya, with the ladle) to make the libation on the burning (stick)[4]. He offers the first libation

[1] According to Kâty. IV, 14, 5 the Adhvaryu illumines the milk with a burning straw; pours some water to it with the sruva or dipping-spoon; then illumines it once more; and lifts up the pot three several times, putting it down each time further north of the fire. Thereupon he warms the two spoons; and wipes them with his hand; and having warmed them once more, he says to the sacrificer, 'I ladle!' The latter, while standing, replies, 'Õm, ladle!'

[2] For the Agnihotra-hava*n*î, or offering-spoon (sru*k*), used at the morning and evening libation, and made of Vikaṅkata wood (Flacourtia Sapida), see p. 67, note 2. In the case of those who make five cuttings from the havis (pa*ñk*âvattin, cf. p. 192 note) he takes five sruva-fuls. Kâty. IV, 14, 10, Comm.

[3] Viz. by the four teats of the udder. Comm.

[4] While holding a billet or kindling-stick (samidh) over the (handle of) the milk-ladle, he [first holds the latter close over the Gârhapatya fire, and thereupon] takes it to the Âhavanîya, keeping

(pûrvâhuti) without putting down (the spoon) beside (the fire, on the grass-bunch). For, were he to put it down beside (the fire), it would be as if, in taking food to somebody, one were to put it down on one's way thither. But when (he makes the libation) without previously putting it down, it is as if, in taking food to somebody, one puts it down only after taking it to him. The second (libation he then makes) after putting it down: he thereby makes these two (libations) of various vigour. Now these two libations are mind and speech: hence he thereby separates mind and speech from each other; and thus mind and speech, even while one and the same (samâna), are still distinct (nânâ).

18. Twice he offers in the fire, twice he wipes (the spout of the spoon), twice he eats (of the milk), and four times he ladles [1];—these are ten (acts), for

---

it on a level with his mouth, except in the middle between the two fires, where he lowers it for a moment to the level of his navel. He then crouches down [bending his right knee, and looking eastwards, by the north-west corner of the Âhavanîya], puts the billet on [the centre of] the fire, and makes the first libation (pûrvâhuti) on the burning stick (see the formula, par. 30. The sacrificer, as usual, pronounces the dedicatory formula, viz. 'This to Agni!' and, 'This to Sûrya!' respectively). Thereupon he lays down the ladle on the kûrka [a grass-bunch, placed behind the Âhavanîya fire-place, to serve as a seat, and to wipe the hands on; according to others, a flat piece of Varana wood], then takes it up again and silently makes the second libation (uttarâhuti) on the north part of the fire. Kâty. IV, 14, 12–17 with Schol.

[1] He ladles four sruva-fuls of milk into the Agnihotra ladle, and makes in the Âhavanîya fire two libations from this milk (so as to leave the larger quantity in the ladle to be eaten). He then wipes twice the spout of the ladle. [In each of the two other fires he thereupon makes likewise two libations with the sruva, of one spoonful each.] The milk left in the ladle he eats, on the completion of the six libations, by twice taking it out with his ring-finger.

of ten syllables consists the virâg stanza, and the sacrifice is virâg (shining): he thereby converts the sacrifice into the virâg.

19. Now what he offers up in the fire, that he offers to the gods; and thereby the gods are (admitted to the sacrifice)[1]. And what he wipes off (the spoons), that he offers to the fathers and plants; and thereby the fathers and plants are (admitted). And what he eats after offering, that he offers to men; and thereby men are (admitted).

20. Verily, the creatures that are not allowed to take part in the sacrifice are forlorn; to those creatures that are not forlorn he thus offers a share at the opening of the sacrifice; and thus beasts (cattle) are made to share in it along with (men), since beasts are behind men[2].

21. On this point Yâgñavalkya said, 'It (the Agnihotra) must not be looked upon as a (havis-) sacrifice, but as a domestic sacrifice (pâkayagña); for while in any other (havis-)sacrifice he pours into the fire all that he cuts off (from the sacrificial dish and puts) into the offering spoon,—here, after offering and stepping outside[3], he sips water and licks out (the milk); and this indeed (is a characteristic) of the domestic offering.' This then is the animal

---

[1] Tasmâd devâh santi; anvâbhaktâh ('allowed to share in the sacrifice') has probably to be supplied here from the next paragraph.

[2] Instead of this paragraph, the Kânva text reads: 'Behind men are beasts; behind the gods are birds, plants, trees, and whatever else exists here. Thus he makes these creatures share in the sacrifice, those that are not forlorn here.' Compare I, 5, 2, 4.

[3] Utsripya is variously explained by the commentators here and on Kâty. IV, 14, 27, as 'having gone out,' or 'having slowly moved forward,' or 'having risen,' or 'having poured out (the milk).'

characteristic[1] of that (Agnihotra), for the domestic offering pertains to beasts (or cattle).

22. Now the first of these libations, doubtless, is the same as that which Pragâpati offered in the beginning[2]; and as those (gods) thereupon continued (to sacrifice)[3],—namely, Agni, that blower (Vâyu), and Sûrya,—so this second libation is offered.

23. What first libation (pûrvâhuti) is made, that is the deity of the Agnihotra[4], and to that (deity) it is accordingly offered; and what second one (uttarâhuti) is made, that indeed is equivalent to the Svishtakrit (Agni, the maker of good offering); whence he offers it on the north part (of the fire), since that is the region of the Svishtakrit[5]. Moreover, this second libation is made in order to effect a pairing, for a couple forms a productive pair.

24. These two libations, then, form a duad: the past and the future, the born and the to-be-born, the actual[6] and the hope, the to-day and the morrow,—(these are) after the manner of that duad.

25. The past is the self, for certain is that which is past, and certain also is that which is a self. The future, on the other hand, is progeny; for uncertain is that which is to be, and uncertain also is progeny.

26. The born is the self, for certain is that which is born, and certain also is the self. The to-be-born,

---

[1] Pasavyam rûpam,—that is to say, its relation to the pasu or animal sacrifice; and hence also to the idâ at the haviryagña; cf. I, 7, 4, 19.

[2] See II, 2, 4, 4 seq.

[3] See II, 2, 4, 18.

[4] That is to say, it represents the chief offering at the haviryagña, which is followed by the (oblation to Agni) Svishtakrit. See I, 7, 2, 1 seq.

[5] See I, 7, 3, 20.

[6] Âgatam, 'what has arrived or come to pass,' 'the accomplished.'

on the other hand, is progeny; for uncertain is what is to be born, and uncertain also is progeny.

27. The actual is the self, for certain is what is actual, and certain also is the self. And hope is progeny, for uncertain is hope, and uncertain also is progeny.

28. The to-day is the self, for certain is what is to-day, and certain also is the self. The morrow is progeny, for uncertain is the morrow, and uncertain also is progeny.

29. Now that first libation is offered on account of the self: he offers it with a sacred text, for certain is the sacred text, and certain also is the self. And that second one is offered on account of progeny: he offers it silently, for uncertain is what (is done) silently, and uncertain also is progeny.

30. [In the evening] he offers (the first libation), with the text (Vâ*g*. S. III, 9, 10), 'Agni is the light, the light is Agni, Svâhâ!' and in the morning with, 'Sûrya (the sun) is the light, the light is Sûrya, Svâhâ!' Thus offering is made with the truth; for, truly, when the sun goes down, then Agni (fire) is the light, and when the sun rises, then Sûrya is the light; and whatever is offered with the truth, that, indeed, goes to the gods.

31. Here now Takshan recited for Âru*n*i[1], who wished to obtain holy lustre (brahmavar*k*asa, inspired nature), 'Agni is lustre, light is lustre;'—'Sûrya is lustre, light is lustre.' Holy lustre, therefore, he obtains whosoever, knowing this, thus offers the Agnihotra.

[1] The Kâ*n*va text has,—Here now Daksha said to Âru*n*i, 'For one wishing to obtain brahmavar*k*asa one should offer with this text, "Agni is lustre, light is lustre;"—"Sûrya is lustre, light is lustre:" a brahmavar*k*asin, then, he becomes for whomsoever they so sacrifice.'

32. That (other text), however, has the characteristic form of generation. In saying, 'Agni is the light, the light is Agni, Svâhâ!' he encloses that seed, the light, on both sides with the deity; and the seed, thus enclosed on both sides, is brought forth: thus enclosing it on both sides he causes it to be brought forth.

33. And when, in the morning, he says, 'Sûrya is the light, the light is Sûrya, Svâhâ!' he encloses that seed, the light, on both sides with the deity, and the seed, thus enclosed on both sides, is brought forth: thus enclosing it on both sides he causes it to be brought forth; and this, indeed, is the characteristic form of generation.

34. But *G*îvala *K*ailaki said[1], 'Âru*n*i merely causes conception to take place, not birth: let him therefore offer with that (text, in par. 32) in the evening.

35. Then, in the morning, by the text, "The light is Sûrya, Sûrya is the light," he places that seed, the light, outside by means of the deity; and the seed thus brought outside he causes to be born.'

36. They also say, 'In the evening he offers Sûrya in Agni, and in the morning he offers Agni in Sûrya[2].' Such, indeed, is the case with those who offer after sunrise; for when the sun sets then Agni is the light, and when the sun rises then Sûrya is the light. Here no offence is committed on his (the sacrificer's) part; but an offence is indeed committed where offering is not made distinctly to that deity (viz. Agni or Sûrya resp.), which is the deity of the Agnihotra.

[1] I have made *G*îvala's speech extend to the end of par. 35, as is done, no doubt correctly, in the Kâ*n*va text.

[2] The Kâ*n*va has,—Now they say, 'In the evening they offer Agni in Sûrya, and in the morning they offer Sûrya in Agni.' But see the formulas (par. 30), where 'light' is to be taken as Sûrya and Agni respectively.

He says[1], 'Agni is the light, the light is Agni, Svâhâ!' and not, 'To Agni Svâhâ!' and in the morning, 'Sûrya is the light, the light is Sûrya, Svâhâ!' and not, 'To Sûrya Svâhâ!'

37. He may also offer (in the evening) with this text (Vâg. S. III, 10), 'Along with the divine Savitri—,' whereby it (the sacrifice) becomes possessed of Savitri for his impulsion; '—along with the Night, wedded to Indra—,' whereby he effects a union with the night, and makes it (the sacrifice) possessed of Indra, for Indra is the deity of the sacrifice; '—may Agni graciously accept! Svâhâ!' whereby he offers to Agni in a direct manner.

38. And in the morning with, 'Along with the divine Savitri—,' whereby it becomes possessed of Savitri for his impulsion; '—along with the Dawn, wedded to Indra,' or 'along with the Day . . . .—,' whereby he effects a union either with the day or the dawn[2], and makes it (the sacrifice) possessed of Indra; for Indra is the deity of sacrifice; '—may Sûrya graciously accept! Svâhâ!' whereby he offers to Sûrya directly: hence he may offer in this way.

39. They then spake, 'Who shall offer this unto us?'—'The priest (brâhmana)!'—'Priest, offer this unto us!'—'What is to be my share then?'—'The residue of the Agnihotra!' Now what he leaves in

[1] Here the Kânva text begins a new paragraph. The author's object seems to be to show that those who offer the Agnihotra after sunrise, commit a mistake in not offering to Sûrya unmistakably; for while before sunrise, Sûrya is still reposing in Agni, and the oblation, in being poured into the fire, is consequently made to Sûrya directly, those offering after sunrise should rather use the formula 'To Sûrya Svâhâ!' Cf. paragraph 9.

[2] Instead of 'ahnâm voshasâm vâ,' I adopt 'ahnâ voshasâ vâ,' from the Kânva reading 'ushasâ vâhnâ vâ.'

the ladle, that is the residue of the Agnihotra; and what remains in the pot, is as (the rice for oblations which) one takes out from the enclosed part (of the cart)[1]. And if any one is to drink it, at least none but a Brâhman must drink it[2]: for it is put on the fire (and thereby consecrated), and hence none but a Brâhman must drink it.

SECOND BRÂHMANA.

1. Verily, in him that exists[3], these deities reside, to wit, Indra, king Yama, Nada the Naishadha[4] (king), Anasnat Sâṅgamana, and Asat Pâmsava.

2. Now Indra, in truth, is the same as the Âhavanîya; and king Yama is the same as the Gârhapatya; and Nada Naishadha is the same as the Anvâhâryapakana (Dakshina fire); and because day by day they take that (fire) to the south, therefore indeed they say that day by day Nada Naishadha carries king Yama[5] (further) south.

3. And again what fire there is in the hall (sabhâ), that is the same as Anasnat Sâṅgamana: Anasvat (not eating) it is for the reason that people

[1] Yathâ parînaho nirvaped evam tat. The Kânva text has: Yathâ (yayâ MS.) koshthâ parînaho vâ nirmimîtaivam tat.

[2] Or, 'anybody may drink it, but none but a Brâhman may drink it.' According to the Schol. on Kâty. IV, 14, 11, the milk which is left in the pot may be drunk by a Brâhman, but by no one else; not even in his own house is a Kshatriya or Vaisya allowed to drink it.

[3] The commentator takes it, 'in whatever (sacrificer) exists.' The (Oxf. MS. of the) Kânva text has nothing corresponding to the second and third Brâhmanas.

[4] The printed text has Naishidha. See Weber, Ind. Stud. I, p. 225 seq.

[5] Here Yama is apparently taken as (the god of) death and destruction, caused, as Professor Weber suggests, by the warlike expeditions of Nada, king of Nishadha, in the south.

approach it before they eat. And that (place) where they throw the ashes they remove (from the fire-places) is the same as Asat Pâ*m*sava. And whosoever knows this, thus gains all those worlds, traverses all those worlds, thinking, 'In me those gods reside.'

4. Now as to rendering homage to (upasthâna, lit. standing near) these (fires). When in the evening and morning (after the Agnihotra) he stands by the Âhavanîya, and sits down by it, that is the homage rendered to that (fire). And when, on stepping back to the Gârhapatya, he either sits or lies down, that is the homage rendered to that (fire). And when, in walking (out of the sacrificial ground), he remembers the Anvâhâryapa*k*ana, and thus, in his mind, tarries near it, that is the homage rendered to that (fire).

5. And again, before taking food in the morning, having sat down for a moment in the hall, he may also, if he like, walk round (the Sabhya or hall-fire), —and this is the homage rendered to that (fire). And when he steps near where lie the ashes removed (from the fire-places) that is the homage rendered to that (fire). And thus homage has been rendered to those deities of his.

6. Now the Gârhapatya (householder's fire) has the sacrificer for its deity; and the Anvâhâryapa*k*ana (southern fire) has his foe for its deity: hence they should not take over that (southern fire) every day (from the Gârhapatya); and he indeed has no enemies, for whomsoever, knowing this, they do not take it over every day. Indeed, it is the Anvâhâryapa*k*ana[1].

[1] That is, the fire on which the Anvâhârya mess of rice, the priests' Dakshi*n*â at the new and full-moon sacrifice, is cooked. See I, 2, 3, 5; p. 49, note 1.

7. Let them only take it over on the fast-day (of the new and full-moon sacrifice), when they are about to sacrifice on this (the Âhavanîya fire): thus that (southern) one is taken over in order to prevent failure on his (the sacrificer's) part.

8. Or they may also take it over to a new dwelling; and let them then cook on it food (other than meat) for the priests to eat. And should he not be able to procure anything to cook, let him order the milk of a cow to be put thereon and let the priests be asked to drink it. And his enemies will indeed fare ill, for whomsoever, knowing this, they do so: let him, therefore, endeavour by all means to do so.

9. Now when it is first kindled, and there is as yet nothing but smoke, then indeed that (fire) is Rudra. And if any one (Kshatriya) desires to consume food (belonging to others),—even as Rudra seeks after these creatures, now with distrust, now with violence, now in striking them down,—let him offer then: and, assuredly, he who, knowing this, offers then (when the fire has just been lighted), obtains that food.

10. And when it burns rather brightly, then indeed that (fire) is Varuna. And if any one desires to consume food,—even as Varuna seeks after these creatures, now, as it were, seizing on them, now with violence, now in striking them down,—let him offer then: and, assuredly, he who, knowing this, offers then, obtains that food.

11. And when it is in full blaze, and the smoke whirls upwards with the utmost speed, then indeed that (fire) is Indra. And if any one wishes to be like Indra in splendour and glory, let him offer then: and, assuredly, he who, knowing this, offers then, obtains that food (object).

12. And when the flame of the waning (fire) gets lower and lower, and (burns) as it were sideways, then, indeed, that (fire) is Mitra. And if any one desires to consume food here through the kindness (maitra, of others),—as one of whom they say, 'Truly, this Brâhman is everybody's friend, he harms not any one,'—let him offer (the Agnihotra) then: and, assuredly, he who, knowing this, offers then (when the fire gets low), obtains that food.

13. And when the coals are glowing intensely, then, indeed, that (fire) is the Brahman. And if anybody wishes to become endowed with holy lustre (brahmavar*k*asin), let him offer then: and, assuredly, he who, knowing this, offers then, obtains that food (object).

14. Let him endeavour to adhere to some one of these (gods or fires) for a year, whether he (the householder) himself offer (the Agnihotra) or some one else offer for him. If, on the other hand, he offers now in this way, now in another, it is just as if, in digging for water or some other food, one were to leave off in the midst of it. But if he offers uniformly, it is just as if, in digging for water or some other food, one lays it open forthwith.

15. Indeed, these offerings are, as it were, the spades for (the digging up of) food; and, assuredly, whosoever, knowing this, offers the Agnihotra, procures food.

16. Now the first libation (pûrvâhuti) represents the gods, and the second (uttarâhuti) represents the men, and what remains in the ladle represents cattle.

17. Only a little he offers for the first libation, somewhat more for the second, and still more he leaves in the ladle.

18. The reason why he offers only a little for the first libation, is that the gods are fewer than men; and why he offers somewhat more for the second libation, is that men are more numerous than the gods; and why he leaves still more in the ladle, is that cattle are more numerous than men. And, verily, whosoever, knowing this, offers the Agnihotra, his cattle will be more numerous than those (human beings) that have to be supported by him: for he, indeed, is in a prosperous condition whose cattle are more numerous than those (human beings) dependent on his support.

THIRD BRÂHMANA.

1. Now when Pragâpati, in creating living beings, created Agni, the latter, as soon as born, sought to burn everything here: and so everybody tried to get out of his way[1]. The creatures then existing sought to crush him. Being unable to endure this, he went to man.

2. He said, 'I cannot endure this: come, let me enter into thee! Having reproduced me, maintain me; and as thou wilt reproduce and maintain me in this world, even so will I reproduce and maintain thee in yonder world!' He (man) replied, 'So be it.' And having reproduced him, he maintained him.

3. Now when he establishes the two fires, he reproduces that (Agni); and having reproduced him, he maintains him; and as he reproduces and maintains him in this world, even so does he (Agni) reproduce and maintain him in yonder world.

4. One must not, therefore, remove it (the sacrificial fire from the hearth) prematurely, for too

[1] Ity âbilam âsa, i.e. 'there was a (general rush) to a hole,' (or perhaps 'to the outlet.')

soon it languishes for him; and as it languishes for him too soon in this world, even so does it languish for him too soon in yonder world: one must not, therefore, remove it prematurely.

5. And when he dies, and they place him on the (funeral) fire, then he is reproduced from out of the fire; and he (Agni) who heretofore was his son[1], now becomes his father.

6. Hence it has been said by the *Ri*shis (Rig-veda I, 89, 9), 'A hundred autumns (may there be) before us, O gods, during which ye complete the life-time of our bodies, during which sons become fathers! do not cut us off, midway, from reaching the full term of life!' for he (Agni) who is the son, now in his turn becomes the father: this, then, is why one must establish the fires.

7. Now yonder burning (sun) doubtless is no other than Death; and because he is Death, therefore the creatures that are on this side of him die. But those that are on the other side of him are the gods, and they are therefore immortal. It is by the rays (or reins, thongs, ra*s*mi) of that (sun) that all these creatures are attached to the vital airs (breaths or life), and therefore the rays extend down to the vital airs.

8. And the breath of whomsoever he (the sun) wishes he takes and rises, and that one dies. And whosoever goes to yonder world not having escaped that Death, him he causes to die again and again in yonder world, even as, in this world, one regards not him that is fettered, but puts him to death whenever one wishes.

[1] Viz. inasmuch as the householder, by the Âdhâna, produces, generates Agni.

9. Now when, in the evening after sunset, he offers two libations, then he firmly plants himself on that Death with those fore-feet of his; and when, in the morning before sunrise, he offers two libations, then he plants himself on that Death with those hind-feet of his. And when he (the sun) rises, then, in rising, he takes him up and thus he (the sacrificer) escapes that Death. This, then, is the release from death in the Agnihotra: and, verily, he who knows that release from death in the Agnihotra, is freed from death again and again.

10. What the arrow-head is to the arrow, that the Agnihotra is to sacrifices. For whither the head of the arrow flies, thither the whole arrow flies: and so are all his works of sacrifice freed by this (Agnihotra) from that Death.

11. Now day and night, revolving, destroy (the fruit of) man's righteousness in yonder world. But day and night are on this side (of the sun) from him (after he has gone up to heaven); and so day and night do not destroy (the fruit of) his righteousness.

12. And as, while standing inside a chariot, one would look down from above on the revolving chariot-wheels, even so does he look down from on high upon day and night: and, verily, day and night destroy not the reward of him who thus knows that release from day and night.

13. [The sacrificer] having gone round the Âhavanîya, (after entering) from the east[1], passes

[1] According to Kâty. IV, 13, 12 [and Schol.], the householder [after taking out the fires and performing his regular twilight adoration (sandhyâ), that is, muttering the Sâvitrî, Rig-veda III, 62, 10 (see *S*at. Br. II, 3, 4, 39), when the sun has half disappeared or until it becomes visible; cf. Â*s*val. G*ri*hyas. XX, 3, 7] passes between the Gârhapatya and Dakshi*n*a fires, or south of them,

between (it and) the Gârhapatya (to his seat). For the gods do not know (this) man[1]; but when he now passes by them between (the fires), they know him, and think, 'This is he that now offers to us.' Moreover, Agni (the fire) is the repeller of evil; and these two, the Âhavanîya and Gârhapatya, repel the evil from him who passes between them; and the evil being repelled from him, he becomes a very light in splendour and glory.

14. On the north side is the door of the Agnihotra[2]: thus (he approaches it) as he would enter (a house) by a door. If, on the other hand, he were to sit down after approaching from the south, it would be as if he walked outside.

15. The Agnihotra, truly, is the ship (that sails) heavenwards. The Âhavanîya and Gârhapatya are the two sides[3] of that same heavenward-bound ship; and that milk-offerer is its steersman.

16. Now when he walks up towards the east, then he steers that (ship) eastwards towards the

---

[enters the Âhavanîya house by the east door], circumambulates the fire from right to left (apadakshi*n*am), and sits down in his place (south of the Âhavanîya fire and altar). The same circumambulation is performed by the wife, who thereupon sits down in her place, south-west of the Gârhapatya.

[1] Or, 'the gods are not aware of (this) man' (na vai devâ manushya*m* vidu*h*). The gods are supposed to be assembled around the altar; see I, 3, 3, 8.

[2] I do not understand this, there being no door on the north side of the Âhavanîya fire-house. According to the commentator this passage is directed against those who make the sacrificer betake himself to the Âhavanîya from (or along) the south; and he quotes the words 'dakshi*n*ena vâ' from Kâtyâyana, apparently IV, 13, 12, where it is said that the sacrificer, in going to the Âhavanîya, has to pass between the two western fires, 'or south of them.'

[3] 'Nauma*nd*e'? according to the commentator=bhittî (the two walls or sides). The Petersb. Dict. proposes 'the two rudders (or oars).'

heavenly world, and he gains the heavenly world by it. When ascended from the north it makes him reach the heavenly world; but if one were to sit down in it after entering from the south, it would be as if he tried to enter it after it has put off and he were left behind and remained outside.

17. And again, the stick which he puts on the fire (corresponds to) a brick, and the formula wherewith he offers is the Ya*g*us-text wherewith he puts on that brick[1]; and when the brick is put on, then a libation is made: hence those same libations of the Agnihotra are offered on his pile of bricks[2].

18. The fire, assuredly, is Pra*g*âpati, and Pra*g*âpati is the year. Year after year, therefore, is his Agnihotra consummated with the piled-up fire-altar; and year after year does he obtain the piled-up fire-altar, whosoever, knowing this, offers the Agnihotra.

19. Seven hundred and twenty eighties of *Ri*k-verses (he should recite at the Agnihotra in the course of a year). When he offers the Agnihotra in the morning and evening, then there are two libations: hence those libations of his, in the course of a year, amount to—

20. Seven hundred and twenty. Thus, indeed, his Agnihotra is accomplished, year after year, with the great chant[3]; and year after year does he obtain

---

[1] Viz. at the Agni*k*ayana, or piling up of the brick-altars at the Soma-sacrifice. As to the putting on of the stick, see II, 3, 1, 17. The Kâ*n*va text of the Vâ*g*. S. (but not that of the Brâhm.) gives the formula 'Agni*g*yotisha*m* (Sûrya*g*yotisha*m*, in the morning) tvâ vâyumatîm,' &c. See Kâty. IV, 14, 13; 15, 9.

[2] After the completion of the fifth, and last, layer of the brick-altar, oblations of various materials are made thereon; especially the *S*atarudriyahoma, consisting of 425 single oblations; *S*at. Br. IX, 1, 1, 1 seq., 2, 1, 1 seq.

[3] The mahad (or, b*ri*had) uktha or great chant, which marks

the great chant, whosoever, knowing this, offers the Agnihotra.

FOURTH BRÂHMANA.

1. Once on a time the gods deposited with Agni all their beasts, both domestic and wild; either because they were about to engage in battle or from a desire of free scope, or because they thought that he (Agni) would protect them as the best protector.

2. Now Agni coveted them, and seizing them he entered the night with them. 'Let us go back thither,' said the gods, and betook themselves to where Agni was concealed. Now they knew that he had entered there, that he had entered the night; and when the night returned in the evening, they approached him and said, 'Give us our beasts! give us back our beasts!' Agni then gave them back their beasts.

3. For this then let him respectfully approach the two fires: the fires are givers, and thereby he supplicates them. Let him approach them in the evening, for in the evening the gods approached (Agni). And whosoever, knowing this, approaches (the two fires), to him, indeed, they grant cattle.

4. Then as to why he should not approach them. Now in the beginning both the gods and men were together here. And whatever did not belong to the men, for that they importuned the gods, saying, 'This is not ours: let it be ours!' Being indignant

the conclusion of the Agnikayana, consists of 3 × 80 trikas (strophes of three verses each), or together 720 verses. On the frequent use of number 80 in the fire-ritual, see Weber, Ind. Stud. XIII, p. 167.

at this importunity, the gods then disappeared. Hence (it may be argued) one should not approach (the fires), fearing lest he should offend them, lest he should become hateful to them.

5. Then as to why he should nevertheless approach (the fires). The sacrifice, assuredly, belongs to the gods, and the prayer for blessing to the sacrificer. Now the (Agnihotra) libation, doubtless, is the same as the sacrifice; and what he does[1] in now approaching (the fires), that indeed is the sacrificer's prayer for blessing.

6. And again, why he should not approach (the fires). Whosoever follows either a Brâhman or Kshatriya, praising him, thinking, 'He will give me gifts, he will build me a house,' to him, if he strives to please him both in speech and deed, that (master of his) will think himself bound to give gifts. Whosoever, on the other hand, says, 'What art thou to me, that givest me nothing?' him that (master) is likely to hate, to become disgusted with. Hence one should not approach (the fire); for by kindling and offering in it, he already supplicates it, and he should not therefore approach (and importune it again).

7. And again, why he should nevertheless approach (the fires). He alone that asks finds a giver; and the master, moreover, knows nothing of his dependent. But when the latter says, 'I am thy dependent: support me!' then he does know him, and feels himself bound to support him. Let him therefore approach (the fires). This then is the

[1] The Kânva text has: 'And when he approaches (the fires), that (represents) the sacrificer's wish for blessing: what there is here for him, that indeed he thereby makes his own (âtmani kurute).'

whole (argument) as to why one should approach (the fires).

8. Now that (fire) being Pragâpati,—when the Agnihotra is offered, he casts the seed of all that he rules over, of all that is after his manner: and by approaching (the fire) one imitates (him in) all this, one reproduces all this[1].

9. He begins to pray[2] with the verse (Vâg. S. III, 11) containing the word 'upon (upa).' Now the word 'upon' means this (earth), and that in a twofold way: for whatever is produced here, that is produced upon (upa-gan) this (earth); and whatever decays, that is buried (upa-vap[3]) in this (earth): hence there is here imperishable, ever-increasing abundance, and with that imperishable abundance he begins.

10. He prays, 'Entering upon the worship—,' worship (adhvara) doubtless means sacrifice: 'entering upon the sacrifice' is what he means to say. '—Let us offer prayer to Agni—,' for he is indeed about to offer prayer to him; '—to him who hears us even from afar!' thereby he means to say, 'Although thou art afar from us, yet do thou hear this our (prayer), do thou so far think well of it!'

11. [He continues, Vâg. S. III, 12], 'Agni, the head,

[1] Or, 'this All' (idam sarvam). The Kânva text has bhûmânam, 'abundance,' instead.

[2] The mode of approaching and worshipping the fires (agnyupasthâna) detailed in pars. 9–41 is ascribed to Vatsaprî (author of Rig-veda IX, 68; X, 45 and 46), and therefore termed vâtsaprâupasthâna. It is, however, also called mahopasthâna (or dîrghopasthâna), or great (long) worship, as distinguished from the so-called kshullakopasthâna (or laghûpasthâna), or little (short) worship, described in II, 4, 1, and ascribed to Âsuri.

[3] Or 'upa-kîryate,' according to the Kânva text.

the summit of the sky; he, the lord of the earth, animates the seeds of the waters.' He thereby follows (and praises) him:—even as a supplicant would speak politely, 'Surely thou art the descendant of so and so! surely thou art able to do this!' so (he does) by this (verse).

12. Thereupon the verse to Indra and Agni (Vâg. S. III, 13), 'You two, O Indra and Agni, I will invoke; you two I will delight together with kindly office; you two, the givers of strength and wealth, —you two I invoke for the obtainment of strength!' Indra, doubtless, is the same as that burning (sun); when he sets, then he enters the Âhavanîya;—hence he now approaches these two that are thus united, thinking, 'May the two, united, grant me favours:' this is why the Indra-Agni (verse is muttered).

13. [He continues, ib. 14 seq.], 'This is thy natural womb, whence born thou shonest forth: knowing this, arise, O Agni, and increase our substance!'—substance, doubtless, means affluence: 'grant to us ever-increasing affluence!' is what he thereby says.

14. 'First was he founded by the founders here, the best offering priest, worthy of praise at the sacrifices; he whom Apnavâna and the Bh*ri*gus kindled[1], shining brightly in the wood, and spreading from house to house:'—even as a supplicant would speak politely, 'Surely thou art the descendant of so and so! surely thou art able to do this!' so in this (verse). And what he (Agni) really is, as such he speaks of him when he says 'spreading from house to house,' for he does indeed spread from house to house.

[1] Or, as Grassmann, in his translation of the *Ri*ksa*m*hitâ, takes it, 'he whom the active Bh*ri*gus kindled.'

15. 'In accordance with his old (pratna) splendour, the dauntless have milked the shining juice from the wise one that giveth a hundredfold.' The richest of gifts, indeed, is the hundredfold gift; and in order to obtain that (giver) he says, 'the wise one that giveth a hundredfold.'

16. This is a hymn of six verses collected (from the *Ri*k); the first of them containing (the word) 'upon,' and the last containing (the word) 'old' (pratna). And this we recited, because she (the earth) is the one that contains the (word) 'upon;' and that which is 'old' doubtless is yonder (sky), for as many gods as there were 'of old,' in the beginning, so many gods there are now, and hence the 'old' means yonder (sky). Now within these two (worlds) all desires are contained; and these two are in accord with each other for his (the sacrificer's) benefit, and concede all his wishes.

17. Thrice he mutters the first (verse) and thrice the last; for of threefold beginning are sacrifices, and of threefold termination: therefore he mutters thrice the first and the last (verses).

18. Now, in offering the Agnihotra, whatever mistake one commits, either in word or deed, thereby he injures either his own body, or his life, or his vigour, or his offspring.

19. Accordingly (he mutters the texts, Vâ*g*. S. III, 17), 'Thou, O Agni, art the protector of bodies: protect my body! Thou, O Agni, art the giver of life: give me life! Thou, O Agni, art the giver of vigour: give me vigour! O Agni, what defect there is in my body, supply that for me!'

20. And whatever mistake he commits, in offering the Agnihotra, either in word or deed, thereby he

injures either his own body, or his life, or his vigour, or his offspring: 'make that up for me!' he thereby says; and accordingly that (defect) is again made up for him.

21. [He continues, Vâg. S. III, 18], 'Kindled, we enkindle thee, the brilliant one, a hundred winters—;' he thereby says, 'may we live a hundred years;' and 'so long we enkindle thee, the great one,' he says, when he says 'we enkindle thee, the brilliant one.' '—We, the vigorous—thee, the invigorating; we, the strong—thee, the giver of strength—;' whereby he says, 'may we be vigorous, mayest thou be invigorating! may we be strong, mayest thou be a giver of strength!' '—We, the uninjured—thee, the uninjurable injurer of enemies!' whereby he says, 'by thine aid may we render our enemies utterly miserable!'

22. 'O thou, rich in lights, may I safely reach thine end!' this he mutters thrice. She that is rich in lights (*k*itrâvasu) doubtless is the night, since the latter, as it were, rests (vas) after gathering together the lights (*k*itrâ): hence (at night) one does not see clearly (*k*itram) from afar.

23. Now it was by means of this same (text) that the *Ri*shis reached safely the end of the night; and because of it the evil spirits, the Rakshas, did not find them: by it, therefore, he also now reaches safely the end of the night; and because of it the evil spirits, the Rakshas, find him not.—This much he mutters while standing.

24. Thereupon, while seated, (he mutters, Vâg. S. III, 19 seq.), 'Thou, O Agni, hast attained to Sûrya's lustre—;' this he says, because, in setting, the sun enters the Âhavanîya; '—to the praise

of the *Ri*shis—;' this he says, because he himself now approaches (and worships, praises, the fire); '—to the favourite abode (or dainty);' his (Agni's) favourite abode doubtless are the offerings: 'to offerings' he thereby says. '—May I attain to long life, to lustre, to offspring, to increase of wealth!' whereby he says, 'Even as thou didst attain to those (qualities), so may I attain to long life, lustre, offspring, affluence,—that is to say, to prosperity.'

25. He then approaches the cow[1], with the text (Vâ*g*. S. III, 20), 'Food ye are: may I enjoy your food! wealth ye are: may I enjoy your wealth!'—whereby he means to say, 'whatever energies are yours, whatever riches are yours, may I enjoy them.'—'Strength ye are: may I enjoy your strength!' whereby he says, 'sap ye are: may I enjoy your sap!'—'Affluence ye are: may I enjoy your affluence!' whereby he says, 'abundance ye are: may I enjoy your abundance!'

26. 'Ye prosperous ones, disport yourselves—;' cattle are prosperous: therefore he says, 'ye prosperous ones, disport yourselves—;' '—in this seat, in this fold, in this place, in this homestead: remain here, go not from hence!' this he says with reference to himself,—'go not away from me!'

27. He then touches the cow, with the text (Vâ*g*. S. III, 22 a), 'Motley thou art, of all shapes;'—for cattle are indeed of all shapes: therefore he calls her all-shaped; '—come to me with sap and possession of cattle!' when he says 'with sap,' he means

[1] Viz. the Agnihotra cow, which has supplied the milk for the morning and evening libation; or any cow, if other material than milk be used.

to say 'with juice;' and when he says 'with possession of cattle,' he means to say 'with abundance.'

28. He then steps up to the Gârhapatya, and renders homage to it, with the text (ib. 22 b), 'Thee, O Agni, illuminer of the night[1], we approach day by day with prayer, paying homage unto thee.' He thus renders homage to it in order that it may not injure him.

29. [He continues, ib. 23 seq.], 'Thee that rulest over the sacrifices, the brilliant guardian of the sacred rite, thriving in thine own house;'—whereby he means to say, 'thine own house is this (house) of mine: make it ever more flourishing for us!'

30. 'O Agni, be thou accessible unto us, even as a father is to his son! lead us unto well-being!'—whereby he says, 'As a father is easy of access to his son, and the latter in no wise injures him, so be thou easy of access to us, and may we in no wise injure thee!'

31. Then the dvipadâ verses (Vâg. S. III, 25, 26), 'O Agni, be ever nigh unto us, a kindly guardian and protector! as wealthy Agni, famed for wealth, come hither and bestow on us glorious riches! Thee, the most bright and resplendent, we now approach for happiness to our friends: be with us, hear our call, and keep us safe from every evil-doer!'

32. Now when he approaches the Âhavanîya, he prays for cattle: he therefore approaches it with metres great and small, since cattle are of great and small size. And when he approaches the Gârha-

[1] Doshâvastar, 'the illuminer of the dusk;' or perhaps, as Professor Ludwig proposes, 'We approach thee, day by day, at dusk and dawn (in the evening and morning), with prayer.'

patya, he prays for men: hence the first tristich is in the gâyatrî metre, since the gâyatrî is Agni's metre, and he thus approaches him with his own metre.

33. Thereupon (he mutters) the dvipadâ (two-footed) verses. The dvipadâ, doubtless, is man's metre, since man is two-footed, and men are therewith prayed for: and as he now prays for men, therefore (he uses) dvipadâ verses. And whosoever, knowing this, approaches (the two fires), becomes possessed both of cattle and men.

34. He then goes (again) to the cow, with the text (Vâ*g*. S. III, 27), 'O I*d*â, come hither! O Aditi, come hither!' for both I*d*â and Aditi are cows. He touches her with, 'Come hither, ye much-desired!'—for men's wishes are fixed on them, and hence he says, 'come hither, ye much-desired;'—'Let there be for me the fulfilment of wishes from you!' whereby he says, 'may I be dear to you!'

35. Thereupon, while standing between the Âhavanîya and Gârhapatya and looking eastward at the (former) fire, he mutters (Vâ*g*. S. III, 28–30), 'O Lord of prayer, make him sweet-voiced, the offerer of Soma, Kakshîvat, U*s*i*g*'s son!—Be he with us, he the opulent, the killer of woe, the bestower of wealth, the increaser of prosperity, he the nimble!—Let not the curse of the evil-doer reach us, nor the guile of the mortal: preserve us, O Lord of prayer!'

36. Now when he approaches the Âhavanîya, he approaches the sky; and when (he approaches) the Gârhapatya, (he approaches) the earth. Hereby now (he approaches) the ether, that being B*ri*haspati's region; and that region he thereby approaches: this is why he mutters the prayer to B*ri*haspati.

37. [He continues, Vâ*g*. S. III, 31–33], 'May the

mighty, the heavenly, the unassailable favour of the three, Mitra, Aryaman, and Varu*n*a, be (with us)! For the wicked enemy lords it not over them (that are protected by these gods), neither at home nor on dangerous paths: for those sons of Aditi bestow undying light on the mortal that he may live!'—In this (prayer) he says, 'nor on dangerous paths;' for dangerous indeed are the paths that lie between heaven and earth: those he now walks, and therefore he says, 'nor on dangerous paths.'

38. Then follows a verse to Indra (Vâ*g*. S. III, 34); for Indra is the deity of the sacrifice, and with Indra therefore he now connects the fire-worship: 'At no time, O Indra, art thou barren; and never dost thou fail the worshipper—;' the worshipper, doubtless, is the sacrificer: 'never dost thou harm the sacrificer,' this is what he thereby says: '—but more and evermore is thy gift increased, O mighty god!' thereby he says, 'do thou make us ever more prosperous here!'

39. Then follows a verse to Savit*ri*[1] (Vâ*g*. S. III, 35),—for Savit*ri* is the impeller (prasavit*ri*) of the gods; and thus all his (the sacrificer's) wishes are fulfilled, impelled as they are by Savit*ri*.—(He mutters), 'May we obtain the glorious light of the divine Savit*ri*, who, we trust, may inspire our prayers!'

40. Thereupon a verse to Agni (Vâ*g*. S. III, 36),—whereby he finally makes himself over to Agni for protection: 'May thine unapproachable chariot, wherewith thou protectest the worshippers, encircle us on every side!' The worshippers, doubtless, are

---

[1] Or, the Sâvitrî, that is, the sacred prayer to Savit*ri*, the sun, also called Gâyatrî, Rig-veda III, 62, 10. Cf. p. 344, note 1.

the sacrificers; and what unassailable chariot he (Agni) possesses, therewith he protects the sacrificers. Hence he thereby means to say, 'what unassailable chariot thou possessest, wherewith thou protectest the sacrificers, therewith do thou guard us on every side.' This (verse) he mutters thrice.

41. He then pronounces his son's name[1]: 'May this son (N. N.) carry on this manly deed of mine!' Should he have no son, let him insert his own name.

Fourth Adhyâya. First Brâhma*n*a.

1. Now after the performance of the Agnihotra he (optionally[2]) approaches the fires with (Vâ*g*. S. III, 37), 'Earth! ether! sky!' In saying 'Earth! ether! sky!' he renders his speech auspicious by means of the truth, and with that (speech) thus rendered propitious he invokes a blessing:—'May I be well supplied with offspring!' whereby he prays for offspring; '—well supplied with men!' whereby he prays for men (heroes); '—well supplied with viands!' whereby he prays for prosperity.

2. That long (form of) fire-worship is a prayer for blessing, and so is this (short) one a prayer for blessing: hence even with this much he obtains all, and he may therefore worship the fires with it. 'Therewith, indeed, we perform,' so spake Âsuri.

3. Now, when he is about to set out on a journey[3], he approaches first the Gârhapatya, and thereupon the Âhavanîya.

---

[1] See I, 9, 3, 21.

[2] For this shorter form of worshipping the fires, see p. 349, note 2.

[3] That is, a journey which will compel him to pass the night beyond the village boundary.

4. The Gârhapatya he approaches with the text (Vâg. S. III, 37 b seq.), 'Thou, that art friendly to man, protect my offspring!' He (Agni Gârhapatya), truly, is the guardian of offspring; and therefore he now makes over to him his offspring for protection.

5. He then approaches the Âhavanîya, with 'Thou, that art worthy of praise, protect my cattle!' He (Agni), truly, is the guardian of cattle, and therefore he now makes over to him his cattle for protection[1].

6. Thereupon he walks or drives off; and having got as far as what he considers to be the boundary[2], he breaks silence. And when he returns from his journey he maintains silence from the moment he sees what he considers to be the boundary. And even though there be a king inside (one's house), one must not go to him (or any other person before one has rendered homage to the fires).

7. He first approaches the Âhavanîya fire, and thereupon the Gârhapatya. The Gârhapatya doubtless is a house (*gri*hâ*h*), and a house is a safe resting-place: so that he thereby (finally[3]) establishes himself in a house, that is, in a safe resting-place.

8. He approaches the Âhavanîya fire, with the text (Vâg. S. III, 38 seq.), 'We have approached (thee), the all-knowing, the most liberal dispenser of

---

[1] The Vâg. S. gives also the formulas with which the Dakshi*n*âgni should be approached, after the other two fires, by the householder, both in starting on, and returning from, his journey. See Kâty. IV, 12, 13; 18. The Kâ*n*va text does not allude to the Dakshi*n*a fire any more than ours.

[2] According to the Paddhati on Kâty. IV, 12, he has to maintain silence as long as he can see the roof of one of his fire-houses; but according to the *S*âṅkhâyana *s*âkhâ he has to do so only as long as he can see one of the fires.

[3] The Kâ*n*va text reads 'antata*h*.'

goods: O Agni, sovereign lord, bestow on us lustre and strength!' Having then sat down he sweeps the blades of grass[1] (into the fire).

9. Thereupon he approaches the Gârhapatya, with the text, 'He, Agni Gârhapatya, is the lord of the house, the most liberal dispenser of goods to our offspring: O Agni, lord of the house, bestow on us lustre and strength!' Having then sat down, he sweeps off the blades of grass. In this way (householders) mostly approach the fires with muttered prayer.

10. However, one may also approach the fires silently,—and that for this reason:—If in the place (where one lives), a Brâhman or noble—in short, a better man—resides, one dares not say to him, 'I am going on a journey, take care of this (property) of mine[2]!' Now in this (sacrificial ground) one's betters indeed reside, viz. the divine Agnis: who, then, would dare to say to them, 'I am going on a journey, take ye care of this (property) of mine!'

11. The gods assuredly see through the mind of man: that (Agni) Gârhapatya therefore knows that he (the householder) now approaches in order to give

---

[1] According to Kâty. IV, 12, 18–19 he [after performing ablutions, and lustrating the Âhavanîya and Dakshi*n*a fire-places, and taking out these fires from the Gârhapatya] approaches the Âhavanîya, while holding pieces of fire-wood in his hand, and mutters the formula given above. He then sits down and silently puts on the fire a piece of wood and the grass that has fallen around the fire. According to the Kâ*n*va text he mutters the second half of the formula ('O Agni,' &c.) while sweeping the grass (into the fire).

[2] In Taitt. Br. I, 1, 10, 6, a householder who is about to start on a journey is apparently recommended to entrust his house to a Brâhman, who may be staying in it.

himself up to him. Silently he approaches the Âhavanîya fire: that (Agni) Âhavanîya knows that he now approaches in order to give himself up to him.

12. Thereupon he walks or drives off; and having got as far as what he considers the boundary line, he releases his speech. And when he returns from the journey, he maintains silence from the moment he sees what he considers to be the boundary. And even though there be a king inside (one's house), one must not go to him.

13. He first approaches the Âhavanîya, and thereupon the Gârhapatya. Silently he approaches the Âhavanîya; and silently he sits down and sweeps away the grass-blades. Silently he approaches the Gârhapatya; and silently he sits down and sweeps away the grass-blades.

14. Then as to the observances in regard to (the entering of) his house. Now when a householder comes home from a journey, his house trembles greatly for fear of him, thinking, 'What will he say here? what will he do here?' It is therefore for fear of him that speaks or does anything on this occasion that the house trembles and is liable to crush his family; but him who neither speaks nor does anything, his house receives with confidence, thinking, 'He has not spoken here, he has not done anything here!' And should he be ever so angry at anything on this occasion, let him rather do on the next day whatever he might wish to say or do. This then is the observance in regard to the house[1].

---

[1] The Kânva text here adds the formulas Vâg. S. III, 41-43, lines 1 and 2, wherewith he approaches (upatishthate) the house. See Kâty. IV, 12, 22. According to Kâty. ib. 23, he then enters

SECOND BRÂHMA*N*A.

III. THE PI*ND*APIT*RI*YA*GÑ*A OR OBLATION OF OBSEQUIAL CAKES TO THE FATHERS.

1. Now the living beings once approached Pra*g*âpati—beings doubtless mean creatures—and said, 'Ordain unto us in what manner we are to live!' Thereupon the gods, being properly invested with the sacrificial cord[1] and bending the right knee, approached him. To them he said, 'The sacrifice (shall be) your food; immortality your sap; and the sun your light!'

2. Then the fathers approached, wearing the cord on the right shoulder, and bending the left knee. To them he said, 'Your eating (shall be) monthly; your cordial (svadhâ) your swiftness of thought; and the moon your light!'

3. Then the men approached him, clothed and bending their bodies. To them he said, 'Your eating (shall be) in the evening and in the morning; your offspring your death; and the fire (Agni) your light!'

4. Then the beasts approached him. To them he granted their own choice, saying, 'Whensoever ye shall find anything, whether in season or out of season,

---

the house with the formula Vâ*g*. S. III, 43, line 3, 'For safety, for peace I resort to thee: be there kindliness, happiness, all-hail, and blessing!' Thereupon, according to the Schol., he is to proceed in accordance with the rules laid down in the G*ri*hya-sûtras; cf. Pârask. G. I, 18; Â*s*v. G. I, 15, 9.

[1] Ya*gñ*opavîtin, 'sacrificially invested,' i.e. wearing the sacrificial cord in the ordinary way, on the left shoulder and under the right arm. In any performance connected with the deceased ancestors, the cord has to be shifted from the left to the right shoulder and under the left arm (prâ*k*înopavîtin, lit. 'eastward invested').

ye shall eat it!' Hence whenever they find anything, whether in season or out of season, they eat it.

5. Thereupon—so they say—the Asuras also straightway[1] approached him. To them he gave darkness (tamas) and illusion (mâyâ): for there is indeed what is called the illusion of the Asuras. Those creatures, it is true, have perished; but creatures still subsist here in the very manner which Pra*g*âpati ordained unto them.

6. Neither the gods, nor the fathers, nor beasts transgress (this ordinance); some of the men alone transgress it. Hence whatever man grows fat, he grows fat in unrighteousness, since he totters and is unable to walk because of his having grown fat by doing wrong. One should therefore eat only in the evening and morning; and whosoever, knowing this, eats only in the evening and morning, reaches the full measure of life; and whatever he speaks, that is (true); because he observes that divine truth. For, verily, that is Brâhmanic lustre (te*g*as), when one knows to keep His (Pra*g*âpati's) law.

7. Now that (lustre) indeed belongs to him who presents (food) to the fathers once a month. When that (moon) is not seen either in the east or in the west, then he presents (food) to them; for that moon doubtless is king Soma, the food of the gods. Now during that night (of new moon) it fails them, and when it fails, he presents (food to them), and thereby establishes concord (between the gods and fathers). But were he to present (food) to them when it is not failing, he would indeed cause a quarrel between the gods and fathers: hence he presents

[1] *S*a*s*vat = 'repeatedly,' Comm.; *s*a*s*vad api, 'endlich auch (at last also),' St. Petersb. Dict.

(food) to them when that (moon) is not seen either in the east or in the west.

8. He presents it in the afternoon. The fore-noon, doubtless, belongs to the gods; the mid-day to men; and the afternoon to the fathers: therefore he presents (food to the fathers) in the afternoon.

9. While seated behind the Gârhapatya, with his face turned toward the south[1], and the sacrificial cord on his right shoulder, he takes that (material for the offering from the cart)[2]. Thereupon he rises from thence and threshes (the rice) while standing north of the Dakshi*n*a fire and facing the south. Only once he cleans (the rice)[3]; for it is once for all that the fathers have passed away, and therefore he cleans it only once.

10. He then boils it. While it stands on the (Dakshi*n*a) fire, he pours some clarified butter on it;—for the gods they pour the offering into the fire; for men they take (the food) off the fire; and for the fathers they do in this very manner: hence, they pour the ghee on it while it stands on the fire.

11. After removing it (from the fire) he offers to the gods two libations in the fire. For, in esta-blishing his sacrificial fires, and in performing the new and full-moon sacrifice, that (householder) resorts to the gods. Here, however, he is engaged in a

[1] Dakshi*n*âsîna*h*; the Commentator interprets it by 'sitting south of the cart.'

[2] The Kâ*n*va text has,—eta*m* *k*aru*m* g*ri*h*n*âti, 'he takes that pot, or potful, (of rice).' Doubtless, he is to take from the cart the quan-tity of rice sufficient for the offerings and put it in the pot (*k*aru). According to Kâty. IV, 1, 5–7 he is to take the but-partly-filled pot, or a spoonful (or, according to the Schol., rather less than a spoonful).

[3] Compare the detailed account in I, 1, 4, 1 seq.

sacrifice to the fathers: hence he thereby propitiates the gods, and being permitted by the gods, he presents that (food) to the fathers. This is why, on removing (the rice), he offers to the gods two libations in the fire.

12. He offers both to Agni and Soma[1]. To Agni he offers, because Agni is allowed a share in every (offering); and to Soma he offers, because Soma is sacred to the fathers. This is why he offers both to Agni and Soma.

13. He offers[2] with the formulas (Vâg. S. II, 29 a, b), 'To Agni, the bearer of what is meet for the wise, svâhâ!' 'To Soma, accompanied by the fathers, svâhâ[3]!' He then puts the pot-ladle on the fire,—that being in lieu of the Svishtakrit[4]. Thereupon he draws (with the wooden sword) one line (furrow) south of the Dakshina fire[5],—that

---

[1] According to Taitt. Br. I, 3, 10, 3, some make a third oblation, viz. as Sâyana states, to Yama (the chief of the fathers), with the formula, 'To Yama, accompanied by the Aṅgiras and fathers, svadhâ! namah!' see note 3.

[2] The commentary on Kâty. IV, 1, 7 supplies the following particulars:—Having removed the pot off the Dakshina fire on the south side, the Adhvaryu takes it, along the east, to the north side of the fire. He then shifts the sacrificial cord to his left shoulder (as he is about to offer to gods), puts three sticks on the fire, and sitting down with his face towards the east offers some boiled rice with the pot-ladle (mekshana).

[3] The Taittirîyas use svadhâ! namah! instead of svâhâ! They also offer first to Soma, with 'To Soma, drank by the fathers' (but cf. Taitt. Br. I, 6, 9, 5), and then to (Yama, and finally to) Agni. Taitt. Br. I, 3, 10, 2-3.

[4] See I, 7, 3, 1 seq.

[5] Or west (gaghanena) of the fire [from north to south], according to the Kânva text; optionally, according to Kâty. IV, 1, 8. Kâty. also gives the text 'Expelled are the Asuras, the Rakshas, seated on the altar' (Vâg. S. II, 29 c) to be muttered during the act.

being in lieu of the altar: only one line he draws, because the fathers have passed away once for all.

14. He then lays down a firebrand at the farther (south) end (of the line). For were he to present that (food) to the fathers, without having laid down a firebrand, the Asuras and Rakshas would certainly tamper with it. And thus the Asuras and Rakshas do not tamper with that (food) of the fathers: this is why he lays down the firebrand at the farther end (of the line).

15. He lays it down, with the text (Vâg. S. II, 30), 'Whatsoever Asuras roam about at will[1], assuming various shapes[2],—be they large-bodied or small-bodied[3],—may Agni expel them from this world!' Agni is the repeller of the Rakshas, and therefore he lays (the firebrand) down in this way.

16. He then takes the water-pitcher and makes (the fathers) wash (their hands)[4], merely[5] saying, 'N. N., wash thyself!' (naming) the sacrificer's father; 'N. N., wash thyself!' (naming) his grandfather; 'N. N., wash thyself!' (naming) his great-grandfather. As one would pour out water (for a guest) when he is about to take food, so in this case.

---

[1] Or, as the Commentator takes svadhayâ, '(attracted) by the svadhâ (offering to the fathers).'

[2] That is, according to the Schol., assuming the shapes of deceased ancestors.

[3] This explanation of the words parâpurah and nipurah, proposed by the Scholiast, is doubtful.

[4] The Adhvaryu (having again shifted the sacrificial cord to his right shoulder) pours water through the "fathers' space" (pitri-tîrtha, i.e. the space between the thumb and fore-finger), from right to left, into the line, at its beginning, centre, and end. Kâty. IV, 1, 10, and Schol.

[5] See paragraph 19.

17. Now those (stalks of sacrificial grass) are severed with one stroke, and cut off near the root;—the top belongs to the gods, the middle part to men, and the root-part to the fathers: therefore they are cut off near the root. And with one stroke they are severed, because the fathers have passed away once for all.

18. He spreads them (along the line) with their tops towards the south. Thereon he presents [to the fathers the three (round) cakes of rice][1]. He presents them thus[2];—for to the gods they offer thus; for men they ladle out (the food in any way they please)[3]; and in the case of the fathers they do in this very way: therefore he presents (the cakes to them) thus.

19. With, 'N. N., this for thee!' he presents (one cake) to the sacrificer's father. Some add, 'and for those who come after thee!' but let him not say this, since he himself is one of those to whom (it would be offered) in common[4]: let him

[1] According to the Paddhati on Kâty. the first ball is to be of the size of a fresh âmalaka, or fruit of the Emblic Myrobalan, and each of the two others is to be larger than the preceding one.

[2] Here the teacher indicated by gesture the part of the hand sacred to the fathers (see p. 365, note 4); and then in the same way that dedicated to the gods, viz. the tip of the fingers.

[3] The Kânva recension reads here also 'thus they take out (the food) for men;' the part of the hand dedicated to man being, according to the commentary on Kâty. IV, 1, 10, the part about the little finger (kanishthikâpradesa).

[4] Svayam vai teshâm saha yeshâm saha. According to the commentary, the author apparently means to say, that if he were to add, 'and those who come after thee (i.e. after his father),' he would include the sacrificer himself, and the latter would consequently offer the pinda to himself. The form of the presentation-formula rejected by our author is the one adopted in Âsval. Sr. II, 6, 15, except that 'atra' is added there ('who here come after thee').

therefore merely say, 'N. N., this for thee!' as to the sacrificer's father; 'N. N., this for thee!' as to his grandfather; and 'N. N., this for thee!' as to his great-grandfather. He presents (the food) in an order (directed) away from the present time, because it is away from hence that the fathers have once for all departed.

20. He then mutters (Vâg. S. II, 31 a), 'Here, O fathers, regale yourselves: like bulls come hither, each to his own share!' whereby he says, 'Eat ye each his own share!'

21. He then turns round (to the left), so as to face the opposite (north) side: for the fathers are far away from men; and thereby he also is far away (from the fathers). 'Let him remain (standing with bated breath) until his breath fail,' say some, 'for thus far extends the vital energy.' However [1], having remained so for a moment—

22. He again turns round (to the right) and mutters (Vâg. S. II, 31 b), 'The fathers have regaled themselves: like bulls they have come each to his own share;' whereby he means to say, 'They have eaten each his own share [2].'

23. Thereupon he takes the water-pitcher and makes them wash themselves [3], merely saying,

---

The Kânva text mentions and rejects the two alternative readings, 'ye *k*a tvâm anvâñ*k*a*h*' and 'yâ*ms* *k*a tvam anvañ asi' ('and those whom thou followest'). In Taitt. Br. I, 3, 10, no presentation-formula is mentioned at all.

[1] The Kânva recension has tad u instead of sa vai.

[2] 'Formerly the gods and men and fathers (deva-manushyâ*h* pitara*h*) drank visibly together, but now they do so invisibly.' *S*at. Br. III, 6, 2, 26.

[3] Viz. by pouring water on the obsequial cakes. According to Â*s*val. *S*r. II, 7, 5, and other treatises, he also puts down some

'N. N., wash thyself[1]!' (naming) the sacrificer's father; 'N. N., wash thyself!' (naming) his grandfather; 'N. N., wash thyself!' (naming) his great-grandfather. Even as one would pour out (water for a guest) when he has taken his meal, so here.

24. He then pulls down the tuck[2] (of the sacrificer's garment) and performs obeisance. The tuck is sacred to the fathers (pitridevatyâ): therefore he performs obeisance to them after pulling down the tuck. Now obeisance means worship (or sacrifice): hence he thereby renders them worthy of worship. Six times he performs obeisance; for there are six seasons, and the fathers are the seasons: for this reason he performs obeisance six times. He mutters (Vâg. S. II, 32 g), 'Give us houses, O fathers!' for the fathers are the guardians (îsate) of houses; and this is the prayer for blessing at this sacrificial performance. After the cakes have been put back (in the dish containing the remains of boiled rice) he (the sacrificer) smells at (the rice); this (smelling) being the sacrificer's share. The

ointment, oil, or butter on the pindas, saying, '(Father), N. N., anoint thyself!' &c.; see Donner, Pindap., p. 25.

[1] See paragraph 19.

[2] Nîvim udvrihya=paridhânîyasya vâsaso dasâ tâm udvrihya visramsya, Sâyana. According to Mahâdeva, he (who presents the pindas, viz. either the Adhvaryu or the sacrificer) has previously to put on a garment with a tuck (nîvimat paridhânam), i.e. with the dasâ, or unwoven edge of the upper garment, tucked up under the waistband. This he is to pull out. Kâtyâyana has the following rules: IV, 1, 15, Having made (them) wash themselves as before, and having loosened (visramsya) the tuck, he makes obeisance with 'adoration to your vigour, O fathers!' &c. (Vâg. S. II, 32 a–f). [According to the Comm., he adds the formula, 'Give us houses, O fathers! we will give to you of what is (ours).' Vâg. S. II, 32, 9.] 16, With 'Put on this your garment, O fathers!' (Vâg. S. II, 32 h), he throws three threads (pieces of

(stalks of sacrificial grass) cut with one stroke he puts on the fire; and he also again throws away the firebrand [1].

THIRD BRÂHMANA.

IV. THE ÂGRAYANESHTI OR OFFERING OF FIRST-FRUITS.

This sacrifice is performed in spring and autumn—generally at new or full moon—at the commencement of the harvest. The oblations, which, as a rule, are prepared from new grain (viz. barley in spring, and rice in autumn), consist of—1. a sacrificial cake contained on twelve potsherds for Indra and Agni; 2. a *k*aru (mess of boiled grains) for the Visve Devâ*h*, prepared with water or milk; and 3. a cake on one potsherd for heaven and earth. Kâty. IV, 6 and comm. According to the Paddhati, the offering of first-fruits takes place after the new-moon offering, and before the full-moon offering. At the beginning of the harvest of Panicum Frumentaceum (syâmâka), in the rainy season or in autumn; and at that of bamboo

---

yarn), one on each cake. 17, Or, woollen fringe [or, wool or fringe (dasâ), according to others]. 18, Or, hairs of the sacrificer (pulled out from the chest near the heart), if he is advanced in years. 19, He pours [the water, left in the pitcher, on the cakes] with 'Ye (O waters) are a refreshing draught, ye, that bring sap, immortal ghee and milk and foaming mead: gladden my fathers!' (Vâg. S. II, 34.) 20, [The Adhvaryu] having laid (the cakes on the dish) the sacrificer smells at them. 21, The firebrand and the once-cut stalks of grass (he throws) into the fire. 22, The wife, if desirous of a son, eats the middle cake with, 'Bestow offspring on me, O fathers, a boy crowned with lotuses; that there may be a man here!' (Vâg. S. II, 33.) [According to the comment, the other two cakes are thrown into the water or fire; or eaten by a priest.] For other variations, see Donner, Pi*nd*apit*ri*yag*ñ*a. The Kâ*n*va recension, on the whole, agrees with our text.

[1] The Kâ*n*va text has as follows: 'Therefore he says, Give us houses, O fathers!' He then smells at the pot (ukhâ): that is the sacrificer's share. They again put down the cakes together (with the rice in the pot! samavadadhati). The once-severed (stalks of grass) they put on the fire. The firebrand he again shifts to (the fire; apy-argati).

in summer, offerings of first-fruits are also made to Soma in the form of a potful of boiled *s*yâmâka or bamboo grains respectively.

1. Now Kaho*d*a Kaushîtaki spake, 'This sap (of the plants) truly belongs to those two, heaven and earth: having offered of this sap to the gods, we will eat it.' 'That is why the offering of first-fruits is performed.'

2. And Yâ*gñ*avalkya also spake:—The gods and the Asuras, both of them sprung from Pra*g*âpati, once contended for superiority. The Asuras then defiled, partly by magic, partly with poison, both kinds of plants—those on which men and beasts subsist—hoping that in this way they might over come the gods. In consequence of this neither did men eat food, nor did beasts graze; and from want of food these creatures well-nigh perished[1].

3. Now the gods heard as to how these creatures were perishing from want of food. They spake unto one another, 'Come, let us rid them[2] of this!'—'By what means?'—'By means of the sacrifice.' By means of the sacrifice the gods then accomplished all that they wanted to accomplish[3]; and so did the *Ri*shis.

4. They then said, 'To which of us shall this belong?' They did not agree (each of them exclaiming), 'Mine (it shall be)!' Not having come to an agreement, they said, 'Let us run a race for this (sacrifice): whichever of us beats (the others), his it shall be!' 'So be it!' they said, and they ran a race.

---

[1] The Kâ*n*va text has: Tâ etâ ubhayya*h* pra*g*â ana*s*anena not parâbabhûvu*h*.

[2] Viz. the plants, according to the reading of the Kâ*n*va text: Hantâsâm oshadhînâ*m* k*ri*tyâ*m* tvad visha*m* tvad apahanâmeti.

[3] The Kâ*n*va text reads kalpyam instead of kalpam.

5. Indra and Agni won, and hence that Indra-Agni cake on twelve potsherds[1]; Indra and Agni having won a share in it. And where Indra and Agni were standing when they had won, thither all the gods followed them.

6. Now, Indra and Agni are the Kshatra (nobility), and all the gods (or, the All-gods) are the Vi*s* (common Âryan people); and wherever the Kshatra conquers, there the Vi*s* is allowed to share. Thus they (Indra and Agni) allowed the Vi*s*ve Devâ*h* (the All-gods) a share (in the offering); and hence that pap of boiled (rice or barley) grain (offered) to the All-gods.

7. 'Let him prepare it from old (grain)[2],' say some; 'for Indra and Agni are the Kshatra (and he should therefore use old grain for the Vai*s*vadeva pap) lest he (the sacrificer) should exalt (the Vi*s*) to the level of the Kshatra.' Nevertheless let both (the cake and *k*aru) consist of new (grain); for (by the very fact that) the one is a cake and the other a pap, the nobility is not equalled (by the people): hence they should both consist of new (grain).

8. The All-gods spake, 'This sap (of the rice and barley plants) truly belongs to those two, heaven and earth: let us, then, allow those two a share in it!' They accordingly assigned that share to them, to wit, the cake on one potsherd offered to heaven

---

[1] The MS. of the Kâ*n*va recension has: Tasmâd esha aindrâgno da*s*akapâla*h* purolâ*s*o bhavati. The commentary on Kâty. IV, 6, 1, on the other hand, makes it a cake on eleven potsherds.

[2] Or, he may do so. Kâty. IV, 6, 7 leaves the option between new and old grain.

and earth[1]. This is why there is a cake on one potsherd (kapâla) for heaven and earth. Now this (earth) is, doubtless, the cup (depository, kapâla) of that (sap)[2]; and she indeed is one only: hence (the cake) consists of one potsherd.

9. An offence (is thereby committed) by him[3]; since, for whatever deity sacrificial food may be taken out, the Svish*t*ak*ri*t (Agni, the maker of good offering) is invariably allowed a share in it after (the respective deity). But that (cake) he offers entire, and he does not cut off a portion for the Svish*t*ak*ri*t: this is an offence, and consequently (that cake), when offered, turns upside down.

10. Hence they say, 'That (cake) contained on one potsherd has turned upside down: it will throw the kingdom into disorder.' No offence (is, however, committed) by him, for the Âhavanîya is the support of oblations; and if, after reaching the Âhavanîya, (the cake) were to turn upside down ten times, he need not heed it. And if others ask as to who would care to incur (the result of) such a combination (of errors), let him offer nothing but butter; for clarified butter is manifestly the sap of

[1] This is a 'low-voiced' oblation, the invitatory and offering prayers thereat (with the exception of the concluding 'Vausha*t*' and 'Om') being pronounced in a low tone. See p. 171, note 1; p. 192, note 1.

[2] The Kâ*n*va text has: 'The reason why it consists of one kapâla is that this earth is a kapâla, and that she is one only.'

[3] The Kâ*n*va recension has as follows:—As to this they say, 'It should not be a one-cup cake, (because) therein a neglect is (involved).' Even so (ida*m* nu): for whatever deity they take out sacrificial food, the Svish*t*ak*ri*t is invariably made to share in it after (the respective deity). That (cake) they offer whole: this is consequently a neglect. Moreover, it turns round (paryâbhavati). As to this they say, 'That (cake) has turned upside down,' &c.

those two, heaven and earth, so that he thereby manifestly gladdens those two with their own sap or essence: hence he need offer nothing but butter.

11. By performing that same sacrifice, the gods removed the magic spell as well as the poison from both kinds of plants,—those on which men and beasts subsist; and henceforward the men ate food and the cattle grazed.

12. Now when he performs that sacrifice, he does so either for the reason that no one will then defile (the plants) either by magic or poison; or because the gods did so. And whatever share the gods assigned (to themselves), that share he thereby makes over to them. Moreover, he thereby renders wholesome and faultless both kinds of plants,—those on which men and beasts subsist; and these creatures subsist on those wholesome and faultless (plants) of his: this is why he performs that sacrifice.

13. The priests' fee for this (sacrifice) consists of the first-born calf (of the season); for that is, as it were, the first-fruits (of the cattle). If he has already performed the new and full-moon offerings, let him first perform those offerings[1], and thereupon the present (offering of first-fruits). If, on the other hand, he has not yet performed (the new and full-moon offerings), let them cook a *k*âtushprâ*s*ya[2] pap on the southern fire, and let the priests eat it.

---

[1] I do not know how to account for the vâ. Sâya*n*a seems to take the passage thus:—'If he be a Soma-sacrificer, or if he be performing the Dar*s*apûr*n*amâsa, [let him first perform that sacrifice, and] let him then perform the present one.' The Oxford MS. of the Kâ*n*va text has:—Etat tasya karma ya î*g*âno vâ syâd dar*s*a-pûr*n*amâsâbhyâ*m* vâ ya*g*etâtha yo 'nî*g*âno 'nvâhâryapa*k*ana evau-danam *k*âtushprâ*s*yam pa*k*et tam brâhma*n*ebhya upanidadhyât.

[2] See II, 1, 4, 4 seq.

14. Verily, there are two kinds of gods: for the gods themselves, assuredly, are gods; and those priests who have studied, and teach Vedic lore, are the human gods. And in like manner as that is offered whereon the Vashat has been pronounced, so is that (offering of first-fruits consecrated by the feeding of the priests). Let him also, at this (sacrifice), give as much as is in his power, for no offering, they say, should be without a dakshinâ. At the Agnihotra (performed at the time of the Âgrayaneshti) let him not offer (milk obtained from the eating of new corn)[1]; for were he to offer such at the Agnihotra, he would cause a conflict (between the deities of the two offerings). The Âgrayana is one thing, and the Agnihotra is another: let him, therefore, not offer (new material) at the Agnihotra.

FOURTH BRÂHMANA.

THE DÂKSHÂYANA SACRIFICE.

This peculiar modification of the new and full-moon sacrifice seems to have been originated and generally to have been practised among the Dâkshâyanas, a royal family which was evidently still flourishing at the time of our author[2].

Here also two days were, as a rule, required for the performance, both at full and new moon; but while, at the ordinary sacrifice,

---

[1] Kâty. has the rules IV, 6, 11: 'In the case of one, who only performs the Agnihotra (and no longer the Darsapûrnamâsa), the evening and morning Agnihotra-oblation (at the time of the Âgrayana) is performed with new (corn).' 12, 'Or with the milk of (a cow) which has been fed with such (new corn).' The Kânva text has: 'Now at the Agnihotra also some offer (milk obtained from new corn), but let him not do so; for he would raise a quarrel were he to offer (such milk).'

[2] See Weber, Ind. Stud. I, p. 223; IV, p. 358; Ludwig, Rigveda III, p. 195.

the first day was completely taken up with the preliminary ceremonies, the Dâkshâyanas spread the special offerings over both days, making each time two separate ishtis of them. The special havis, or sacrificial dishes, were, at the ordinary full-moon sacrifice, a rice-cake (to Agni, and another) to Agni and Soma; and at the new-moon sacrifice, a cake (to Agni, and another) to Indra and Agni, or, as an alternative, a dish of curds (sânnâyya) prepared of sweet and sour milk, offered to Indra (or Mahendra). The Dâkshâyanas, on the other hand, offered the Agni-Soma and Indra-Agni cakes in the fore-noon of the first day, that of full and new moon respectively. The afternoons of the same days were then taken up with preliminary rites, such as the eating of fast-day food, the cutting of a palâsa branch, driving away of the calves from the cows, &c. The second day's performance commences (after the Agnihotra) with the election of the Brahman. The chief oblations of the day are (a cake to Agni, and) sour and sweet milk, offered separately to Indra at full moon; and mixed (as sânnâyya or payasyâ) to Mitra and Varuna at new moon.

At full moon some authorities add a special ishti to Indra Vimridh ('the Averter of evil'). The new-moon performance concludes with libations of whey to the divine coursers (the horses of the gods); and, optionally, with an ishti to Âditya.

The performance of the Dâkshâyana sacrifice was held to be obligatory only for a period of fifteen years (see XI, 1, 2, 13), whereas the ordinary new and full-moon offerings had to be performed for double that period from the setting up of the sacred fires. Nay, even the daily performance of it with certain modifications, for a whole year, was supposed to acquit the householder of any further obligation in this respect; his sacrificial duties being henceforth limited to the performance of the Agnihotra, or morning and evening libations. The daily performance of the Dâkshâyana is so regulated that an afternoon and following forenoon are alternately assigned to the two days' ceremonies of the ordinary fortnightly Dâkshâyana sacrifice.

1. In the beginning Pragâpati, being desirous of offspring, sacrificed with this sacrifice: 'May I abound in offspring and cattle; may I obtain prosperity; may I become glorious; may I become an eater of food!' so he thought.

2. Now he was indeed Daksha: and because

he sacrificed in the beginning with this sacrifice, it is called Dâkshâyana-sacrifice. Some, however, call it the Vasishtha-sacrifice; for he (Pragâpati) is indeed vasishtha (the best)[1], and after him they call it. He sacrificed with that sacrifice; and what race, what prosperity of Pragâpati was then produced through his performing that sacrifice, that same race he procreates, that same prosperity he obtains, whosoever, knowing this, performs that sacrifice: let him therefore perform that sacrifice.

3. Now that same sacrifice was afterwards performed by Pratîdarsa Svaikna; and he indeed was an authority[2] to those who emulated him. An authority, therefore, he will become, whosoever, knowing this, performs that sacrifice: let him, therefore, perform that sacrifice.

4. Him Suplan Sârñgaya approached for the sake of sanctity; and accordingly he was taught that sacrifice and another[3]; and having learnt it he went back to the Sriñgayas. Now they knew that he was coming to them after studying the sacrifice for their sake. They said, 'Verily, with the gods (saha devaih) he has come to us who has come after studying the sacrifice:' thus he (was called) Sahadeva Sârñgaya; and even now the saying is, 'Lo, Suplan has taken another name!' He performed that sacrifice; and what race and prosperity of the Sriñgayas was then produced through his performing that sacrifice, that same race he procreates, that same prosperity he obtains, whoso-

[1] The Kânva text has:—Sa u vâ ekena nâmnâ vasishthas, 'and with one of his names he (Pragâpati) is indeed (called) Vasishtha.'

[2] Vivakanam; vivâkanam, Kânva recension.

[3] Viz. the Sautrâmanî-sacrifice, according to XII, 8, 2, 3.

ever, knowing this, performs that sacrifice: let him, therefore, perform that sacrifice.

5. That same sacrifice was afterwards performed by Devabhâga *S*rautarsha. He was Purohita both to the Kurus and the *S*riñgayas. Now a very high position (is held by him) who is the Purohita of one kingdom: how much higher, then, is the position (of one) who (is the Purohita) of two (kingdoms). A very high position accordingly he obtains, whosoever, knowing this, performs that sacrifice: let him, therefore, perform that sacrifice.

6. That same sacrifice was afterwards performed by Daksha Pârvati; and even to this day these (descendants of his) the Dâkshâya*n*as are possessed of the royal dignity: royal dignity he, therefore, here obtains, whosoever, knowing this, performs that sacrifice: let him, therefore, perform that sacrifice.—Day by day there is one cake[1]: thereby Fortune (*s*rî) is (wedded) to him without a rival wife and undisturbed. He offers on two days of the full moon and on two of the new moon: for two means a pair, so that a productive pair is thereby obtained.

7. Now when[2], at full moon, he offers a (cake) to Agni and Soma on the first day,—these are two deities, and two means a pair: hence a productive pair is thereby obtained.

8. And on the morrow there are Agni's cake and Indra's Sânnâyya[3],—these are two deities, and two means a pair, so that a productive pair is thereby obtained.

---

[1] Viz. on the first day of the full moon a cake to Agni-Soma; on that of new moon a cake to Indra-Agni; and on the second day of either ceremony the (ordinary) cake to Agni.

[2] Or, 'Now, as to the reason why' (yad) here and in the sequel.

[3] See I, 6, 4, 9 seq.

9. Again when, at new moon, he offers a (cake) to Indra and Agni on the first day,—these are two deities, and two means a pair, so that a productive pair is thereby obtained.

10. Then on the morrow there are Agni's cake and Mitra and Varuna's curds. Now Agni's cake (is offered), for the sole purpose that it may not forsake the sacrifice[1]. Then those two, Mitra and Varuna, are two deities, and two means a pair: hence a productive pair is thereby obtained; and thus is (produced) that form (of the sacrifice) whereby he becomes many, whereby he is reproduced.

11. And when, at full moon, he offers the Agni-Soma (cake) on the first day, then this is for him that victim which they slaughter for Agni and Soma on the fast-day (of the Soma-sacrifice)[2].

12. And on the morrow there are Agni's cake and Indra's Sânnâyya. Now Agni's cake is for him what the morning libation is (at the Soma-sacrifice), for the morning libation is indeed sacred to Agni; and the Sânnâyya is for him the mid-day libation, for the mid-day libation is indeed sacred to Indra.

13. And again when, at new moon, he offers the Indra-Agni (cake) on the first day, that is for him the same as the third (or evening) libation; for the third libation is sacred to the All-gods, and Indra and Agni truly are all the gods[3].

14. And on the morrow there are Agni's cake and Mitra and Varuna's curds. Now Agni's cake is (offered) for the sole purpose that it should not

[1] See I, 6, 2, 6, with note.

[2] On the upavasatha (fast-day, or day of preparation) preceding the Soma-sacrifice a he-goat is sacrificed to Agni and Soma.

[3] Compare II, 4, 3, 5 seq.

forsake the sacrifice; and that dish of curds (payasyâ) is to him the same as that barren cow, the anûbandhyâ, which has to be slaughtered for Mitra and Varuna (at the Soma-sacrifice)[1]: thus by performing the full and new-moon offering one gains as much as is gained by performing a Soma-sacrifice; and that (offering) is indeed a great sacrifice.

15. And again when, at full moon, he offers the Agni-Soma (cake) on the first day,—it was by that (offering) that Indra slew Vritra[2]; it was thereby he gained that supreme authority which he now wields[3]: and so does he (the sacrificer) thereby slay his wicked spiteful enemy and gain the superiority. And as to his mixing (sweet and sour milk),—the Sânnâyya is (the oblation) of the new moon (amâ-vâsyâ)[4], and the new moon[5] means being far away: to him who had slain Vritra this was forthwith (offered), and him they regaled with that draught. He therefore who, knowing this, prepares the Sânnâyya at full moon, forthwith

---

[1] In connection with the so-called udayanîyâ ishti, or concluding offering, of the Soma-sacrifice, a barren cow, called anûbandhyâ (literally, 'to be bound afterwards'), is offered to Mitra and Varuna. In default of such a cow, an ox, or even a dish of curds (payasyâ) serves the same purpose. See Kâty. Sr. X, 9, 12–15; Sat. Br. IV, 5, 2, 1 seq.

[2] See I, 6, 4, 12.

[3] Thus the frequently-occurring phrase 'vyagayata yâsyeyam vigitis tâm' (literally, 'he conquered that conquest which is now theirs') has been translated throughout.

[4] On the derivation of amâ-vâsyâ ('dwelling at home, or together'), see I, 6, 4, 3 seq.

[5] Or, 'the dwelling at home,' or '(Indra's) dwelling together (with Agni) means (Indra, the Vritra-slayer) being far away.'

drives away evil. Now that moon doubtless is king Soma, the food of the gods: they extract it on the first day, intending to consume it on the next day; consequently when that (moon) wanes, it is being consumed by them.

16. And when, at full moon, he offers the Agni-Soma (cake) on the first day, he thereby (as it were) extracts that (Soma); and, when extracted, he adds that juice to it, and makes it strong by means of that juice[1]. Whosoever, then, knowing this, prepares the Sânnâyya at full moon, renders his offering palatable to the gods, and his offering is palatable to the gods.

17. And again as to why, at new moon, he offers the Indra-Agni (cake) on the first day. Indra and Agni doubtless are the deities of the new and full moon: it is to these, therefore, that he offers directly and expressly; and directly to the new and full moon is offering made by him who thus knows this.

18. And on the morrow there is Agni's cake and Mitra and Varu*n*a's curds. Now Agni's cake is (offered) for the sole purpose that it may not forsake the sacrifice. Mitra and Varu*n*a, on the other hand, are the two half-moons: the waxing one is Varu*n*a, and the waning one is Mitra. During that night (of new moon) these two meet, and when they are thus together he pleases them with that (cake-offering): and, verily, all is pleased with him, all is obtained by him who thus knows this.

19. In that same night Mitra implants seed in Varu*n*a, and when it (the moon) wanes, then it is

[1] See I, 6, 4, 6 seq.

produced from that seed. Now as to why that oblation of curds (payasyâ) to Mitra and Varu*n*a is here exactly analogous (to the Sânnâyya offered at new moon)[1].

20. The new moon doubtless is entitled to the Sânnâyya: it is prepared both then and at full moon. Now were he also here (at the full-moon offering) to mix together (the sweet and sour milk), he would commit a repetition and cause a quarrel (between the respective gods)[2]. Having collected that (Soma or moon) from the waters and plants, he causes him to be born from out of the oblations; and on being born from the oblations, he is visible in the western (sky).

21. It is through union that he produces him: the curds (payasyâ, fem.) are female, and the whey is seed. Now what is produced by union is (produced) properly: hence he thereby produces him by a productive union; and therefore there is an offering of curds.

---

[1] Or, to the offering of sour and sweet milk at full moon; see next note. The Kâ*n*va text has: 'Now as to why the oblation of curds is here made exactly analogous (at the full and new-moon ceremonies).' Perhaps it may also refer to the exact correspondence of the offering of curds to Mitra and Varu*n*a at new moon and at the Soma-sacrifice.

[2] At the new-moon offering of the Dâkshâya*n*a, the sânnâyya or payasyâ offered to Mitra and Varu*n*a is prepared in the ordinary way (as at the new-moon ceremony), by fresh (boiled or unboiled) milk being added to the sour milk of the preceding night's milking. At the full-moon offering, on the other hand, the sour and sweet milk remain separate, and constitute two different havis, or sacrificial dishes, dedicated to Indra. The terms san-nî ('to bring together') and sânnâyya are here likewise applied to the offering of the separate substances.

22. He then offers the whey[1] to the (divine) Coursers. Now the Coursers are the seasons, and the whey is seed: and thus the seed is cast properly, and the seasons bring forth the seed so cast in the form of these creatures. This is why he offers the whey to the Coursers.

23. He offers, as it were, behind the sacrifice: for it is from behind that the male approaches and impregnates the female. He first offers in the east. With 'O Agni, accept . . . !' he repeats the Vasha*t*, —this is in lieu of the Svish*t*ak*ri*t; and (the latter)[2] he offers in the east.

24. He then sprinkles (the whey) in the several quarters, with the texts (Vâ*g*. S. VI, 19 b–g), 'The quarters!—The fore-quarters (pra-dis)!—The by-quarters (â-dis)!—The intermediate quarters (vi-dis)! The upper quarters (ud-dis)!—To the quarters,—Svâhâ[3]!' Five are the quarters, and five the

---

[1] Before the oblations of curds are made, the whey is poured off into a vessel (then optionally sprinkled with butter), and placed on the utkara, or heap of rubbish. After the stalk of grass has been thrown into the fire (see I, 8, 3, 19), or after the dismissal of the spoons (I, 8, 3, 27), the Adhvaryu takes the whey and sprinkles the barhis (the grass covering on the altar) with it. He then pours the remaining whey into the *g*uhû spoon and calls on the Hot*ri* to recite the invitatory prayer to the Coursers. Thereupon he betakes himself with the spoon to the north of the fire, calls on the Hot*ri* for the offering-formula, and at the two concluding Vasha*t*s pours some of the whey into the east part of the fire. He then sits down and sprinkles the whey on the fire according to the several quarters, beginning in the east, and moving around from left to right (pradakshi*n*am), with the respective texts, Vâ*g*. S. VI, 19 b–e; after which he makes two more libations in the centre and east part of the fire, with VI, 19 f and g.

[2] The Kâ*n*va text has tadu instead of sa vai. On the oblation to Agni as 'the maker of good offering,' see I, 7, 3, 1 seq.

[3] Svâhâ is uttered after each formula,—'The quarters, Svâhâ!' &c.

seasons: he thus effects a union between the quarters and the seasons [1].

25. Five partake of that (whey remaining in the spoon),—viz. the Hot*ri*, the Adhvaryu, the Brahman, the Âgnîdhra, and the Sacrificer; for five are the seasons, so that the characteristic nature of the seasons is thereby obtained; and the seed that is cast is firmly implanted in the seasons. The sacrificer partakes of it first, thinking, 'May I first obtain seed!' But also last (he partakes of it)[2], thinking, 'May seed remain in me last of all!' By saying, 'Invited,—invite thou[3]!' they make it (the whey to resemble) the Soma.

FIFTH ADHYÂYA. FIRST BRÂHMA*N*A.

V. THE *K*ÂTURMÂSYÂNI OR SEASONAL SACRIFICES.

A. THE VAI*S*VADEVA.

The three seasonal or four-monthly sacrifices are performed at the parvans, or commencement of the three seasons (spring, rainy

---

[1] *Ri*tûn evaitad digbhir mithunân karoti, Kâ*n*va recension.

[2] The author does not express himself quite clearly. The sacrificer is to partake of the whey before the priests and also (or, as an alternative) after them. According to Kâty. IV, 4, 26–27, the sacrificer is to eat either last of all, or first and last. The Kâ*n*va text has: Prathamo ya*g*amâno bhakshayati prathamo reta*h* parig*ri*h*n*âmîty athottamo mayy uttama*m* reta*h* pratitish*th*âd iti,—accordingly he is to eat first and last.

[3] Each of them, in his respective order, takes the spoon, calls on the others in the same order with 'O sacrificer (Hot*ri*, Adhvaryu, &c.) invite!' Their permission having been given by 'Invited (thou art)!' he then takes some of the whey, with one of the texts: 'I eat thee, the courser (or whey, vâ*g*inam) of the seasons, the coursers!' 'I, the courser (or, mighty one) eat, invited, of the invited, to the whey.' 'May I be a racer in the race!' Kâty. IV, 4, 13–15.

season, and autumn), viz. the Vaisvadeva generally on the full moon of Phâlguna; the Varunapraghâsâh on that of Âshâdha; and the Sâkamedhâh on that of Kârttika. As a fourth Kâturmâsya, ritual authorities add the Sunâsîrîya, though they are at variance as to the exact time of its performance; and neither is its true significance clearly indicated. It apparently marks merely the conclusion of the seasonal offerings (which, as a rule, are only performed once, cf. II, 6, 3, 12 seq.); but while the author of the Satapatha allows it to be performed at any time (within four months) after the Sâkamedhâh, other ritualists hold that its performance should take place on the fifth full moon after the Sâkamedhâh, or, in other words, exactly a year after the Vaisvadeva. See Weber, Nakshatra, II, p. 334 seq.

1. Verily, in the beginning, Pragâpati alone existed here[1]. He thought within himself, 'How can I be propagated?' He toiled and practised austerities. He created living beings[2]. The living beings created by him passed away: they are those birds. Now man is the nearest to Pragâpati; and man is two-footed: hence birds are two-footed.

2. Pragâpati thought within himself, 'Even as formerly I was alone, so also am I now alone.' He created a second (race of beings); they also passed away: they are those small crawling reptiles other than snakes. He created a third (race), they say; they also passed away: they are those snakes. Yâgñavalkya, on his part, declared them to be of two kinds only; but of three kinds they are according to the Rik.

3. While praising and practising austerities, Pragâ-

[1] Or, Pragâpati alone was this (universe). Cf. Muir, Original Sanskrit Texts, p. 70.

[2] By pragâh, or (living) beings, mammalia—especially man and domestic animals—seem to be understood.

pati thought within himself, 'How comes it that the living beings created by me pass away?' He then became aware that his creatures passed away from want of food. He made the breasts in the fore-part of (their) body[1] teem with milk. He then created living beings; and by resorting to the breasts, the beings created by him thenceforward continued to exist: they are these (creatures) which have not passed away.

4. Hence it has been said by the *Ri*shi[2],—'Three generations have passed beyond,'—this is said regarding those that passed away;—'Others settled down around the light (arka, the sun)'—the light doubtless is the fire: those creatures which did not pass away, settled down around the fire; it is with regard to them that this is said.

5. 'The great one (neut.)[3] remained within the worlds'—it is with regard to Pra*g*âpati that this is said.—'The blower (or, purifier) entered the regions'—the regions doubtless are the quarters, and these were indeed entered by that blowing wind: it is with regard to them that this verse was uttered. And in like manner as Pra*g*âpati created these living beings, so they are propagated: for whenever the breasts of woman and the udder of cattle swell, then whatever is born is born; and by resorting to the breasts these (beings) continue to exist.

6. Now that milk is indeed food; for in the beginning Pra*g*âpati produced it for food. But that

---

[1] Âtmana evâgre; the Kâ*n*va text has âtmany evâgre.

[2] Rig-veda VIII, 90, 14.

[3] Or perhaps better, as Ludwig takes it, 'On high he took his place within the worlds.'

food also means living beings (progeny), since it is by food that they exist: by resorting to the breasts of those who have milk, they continue to exist. And those who have no milk are nursed by the former as soon as they are born; and thus they exist by means of food, and hence food means progeny.

7. He who is desirous of offspring, sacrifices with that oblation, and thereby makes himself the sacrifice, which is Pragâpati[1].

8. In the first place[2] there is a cake for Agni on eight potsherds. Agni indeed is the root, the progenitor of the deities; he is Pragâpati ('lord of creatures'): hence there is a cake for Agni.

9. Then follows a potful of boiled rice (*k*aru) for Soma. Soma doubtless is seed, and that in Agni, the progenitor; he (Agni) casts the seed Soma: thus there is at the outset a productive union.

10. Then follows a cake on twelve or eight potsherds[3] for Savitri. Savitri indeed is the impeller (pra-savitri) of the gods; he is Pragâpati, the intermediate[4] progenitor: hence the cake to Savitri.

11. Then follows a potful of boiled rice for Sarasvatî; and another for Pûshan. Sarasvatî doubtless is a woman, and Pûshan is a man: thus there is again a productive union. Through that twofold productive union Pragâpati created the living beings,—

[1] ? Or, Pragâpati, the real, the existent, 'Pragâpatim bhûtam.'

[2] Instead of the preliminary Anvârambhanîyâ-ishti (see p. 7), a special ishti may be performed on this occasion, with a cake on twelve potsherds to Agni Vaisvânara, and a potful of boiled rice (*k*aru) to Parganya, for oblations. Kâty. V, 1, 2–4.

[3] According to Taitt. S. I, 8, 2, it is one on twelve potsherds.

[4] Madhyatah, lit. 'from the middle.'

through the one (he created) the upright, and through the other those looking to the ground. This is why there are these five oblations[1].

12. After that (follows), as a foundation for the curds, a cake on seven potsherds for the Maruts. The Maruts indeed are the people (visah), the people of the gods. They roamed about here entirely unimpeded. Having approached Pragâpati, when he was sacrificing, they said, 'We shall destroy those creatures of thine which thou art about to create by means of this offering[2].'

13. Pragâpati reflected, 'My former creatures have passed away; and if those (Maruts) destroy these (creatures), then nothing will be left.' He accordingly set aside for them that share, the Maruts' cake on seven potsherds; and that is this same cake on seven potsherds for the Maruts. The reason why it is one of seven potsherds, is that the host of the Maruts is (distributed in troops) of seven each[3]. This is why there is a cake on seven potsherds for the Maruts.

14. Let him offer it to the 'self-strong' (Maruts); since they gained that share for themselves. [If], however, they (the priests) do not find an invitatory and an offering prayer (addressed) to the 'self-strong' (Maruts)[4], let it be (offered) simply to the

---

[1] While the five preceding oblations are common to all the seasonal offerings (Kâty. V, 1, 15), the succeeding ones are peculiar to the Vaisvadeva.

[2] The Kânva text adds, 'if thou wilt not assign a share to us.'

[3] In Rig-veda VIII, 96, 8, the Maruts are said to be sixty-three in number, divided into nine troops of seven each.

[4] The Kânva text has: Tad uta yâgyânuvâkye svatavatyau na vindanti; yadi yâgyânuvâkye svatavatyau na vinded api mârutyâv eva syâtâm.

Maruts. It is offered for the safety of creatures: hence it is offered to the Maruts.

15. Thereupon follows the oblation of curds (payasyâ). Now it is on milk that the creatures subsist, it was by means of milk that they were preserved: hence he now offers to them that by which they were preserved, and whereon they subsist; and the beings whom he creates by means of the foregoing offerings, subsist on that milk, on that oblation of curds.

16. Therein a union takes place: the curdled milk (payasyâ, fem.) is female, and the whey is seed. From that union the infinite All was gradually generated; and since the infinite All was gradually generated from that union, therefore it (the offering of curds) belongs to the All-gods.

17. Then follows a cake on one potsherd for Heaven and Earth. Now when Pragâpati had created the living beings by those offerings, he enclosed them within heaven and earth; and so they are now enclosed within heaven and earth. And in like manner he, who by means of those oblations creates living beings, thereby encloses them within heaven and earth: this is why there is a cake on one potsherd for Heaven and Earth.

18. Now as to the course of proceeding. They do not raise an uttara-vedi[1] in order that it (the sacred work) may be unobstructed, that it may be entire, that it may be (worthy) of the All-gods.—The barhis is tied up in three (bunches), and then

[1] The uttara-vedi, or northern (or upper) altar, is not required at the performance of the Vaisvadeva, but at that of the Varuna-praghâsâh; see II, 5, 2, 5 seq.

again in one[1]; for such is the characteristic form of generation, since father and mother are a productive (pair), and what is born forms a third element: hence that which is threefold is again (made) one. Thereto flowering shoots (of sacrificial grass) are tied: these he uses for the prastara[2]; for this is a productive union, and productive indeed are flowering shoots: this is why he takes flowering shoots for the prastara.

19. On putting the sacrificial dishes in their place, they churn the fire[3]. For it was after Agni was born that Pra*g*âpati's offspring was born; and so for this (sacrificer) also offspring is born after Agni (the fire) has been produced: this is why they churn the fire, after they have deposited the sacrificial dishes in their place.

---

[1] Three bunches of sacrificial grass are tied together with one band. Kâty. V, 1, 25.

[2] For the prastara, or bunch of grass representing the sacrificer, see I, 3, 3, 5 seq.; I, 8, 3, 11 seq.

[3] Kâty. V, 1, 27 seq. supplies the following details:—With the text (Vâ*g*. V, 2 a, &c.), 'Agni's birth-place art thou,' the Adhvaryu takes up a piece of wood and puts it on the altar. With 'the two testicles are ye' he lays on it two stalks of sacrificial grass. With 'Urva*s*î thou art' he places the lower ara*n*i (see p. 294, note 3) thereon. With 'Âyus (old age, or the son of Purûravas and Urva*s*î) thou art' he touches the butter in the pot with the upper ara*n*i; and with 'Purûravas thou art' he puts it down on the lower ara*n*i. He then calls on the Hot*ri* to recite 'to the fire being churned out.' With the three formulas 'with the gâyatrî (trish*t*ubh, *g*agatî) metre I churn thee!' he churns thrice from left to right, and then alternately both ways until fire is produced. He then calls on the Hot*ri* to recite 'to the born fire' (Sâṅkh. III, 13, 21); and in carrying the fire towards the Âhavanîya he makes him recite 'to (the fire) being carried forward.' With the text V, 3, he throws it down on the Âhavanîya hearth; and (having put a kindling-stick on it) he makes two libations of butter thereon with V, 4.

20. [At the Vaisvadeva-offering] there are nine fore-offerings and nine after-offerings[1]. Now the virâg metre consists of ten syllables: hence he obtains both times an inferior (incomplete) virâg for the sake of production, because it was from that inferior (lower) source of production[2] that Pragâpati twice produced creatures—both the upright and those looking to the ground. This is why (the Vaisvadeva) has nine fore-offerings and nine after-offerings.

21. There are three Samishtayagus[3]; for this (offering) is decidedly greater than an (ordinary) havir-yagña[4], since it has nine fore-offerings and nine after-offerings. However, there may also be only a single Samishtayagus, since this is a havir-yagña. The priest's fee for it (consists of) the first-born calf (of the season).

22. And what race, what prosperity accrued to Pragâpati from his offering this sacrifice, that same race he produces, that same prosperity he attains

---

[1] The same number of prayâgas and anuyâgas are prescribed for the Varunapraghâsâh (see II, 5, 2, 30 and 41, with notes) and for the Mahâhavis of the Sâkamedhâh. Kâty. V, 2, 8.

[2] Or rather, from that productive nyûna (womb, lit. defective, lower); see II, 1, 1, 13.

[3] See I, 9, 2, 25 seq. The formula used, if there be only one Samishtayagus, is the same as at the Darsapûrnamâsa, viz. II, 21 b (VIII, 21). If there are three, they are offered to the wind (vâta), the sacrifice, and the lord of sacrifice respectively; the formulas Vâg. S. VIII, 22 a b being used with the second and third. Kâty. V, 2, 9. For the Varunapraghâsâh and Sâkamedhâh three Samishtayagus are prescribed, and for the Sunâsîrîya only one.

[4] Viz. such as the new and full-moon sacrifice, which serves as the model sacrifice, and at which there are only five fore-offerings and three after-offerings. See I, 5, 3, 1 seq.; I, 8, 2, 7 seq.

whosoever, knowing this, offers this sacrifice: let him therefore perform this sacrifice.

SECOND BRÂHMANA.

B. THE VARUNAPRAGHÂSA OFFERINGS.

1. Now it was by means of the Vaisvadeva that Pragâpati produced living beings. The beings produced by him ate (ghas) Varuna's barley corn; for originally the barley belonged to Varuna. And from their eating Varuna's barley corn the name Varunapraghâsâh (is derived).

2. Varuna seized them; and on being seized by Varuna, they became rent all over[1]; and they lay and sat them down breathing in and breathing out. The out-breathing and in-breathing forsook them not, but all the other deities[2] forsook them; and owing to these two, the creatures did not perish.

3. Pragâpati healed them by means of that oblation: both the creatures that were born and those that were unborn he delivered from Varuna's noose; and his creatures were born without disease and blemish.

4. Now when this (sacrificer) performs these offerings in the fourth month (after the Vaisvadeva), he does so either because thus Varuna does not seize his offspring, or because the gods performed (the same offering); and both the children that have been born to him and those that are yet unborn he thereby delivers from Varuna's noose, and his children are born without disease and blemish. This is why he performs these offerings in the fourth month.

---

[1] Paridîrna, i.e. swollen, dropsical.

[2] In the St. Petersb. Dict. devatâ is here taken as 'organ of sense.

5. At this (sacrifice) there are two altars and two fires [1]. The reason why there are two altars and two

[1] For the performance of the Varunapraghâsâh the Adhvaryu and his assistant, the Pratiprasthâtri, have to prepare,—to the east of the Âhavanîya, and at the distance of at least three steps (prakrama) from it,—two altars, separate from each other by about a span (of thumb and fore-finger), one south of the other. The northern one, belonging to the Adhvaryu, is to measure between four and five cubits along the west side, and between three and four cubits along the east side; the two sides being between six and eight cubits distant from each other. The southern altar, reserved for the Pratiprasthâtri, is to be of the usual size of the altar at the haviryagñâ. The ceremonies, detailed in I, 2, Brâhmanas 4 and 5, have to be performed also on the present occasion. In the middle of the east side of the northern altar a stake is fixed in the ground. On the north side of the northern altar, and contiguous with it, a pit (kâtvâla), 1⅓ cubits (the length of the wedge) square, is dug, so as to be separated on the west from the utkara (heap of rubbish) by a narrow passage. With the mould dug up from the pit, the so-called uttara-vedi (upper or north altar) is raised on the northern altar, either of the same dimensions as the pit (1⅓ cubits square) or one third of the area of the northern altar, and so that the stake marks the middle of its east side. In the centre of this mound he makes a hollow (or 'navel'), a span square; and the whole mound is then bestrewed with fine gravel. The texts used while tracing the sides of the pit, thrice throwing the wooden sword within the marked-off space, and raising the uttara-vedi, are given Vâg. S. V, 9–10. During the night the uttara-vedi remains covered with udumbara or plaksha branches or with sacrificial grass. Next morning the two fires for the newly-constructed fire-places are taken from the Âhavanîya, either by dividing the latter into two equal parts, or by means of two bundles of firewood (threefold bound, see p. 389, note 1), lighted at it, and carried eastwards in a pan covered with sand or mould. While the fires, together with the lustral water and a spoonful of ghee, taken from the pot by five ladlings with the sruva, are taken eastward, the Hotri thrice recites the verse 'Pra devyam deva,' &c.; and the Pratiprasthâtri draws, with the wooden sword, a line from the Âhavanîya to the south-west corner (or 'right hip') of the northern altar, or to the uttara-vedi. The Adhvaryu, standing between the two altars, then besprinkles the uttara-vedi with water, while muttering the

fires, is that thereby one frees the creatures from Varuna's noose both ways,—on the one side (he frees) the upright, and on the other those looking to the ground: this is why there are two altars and two fires.

6. On the northern (uttara) altar he raises the uttara-vedi (upper or north altar), not on the southern one. Varuna, doubtless, is the nobility, and the Maruts are the people: he thus makes the nobility superior (uttara) to the people; and hence people here serve the Kshatriya, placed above them. This is why he raises the uttara-vedi on the northern, not on the southern altar.

7. In the first place there are those five oblations[1]. For by means of those five oblations Pragâpati produced the creatures, with them he freed the creatures both ways from Varuna's noose,—on the one side (he freed) the upright, and on the other those that tend to the ground: this is why there are those five oblations.

8. Then follows a cake on twelve potsherds for Indra and Agni. Indra and Agni indeed are the out-breathing and in-breathing: thus this is like

---

texts Vâg. S. V, 11; whereupon he pours out on it crosswise the spoonful of clarified butter, with the texts V, 12; and lays, with the mantras V, 13, three enclosing-sticks (paridhi) of pîtadâru wood round the 'navel' (see I, 3, 4, 2 seq.), and puts bdellium, fragrant reed-grass, and the front-hair of a ram on the 'navel' as a foundation (sambhâra, see II, 1, 1, 1 seq.) for the fire, which is then laid down thereon. On a hearth-mound (khara), a cubit square, formed on the southern altar, the Pratiprasthâtri also lays down his fire, after performing the usual fivefold lustration (see p. 2). Thereupon the pranîtâ-water is brought forward in the way set forth at I, 1, 1, 12 seq. Kâty. V, 3, 9–4, 21. For a different mode of transferring the fire to the special fire-places, see p. 396, note 1.

[1] See II, 5, 1, 11, with note.

doing a good turn to one who has done him a good turn; for it is owing to these two that his creatures[1] did not perish. Hence he now restores his creatures by means of the out-breathing and in-breathing, bestows out-breathing and in-breathing on them: this is why there is a cake on twelve potsherds for Indra and Agni.

9. On both (fires) there is an oblation of curds. It is on milk that the creatures subsist and by means of milk that they were preserved: hence it is with that by which they were preserved and whereon they subsist, that he delivers them both ways from Varu*n*a's noose,—on the one side (he delivers) the upright and on the other those looking to the ground. This is why there is an oblation of curds on both (fires).

10. The northern one is offered to Varu*n*a, since it was Varu*n*a who seized his (Pra*g*âpati's) creatures: hence he thereby directly delivers them from Varu*n*a's noose. The southern one is offered to the Maruts. It is for the sake of diversity that it is offered to the Maruts; for a repetition he would undoubtedly commit, were he to offer both to Varu*n*a. Moreover, it was from the south that the Maruts intended to slay his (Pra*g*âpati's) creatures, and with that share he propitiated them: for this reason the southern (oblation of curds) belongs to the Maruts.

11. Upon both (dishes of curds) he scatters karîra-fruits[2]; for with karîra-fruits Pra*g*âpati

---

[1] That is, his offspring and cattle.

[2] The fruit of Capparis Aphylla. According to Sâya*n*a, on Taitt. I, 8, 3, it is karîra-shoots—which he says resemble the Soma-creeper (somavallî)—that are so used; but he also mentions that some authorities take karîra to mean the fruit. According to a sûtra he

bestowed happiness (ka) on the creatures, and so does he (the sacrificer) thereby bestow happiness on the creatures.

12. Upon both of them he also scatters *s*amî-leaves; for with *s*amî-leaves Pra*g*âpati bestowed bliss (*s*am) on the creatures, and so does he now thereby bestow bliss on the creatures.

13. Then follows a cake on one potsherd for Ka (Pra*g*âpati); for by that cake on one potsherd to Ka Pra*g*âpati indeed bestowed happiness (ka) on the creatures, and so does he (the sacrificer) now bestow happiness on the creatures by that one-cup cake: this is why there is a cake on one potsherd for Ka.

14. And on the first day, after husking and slightly roasting barley on the Dakshi*n*âgni, they prepare therewith as many dishes of karambha[1] as there are members of the (sacrificer's) family, exceeded by one.

15. At the same time they also prepare a ram and a ewe; and if he be able to procure wool other than from e*d*aka sheep, let him wash it and stick it on both the ram and the ewe; but should he not be able to procure wool other than from e*d*aka sheep, tufts of ku*s*a grass may also be (used).

16. The reason why there are a ram and a ewe is that the ram manifestly is Varu*n*a's victim, so that he thereby manifestly delivers the creatures from Varu*n*a's noose. They are made of barley, because it was when they (the creatures) had eaten barley that Varu*n*a seized them. A pair they form, so that he

---

quotes, above a hundred *s*amî-leaves and above a thousand karîras should be strewn over the two dishes of curds. Cf. Taitt. Br. I, 6, 5, 5.

[1] A kind of porridge prepared with roasted barley, coarsely ground, and sour curds.

delivers the creatures from Varu*n*a's noose through conjugal union.

17. The ewe he places on the southern, and the ram on the northern dish of curds; for in this way alone a proper union is effected, since the woman lies on the left (or north) side of the man.

18. The Adhvaryu places all the (other) sacrificial dishes upon the northern altar; and the Pratiprasthât*ri* places on the southern altar that dish of curds (belonging to the Maruts).

19. Having thus placed the sacrificial dishes, he churns the fire; and having churned it and placed it on (the hearth)[1], he offers thereon. The Adhvaryu in the first place says (to the Hot*ri*)[2], 'Recite to the fire that is being kindled!' Both (the Adhvaryu and the Pratiprasthât*ri*) then put firewood on (the fire) and both reserve one kindling-stick each; and they both pour out the first libation (âghâra). Thereupon the Adhvaryu says, 'Agnîdh, trim the fire!' Although the summons is given, the trimming does not take place (immediately)[3].

20. Thereupon the Pratiprasthât*ri* returns (to where the sacrificer's wife is seated). When he is about to lead the wife away, he asks her, 'With

---

[1] The author here apparently alludes to a different way of transferring the fire to the new fire-places from that detailed by Kâtyâyana (see p. 392, note 1). The same mode seems to be referred to by the Paddhati on Kâty. V, 4 (p. 467). According to this mode (called samâropa*n*a, or mounting of the fire), the old fires are 'taken up' by means of the two ara*n*is being lighted, or rather heated, at them, and then 'churned out' and placed on the newly-prepared hearth-mounds.

[2] For the detailed course of procedure, see I, 3, 5, 1 seq.

[3] Asa*m*s*ri*sh*t*am eva bhavati sampreshitam. The Kâ*n*va recension reads, asa*m*s*ri*sh*t*a evâgnir bhavati sampreshita*h*. Cf. par. 30.

whom holdest thou intercourse?' Now when a woman who belongs to one (man) carries on intercourse with another, she undoubtedly commits (a sin) against Varu*n*a. He therefore thus asks her, lest she should sacrifice with a secret pang in her mind; for when confessed the sin becomes less, since it becomes truth; this is why he thus asks her. And whatever (connection) she confesses[1] not, that indeed will turn out injurious to her relatives.

21. He then makes her say the text (III, 44), 'We invoke the Maruts, the voracious consumers of enemies, delighting in their porridge.' This (verse) is (of like import) as the invitatory prayer: she therewith invites them to these dishes[2].

22. Of these (dishes) there is one for each descendant; as many (children) as there are in the (sacrificer's) family, so many (dishes) there are, exceeded by one. There being one for each descendant, he thereby delivers from Varu*n*a's noose one by one the children born to him; and there being an additional one, he thereby delivers from Varu*n*a's

---

[1] According to Kâty. V, 5, 7–9, she is either to give the total number or the names of her lovers, or to hold up as many stalks of grass. [If she have none, she is to reply, 'with no one else.' Comm.]—'He makes the wife speak (confess): (thereby) he renders her pure, and then he leads her to penance. Were she not to reveal (the name of) a paramour she has, she would harm a dear relative. Let her declare "N. N. is my paramour," by thus declaring (any one) she causes him to be seized by Varu*n*a.' Taitt. Br. I, 6, 5, 2.

[2] According to the Black Yagus, the Pratiprasthât*ri* mutters this formula, while leading the mistress to the place of offering. The sacrificer then recites as the invitatory prayer the verse given in par. 28 (Vâg. S. III, 46); while the offering-prayer (Vâg. S. III, 45) and the text III, 47 (par. 29) are muttered by both the husband and wife. Taitt. I, 6, 5, 3 argues against the practice of the wife being made to pronounce the anuvâkyâ.

noose those children of his that are as yet unborn: this is why there are (the same number of dishes) exceeded by one.

23. (In the form of) dishes they are, because it is from dishes that food is eaten; and of barley they are prepared, because it was when they (the creatures) had eaten the barley corn that Varuna seized them. From the winnowing basket she offers, because food is prepared by means of the winnowing basket. The wife offers (together with her husband): thus he delivers his offspring from Varuna's noose through conjugal union.

24. She offers previously to the sacrifice, previously to the oblations, since the people do not eat offerings, and the Maruts are the people. Now when Pragâpati's creatures, being seized by Varuna, became rent all over, and sat and lay them down, breathing in and breathing out, then the Maruts destroyed their sin; and so do the Maruts now destroy the sin of his (the sacrificer's) offspring. This is why she offers previously to the sacrifice, previously to the oblations.

25. He[1] offers in the southern fire, with the text (III, 45), 'Whatever (sin we have committed) in the village and forest,'—for both in the village and in the forest sin is committed;—'whatever in society and in our own self,'—by 'whatever (we have committed) in society,' he means to say 'against man;' and by 'whatever in our own self' (indriya), he means to say 'against the gods;'—'whatever sin

[1] According to Kâty. V, 5, 11, either the mistress alone offers, or she together with her husband. In the latter case, the offering-formula (as well as the dedicatory formula, 'This to the Maruts') is pronounced by both.

we have here committed, that we expiate by offering, Svâhâ!'—whereby he says 'whatsoever sin we have committed, from all that we rid ourselves.'

26. Thereupon he mutters the (verse) addressed to Indra and referring to the Maruts.—Now when the Maruts destroyed the sin of Pra*g*âpati's creatures, he thought within himself, 'I hope they will not destroy my creatures.'

27. He muttered that (verse) addressed to Indra and referring to the Maruts. Indra indeed is the nobility, and the Maruts are the people; and the nobility are the controllers of the people: 'They shall be controlled,' he thought; and therefore (that verse, Vâ*g*. S. III, 46) is addressed to Indra.

28. 'Let there not, O Indra, be (fight) for us here in battles with the gods, since there is a share for thee in the sacrifice, O fiery one!—for thee, the mighty showerer of gifts, whose Maruts the song of the offerer stream-like celebrates.'

29. He then makes her say the text (Vâ*g*. S. III, 47), 'The men skilled in the work have done the work,'—those skilled in the work have indeed done the work;—'with pleasing song;'—for with song they have done it. 'Having done the work for the gods;'—for the gods indeed they have done the work;—'go home, ye companions!'—they are now together with her while she is led thither from an other place: hence she says, 'ye companions' (sa*k*âbhû, 'being together'). 'Go home,' she says, because that wife doubtless is the hind part of the sacrifice, and he has just now made her take her seat to the east of the sacrifice. 'Home' doubtless means the house, and the house is a resting-place: hence he thereby makes her rest in that resting-place, the house.

30. Having led her back (to her seat) the Pratiprasthâtri returns (to his place by the side of the southern altar). They now trim the fire[1]. When the fire has been trimmed, both (the Adhvaryu and Pratiprasthâtri) make the second libation (of butter). Thereupon the Adhvaryu, having called (on the Âgnîdhra) for the 'Sraushat,' chooses the Hotri. The chosen Hotri then seats himself on the Hotri's seat beside the northern altar; and having seated himself, he urges (the Adhvaryu and Pratiprasthâtri) to proceed. Being thus urged to proceed, they both take up the spoons and step across (to the south side of the fires). After stepping across and calling for the 'Sraushat,' the Adhvaryu says (to the Hotri), 'Pronounce the offering-prayer on the kindling-sticks!' and 'Pronounce the offering-prayer!' at each (subsequent fore-offering). Pouring (the butter in the spoons) together (into the guhû) at the fourth[2], they both proceed with the nine fore-offerings[3].

31. Thereupon the Adhvaryu says (to the Hotri),

[1] The Kânva text has more correctly, 'He trims both fires;' since it is the Âgnîdhra who has to trim both the northern and southern fires. See par. 19.

[2] The recipients of the first four fore-offerings are the same as at the normal haviryagña (cf. p. 146 note), viz. 1. the kindling-sticks (samidhs); 2. Tanûnapât (or Narâsamsa); 3. the Ids; 4. the Barhis. The remaining ones are—5. the doors (of heaven); 6. dawn and night; 7. the two divine Hotris; 8. the three goddesses (Sarasvatî, Idâ, and Bhâratî); 9. all the deities to whom offering is made during the sacrifice (see I, 5, 3, 22 seq.). The objects of the first eight offerings are identical with those of the first eight verses of the Âprî hymns.

[3] Or, 'at every fourth (fore-offering)?' According to the Paddhati on Kâty. V, 5, the butter is poured together at the fourth and seventh prayâgas. See also I, 5, 3, 16.

'Pronounce the invitatory prayer to Agni!' referring to Agni's butter-portion[1]. Both (the Adhvaryu and Pratiprasthâtri) having taken four 'cuttings' of butter, they step across (to the north side of their respective fires). Having stepped across and called for the '*S*raushat,' the Adhvaryu says (to the Hotri), 'Pronounce the offering-formula to Agni!' After the 'Vashat' has been uttered, they both pour out the oblation.

32. The Adhvaryu then says, 'Pronounce (the invitatory prayer) to Soma!' referring to Soma's butter-portion. Both having taken four cuttings of butter, they step across. Having stepped across and called for the '*S*raushat,' the Adhvaryu says (to the Hotri), 'Pronounce the offering-prayer to Soma!' After the 'Vashat' has been uttered, they both pour out the oblation.

33. Thus whatever has to be done by speech, that the Adhvaryu does, and not the Pratiprasthâtri. Now as to why the Adhvaryu alone calls for the '*S*raushat.' Here indeed when the 'Vashat' is pronounced,—

34. The Pratiprasthâtri is merely the imitator of what is done (by the Adhvaryu). For Varuna is the nobility, and the Maruts are the people: hence he thereby makes the people the imitators, the followers of the nobility. But were the Pratiprasthâtri also to call for the '*S*raushat,' he would doubtless make the people equal in power to the nobility: for this reason the Pratiprasthâtri does not call for the '*S*raushat.'

35. The Pratiprasthâtri sits down, after taking the two offering-spoons in his hand. The Adhvaryu then

[1] See I, 6, 1, 20 seq.

proceeds with those oblations,—viz. Agni's cake on eight potsherds, Soma's pap, Savitri's cake on twelve or eight potsherds, Sarasvatî's pap, Pûshan's pap, and Indra and Agni's cake on twelve potsherds.

36. Thereupon, being about to proceed with those two oblations of curds, (the Adhvaryu and Pratiprasthâtri) exchange (the ram and ewe): the ram which was on the Maruts' (dish of curds) he (the Adhvaryu) places on that of Varuna; and the ewe which was on Varuna's (dish of curds) he (the Pratiprasthâtri) places on that of the Maruts. Now the reason why they make this exchange, is this,—Varuna is the nobility, and the male represents energy: hence they thereby bestow energy on the nobility. The female, on the other hand, is without energy; and the Maruts are the people: hence they thereby cause the people to be without energy. This is why they make this exchange.

37. The Adhvaryu now says (to the Hotri), 'Pronounce the invitatory prayer to Varuna!' He then pours an 'under-layer' of butter (into the guhû), takes two cuttings from Varuna's curds, and with either of the two cuttings puts the ram (in the spoon). He then pours butter thereon, replenishes (the place whence) the two cuttings (have been made), and steps across (to the south side of the fire). After stepping across and calling for the 'Sraushat,' he says (to the Hotri), 'Pronounce the offering-prayer to Varuna!' and, on the 'Vashat' being uttered, he pours out the oblation.

38. Thereupon the Adhvaryu takes both spoons in his left hand; and taking hold of the Pratiprasthâtri's garment, says (to the Hotri), 'Pronounce the invitatory prayer to the Maruts!' The

Pratiprasthât*ri* then makes an 'under-layer' of butter (in his *g*uhû), and two cuttings from the curds of the Maruts, and with either of the two cuttings puts the ewe (in the spoon). He then pours butter thereon, replenishes (the place of) the two cuttings, and steps across (to the south of the fire). The Adhvaryu, having called for the '*S*rausha*t*,' says (to the Hot*ri*), 'Pronounce the offering-prayer to the Maruts!' and on the 'Vasha*t*' being uttered, (the Pratiprasthât*ri*) he pours out the oblation.

39. The Adhvaryu then proceeds with the cake on eleven potsherds for Ka; and having made that offering, he says, 'Pronounce the invitatory prayer to Agni Svish*t*ak*ri*t ("the maker of good offering")!' The Adhvaryu then takes cuttings from all (his) oblations, one from each; and the Pratiprasthât*ri* also takes one cutting from that oblation of curds (to the Maruts). They then pour twice butter upon (the portions), and step across (to the south side of the fires). On stepping across and calling for the '*S*rausha*t*,' the Adhvaryu says, 'Pronounce the offering-prayer to Agni Svish*t*ak*ri*t; and after the (concluding) 'Vasha*t*,' they both pour out the oblation.

40. The Adhvaryu now cuts off the fore-portion. Having then cut off the I*d*â piece by piece, he hands it to the Pratiprasthât*ri*; and the Pratiprasthât*ri* puts thereon two cuttings from the Maruts' curds. He (the Adhvaryu) then pours twice butter thereon. After invoking (the I*d*â), they cleanse themselves[1].

41. Thereupon the Adhvaryu says, 'O Brahman, shall I step forward?' Having put on the (remaining) kindling-stick[2], he says, 'Agnîdh, trim the fire!'

[1] See I, 8, 1, 18-43.

[2] See II, 5, 2, 19, and I, 8, 2, 3.

He, the Adhvaryu, then pours the clotted butter[1] (in the prishadâgya-upabhrit) into the two spoons (the guhû and upabhrit); and the Pratiprasthâtri also, if he have any clotted butter, divides it into two parts and pours it (into the two spoons); but if there is no clotted butter, he divides the butter in the upabhrit in two parts and pours them out separately. Then both step across (to the south side of the fires). The Adhvaryu, having stepped across and called for the '*S*raushat,' says (to the Hotri), 'Pronounce the offering-formula to the gods!' and, 'Pronounce the offering-formula!' at each (subsequent after-offering). Thus they both perform the nine after-offerings[2], pouring together (the butter from the spoons) at the (or at every) fourth after-offering. The reason why there are nine fore-offerings and nine after-offerings, is that he thereby delivers the creatures both times from Varuna's noose,—by the former (he delivers) the upright and by the latter those looking to the ground: for this reason there are nine fore-offerings and nine after-offerings.

42. They both then separate the spoons[3], after laying them (on the altars). Having separated the spoons, and anointed the enclosing-sticks; and having thereupon taken hold of the (middle) enclosing-

[1] Prishad-âgya (lit. mottled butter) is clarified butter mixed with sour milk.

[2] The recipients of the nine after-offerings are as follows: 1. The divine Barhis; 2. the divine doors; 3. the divine dawn and night; 4. the two divine benefactresses (goshtrî); 5. the two goddesses of potent sacrifice (ûrgâhutî); 6. the two divine Hotris; 7. the three goddesses; 8. the divine Narâsamsa; 9. the divine Agni Svishtakrit. Cf. p. 400, note 2.

[3] See I, 8, 3, 1 seq.

stick, and called for the (Âgnîdhra's) '*S*raushа*t*,' the Adhvaryu thus addresses (the Hot*ri*)[1], 'The divine Hot*ri*s are summoned for the proclamation of success; the human is called upon for the song of praise!' The Hot*ri* then intones the song of praise (sûktavâka). Thereupon both seize their prastara-bunches and throw them (into the fires); both take a single straw each therefrom and remain sitting by (the fires); when the Hot*ri* recites the song of praise,—

43. The Âgnîdhra says, 'Throw after!' Both (the Adhvaryu and Pratiprasthât*ri*) throw (the stalk) after (the prastara); and both touch themselves.

44. He (the Âgnîdhra) then says[2], 'Discourse (with me)!' [The Adhvaryu asks,] 'Has he gone (to the gods), Agnîdh?'—'He has gone!'—'Bid (the gods) hear!'—'Yea, may (one) hear!'—'Good-speed to the divine Hot*ri*s! Success to the human!' —The Adhvaryu also (afterwards)[3] says (to the Hot*ri*), 'Pronounce the "All-hail and blessing!"' They both throw the enclosing-sticks (into the fire); and after taking up the spoons together, they both place them on the wooden sword[4].

45. Thereupon the Adhvaryu returns (to the Gârhapatya fire) and performs the Patnîsa*m*yâ*g*as[5]. The Pratiprasthât*ri*, in the meantime,

---

[1] See I, 8, 3, 10 seq. [2] See I, 8, 3, 20 seq.

[3] In thus briefly recapitulating the chief points of the course of sacrificial performance, the author's object is merely to assign to each officiating priest—especially to the Adhvaryu and his assistant, the Pratiprasthât*ri*—his special share of business. In the actual performance, the pronunciation of the formula of 'All-hail and blessing' (see I, 9, 1, 26), of course, comes after the throwing of the enclosing-sticks into the fire (see I, 8, 3, 22).

[4] See I, 8, 3, 26. [5] See I, 9, 2, 1.

remains waiting. After performing the Patnîsa*m*yâ*g*as, the Adhvaryu steps up (to the northern fire).

46. He (the Adhvaryu) performs the three Samish*t*aya*g*us (with the respective texts)[1]; the Pratiprasthât*ri* takes up his spoon (and performs those oblations) silently.—The same garments, worn by the sacrificer and his wife at the Vai*s*vadeva, should be put on also on this occasion. They now take (the havis) mixed with the burnt scrapings of the Varu*n*a curds, and betake themselves to (the place of) the expiatory bath (avabh*ri*tha). This (ablution) stands in relation to Varu*n*a, (being performed) with a view to deliverance from Varu*n*a's power. No Sâman-hymn is sung on this occasion, for at this (sacrifice) nothing whatever is performed with a Sâman-hymn. Having silently walked thither and entered (the water), he (the Adhvaryu) immerses (the vessel containing the scrapings).

47. With the text (Vâ*g*. S. III, 48), 'O laving bath, laving thou glidest along: with the help of the gods may I wipe out the sin committed against the gods, and with the help of mortals the sin committed against mortals! Preserve me, O God, from injury from the fiercely-howling (demon)!' Those (garments worn while bathing)[2] he may give

---

[1] See p. 390, note 3.

[2] Kâty. V, 5, 30–33, and the scholiasts supply the following particulars: The sacrificer and his wife, accompanied by the priests, are to repair to some quiet part of flowing water. The Adhvaryu then takes the sacrificer by the arm and makes him enter the water. Thereupon he himself enters, strews sacrificial grass on the water, puts a stick on it, and thereon offers a spoonful of butter to Agni. Then follow six oblations, viz. four fore-offerings, performed in the usual way (the one to the Barhis being omitted);

to whichever (priest) he chooses, since they are not the garments of an initiated person. Even as a snake casts its skin, so does he cast away all his sin.

48. Thereupon they shave (the sacrificer's) hair and beard; and take up the two fires[1],—for only after changing his place (to the ordinary sacrificial ground) he performs that (other) sacrifice[2], since it is not proper that he should perform the Agnihotra on the uttaravedi: for this reason he changes his place. Having gone to the house[3] and 'churned out' the fires, he performs the full-moon offering. These seasonal offerings doubtless are detached sacrifices; whereas the full-moon offering is a regular, established sacrifice: hence he finally establishes himself by means of that regular sacrifice; and therefore he changes his place (to the ordinary sacrificial ground).

---

an oblation of butter to Varuna, and another of the scrapings of curds to Agni and Varuna. Other authorities offer ten oblations instead of six, viz. four fore-offerings, two 'butter-portions' to Agni and Soma, the two oblations to Varuna and Agni-Varuna, and two after-offerings. The Adhvaryu then immerses the butter-pot, with the text Vâg. S. III, 48. Thereupon the sacrificer and his wife bathe without diving, but wash each other's back. They then come out of the water and put on fresh clothes.

[1] Viz. by lighting (or heating) at them two aranis or churning-sticks, by means of which the fires are transferred to the old hearths. According to the Paddhati, the remaining ceremonies of the ishti, from the offering of the Barhis (see I, 9, 2, 29) to the end, are performed previously to the lifting of the fires.

[2] Viz. the full-moon sacrifice, see II, 6, 2, 19, where, however, agnau instead of agnî. The construction here is quite irregular. The Kânva text has: kesasmasrûptvâgnî samârohayata udavasâya hy etena yagate.

[3] That is, to the ordinary sacrificial ground.

THIRD BRÂHMA*N*A.

C. THE SÂKAMEDHA OFFERINGS[1].

1. Verily, by means of the Varu*n*apraghâsâ*h* Pra*g*âpati delivered the creatures from Varu*n*a's noose; and those creatures of his were born without disease and blemish. Now with these Sâkamedha offerings,—therewith indeed the gods slew V*ri*tra, therewith they gained that supreme authority which they now wield; and so does he now therewith slay his wicked, spiteful enemy and gain the victory: this is why he performs these offerings in the fourth month (after the Varu*n*apraghâsâ*h*). He performs them on two successive days.

2. On the first day he offers a cake on eight potsherds to Agni Anîkavat[2]. For it was after

[1] The performance of the Sâkamedha offerings requires two days. In the first place—after the Âhavanîya has been 'taken out' from the Gârhapatya—both fires are taken up by means of (or 'made to mount') the two kindling-sticks, and transferred (by 'churning out') to another altar (the uttaravedi). On the first day oblations are then made to Agni Anîkavat, the Maruta*h* Sântapanâ*h* and the Maruto G*ri*hamedhina*h*, these being completed on the next morning by a Darvihoma to Indra, and an oblation of cake to the Maruta*h* Krî*d*ina*h*. Then follows the Mahâhavis, consisting—besides the five constant oblations—of oblations to Indra-Agni, Mahendra, and Vi*s*vakarman. In the afternoon takes place the Mahâpit*ri*ya*gñ*a, or (Great) sacrifice to the Manes (performed on a special altar and fire-place, south of the Dakshi*n*âgni); which is succeeded by the Traiyambaka-homa, or offering to Rudra Tryambaka, performed on a cross-way somewhere north of the sacrificial ground.

[2] That is, Agni, the 'sharp-pointed' or 'sharp-edged;' an epithet apparently referring to the pointed flames or tongues of Agni. The St. Petersburg Dict. takes it to mean 'Agni, possessed of a face.' Perhaps it may mean, 'Agni, constituting the front or van of the army.' In *S*at. Br. III, 4, 4, 14, Agni is likened to the point (anîka) of the thunderbolt, Soma to its shaft (*s*alya), and Vish*n*u

shaping Agni into a sharp point[1], that the gods rushed forward, intent on slaying V*ri*tra; and that sharp point, Agni, swerved not. And so does he (the Sacrificer) now rush forward, after shaping Agni into a sharp point, intent on slaying his wicked, spiteful enemy; and that sharp point, Agni, swerves not: this is why he sacrifices to Agni Anîkavat.

3. Thereupon, at midday, he offers a potful of boiled grain (*k*aru) to the Maruts, the Scorchers (Sântapanâ*h*), for at midday indeed the scorching winds scorched V*ri*tra; and thus scorched he lay panting and gasping, being rent all over. And so do the scorching winds scorch his (the Sacrificer's) wicked, spiteful enemy: hence (he sacrifices) to the Maruts, the Scorchers.

4. Thereupon, (in the evening, he offers a potful of boiled grain) to the Maruts, the Householders (G*ri*hamedhina*h*). That pap he cooks after driving

---

to the part where the point is fixed on the shaft (kulmala). Compare the corresponding passage in Taitt. Br. I, 6, 6: 'The gods and Asuras were contending. Agni spake, "My body is anîkavat (possessed of an army, acc. to Sâya*n*a): satisfy it and you will overcome the Asuras!" The gods prepared a cake on eight potsherds for Agni Anîkavat. Agni Anîkavat, being pleased with his share, produced for himself four anîkas; and thereby the gods prevailed and the Asuras were defeated. . . . Now Agni Anîkavat is yonder sun: his rays are the anîkas.' Here anîka would rather seem to mean either 'dart' or 'face.' [In Taitt. Br. I, 6, 2, 5, in the battle between the gods and Asuras, Agni is represented as the mukham of the gods, which Sâya*n*a takes to mean the 'van-guard' or 'the champion' of the gods. Compare also *S*at. Br. II, 6, 4, 2; XI, 5, 2, 4]. Acc. to the Black Ya*g*us, the cake to Agni Anîkavat is to be prepared (or offered) simultaneously (sâkam) with the rising of the sun; whence is probably derived the term 'Sâkam-edha.'

[1] I. e. into a sharp-pointed weapon; or, perhaps, 'after appointing Agni their leader.' Cf. p. 449 note; and *S*at. Br. V, 3, 1, 1.

away the calves (from the cows) with the (palâsa-) branch, and having (all the cows) milked into the pot containing the strainers. Now, whenever (in preparing the pap) they use (whole) rice-grains, then that is a *k*aru: this nourishment[1] the gods took when they were about to slay V*ri*tra on the morrow; and so does he (the Sacrificer) now take that nourishment, being about to slay his wicked, spiteful enemy. The reason, then, why it is milk-pap, is that milk is nourishment, and rice-grains are nourishment, and that he thus puts into him (âtman) that twofold nourishment. For this reason it is a rice-pap (prepared) with milk.

5. The practice, in regard to this (pap, is as follows). The same altar covered (with sacrificial grass) which served for the (oblation to) the Maruts, the Scorchers, is (now used)[2]. Near this covered altar they lay down the enclosing-sticks and pieces of wood. Having had (the cows) milked in the same way (as before), he (the Adhvaryu) cooks the pap; and having cooked it and basted it with butter, he removes it from the fire.

6. They then rinse either two plates or two dishes, and put that (pap) thereon in two equal

[1] That is, strengthening food. Instead of medhas, the Kâ*n*va recension has throughout medham (as once in our text).

[2] At the preceding offering, that to the Marutah Sântapanâ*h*, the ish*t*i is either to be interrupted at the end of the Samish*t*ayagus (see I, 9, 2, 25–28), or only the offering of the Barhis (I, 9, 2, 29–31) is to be omitted. The concluding ceremonies are to be performed either on the same day, after the offering to the Maruto G*ri*hamedhina*h*—which itself concludes with the I*d*â, and (acc. to Taitt. Br. I, 6, 6, 6) has neither fore-offerings nor after-offerings—or the following morning after the Darvihoma (see par. 17). Kâty. V, 6, 3–5 2–33.

parts. Having then made a hollow in each (pap), he (the Adhvaryu) pours clarified butter therein, and wipes both the dipping-spoon and the offering-spoon. Thereupon he takes the two dishes of pap, and walks up (to the altar); and again, he takes the dipping and offering spoons, and walks up; and having touched[1] the covered altar, and laid the enclosing-sticks round (the fire)[2], he puts on as many pieces of firewood as he thinks fit. He then deposits those two dishes of pap, and the dipping and offering spoons, in their places (outside the altar). The Hot*ri* sits down on the Hot*ri*'s seat. Taking the dipping and offering spoons, he (the Adhvaryu) says,—

7. 'Pronounce the invitatory prayer to Agni!' with reference to Agni's butter-portion. He then takes four 'cuttings' of butter from the hollow of the southern pap, and steps over (to the south side of the fire). Having stepped over, and called for the (Âgnîdhra's) '*S*rausha*t*,' he says (to the Hot*ri*), 'Pronounce the offering-prayer to Agni!' and pours out the oblation, as soon as the Vasha*t* has been uttered.

8. He then says, 'Pronounce the invitatory prayer to Soma!' with reference to Soma's butter-portion. He then takes four cuttings of butter from the hollow of the northern pap, and steps over. Having stepped over and called for the '*S*rausha*t*,' he says, 'Pronounce the offering-prayer to Soma!' and pours out the oblation, as soon as the Vasha*t* has been uttered.

9. He then says, 'Pronounce the invitatory prayer

[1] According to Kâty. V, 6, 14, he is to do so either silently, or with the text (Vâ*g*. S. II, 2) used in spreading the sacrificial grass on the altar. See I, 3, 3, 11.

[2] See I, 3, 3, 13; 3, 4, 1 seq.

to the Maruts, the Householders!' He makes an 'under-layer' of butter (in the offering-spoon) from the hollow of the southern pap, takes two cuttings from the latter, pours some butter thereon, and steps across. Having stepped across and called for the 'Sraushat,' he says, 'Pronounce the offering-prayer to the Maruts, the Householders!' and pours out the oblation as soon as the Vashat has been uttered.

10. He then says, 'Pronounce the invitatory prayer to Agni Svishtakrit[1]!' He makes an under-layer of butter from the hollow of the northern pap, takes two cuttings from the latter, pours some butter thereon, and steps across. Having stepped across and called for the 'Sraushat,' he says, 'Pronounce the offering-prayer to Agni Svishtakrit!' and pours out the oblation as soon as the Vashat has been uttered. Thereupon he cuts off the Idâ[2], but no fore-portion[3]. Having invoked (the Idâ), they cleanse themselves. This is one mode of performance.

11. Then there is this other. The same altar covered (with sacrificial grass) which has served for the Maruts, the Scorchers, is (used now). Near this covered altar they lay down the enclosing-sticks and pieces of firewood; and having had (the cows) milked in the same way (as before) he cooks the rice-pap. The butter he puts on so as to be no mere accessory[4]. Having cooked (the pap) and basted

---

[1] See I, 7, 3, 1 seq.

[2] See I, 8, 1, 1 seq.

[3] See I, 7, 4, 6 seq.

[4] Ned eva pratives*am âgyam adhisrayati. There seems to be some mistake here. The commentary on Kâty. V, 6, 6 has 'tad eva' instead of 'ned eva.' Sâyana says that the butter is put on the Dakshinâgni; but according to Kâty. V, 6, 24, it is put on the fire together with the pap. The Kânva text has, abhyardha âgyam

it, and removed it (from the fire), he anoints it. He then removes the butter in the pot (from the fire), and wipes the dipping and offering spoons. Thereupon, taking the dish with the pap, he walks up (to the altar); and again, taking the butter in the pot, he walks up; and again, taking the dipping and offering spoons, he walks up (to the altar). He then touches that covered altar, lays the enclosing-sticks round (the Âhavanîya fire), and puts on as many pieces of wood as he thinks fit. He then deposits successively[1] (in their respective places) the dish with the pap, the pot with butter, and the dipping and offering spoons. The Hotri sits down in the Hotri's seat. Taking the dipping and offering spoons, he (the Adhvaryu) says,—

12. 'Pronounce the invitatory prayer to Agni!' with a view to (offering) Agni's butter-portion. He then takes four 'cuttings' of butter from the pot and steps across (to the offering-place on the south side of the fire). Having stepped across and called for the (Âgnîdhra's) *S*raushat, he says (to the Hotri), 'Pronounce the offering-prayer to Agni!' and pours out the oblation, as soon as the Vashat has been uttered.

13. He then says, 'Pronounce the invitatory prayer to Soma!' with a view to Soma's butter-portion. He then takes four cuttings of butter from the pot, and steps across. Having stepped

---

sthâlyâm adhisrayati, 'he puts on the butter in the pot on the near side.'

[1] In the original this is expressed by repetition of the verb, as was the case in the last sentence but one, where the original construction is retained. The Kânva text has merely, 'Having taken (the pap) with the dish, he hastes up (udâdravati).'

across, and called for the *S*raushat, he says, 'Pronounce the offering-formula to Soma!' and pours out the oblation, as soon as the Vashat has been uttered.

14. Thereupon he says, 'Pronounce the invitatory prayer to the Maruts, the Householders!' He then makes an 'under-layer' of butter (in the guhû), takes two cuttings from that pap, pours some butter thereon, re-anoints (replenishes with butter the parts of the sacrificial dish from which he has made)[1] the two cuttings, and steps across (to the offering-place). Having stepped across and called for the *S*raushat, he says, 'Pronounce the offering-prayer to the Maruts, the Householders!' and pours out the oblation, as soon as the Vashat has been uttered.

15. Thereupon he says, 'Pronounce the invitatory prayer to Agni Svishtakrit!' He then makes an under-layer of butter, takes one cutting from the pap, pours twice butter thereon, without, however, re-anointing the (place of the) cutting; and steps across. Having stepped across, and called for the *S*raushat, he says, 'Pronounce the offering-prayer to Agni Svishtakrit!' and pours out the oblation, as soon as the Vashat has been uttered.

16. He then cuts off the Idâ, but no fore-portion. Having invoked (the Idâ), they (the priests) eat it. As many members of (the sacrificer's) household as are entitled to partake of the remains of sacrificial

[1] 'Pratyanakti' is probably the same as 'pratyabhighârayati,' generally applied to the basting of the avadâna-sthâna, or that part of the havis from whence the cuttings have been made (Kâty. I, 9, 11; the 'replenishing' of the havis in *S*at. Br. I, 7, 3, 6 refers to the same thing). See, however, Kâty. V, 6, 22, where it is ruled that no pratyabhighâra*n*a is to take place at the present sacrifice. The Kâ*n*va MS., on the other hand, reads, 'he does not re-anoint the two cuttings.' Perhaps he is to anoint separately the two cut-off pieces.

food[1] may eat (of the pap); or the officiating priests may eat it; or, if there be abundant pap, other Brâhmans also may eat of it. The pot having then been covered, before it is quite emptied, they put it away in a safe place, for the 'full-spoon ceremony.' Thereupon they let the calves together with their mothers; and thus the cattle take that nourishment. That night he performs the Agnihotra with rice-gruel. In the morning they milk a cow, which suckles an adopted calf[2], for the purpose of the offering to the fathers.

17. Thereupon, in the morning, either after or before the performance of the Agnihotra—whichever he pleases—he cuts out (the remaining rice-pap) with the darvi-spoon[3] from the unemptied pot, with the text (Vâg. S. III, 49), 'Full, O spoon, fly away, well filled fly back to us!

---

[1] That is, those who have been invested with the sacrificial cord. According to Taitt. Br. I, 6, 7, 1 the mistress of the house is not to eat of it, but an additional (prativesa) pap is to be cooked specially for her on the Dakshina fire.

[2] 'In the morning they tie up the (adopted) calf of a nivânyâ (cow suckling a strange calf),' Kânva text.

[3] The Darvi-homa, or oblation of a darvi-spoonful of boiled rice to Indra, the associate of the Maruts, may be considered as part of the Grihamedhîyâ ishti, being, as it were, an offering of remains (or scrapings, nishkâsa, Taitt. Br. I, 6, 7, 3); cf. Kâty. V, 6, 33. Like all Guhoti-offerings, the darvi-homa is performed by the Adhvaryu while seated on the north side of the fire. According to Taitt. Br. I, 6, 7, 3, it is to be offered in the Gârhapatya, but according to Kâty. V, 6, 38 (comm.) in the Âhavanîya. If the concluding ceremonies of the Sântapanîyâ ishti (from the offering of the Barhis) have not already been performed on the previous night, they have to be performed after the conclusion of the darvi-homa. If, however, only the offering of the Barhis was then omitted, the darvi-homa, if performed before the Agnihotra, is followed immediately by that oblation.

O thou (Indra), of a hundredfold powers, let us two barter food and drink, like wares!' In like manner as an invitatory prayer (is used at offerings) so does he by this (verse) invite him (Indra) to that share.

18. Let him then tell (the Sacrificer) to make a bull roar. 'If it roars,' say some, 'then that (sound) is the Vashat; let him offer after that Vashat.' And in this way indeed he calls Indra in his own form to the slaying of Vritra[1]; for the bull is indeed Indra's form: hence he thereby calls Indra in his own form to the slaying of Vritra. If it roars, then one may know that Indra has come to his sacrifice, that his sacrifice is with Indra. And should it not roar, let the priest, seated on the south side (viz. the Brahman), say, 'Sacrifice!'—this, indeed, is Indra's voice.

19. He offers with the text (Vâg. S. III, 50), 'Give unto me, (and) I give unto thee. Bestow (gifts) on me, (and) I bestow on thee[2]! And mayest thou give me guerdon, (and) I will give thee guerdon! Svâhâ!'

20. He then offers a cake on seven potsherds to the sportive (Krîdinah) Maruts. For when Indra went forward in order to slay Vritra, the sportive Maruts were sporting around him singing his praises; and even so do they sport around this (Sacrificer), singing his praises, now that he is about to slay his wicked, spiteful enemy: this

---

[1] On the symbolic connection of the seasonal offerings, especially the Sâkamedhâh, with the slaying of Vritra, the evil spirit of drought, see II, 6, 4, 1.

[2] According to Mahîdhara, this first line is spoken by Indra to his worshipper; the second line containing the latter's reply.

is why (he sacrifices) to the sportive Maruts[1]. Thereupon (follows the performance) of the Great Oblation (Mahâ-havis): this (performance) is in accordance with that of the great (seasonable) oblation[2].

FOURTH BRÂHMANA.

1. Verily, by means of the Great Oblation the gods slew Vritra[3]; by means of it they gained that supreme authority which they now wield; and so does he (the Sacrificer) thereby now slay his wicked, spiteful enemy, and gain the victory: this is why he performs this sacrifice.

2. The mode of its performance (is as follows): They raise an uttara-vedi[4]; they use clotted butter[5]; and they churn the fire. There are nine

---

[1] Comp. Taitt. Br. I, 6, 7, 4: When Indra had slain Vritra (with the thunderbolt) he went to the farthest distances, thinking that he had missed (his aim). He said, 'Who will know this' [viz. whether Vritra is really dead or not, comm.]? The Maruts said, 'We will choose a boon, then we will know (find it out): let the first oblation be prepared for us! They sported (danced about) on him (Vritra, and thereby found out that he was dead).

[2] That is to say, the Mahâ-havis, or Great Oblation, though apparently only an integral part of the Sâkamedhâh, is in reality its chief ceremony, and may therefore be considered as being itself on a par with the other seasonal offerings; hence it requires the five oblations common to all the Kâturmâsyas; see II, 5, 1, 8–11. The Black Yagus it seems does not use the term Mahâ-havis, but assigns more importance to the Mahâ-pitriyagña (see II, 6, 1, 1 seq.). See Âpastamba's Paribhâshâs, 80, 81 (M. Müller, Zeitschrift der Deutschen Morg. Ges. IX), according to which the sacrifice to the Manes belongs to the Mahâyagñas.

[3] See p. 416, note 1.

[4] See p. 392, note 1. The southern altar is not required at the present ceremony.

[5] See p. 404, note 1.

fore-offerings and nine after-offerings[1], and three Samish*t*ayag*u*s. In the first place there are those five oblations[2].

3. Now as to why there is a cake on eight potsherds for Agni. With Agni, (shaped into) a sharp point (te*g*as)[3], indeed, they (the gods) slew him (V*ri*tra); and Agni, that sharp point, swerved not: hence there is (a cake) for Agni.

4. Then as to why there is a rice-pap for Soma. With the aid of Soma, the king, indeed they slew him, they who have Soma for their king: hence there is a pap for Soma.

5. Then as to why there is a cake on twelve, or eight[4], potsherds for Savit*ri*. Savit*ri*, indeed, is the impeller (prasavit*ri*) of the gods; and impelled by Savit*ri* they slew him: hence there is (a cake) for Savit*ri*.

6. Then as to why there is a rice-pap for Sarasvatî. Sarasvatî in truth is Speech; and Speech indeed it was that cheered them up, saying, 'Strike! slay[5]!' Hence there is a pap for Sarasvatî.

7. Then as to why there is a rice-pap for Pûshan. Pûshan doubtless is this earth[6], and this

[1] See II, 5, 2, 30 and 41.

[2] See II, 5, 1, 11, with note 9.

[3] See II, 5, 3, 2. This cake, again, is to be prepared (or offered) simultaneously with the rising of the sun; see p. 409 note.

[4] According to Taitt. S. I, 8, 4 it is to be one on twelve potsherds.

[5] The Kâ*n*va text has, 'Attack (abhipadyasva)! strike! slay!'

[6] This identification of Pûshan with the earth is very strange, the more so as, at II, 5, 1, 11, special stress is laid on the male nature of Pûshan. Perhaps it is in his character of bountiful bestower of food and cattle, or as the tutelary god of travellers, that he is so identified.

earth, indeed, gave him (Vritra) up to slaughter; and they slew him, thus given up by her: hence there is a rice-pap for Pûshan.

8. Then follows a cake on twelve potsherds for Indra and Agni; for by means of that they slew him, since Agni means fiery glow (tegas), and Indra means manly power, and by means of these two powers they did indeed slay him. Moreover, Agni is the priesthood, and Indra is the nobility; having allied these two, having closely united the priesthood with the nobility, they (the gods) slew him by means of these two powers: hence there is a cake on twelve potsherds for Indra and Agni.

9. Then follows a rice-pap for Mahendra. For before the slaying of Vritra he was indeed Indra; but after slaying Vritra he became Mahendra (the great Indra), even as (a king becomes) a mahârâga, after obtaining the victory: hence there is a rice-pap for Mahendra. And thereby indeed he renders him great (strong), for the slaying of Vritra: for this reason also there is a rice-pap for Mahendra.

10. Then follows a cake on one potsherd for Visvakarman. To the gods, indeed, on performing the Sâkamedha-sacrifice and obtaining the victory (over Vritra), that sacred work (karman) was made complete (visva), and all was conquered; and so is that sacred work made complete, and all is conquered, by him who has performed the Sâkamedha-sacrifice and obtained the victory: hence there is a cake on one potsherd for Visvakarman.

11. And, verily, by performing this sacrifice the gods became what race, what prosperity of the gods there now is; and that same race he propagates,

that same prosperity he attains, whosoever, knowing this, performs this sacrifice. Let him therefore perform this sacrifice.

SIXTH ADHYÂYA. FIRST BRÂHMAVA.

1. Verily, by means of the Great Oblation the gods slew Vritra, and gained that supreme authority which they now wield. And by means of the sacrifice to the fathers they then recalled to life those of them that had been slain in this battle; and they, indeed, were the fathers: hence the name Pitriyagña[1] (sacrifice to the Manes).

2. Now the spring, the summer, and the rainy season,—they are those who vanquished (Vritra); and the autumn, the winter, and the dewy season,—they are those whom they (the gods) recalled to life[2].

3. Now when he performs that sacrifice, he does so, hoping that thus they (the Asuras) will not slay any of his, or because the gods did so (perform it). Moreover he thereby offers to those (fathers) the share which the gods assigned to them; and thus he gratifies those whom the gods recalled to life, and leads his own fathers up to a better world; and whatever injury or loss he suffers through his own unrighteous conduct (or wrong sacrificial performance)[3] that is thereby made good to him: that is why he performs this sacrifice (to the fathers).

[1] This is generally called the Mahâpitriyagña, as distinguished from the ordinary monthly Pitriyagña of the new-moon sacrifice; for which see II, 4, 2, 1 seq.

[2] See II, 1, 3, 1 seq.

[3] Instead of 'ákaranena,' the Kânva MS. has 'karanéna (!).' Cf. Sâyana's interpretation 'anukaranena anugamanena ka.'

4. He offers a cake on six potsherds to the Pitarah Somavantah, or to Soma Pitrimat[1] Six doubtless are the seasons, and the fathers are the seasons: hence it is one of six potsherds.

5. Thereupon they parch barley-grain on the Anvâhâryapakana (or Dakshinâgni) for the Pitaro Barhishadah[2]. They then grind one half of it; and (the other) half remains thus unground,—this is the parched grain for the Barhis-seated fathers.

6. Then a porridge is (prepared) for the Pitaro 'gnishvâttâh[3] (by the ground half of the parched grain) being mixed with the milk of a cow suckling an adopted calf, by stirring it once with a single splinter. It is indeed once for all that the fathers have departed, and hence it is stirred but once. These are the oblations.

7. Now those (fathers) who have sacrificed with Soma are the Pitarah Somavantah; and those who gain the world (of the gods) by means of cooked (sacrificial food) offered by them are the Pitaro Barhishadah; and they who (have offered) neither the one nor the other, and whom Agni consumes by burning, they are the Pitaro 'gnishvâttâh. These, then, are the fathers[4].

8. He takes out [the rice for] that cake of six potsherds, while seated behind the Gârhapatya, and looking southwards, with the sacrificial cord over his right shoulder. From thence he rises and

---

[1] That is, either to 'the fathers, accompanied by Soma (or possessed of Soma),' or to 'Soma, accompanied by the fathers.' The Black Yagus assigns the oblation to Soma Pitrimat.

[2] That is, 'the fathers seated on the barhis.'

[3] That is, 'the fathers consumed by the fire.'

[4] 'These, then, are the three kinds of fathers,' Kânva recension.

threshes (the rice), while standing north of the Dakshina-fire, with his face towards the south. He cleans it but once[1]; since it is once for all that the fathers have departed.

9. He places the two mill-stones on (the black antelope skin, so as to be inclined) towards the south[2]; and puts the six potsherds on the south part of the Gârhapatya hearth. The reason why they keep the southern direction is because that is the region of the fathers: this is why they keep the southern direction.

10. Thereupon he raises a square altar south of the Dakshinâgni[3]. He makes the corners point towards the intermediate quarters. There are doubtless four intermediate quarters, and the fathers are the intermediate quarters: this is why he makes the corners point towards the intermediate quarters.

11. In the centre of this (altar) he lays down the fire. From the east, indeed, the gods came westwards to the men: hence one offers to them while standing

---

[1] Not thrice, as at an ordinary ishti; see I, 1, 4, 23.

[2] Not towards the east, as at the Darsapûrnamâsa; cf. p. 38, note 3. At offerings to the Manes the south, as a rule, takes the place of the east, the west that of the south, &c.

[3] At the conclusion of the Âptya ceremony (cf. I, 2, 2, 18–3, 5) he erects south of the (ordinary) Dakshina-fire a (quadrangular) shed (see further on, paragraph 20) with a door on the north side. Inside it he prepares a quadrangular altar (of the same size as at the Darsapûrnamâsa; cf. I, 2, 5, 14) with the corners towards the intermediate quarters, in the centre of which he makes the (new) Dakshinâgni hearth. [According to Taitt. Br. I, 6, 8, 5–6 no digging takes place in preparing the altar (which is to be square) at the Pitriyagña.] When the Dakshina-fire is transferred to the new fire-place, the Pranîtâ-water (see p. 9, note) is carried after it, followed by the Brahman and Sacrificer, and placed east (not north) of the hearth. The laying down of the fire is preceded by the usual fivefold lustration of the hearth (see p. 2).

with his face towards the east. On all sides are the fathers, for the fathers are the intermediate regions, and the intermediate regions are indeed on all sides: this is why he lays down the fire in the centre.

12. From thence he throws the grass-bush (stambayagus) eastwards[1]. Having thrown away the grass-bush, he first encloses (the altar) thus (viz. on the west side), then thus (viz. on the north side), then thus (on the east side). Having enclosed it with the first line of enclosure, he (the Adhvaryu) draws (three) lines (across the altar)[2] and [the Âgnîdhra] removes (from them the dust) which has to be removed. In the same way he encloses it with the second line of enclosure; and having enclosed it with the second line of enclosure, and smoothed it down, he says, 'Place the sprinkling water on (the altar)!' They accordingly place the sprinkling water on (the altar); and the firewood and barhis they lay down beside it[3]. He (the Âgnîdhra) wipes the spoons. He then walks up (to the altar) with the butter (and

---

[1] Instead of northwards, as is done at the normal ishti; see I, 2, 4, 12 seq.

[2] After tracing the first line of enclosure, the Adhvaryu draws three lines across the altar, either from west to east or from south to north; and says to the Âgnîdhra, 'Take thrice!' The latter then takes the dust from the lines and throws it on the utkara (the heap of rubbish, formed north of the altar in preparing the latter), and thereupon again obliterates them. According to Kâty. II, 6, 29, the same ceremony may be performed at the Darsapûrnamâsa; but there no mention is made of it by our author (see I, 2, 5, 12).

[3] Viz. the Âgnîdhra lays them down between the altar and the pranîtâh (see p. 422, note 3); the firewood behind (west of) the sacrificial grass (barhis), and both with the tops towards the south. The wooden sword also has been previously put down by the Adhvaryu close behind the pranîtâh.

puts it down thereon[1], north of the sprinkling water). He (the Adhvaryu) takes butter, while 'sacrificially-invested[2].'

13. Here now they say, 'Let him take butter in the upabhrit (by) twice (ladling with the dipping spoon); since there are two after-offerings[3] at this (sacrifice).' Let him, nevertheless, ladle eight times into the upabhrit: let him do so, lest he should depart from the manner of the sacrifice. After ladling out butter, and shifting his cord back to the right shoulder,—

14. The Adhvaryu takes the lustral water, and sprinkles first the firewood, and then the altar[4]. Thereupon they hand the sacrificial grass[5] to him, and he puts it down (on the altar) with the knot to the east. Having thereupon sprinkled it and

[1] The lady of the house not being present at the sacrifice to the Manes, neither the ceremony of girding (I, 3, 1, 12 seq.), nor that of her looking at the butter—while it is taken from the Gârhapatya fire, along the east side of the Âhavanîya to the altar—takes place on this occasion. According to the commentators on Kâty. V, 8, 25 (Paddh. p. 519), however, the Adhvaryu has to look down on the butter, with the same text (Vâg. S. I, 30) which was used by the sacrificer's wife. For some details to be supplied here, see I, 3, 1, 22–28.

[2] He has hitherto worn his sacrificial cord on the right shoulder and under the left arm ('eastward-invested'), and now shifts it so as to be on the left shoulder and under the right arm ('sacrificially-invested'). As to the taking or ladling of butter into the offering-spoons, see I, 3, 2, 1 seq.

[3] See I, 3, 2, 9.

[4] See I, 3, 3, 1 seq.

[5] The barhis, on this occasion, must have been cut close to the root (upamûlam, II, 4, 2, 17; ûpamûle ditam, Kânva rec.). According to Taitt. Br. I, 6, 8, 6–7, on the other hand, it has apparently to be torn up with the roots (yat parushi dinam tad devânâm, yad antarâ tan manushyânâm, yat samûlam tat pitrînâm).

poured out (the lustral water on the lower ends of the grass-stalks), and untied the knot, he (at once) seizes the knot, not the prastara[1];—it is once for all that the fathers have departed: hence he does not take the prastara.

15. After undoing the band, he moves thrice[2] round from right to left, spreading the sacrificial grass all over (the altar); while spreading it all over from right to left in three layers, he reserves as much as may serve for the prastara-bunch. He then moves again thrice round (the altar) from left to right. The reason why he again moves thrice round from left to right, is that, while the first time he went away from here after those three ancestors of his, he now comes back again from them to this, his own world: that is why he again moves thrice round from left to right.

16. He lays the enclosing-sticks along (the fire, with their tops) towards the south[3]; and the prastara also he spreads (with the grass-tops) towards the south; nor does he lay down the two vidh*ri*tis between (the barhis and the prastara). Once for all the fathers have departed from hence: therefore he lays no vidh*ri*tis between.

---

[1] As he did on the former occasion, I, 3, 3, 5.

[2] According to Taitt. Br. I, 6, 8, 7, because the fathers abide in the third world from here (*tri*tîye vâ ito loke pitara*h*).

[3] Viz. he is to lay down the enclosing-sticks along the north, west, and east sides, the last two with their tops towards the south. The third text (cf. I, 3, 4, 4) has, of course, to be changed to 'May Mitra-Varu*n*a lay thee around in the east,' &c.; as has also the one he mutters after putting the two sticks on the fire, to 'May the sun guard thee from the south against any imprecation!' (I, 3, 4, 8.) According to Taitt. Br. I, 6, 8, 8–9, on the other hand, he is to lay down only two enclosing-sticks (viz. the middle or western, and the northern one, cf. Sâya*n*a on Taitt. S. II, p. 72).

17. Thereon he lays the guhû, and east of it (on the barhis) the upabhrit. Having then put down the dhruvâ, the cake, the parched grain, and the porridge (each east of the preceding one), he touches the oblations.

18. All of them having now become 'sacrificially-invested,' the Sacrificer and Brahman (being) thus (invested) walk round (from the east, along the south) to the west side; and the Âgnîdhra (from the west) to the east side (of the fire)[1].

19. They perform this (sacrifice) in a low voice. Secret, indeed, are the fathers, and secret also is (what is spoken) in a low voice: hence they perform (the offering) in a low voice.

20. They perform it in an enclosed place. Secret, indeed, are the fathers, and secret also is that which is enclosed: hence they perform in an enclosed place.

21. While putting firewood (on the fire), he then says (to the Hotri), 'Recite to the fire, as it is being kindled!' Only (this) one kindling-verse the Hotri recites[2], (and that) thrice;—the fathers have departed once for all: hence the Hotri recites thrice only one kindling-verse.

22. He recites, 'Loving we deposit thee (O Agni), loving we enkindle thee: O loving one, bring

[1] Here he remains standing, while the Sacrificer and Brahman sit down facing the east.

[2] Instead of the ordinary eleven verses, the first and last of which are recited thrice; see I, 3, 5, 6. According to Taitt. Br. I, 6, 9, 1, the Adhvaryu summons the Hotri with 'Recite to the fire, as it is being kindled for the gods (and) fathers!' The bunch of firewood, with the exception of one stick, which is reserved for the after-offerings, is divided into three parts, one of which is thrown on the fire at the same time when the syllable 'om' is pronounced by the Hotri at the end of the kindling-verse.

hither the loving fathers to eat their oblation!' Thereupon he says, 'Bring Agni hither[1]! bring Soma hither! bring hither the fathers, accompanied by Soma! bring hither the fathers, seated on the barhis! bring hither the fathers, consumed by Agni! bring hither the butter-drinking gods! bring hither Agni for the Hotriship! bring hither (thine) own greatness[2]!' Having thus called on (Agni) to bring hither (the fathers and gods), he sits down.

23. Having then called[3] for the (Âgnîdhra's) '*S*raushat,' he does not elect the Hotri; for this being a sacrifice to the Manes, he does not elect the Hotri[4], lest he should consign the Hotri to the Manes. He says, 'Hotri, seat thyself!' and takes his seat. The Hotri, having sat down on the Hotri's seat, urges (the Adhvaryu) to proceed; and thus urged, the Adhvaryu takes the two spoons and steps across to the west (of the fire); and having stepped across and called for the '*S*raushat,' he says, 'Pronounce the offering-prayer to the kindling-sticks!' He performs four fore-offerings[5],

---

[1] The Kânva MS. reads, 'Bring Agni hither, O Agni!' Before this, Â*s*val. II, 19, 7 inserts, 'Bring hither the gods (and) fathers for the sacrificer!' See I, 4, 2, 16.

[2] According to the Kânva text he adds here the same formula as at ordinary ishtis (I, 4, 2, 17), 'Bring (them) hither, O *G*âtavedas, and offer up a good offering!' For the formulas 'Bring hither Agni for the Hotriship! bring hither thine own greatness!' Â*s*val. II, 19, 8 apparently substitutes 'Bring hither Agni Kavyavâhana!' cf. further on, par. 30.

[3] 'The Adhvaryu, having offered the two libations of butter, and called for the *S*raushat,' Kânva recension.

[4] On the pravara, or election of the (divine and human) Hotri, see I, 4, 2, 1 seq., 5, 1, 1 seq. The call 'Hotri, seat thyself!' here takes the place of the formulas given I, 5, 1, 5 seq.

[5] See I, 5, 3, 1 seq.

omitting the one to the Barhis; for the barhis means offspring, and he therefore performs the four fore-offerings without the one to the barhis, lest he should consign his offspring to the fathers. Thereupon they proceed with the two butter-portions; and having offered the two butter-portions,—

24. They all shift their sacrificial cord over to the right shoulder, being now about to proceed with those (chief) oblations. The Sacrificer and Brahman, (being) thus (invested), step across (from the west) to the east side, and the Âgnîdhra (from the east) to the west side (of the fire). And furthermore, the (Adhvaryu's) call for the '*S*raushà*t*' is '*Õm* svadhâ!' and the (Âgnîdhra's) response is 'Astu svadhâ[1]!' and the Vasha*t*-call is 'Svadhâ nama*h*!'

25. As to this, Âsuri said, 'Let them call for the *S*rausha*t* (by "Õ *S*râvaya"), and let them respond with the "(Astu) *S*rausha*t*," and let them pronounce the "Vasha*t*," lest we should depart from the manner of the sacrifice.'

26. [The Âdhvaryu] then says, 'Pronounce the invitatory prayer to the fathers, accompanied by Soma!' or '—to Soma, accompanied by the fathers'!—Two invitatory prayers he (the Hot*ri*) pronounces (at the offerings), because it is with one that one moves the gods, and with two the fathers, since the fathers have departed once (for all)[2]: hence he pronounces two invitatory prayers.

---

[1] At the sacrifice to the Manes, the Âgnîdhra, when uttering his response, stands south of the Adhvaryu. See p. 132, note. The first syllable of 'svadhâ' is protracted. According to the comm. on Kâty. V, 9, 12, the offering formulas also begin with 'Yĕ svadhâmahe,' instead of 'Yĕ yag*â*mahe' (see I, 5, 2, 16 and note).

[2] I do not quite see the pertinency of the reason here alleged, unless it be that the author means to say that once (by the first

27. [The Adhvaryu] makes an 'under-layer' of butter (in the *g*uhû or offering-spoon). He then cuts a piece from the cake, and together therewith some of the parched grain and the porridge[1]. This he puts down at the same time (in the *g*uhû); makes two sprinklings of butter thereon; and re-anoints (replenishes with butter, the parts of the sacrificial dishes from which he has made) the cuttings. He does not walk over (to the south side of the fire); but having risen and stepped up (to the fire) on the same side (where he was seated), and called (on the Âgnîdhra) for the '*S*raushat,' he says (to the Hot*ri*), 'Pronounce the offering-prayer to the fathers, accompanied by Soma!' and pours the oblation (into the fire) as soon as the Vasha*t*[2] has been uttered.

act) the fathers have departed, and by a second act they return hither. According to Â*s*val. II, 19, 22, the two invitatory prayers to the Pitara*h* Somavanta*h* are Rig-v. X, 15, 1; IX, 96, 11; to Soma Pit*ri*mat, Rig-v. I, 91, 1; 20; to the Pitaro Barhishada*h*, Rig-v. X, 15, 4; 3; to the Pitaro 'gnishvâttâ*h*, Rig-v. X, 15, 11; 13; [to Yama X, 14, 4; 5.]—The offering-prayers being respectively, Rig-v. X, 15, 5; VIII, 48, 13; X, 15, 2; X, 15, 14; [X, 14, 1.]

Somewhat different the Black Yagus; viz. Soma Pit*ri*mat, anuvâkyâs Rig-v. I, 91, 1; IX, 96, 11; yâ*g*yâ VIII, 48, 13; Pitaro Barhishada*h*, anuvâkyâs X, 15, 4; 3; yâ*g*yâ X, 15, 5; Pitaro 'gnishvâttâ*h*, anuvâkyâs X, 15, 11; 14 (ye 'gnishvâttâ*h*, &c.!); yâ*g*yâ 'vânyâyai dugdhe,' &c. [Then either upahoma with the formulas X, 15, 1; 2; IV, 2, 16; or] an oblation to Agni Kavyavâhana (anuvâkyâs, 1. 'yad agne kavyavâhana,' 2. X, 15, 12; yâ*g*yâ X, 14, 3) [and another to Yama Aṅgirasvat Pit*ri*mat (anuv. X, 14, 4; 5; yâ*g*yâ X, 14, 6).] Taitt. S. I, 8, 5; II, 6, 12; Taitt. Br. I, 6, 9.

[1] From the centre of each sacrificial dish he makes one 'cutting' with the *sri*tâvadâna, shaped like a cow's ear. Kâty. V, 9, 2, and Schol.

[2] Or rather the 'Svadhâ nama*h*,' cf. par. 24. The Adhvaryu makes the oblation with his left hand, while looking towards the south. Paddh. on Kâty. V, 9.

28. Thereupon he says, 'Pronounce the invitatory prayer to the fathers, seated on the barhis!' He then makes an under-layer of butter, takes a 'cutting' from (the north part of) the parched grain, and together therewith some of the porridge and the cake; puts down all this at the same time (in the *g*uhû); makes two sprinklings of butter thereon, and re-anoints (the places of) the cuttings. He does not walk across; but having stepped up (to the fire) on the same side and called for the '*S*rausha*t*,' he says, 'Pronounce the offering-prayer to the fathers, seated on the barhis!' and pours out the oblation as soon as the Vasha*t* has been uttered.

29. Thereupon he says, 'Pronounce the invitatory prayer to the fathers, consumed by the fire!' He then makes an under-layer of butter, takes a cutting from (the south part of) the porridge, and therewith some of the cake and the parched grains; puts down all this at the same time (in the *g*uhû); makes two sprinklings of butter thereon, and re-anoints (the places of) the cuttings. He does not walk across; but having stepped up (to the fire) on the same side, and called for the '*S*rausha*t*,' he says, 'Pronounce the offering-prayer to the fathers, consumed by the fire!' and pours out the oblation as soon as the Vasha*t* has been uttered.

30. Thereupon he says, 'Pronounce the invitatory prayer to Agni Kavyavâhana!' that being for (Agni as) the Svish*t*ak*ri*t ('maker of good offering'). For to the gods indeed he is havyavâhana ('bearer of oblations'), and to the fathers he is kavyavâhana ('the bearer of what is meet for the wise'): hence he says, 'Pronounce the invitatory prayer to Agni Kavyavâhana!'

31. He makes an under-layer of butter (in the offering-spoon); then cuts a piece from (the front part of) the cake, and therewith some of the parched grain and the porridge; puts down all this at the same time; and makes two sprinklings of butter thereon. The (places from which he has made the) cuttings he does not replenish with butter, nor does he walk across; but having stepped up (to the fire) on the same side (where he was seated), and called for the '*S*raushat,' he says, 'Pronounce the offering-prayer to Agni Kavyavâhana!' and pours out the oblation, as soon as the Vashat has been uttered.

32. Now the reason why he does not walk across (to the ordinary place of offering), but pours out the oblation after stepping up (to the fire) on the same side, is that the fathers have departed once for all; and the reason also, why he cuts but once from each of the sacrificial dishes, is that the fathers have departed once for all. And the reason why in making the cuttings, he keeps them together, is that the fathers are the seasons;—he thus keeps the seasons together, joins them to one another: that is why in making the cuttings, he keeps them together.

33. Here now some hand over that entire (remaining) porridge to the Hot*ri*; and the Hot*ri*, having invoked it[1], smells it and hands it to the

[1] According to the comm. on Kâty. V, 9, 13, 'mantha*h*' is, in that case, substituted for 'i*d*â' in the invocation, see I, 8, 1, 19 seq. The Kâ*n*va MS. has as follows: Thereupon, by way of i*d*â, they place that same porridge into the hand of the Hot*ri*. The Hot*ri*, having invoked it, smells it. They hand it to the Âgnîdhra. The Âgnîdhra smells it. They hand it to the Brahman. The Brahman smells it. As to this Âsuri said, 'As from any other oblation they cut off the "i*d*â" and the fore-portion, so let them cut off and smell,

Brahman. The Brahman smells it and hands it to the Âgnîdhra; and the Âgnîdhra also smells it. And so indeed they do this. But, as from any other oblation they cut off the Idâ and the fore-portion, so let them cut from this also; and having invoked it (the Idâ) they smell it, but do not eat it. 'But,' said Âsuri, 'we think that some should be eaten, of whatever is offered up in the fire.'

34. Now he who is about to present (the obsequial cakes to the fathers),—either the Adhvaryu or the Sacrificer,—takes the vessel of water and walks thrice round (the altar) from right to left sprinkling all about (the altar). He then, with the text, 'N. N., wash thyself[1]!' pours out water (in the north-west corner of the altar) for the Sacrificer's father[2] to wash himself; and (in the south-west corner), with 'N. N., wash thyself!' for the grandfather; and (in the south-east corner), with 'N. N., wash thyself!' for the great-grandfather.

---

but not eat: some indeed must be eaten of that of which offering is made in the fire.'

[1] See II, 4, 2, 16 seq. According to the comm. on Kâty. V, 9, 17, some sprinkle three times round the altar for each of the three ancestors. But according to the Paddhati, he sprinkles once round the altar, beginning from the north-west corner; then he sits down and pours out water in that corner for the father. Thereupon, after walking round in the opposite direction (from left to right) to the south-west corner, he again sprinkles all round, and in the same way pours out water in that corner for the grandfather; and after retracing his steps as far as the south-east corner, he performs the same circumambulation, and pours out water in that corner for the great-grandfather; whereupon he again retraces his steps up to the west of the altar.

[2] In the case of a sacrificer whose father is still alive, these ceremonies are performed in honour of the father's father, grandfather, and great-grandfather.

As one would pour out water for (a guest) who is to take food with him, so in this case.

35. Thereupon he takes one 'cutting' from the cake and puts it in his left hand; from the parched grain also he takes one cutting and puts it in his left hand; and from the porridge also he takes one cutting and puts it in his left hand.

36. And in the corner (of the altar) opposite this intermediate quarter (viz. the north-west), he then presents (an obsequial cake[1]) to the Sacrificer's father, with the formula, 'N. N., this for thee!' And in the corner opposite this intermediate quarter (the south-west), he presents one to the Sacrificer's grandfather, with 'N. N., this for thee!' And in the corner opposite this intermediate quarter (the south-east), he presents one to the Sacrificer's great-grandfather, with 'N. N., this for thee!' And in the corner opposite this intermediate quarter (the north-east), he cleanses (his hands), with the text (Vâg. S. II, 31), 'Here, O Fathers, regale yourselves! Like bulls come hither, each to his own share!' whereby he means to say, 'Eat ye each his share!' And the reason why he thus presents (food) to the Fathers is that in this way he does not exclude his own fathers from this sacrifice.

37. Thereupon they all, being sacrificially invested, walk out (of the shed) on the north side, (pass along the east side of, and) stand by the (north) side of, the Âhavanîya fire. For he who has established his fires, and performs the New and Full-moon sacrifices, approaches the gods; but they have just been

[1] He mixes the three pieces (about as much as a thumb's joint each) cut from the sacrificial dishes, and forms them into three pi*nd*as or round cakes.

performing the sacrifice to the Manes, and therefore they now propitiate the gods.

38. They stand by the Âhavanîya fire (worshipping) with two (verses) addressed to Indra [viz. Rig-veda I, 82, 2–3; Vâg. S. III, 51–52], since the Âhavanîya is Indra. 'The friends have eaten, and regaled themselves, and have shaken off (the enemies)[1]; the self-shining bards have extolled (thee) with their newest hymn: yoke, then, thy pair of bay steeds, O Indra!—To thee, the splendid, we will sing praises, O bountiful one! Thus praised, do thou now issue forth, with well-filled car, agreeably to our desire! yoke, then, thy pair of bay steeds, O Indra!'

39. Thereupon they return to the Gârhapatya and stand by it worshipping with the verses (Rig-veda X, 57, 3–5; Vâg. S. III, 53–55), 'We invoke the Mind with man-lauding strain[2], and with the hymns of the fathers.—May the Mind come back to us for (us to obtain) wisdom, vigour, and life, and that we may long see the sun!—May the divine race restore to us the Mind, O Fathers, that we may abide with the living kind!' They have indeed been performing the sacrifice to the Manes; but now they return to the (land of the) living: hence he says, 'That we may abide with the living kind!'

40. Thereupon he who has presented (the obsequial cakes) again shifts his sacrificial cord to the right shoulder and betakes himself (to the fire in the shed), and mutters (Vâg. S. II, 31), 'The

[1] '—the friends have shaken off (their intoxication),' Ludwig; '—they showered down upon us delightful gifts,' Grassmann; 'they shook their dear (bodies),' Sâyana; '—have trembled through their precious (bodies),' Wilson.

[2] The Rig-veda has 'somena' instead of 'stomena.'

Fathers have regaled themselves: like bulls they came each to his share:' whereby he means to say, 'they have eaten each his own share.'

41. He now takes the vessel of water and again, while sprinkling, walks thrice round (the altar) from left to right (sunwise). With 'N. N., wash thyself!' he pours out water (in the respective corner) for the Sacrificer's father to wash himself; with 'N. N., wash thyself!' for the grandfather; with 'N. N., wash thyself!' for the great-grandfather. As one would pour out water for (a guest) who has taken food with him, so in this case. And as to his again walking thrice round from left to right, while sprinkling,—they think, 'This holy work of ours shall be accomplished sunwise[1],' and hence he walks thrice round from left to right, while sprinkling.

42. He then pulls down the tuck (of the nether garment)[2] and makes obeisance (to the Fathers). The tuck, doubtless, is sacred to the Fathers: hence he makes obeisance to them after pulling down the tuck; and obeisance means worship: hence he thereby recognises them as entitled to worship. Six times he makes obeisance to them, since there are six seasons, and the Fathers are the seasons: hence he thereby establishes his sacrifice in the seasons,—that is why he makes obeisance six times[3]. 'Give houses

[1] The Kâ*n*va text has, 'The reason why he moves thrice round, sprinkling from left to right, is that, after going after those three ancestors of his, he thereby leaves them, and returns to this, his own, world.' See II, 6, 1, 15.

[2] On the nîvi, or unwoven end of the waist-cloth (Hindi dhotî, Mahr. dhotar), which had to be passed under and tucked up behind, at the beginning of the present ceremony, see p. 368, note 2. Cf. Âpast. Dharmas. I, 2, 6, 19.

[3] For the six formulas used for this purpose, see p. 368, note 2.

unto us, O Fathers!' he (further) says, because the Fathers are the guardians of houses;—and this is the prayer for blessing at this sacred performance.

43. Being now about to proceed with the after-offerings, they all invest themselves sacrificially (by shifting the cord over to the left shoulder); and thus (invested) the Sacrificer and Brahman walk round to the west, and the Âgnîdhra to the east, side; and the Hot*ri* sits down on the Hot*ri*'s seat.

44. He (the Adhvaryu) then says, 'Brahman, I shall step forward.' Thereupon he puts the stick (reserved at the time of kindling) on (the fire), and says, 'Agnîdh, trim the fire!' He then takes the two spoons and crosses over to the west side. After crossing over and calling for the '*S*rausha*t*,' he says (to the Hot*ri*), 'Pronounce the offering-prayer to the gods!' He performs two after-offerings, omitting the one to the Barhis; for the Barhis means offspring: hence he performs two after-offerings, omitting the one to the Barhis, lest he should consign his offspring to the Fathers.

45. He then separates the two spoons[1], after laying them down (in their respective places on the altar); and having separated them, and anointed the enclosing-sticks, he takes one enclosing-stick, calls for the '*S*rausha*t*,' and says, 'The divine Hot*ri*s are summoned for the proclamation of success, the human is called upon for the song of praise!' The Hot*ri* intones the 'song of praise (sûktavâka).' The Adhvaryu, on the other hand, does not seize the prastara-bunch, but watches while the Hot*ri* recites the song of praise.

[1] See I, 8, 3, 1 seq.

46. Thereupon the Âgnîdhra says, 'Throw it after[1]!' He (the Adhvaryu) throws nothing after, but silently touches himself.

47. He (the Âgnîdhra) then says, 'Discourse together!' [The Adhvaryu asks], 'Has he gone (to the gods), Agnîdh?'—'He has gone!'—'Bid (the gods) hear!'—'May one (or, they) hear!'—'Good-speed to the divine Hotris! Success to the human!—Pronounce the All-hail and blessing!' Thus saying, he merely touches the enclosing-sticks, but does not (now) throw them (into the fire). The Barhis and enclosing-sticks he throws in afterwards[2].

48. And here some throw also the remaining sacrificial food into the fire; but let him not do so; for that (remaining havis) is the residue of an offering; and lest he should offer the residue of an offering, let them (the priests) rather throw it into the water or eat it.

SECOND BRÂHMANA.

1. Verily, by means of the Great Oblation the gods slew Vritra; by it they gained that supreme authority which they now wield. Now whichever of them were hit by (the Asuras') arrows in that battle, those same darts they extracted, those they pulled out, by performing the Tryambaka-offerings.

2. And, accordingly, when he performs those offerings, he either does so hoping that thus no arrow

---

[1] See I, 8, 3, 19 seq.

[2] Viz. after the strewing of the Veda,—see I, 9, 2, 24, the formulas being pronounced by the Hotri on this occasion,—at the time when the Samishtayagus, which is here omitted, would have to be performed in an ordinary ishti.

(misfortune) will hit any of his, or because the gods did so. And thereby he delivers from Rudra's power both the descendants that are born unto him and those that are unborn; and his offspring is brought forth without disease and blemish. This is why he performs these offerings.

3. They are (offered) to Rudra: Rudra's, indeed, is the dart; and hence (these offerings) belong to Rudra. They consist of (cakes) on one potsherd: 'To one deity they shall belong!' so (he thinks, and) therefore they consist of (cakes) on one potsherd.

4. There is one for each individual,—as many as he has descendants,—exceeded by one. (There being) one for each individual, he thereby delivers from Rudra's power the descendants that are born unto him; and there being an additional one, he thereby delivers from Rudra's power the descendants that are not yet born to him: this is why there are (as many cakes as there are descendants) exceeded by one.

5. He takes out (the rice for) those (cakes), while seated behind the Gârhapatya, sacrificially invested and facing the north. From thence he rises and threshes (the rice), while standing with his face towards the north. He places the two mill-stones on (the black antelope skin, so as to incline) towards the north; and puts the potsherds on the north side of the Gârhapatya hearth. As to why they keep the northern quarter,—that indeed is the quarter of that god (Rudra), and hence they keep the northern quarter.

6. They (the cakes) may be anointed (with ghee),—for the havis is anointed[1];—but let them rather be

[1] This refers to the so-called prânadâna, or 'bestowal of life

unanointed; for, indeed, Rudra would be hankering after the (sacrificer's) cattle, if he were to anoint (the cakes): let them therefore be unanointed.

7. Having removed all (the cakes from the potsherds) into one dish, and taken a fire-brand from the Dakshina-fire, he walks aside towards the north—for that is the region of that god—and offers. He offers on a road,—for on roads that god roves; he offers on a cross-road,—for the cross-road, indeed, is known to be his (Rudra's) favourite haunt[1]. This is why he offers on a cross-road.

8. He offers with the central leaflet of a palâsa-leaf. The palâsa-leaf, truly, is the Brahman (priesthood)[2]: with the Brahman, therefore, he offers. He takes a cutting from (the northern part of) all the cakes; from the additional one alone he takes no cutting.

(or soul),' that is, the anointing of the sacrificial dishes with ghee, previously to their being placed on the altar. The anointing takes place with the text (Vâg. S. ed. p. 35), 'That life (or soul, prâna) of thine which has entered into the cattle, and becomes diffused through the various forms of the gods,—endowed with (that) life (âtmanvân)—for thou art laden with ghee—go to Agni, O Soma! and obtain bliss (svar) for the Sacrificer!' Kâty. II, 8, 14. At the new and full-moon sacrifice, this ceremony is not even alluded to in our Brâhmana, either in this or the Kânva recension. See I, 3, 4, 16. The Kânva text reads, 'They may be anointed,' so they say, &c.

[1] 'He offers on a cross-road, for such is the halting-place (padbîsa) of the Agnis,' Taitt. Br. I, 6, 10, 3.

[2] 'The central leaflet of the palâsa-leaf is the Brahman,' Kânva text. The leaf of the palâsa (Butea Frondosa) consists of three leaflets,—leathery, above shining and pretty smooth, and below slightly hoary; the central (or terminal) one being obovate and considerably larger than the lateral ones (which, according to Roxburgh, Flora Ind., III, p. 244, are from 4 to 6 inches long, and from 3 to 4½ broad). 'Palâsasâkhâyâm yâni trîni parnâni tatra madhyamam parnam prasastayâ srugrûpam,' Sây. on Taitt. S. I, 8, 6.

9. He offers[1], with the text (Vâg. S. III, 57 a), This is thy share, O Rudra! graciously accept it together with thy sister Ambikâ! Svâhâ!' Ambikâ[2], indeed, is the name of his (Rudra's) sister; and this share belongs to him conjointly with her; and because that share belongs to him conjointly with a woman (strî), therefore (these oblations) are called Tryambakâh. Thereby, then, he delivers from Rudra's power the descendants that have been born unto him.

10. Now as to that additional (cake),—he buries it in a mole-hill[3], with the text (Vâg. S. III, 57 b), 'This is thy share, O Rudra! the mole is thy animal (victim).' He thus assigns to him the mole as the only animal[4], and he (Rudra) does not therefore injure any other animal. Then as to why he buries (the cake): concealed, indeed, are embryos, and concealed also is what is buried,—that is why he buries it. By this (offering) he delivers from the power of Rudra those descendants of his, that are not yet born.

[1] He consecrates, by the usual fivefold lustration, some spot on a cross-way, to the north of the sacrificial ground, and after laying down the fire-brand taken from the Dakshinâgni, he offers thereon, using the central leaflet of a palâsa-leaf as the offering-spoon.

[2] In Taitt. Br. I, 6, 10, 4, this sister of Rudra is identified with the autumn, wherewith the god is wont to kill (viz. by means of catarrh, fever, &c., Sây.). See also Weber, Ind. Stud. I, 183; Muir, Original Sanskrit Texts, vol. iv. p. 321.

[3] 'Âkhûtkara;' 'âkhukarîsha,' Kânva text. Possibly a mouse-hole, or the earth thrown up by a mouse, is meant. See p. 278, note 3. Cf. Taitt. Br. I, 6, 10, 2: 'N. N. is thy victim,' thus saying, let him indicate the one he (the Sacrificer) hates; thereby he delivers over to him (Rudra) the one he hates. If he hate no one, let him say, 'the mole (mouse) is thy victim.'

[4] 'Thus he makes over to him only the mole as victim, and puts it into his mouth,' Kânva text.

11. Thereupon they return (to the fire) and mutter (Vâg. S. III, 58, 59), 'We have satisfied the claims of Rudra, satisfied the divine Tryambaka, that he may make us richer, that he may make us more prosperous, that he may render us steady in our purpose. —Thou (O Rudra) art a remedy for the cow, a remedy for the horse, a remedy for man; a blessing for the ram and the ewe.' This is the prayer for blessing at this performance.

12. They then walk thrice round the altar not sunwise, beating their left thighs (with the right hand), with the text (Vâg. S. III, 60 a), 'We worship Tryambaka, the fragrant increaser of prosperity. Even as a gourd (is severed) from its stem, so may I be severed from death, not from immortality!' This is the prayer for blessing at this performance: thereby they invoke a blessing (upon the Sacrificer), for verily blessed is he who shall be severed from death, not from immortality. That is why he says, 'May I be severed from death, not from immortality.'

13. Let the maidens then also walk round, thinking, 'May we enjoy prosperity!' That sister of Rudra, named Ambikâ, indeed is the dispenser of happiness: hence the maidens also should walk round, thinking, 'May we enjoy prosperity!'

14. The text (prescribed) for them is (Vâg. S. III, 60 b), 'We worship Tryambaka, the fragrant bestower of husbands. Even as a gourd (is severed) from its stem, so may I be severed from this (world), not from thence (yonder world)!' By saying 'from this,' she means to say 'from my relatives;' and by saying 'not from thence,' she means to say 'not from husbands.' Husbands, doubtless, are the support of woman: hence she says 'not from thence.'

15. Then they (the Sacrificer and priests) again walk round thrice sunwise, beating their right thighs, with the same text. As to why they again walk round thrice sunwise,—they think, 'Sunwise this sacred work of ours shall be accomplished,' and therefore they again walk thrice round sunwise.

16. The Sacrificer now takes those (remains of the cakes) into his joined palms and throws them upwards higher than a cow can reach[1]. Thereby they cut out his (Rudra's) darts from their bodies. If they fail to catch them[2], they touch (those that have fallen to the ground). Thereby they make them medicine, and hence, if they fail to catch them, they touch them.

17. Having then packed them into two net-work baskets and tied them to the two ends of either a bamboo staff or the beam of a balance, he steps

---

[1] 'Yathâ gaur nodâpnuyât.' 'Yâvad gaur nodâpnuyât tâvat,' Kânva text. Sâyana takes go to mean 'earth,' and interprets, 'in such a way that the earth does not obtain it (i. e. that they do not fall to the ground).' Kâty. prescribes, V, 10, 18, The Sacrificer, with his joined open hands, throws the Rudra-cakes upwards as high as not to be reachable by a cow (agohprâpanam); 19, He catches them; 20, If they cannot be (caught), then touching (of those that have fallen on the ground).

[2] I adopt (not without reluctance) Sâyana's interpretation of vilipsantah (=labdhum asaktâh), which seems to be that of Kâtyâyana also. The St. Petersburg Dict. takes it in the sense of '(if they are) desirous of distributing them.' Taitt. Br. I, 6, 10, 5 has merely 'utkiranti bhagasya lîpsante,' 'they throw (them) up, (whereby) they desire to obtain prosperity.' Âpastamba, as quoted by Sây. on Taitt. S. I, 8, 6, says,—Having thrown up the cakes and caught them again (pratilabhya), and having, with 'We worship Tryambaka,' put them into the Sacrificer's joined palms; and having taken them up separately (? apâdâya), with (or thinking) 'We desire to obtain you of (? from) Bhaga;' let them put them together (samâvapeyuh) thrice in this way.

aside towards the north; and if he meets with a tree or a stake or a bamboo or an ant-hill, he fastens them thereon, with the text (Vâ*g*. S. III, 61), 'These, O Rudra, are thy provisions; therewith depart beyond the Mû*g*avats!'—(supplied) with provisions people indeed set out on a journey: hence he thereby dismisses him supplied with provisions whithersoever he is bound. Now in this case his journey is beyond the Mû*g*avats: hence he says, 'Depart beyond the Mû*g*avats!'—'with thy bow unstrung and muffled up—,' whereby he means to say, 'Depart propitious, not injuring us[1];' 'Clad in a skin,'—whereby he lulls him to sleep[2]; for while sleeping he injures no one: hence he says, 'Clad in a skin.'

18. They then turn to the right about, and return (to the uttaravedi) without looking back. Having returned thither, they touch water; for they have been performing a ceremony relating to Rudra[3], and water is (a means of) purification: with water, that (means of) purification, they accordingly purify themselves.

19. Thereupon he shaves his hair and beard, and takes up the fire (of the uttaravedi),—for only after changing his place (to the ordinary sacrificial ground) he performs the (Full-moon) sacrifice on that fire, since it is not proper that he should perform the

[1] In the Vâ*g*. Sa*m*hitâ this forms part of the text, but it is clearly a gloss taken from the Brâhma*n*a. The Kâ*n*va recension of the Brâhma*n*a has '—pinâkâvasa ity ahi*m*san na*h* *s*iva*h* *s*ânto 'tîhîty evaitad âha,' which has likewise found its way into the Sa*m*hitâ of that school. On the Mû*g*avats, see Muir, Orig. Sanskrit Texts, vol. ii. p. 352.

[2] According to Kâty. V, 10, 22, he mutters the word 'skin-clad' while steadying the two baskets.

[3] See p. 2, note 2.

Agnihotra on the uttaravedi: for this reason he changes his place. Having gone to the house, and 'churned out' the fires [1], he performs the Full-moon offering. The Seasonal offerings, doubtless, are detached sacrifices; whereas the Full-moon offering is a regular, established sacrifice: hence he finally establishes himself by means of that regular sacrifice, and therefore changes his place (to the ordinary sacrificial ground).

THIRD BRÂHMANA.

1. Verily, imperishable is the righteousness of him that offers the Seasonal sacrifices; for such a one gains the year, and hence there is no cessation for him. He gains it (the year) in three divisions, he conquers it in three divisions. The year means the whole, and the whole is imperishable (without end): hence his righteousness is indeed imperishable. Moreover, he thereby becomes a Season, and as such goes to the gods; but there is no perishableness in the gods, and hence there is imperishable righteousness for him. This, then, is why he offers the Seasonal sacrifices.

2. Then as to why he should perform the Sunâsîrya offering. The prosperity (srî) that accrued to the gods on performing the Sâkamedha offerings, and gaining the victory (over Vritra), is suna; and the essence (rasa) that belonged to the year gained by them is sîra [2]. Now that same prosperity which

[1] See II, 5, 2, 48.

[2] The author identifies sîra (plough) with sâra, 'essence, sap;' and takes suna, ploughshare (?), as identical with sunam, 'successfully, prosperously.' See next page, note 3.

accrued to the gods on performing the Sâkamedha offerings, and that same essence which belonged to the year gained by them,—both these he takes possession of and makes his own: that is why he performs the *S*unâsîrya.

3. The mode of its performance (is as follows): They prepare no uttaravedi; they do not use clotted butter; nor do they churn the fire[1]. There are five fore-offerings, three after-offerings, and one Samish*t*aya*g*us.

4. Then, in the first place, there are those five (regular) oblations[2]. By means of these oblations, indeed, Pra*g*âpati produced creatures; with them he delivered the creatures both ways from Varu*n*a's noose; with them the gods slew V*ri*tra and gained that victory which was gained by them. And so does he, by means of them, obtain and make his own, both that prosperity which accrued to the gods from performing the Sâkamedha offerings, and that essence of the year which was gained by them. This is why those five oblations are (offered).

5. Then follows a *S*unâsîrya[3] cake on twelve

[1] But see XI, 5, 2, 8, 'At all four of these (*K*âturmâsya offerings) they churn the fire.' On account of this contradiction, the commentators, on Kâty. V, 11, 3, consider the churning of the fire as optional. But, if the fires were produced by 'churning,' nine fore-offerings and after-offerings would have to be performed, as at the other Seasonal sacrifices, which is expressly forbidden in the above passage. According to Kâty. himself, the *S*unâsîrya is to be treated like an ordinary ish*t*i, except that the barhis is to be tied together in the way prescribed for the Seasonal offerings; see II, 5, 1, 18.

[2] See II, 5, 1, 8–11.

[3] That is, according to Kâty. V, 11, 5, to *S*una and Sîra,—probably the ploughshare and plough, considered as two tutelary deities of agricultural pursuits (Rig-veda IV, 57, 5–8); but by Yâska identified with Vâyu and Âditya;—or, according to Taitt. S. I, 8,

potsherds. The import of this Sunâsîrya oblation is what we have stated before.

6. After that there is an (oblation of) milk[1] to Vâyu. Now it is to milk that living beings readily take, when they are born: 'May the creatures readily take to me—now that I have gained the victory (by means of the Sâkamedha offerings)—for my prosperity, glory, and support!' so he thinks, and hence that (oblation of) milk.

7. Then as to why it is (offered) to Vâyu. Now Vâyu, indeed, is yonder blowing (wind); it is he that makes swell whatever rain falls here. But it is by the rain that plants grow; and on the plants being eaten and the water drunk, milk is produced out of that water. Hence it is he (Vâyu) that produces it; and for this reason it is (offered) to Vâyu.

8. Then follows a cake on one potsherd for Sûrya. Now Sûrya, indeed, is yonder scorching (sun); it is he that governs all this (world), now by means of a good, now by a bad (king)[2]; he assigns its place to everything here, now under a good, now under a bad (king): 'Now that I have obtained the victory, may he, in his pleasure, govern me through a good (king), may he assign to me a place under a good (king)!' thus he thinks; and for this reason there is a cake on one potsherd for Sûrya.

9. The priests' fee for this (oblation to Sûrya)

7, 1, Taitt. Br. I, 7, 1, 1, to Indra Sunâsîra (i.e. Indra, accompanied by Suna and Sîra, Sây.).

[1] According to Kâty. V, 11, 6-10, the milk, in this case, is to be offered quite fresh (and warm) from the cow, without having been put on the fire. Rice-gruel may, however, be offered instead.

[2] Or, 'now by good, now by bad (means).'

is a white horse[1]; whereby it is made of the characteristic form of yonder scorching (sun). If he be unable to procure a white horse, it may be a white bull; whereby it is likewise made of the characteristic form of yonder scorching (sun).

10. He may offer the *S*unâsîrya at the same time when he performs the Sâkamedha offerings. By offering (Seasonal sacrifices) three times in the year, he indeed obtains the (whole) year: he may therefore offer (the *S*unâsîrya) at any time[2].

11. Here now some wish to take possession of the nights; and should he wish to take possession of the nights, let him offer the *S*unâsîrya (on the day) when, previously to the full-moon of Phâlguna, (the new moon) becomes visible in yonder sky.

12. Let him then get consecrated (for the Soma-sacrifice), lest the Phâlguna full-moon again pass by without his offering (Soma). For were the Phâlguna full-moon again to pass by without his having

---

[1] According to Taitt. S. I, 8, 7, Taitt. Br. I, 7, 1, 2, the Dakshi*n*â consists of a plough yoked with twelve oxen.

[2] That is to say, he may perform the *S*unâsîrya, either immediately after the Sâkamedhâ*h*, or at any time within four months after that sacrifice (comm. on Kâty. V, 11, 3). Our author, however, evidently favours the views set forth in the succeeding paragraphs. According to these, the householder who wishes to discontinue the Seasonal offerings after the first round, and to become a Soma-sacrificer, is to perform the *S*unâsîrya on the first day of the waxing moon of Phâlguna, and then to undergo the dîkshâ, or rite of consecration for the Soma-sacrifice (see III, 1, 2, 1 seq.), either immediately or before the approaching full-moon, when he is to perform the Agnish*t*oma (or an animal offering to Agni and Soma or an Âgneyî ish*t*i, Kâty. V, 11, 15). If, on the other hand, he intends to continue the *K*âturmâsyas for another year (or more), he is to perform the *S*unâsîrya on the upavasatha, or day preceding the full-moon.

offered (Soma), he would certainly have to begin anew (to perform the Seasonal offerings): hence the Phâlguna full-moon should not again pass by without his offering Soma. Such (is the rule) for him who discontinues (the Seasonal offerings).

13. And in the case of one who recommences (the Seasonal offerings),—let him perform the Sunâsîrya on the day preceding the Phâlguna full-moon, and on the following day the Vaisvadeva, and after that the Full-moon offering. This, then, (is the rule) for him who recommences (the Seasonal offerings).

14. Then as to (the Sacrificer) shaving his head all round[1]. Now yonder sun, indeed, faces every quarter; it drinks up whatever (moisture) it dries up here: hence this (Sacrificer) thereby faces every quarter and becomes a consumer of food.

15. This fire also faces every quarter, since it burns all they put into it from whatsoever quarter: hence this (Sacrificer) thereby faces every quarter and becomes a consumer of food.

16. This man, on the other hand, faces but one quarter; but by shaving his head all round he comes to face every quarter; and whosoever, knowing this, has his head shaved all round, becomes just such a consumer of food as those two: let him therefore have his head shaved all round.

17. And on this point Âsuri said, 'What in the world has it to do with his face, even if he were to shave off all the hair of his head! It is by offering

[1] 'Parivartayate' ('nivartayate,' Kânva), lit. 'he causes himself to be turned round,' is the technical expression for having one's head shaved all round (the sikhâ, or lock of hair on the crown of the head).

thrice in the year that he comes to face all the quarters and becomes a consumer of food: let him therefore not trouble himself about shaving his head.'

FOURTH BRÂHMANA.

1. Now when it is said, that the gods, by means of the Sâkamedha offerings, slew Vritra and gained that supreme authority which they now wield,—it is rather by means of all the Seasonal sacrifices that the gods slew Vritra; it is by all of them that they gained that supreme authority which they now wield.

2. They spake, 'With what king, with what leader[1] shall we fight?' Agni spake, 'With me for your king, with me for your leader!' With Agni for their king, with Agni for their leader, they gained four months; and with the Brahman (sacerdotium) and the threefold science they encompassed them.

3. They spake, 'With what king, with what leader shall we fight?' Varuna spake, 'With me for your king, with me for your leader!' With Varuna for their king, with Varuna for their leader, they gained other four months; and with the Brahman and the threefold science they encompassed them.

4. They spake, 'With what king, with what leader shall we fight?' Indra spake, 'With me for your king, with me for your leader!' With Indra for their king, with Indra for their leader, they gained other four months; and with the Brahman and the threefold science they encompassed them.

[1] Anika (? 'van-guard'), cf. V, 3, 1, 1 'senâyâh senânîr anîkam;' II, 5, 3, 2.

5. And, accordingly, when he performs the Vaisvadeva, he thereby gains four months, with Agni for his king, with Agni for his leader. Then (in shaving) are used a porcupine's quill spotted in three places, and a copper razor; that three-spotted porcupine's quill resembles the threefold science, and the copper razor resembles the Brahman; for the Brahman is fire, and fire is of reddish (lohita) colour: hence a copper (loha) razor is used. Therewith he has (his head) shaved all round[1]; and thus he (the Adhvaryu) encompasses him with the Brahman and the threefold science.

6. And when he performs the Varunapraghâsa offerings, he thereby gains other four months, with Varuna for his king, with Varuna for his leader. Then a three-spotted quill of a porcupine and a copper razor are used, wherewith he has himself shaved all round; and thus he (the priest) encompasses him with the Brahman and the threefold science.

7. And when he performs the Sâkamedha offerings, he thereby gains other four months, with Indra for his king, with Indra for his leader. Then a three-spotted quill of a porcupine and a copper razor are used, wherewith he has himself shaved; and thus he (the priest) encompasses him with the Brahman and the threefold science.

8. And when he performs the Vaisvadeva, then he becomes Agni, and attains to union with Agni and to co-existence in his world. And when he performs the Varunapraghâsa offerings, then he becomes Varuna, and attains to union with Varuna

[1] See p. 448, note 1.

and to co-existence in his world. And when he performs the Sâkamedha offerings, then he becomes Indra, and attains to union with Indra and to co-existence in his world [1].

9. And in whatever season he goes to yonder world, that season passes him on to the next season, and that season again passes him on to the next season,—he who performs the Seasonal sacrifices reaches the highest place, the supreme goal. Wherefore it is said, 'They find not him that offereth the Seasonal offerings, for verily he goeth unto the highest place, to the supreme goal [2].'

---

[1] The Kâ*n*va text adds: And when he performs the *S*unâsîrîya, then he becomes Vâyu, and attains to union with Vâyu and to co-existence in his world.

[2] The Kâ*n*va text has: In whatever season the performer of Seasonal offerings goes to yonder world, that season passes him on to the next season, and that next one to the next one,—him the seasons, by transmission, make thus attain to the highest station, to the highest world. Wherefore is it said, 'They find not him that offereth the Seasonal offerings, for he conquereth the highest world, the highest conquest (parama*m* hy eva lokam paramâ*m* *g*itim *g*ayatîti).'

ADDITIONS AND CORRECTIONS.

Page 15, note 1. The pole of Indian carts is itself firmly bound with thongs.

P. 27, paragraph 10. Read,—Vâ*g*. S. I, 15 b; I, 15 c.

P. 28, par. 12, and note 2. The Kâ*n*va text has the correct order of castes: 'tâny etâni *k*atvâri vâ*k*a ehîti brâhma*n*asyâgahy âdraveti râ*g*anyasya *k*a vai*s*yasya *k*âdhâveti *s*ûdrasya.'

P. 47, par. 1. The Taitt. S. (II, 6, 6) has a somewhat different version of this legend :—Agni had three elder brothers. While carrying the oblations to the gods, they perished. Agni was afraid, 'In like manner this one will meet with destruction (ârtim ârishyati).' He concealed himself. He entered the waters. The gods wished to find him. A fish betrayed him. He cursed it, 'May (people) kill thee by whatever means they can devise (dhiyâ-dhiyâ), who hast betrayed me!' Hence they kill the fish by whatever means they can devise, for he is accursed. They found him, and said to him, 'Come back to us and carry our oblation!' He said, 'I will ask a boon : whatever portion of the taken (ghee) shall fall outside the enclosing-sticks, before it is offered, that shall be my brothers' portion!' Hence whatever portion of the taken (ghee) falls outside the enclosing-sticks, that is their portion: with that he satisfies them.

P. 47, par. 2. The Kâ*n*va text reads,—'They followed Indra even as now-a-days also a Brâhman follows a Kshatriya blessing him (â*s*a*m*samâno 'nu*k*arati).'

P. 85, par. 6. Read,—for this represents the fringe (of the Sacrificer's nether garment), and it is on the right side that the fringe (is tucked in) . . . . for the fringe also is covered (by being tucked in). Cf. below to p. 368.

P. 118, line 18. Read,—'Thine' instead of 'Your.'

P. 164, par. 2. Professor Delbrück, Syntaktische Forschungen II, p. 118, translates, 'And from the mouth which had been drinking surâ, the sparrow sprang: hence the latter sings so merrily, for indeed he sings so merrily as if it had drank surâ.' Differently, however, ibid. III, p. 64.

P. 175, par. 1. Compare also the corresponding legend in Taitt. Br. I, 6, 7, 4:—Indra, having slain V*ri*tra, went to the farthest distance, thinking 'I have committed a sin (aparâdham, ? I have missed him).' He said, 'Who will find this out?' The Maruts said, 'We will choose a boon, then we shall know: let the first offering be made to us!' They sported on him (V*ri*tra), &c. (According to Sâya*n*a, on Taitt. S. I, 8, 4, Indra flees from fear and says, within the Marut's hearing, 'Is V*ri*tra dead or not? Who will go near him and find it out?' &c.)

P. 183, par. 1. According to Sâya*n*a, on Taitt. Br. I, 1, 3, 10, it was the Soma-plant (soma-vallî) that was carried off by Gâyatrî devatâ, and one of its leaves (par*n*a) was broken off, and on falling to the ground became a palâ*s*a tree. See also Taitt. S. VI, 1, 6; *S*at. Br. III, 2, 4, 1 seq.; Weber, Ind. Stud. II, 312 seq.

P. 184, note 4. Add,—Compare Max Müller, Hist. of Anc. Sansk. Lit., p. 352.

P. 206, par. 19. Correct,—'Bhâllaveya' (also II, 1, 4, 6).

P. 288, note 2. On the etymology of nakshatra, see also Max Müller, Rig-veda-Sa*m*hitâ IV, p. lxvi note.

P. 310, pars. 8–9. Correct,—'And whichever (of the Asuras) they (the gods) slew, he indeed remained the same (viz. alive). In consequence of this the gods were left inferior.'

P. 313, par. 20. The paragraph should have been rendered thus:—To Aru*n*a Aupave*s*i his kinsmen said, 'Thou art advanced in years: establish thou the fires!' He replied, 'Thereby ye tell me, "keep silence!" he who has established his fires must not speak an untruth, and only by not speaking at all one speaks no untruth: to that extent the service (of the consecrated fire) consists in truth.' Similarly the Kâ*n*va text,—aru*n*a*m* haupave*s*i*m* *g*ñâtaya û*k*u*h* sthaviro vâ asy agnî âdhatsveti.—sa hovâ*k*a tan maitad brûtha vâ*k*a*m*-yama evaidhîti mâ brûtheti na hy agnî âdhâya m*ri*shâ vaden no vâ*k*â vadato 'm*ri*shodyam asti tasmâd u satyam eva vivadishet. See Delbrück, Syntaktische Forschungen III, p. 29.

P. 368, par. 24. Read,—He (the Sacrificer) then pulls down the tuck of his (nether garment) and performs obeisance. Cf. p. 435, note 2.

TRANSLITERATION OF ORIENTAL ALPHABETS ADOPTED FOR THE TRANSLATIONS OF THE SACRED BOOKS OF THE EAST.

CONSONANTS.	MISSIONARY ALPHABET.			Sanskrit.	Zend.	Pehlevi.	Persian.	Arabic.	Hebrew.	Chinese.
	I Class.	II Class.	III Class.							
Gutturales.										
1 Tenuis	k	...	...	क	𐬐	[illegible]	ك	ك	כּ	k
2 " aspirata	kh	...	...	ख	𐬑	[illegible]	...	...	כ	kh
3 Media	g	...	...	ग	𐬔	[illegible]	گ	...	גּ	...
4 " aspirata	gh	...	...	घ	𐬖	[illegible]	...	...	ג	...
5 Gutturo-labialis	q	...	...	...	...	...	ق	ق	ק	...
6 Nasalis	ṅ (ng)	...	...	ङ	{ 𐬧 (ng) / 𐬣 (N) }	...	...	...	...	...
7 Spiritus asper	h	...	...	ह	𐬵 (𐬒 *hv*)	[illegible]	ه	ه	ה	h, hs
8 " lenis	'	...	...	...	...	...	ا	ا	א	...
9 " asper faucalis	'h	...	...	...	...	...	ح	ح	ח	...
10 " lenis faucalis	'h	...	...	...	...	...	ع	ع	ע	...
11 " asper fricatus	...	*'h*	...	...	...	...	خ	خ	ח	...
12 " lenis fricatus	...	*'h*	...	...	...	...	...	...	...	...
Gutturales modificatae (palatales, &c.)										
13 Tenuis	...	*k*	...	च	𐬗	[illegible]	چ	...	...	*k*
14 " aspirata	...	*kh*	...	छ	...	...	...	...	...	*kh*
15 Media	...	*g*	...	ज	𐬘	[illegible]	ج	ج	...	...
16 " aspirata	...	*gh*	...	झ	...	...	غ	غ	...	...
17 " Nasalis	...	*ñ*	...	ञ	...	...	...	...	...	...

CONSONANTS (*continued*).	MISSIONARY ALPHABET. I Class.	II Class.	III Class.	Sanskrit.	Zend.	Pehlevi.	Persian.	Arabic.	Hebrew.	Chinese.
18 Semivocalis	y	...	....	य	𐬌𐬌 𐬫 𐬎 init.	[illegible]	ي	ي	י	y
19 Spiritus asper	...	($\grave{y}$)	....	...	....	...	...	...	...	...
20 " lenis	...	($\acute{y}$)	....	...	....	...	...	...	...	...
21 " asper assibilatus	...	*s*	....	श	𐬴	[illegible]	ش	ش	...	...
22 " lenis assibilatus	...	*z*	....	...	𐬲	[illegible]	ژ	...	...	*z*
Dentales.										
23 Tenuis	t	...	....	त	𐬙	[illegible]	ت	ت	תּ	t
24 " aspirata	th	...	....	थ	𐬚	...	...	...	ת	th
25 " assibilata	...	...	TH	...	....	...	ث	ث	...	...
26 Media	d	...	....	द	𐬛	[illegible]	د	د	דּ	...
27 " aspirata	dh	...	....	ध	𐬜	...	...	...	ד	...
28 " assibilata	...	...	DH	...	....	...	ذ	ذ	...	...
29 Nasalis	n	...	....	न	𐬥	[illegible]	ن	ن	נ	n
30 Semivocalis	l	...	....	ल	....	[illegible]	ل	ل	ל	l
31 " mollis 1	...	*l*	....	ळ	....	...	...	...	...	...
32 " mollis 2	...	...	L	...	....	...	...	...	...	...
33 Spiritus asper 1	s	...	....	स	𐬯	[illegible]	س (ث)	س	שׂ	s
34 " asper 2	...	...	s (ʃ)	...	....	...	...	...	ס	...
35 " lenis	z	...	....	...	𐬰	[illegible]	ز (ذ)	ز	ז	z
36 " asperrimus 1	...	...	z (ʒ)	...	....	...	ص	ص	צ	ʒ, ʒh
37 " asperrimus 2	...	...	ẓ (ʒ)	...	....	...	ض	...	...	...

Dentales modificatae (linguales, &c.)										
38 Tenuis	...	*t*	....	ट	....	...	ط	ط	ט	...
39 „ aspirata	...	*th*	....	ठ	....	...	ظ	ظ	...	...
40 Media	...	*d*	....	ड	[illegible]	[illegible]	...	...	...	...
41 „ aspirata	...	*dh*	....	ढ	....	...	...	ض	...	...
42 Nasalis	...	*n*	....	ण	[illegible]	...	...	...	...	...
43 Semivocalis	r	...	....	र	[illegible]	[illegible]	ر	ر	ר	...
44 „ fricata	...	*r*	....	...	....	...	...	...	...	*r*
45 „ diacritica	...	...	R	...	....	...	...	...	...	...
46 Spiritus asper	sh	...	....	ष	[illegible]	[illegible]	...	...	...	sh
47 „ lenis	zh	...	....	...	....	...	...	...	...	...
Labiales.										
48 Tenuis	p	...	....	प	[illegible]	[illegible]	پ	...	פּ	p
49 „ aspirata	ph	...	....	फ	....	...	...	...	פ	ph
50 Media	b	...	....	ब	[illegible]	[illegible]	ب	ب	בּ	...
51 „ aspirata	bh	...	....	भ	....	...	...	...	ב	...
52 Tenuissima	...	*p*	....	...	....	...	...	...	...	...
53 Nasalis	m	...	....	म	[illegible]	[illegible]	م	م	מ	m
54 Semivocalis	w	...	....	...	[illegible]	...	...	...	...	w
55 „ aspirata	hw	...	....	...	....	...	...	...	...	...
56 Spiritus asper	f	...	....	...	[illegible]	[illegible]	ف	ف	...	f
57 „ lenis	v	...	....	व	»	[illegible]	و	و	ו	...
58 Anusvâra	...	*m*	....	अं	[illegible] ã	...	...	...	...	...
59 Visarga	...	*h*	....	अः	....	...	...	...	...	...

VOWELS.	MISSIONARY ALPHABET. I Class.	II Class.	III Class.	Sanskrit.	Zend.	Pehlevi.	Persian.	Arabic.	Hebrew.	Chinese.
1 Neutralis	0	...	...	...	...	...	...	...	ְ	ă
2 Laryngo-palatalis	ĕ	...	...	...	...	...	...	...	...	...
3 „ labialis	ŏ	...	...	...	...	ا fin.	...	...	...	...
4 Gutturalis brevis	a	...	...	अ	𐬀	𐬀 init.	ـَ	ـَ	ַ	a
5 „ longa	â	(*a*)	...	आ	𐬁	𐬀	ـَا	ـَا	ָ	â
6 Palatalis brevis	i	...	...	इ	𐬌	[illegible]	ـِ	ـِ	ִ	i
7 „ longa	î	(*i*)	...	ई	𐬍	[illegible]	ـِي	ـِي	ִי	î
8 Dentalis brevis	*li*	...	...	ऌ	...	...	...	...	...	...
9 „ longa	*lî*	...	...	ॡ	...	...	...	...	...	...
10 Lingualis brevis	*ri*	...	...	ऋ	...	...	...	...	...	...
11 „ longa	*rî*	...	...	ॠ	...	...	...	...	...	...
12 Labialis brevis	u	...	...	उ	𐬎	...	ـُ	ـُ	ֻ	u
13 „ longa	û	(*u*)	...	ऊ	𐬏	ا	ـُو	ـُو	וּ	û
14 Gutturo-palatalis brevis	e	...	...	...	𐬈(e) 𐬉(*e*)	...	...	...	ֶ	e
15 „ longa	ê (ai)	(*e*)	...	ए	𐬉, 𐬉	ↄ	...	...	ֵ	ê
16 Diphthongus gutturo-palatalis	âi	(*ai*)	...	ऐ	...	...	ـَىْ	ـَىْ	...	âi
17 „ „	ei (ĕi)	...	...	...	...	...	...	...	...	ei, êi
18 „ „	oi (ŏu)	...	...	...	...	...	...	...	...	...
19 Gutturo-labialis brevis	o	...	...	...	𐬊	...	...	...	ָ	o
20 „ longa	ô (au)	(*o*)	...	ओ	𐬋	ا	...	...	וֹ	...
21 Diphthongus gutturo-labialis	âu	(*au*)	...	औ	𐬈𐬎 (*au*)	...	ـَوْ	ـَوْ	...	âu
22 „ „	eu (ĕu)	...	...	...	...	...	...	...	...	...
23 „ „	ou (ŏu)	...	...	...	...	...	...	...	...	...
24 Gutturalis fracta	ä	...	...	...	...	...	...	...	...	...
25 Palatalis fracta	ï	...	...	...	...	...	...	...	...	...
26 Labialis fracta	ü	...	...	...	...	...	...	...	...	ü
27 Gutturo-labialis fracta	ö	...	...	...	...	...	...	...	...	...